Prophecy and Hermeneutic
in Early Christianity

E. Earle Ellis

BakerBooks

A Division of Baker Book House Co.
Grand Rapids, Michigan 49516

D0920271

Published by Baker Books,
a division of Baker Book House Company
PO Box 6287, Grand Rapids, Michigan 49516-6287

Printed in the United States of America

First published 1978 as vol. 18 in the series *Wissenschaftliche Untersuchungen zum Neuen Testament.* First American paperback edition published July 1978 by William B. Eerdmans Company by special arrangement with J. C. B. Mohr (Paul Siebeck), Tübingen, Federal Republic of Germany

Library of Congress Cataloging-in-Publication Data

Ellis, E. Earle (Edward Earle)
    Prophecy and hermeneutic in early Christianity / E. Earle Ellis.
       p.   cm.
    "First published 1978 as vol. 18 in the series Wissenschaftliche Untersuchungen zum Neuen Testament. First American paperback edition published July 1978 by William B. Eerdmans Company by special arrangement with J. C. B. Mohr (Paul Siebeck), Tübingen, Federal Republic of Germany"—T. p. verso.
    Includes bibliographical references and index.
    ISBN 0-8010-3222-9
    1. Prophets in the New Testament.   2. Bible. N. T.—Criticism, interpretation, etc.
3. Bible. N. T.—Hermeneutics. 4. Prophecy—Christianity. I. Wissenschaftliche Unter-suchungen zum Neuen Testament ; 18. II. Title.
BS2545.P72E44 1993
225.1'5—dc20   *#28293016*   93-4352

FOR
OSCAR CULLMANN

ὑπηρέτης Χριστοῦ καὶ
οἰκονόμος μυστηρίων Θεοῦ

PREFACE

This volume represents the preliminary work, the results and elaboration of research done at the University of Göttingen in 1968—69. One chapter, Prophecy and Hermeneutic in Jude, is previously unpublished. The others have appeared singly in anniversary volumes[1], journals[2] and symposia[3], to whose editors and publishers a word of acknowledgement and appreciation is here happily given.

Although the essays were composed separately, they are unified by two themes that have had a continuing attraction for me and that are of current interest in the world of scholarship and in the churches. They have occasionally been altered in title or wording to fit them to the present format and to express a change of mind. Unavoidably they contain some repetitions that, nevertheless, may have the beneficial effect of clarifying the issues under consideration. All have been written in the abiding conviction that the New Testament presents to us not merely the opinions of Christian writers but also

---

[1] Chapters 3, 4, 5, 6, 8, 12, 13, 15, 17, respectively, in *Jesus und Paulus ... für W. G. Kümmel,* edd. E. E. Ellis und E. Grässer, Göttingen 1975, 109—128 (ET: *TB* 25, 1974, 82—98);*Christ and Spirit in the New Testament [for] C. F. D. Moule,* edd. B. Lindars and S. S. Smalley, Cambridge 1973, 269—277; *Reconciliation and Hope [for] L. L. Morris,* ed. R. Banks, Exeter und Grand Rapids 1974, 69—75; *Christianity, Judaism and other Greco-Roman Cults... for M. Smith,* ed. J. Neusner, 4 vols., Leiden 1975, I, 264—298; *Apostolic History and the Gospel [for] F. F. Bruce,* ed. W. W. Gasque and R. P. Martin, Exeter and Grand Rapids 1970, 55—67; *Neotestamentica et Semitica [for] M. Black,* ed. E. E. Ellis and M. Wilcox, Edinburgh 1969, 61—69; *Melanges Bibliques B. Rigaux,* ed. A. Descamps et A. de Halleux, Gembloux 1970, 303—312; *Grace upon Grace [for] L. Kuyper,* ed. J. I. Cook, Grand Rapids 1975, 137—142; *Jesus Christus in Historie und Theologie ... für H. Conzelmann,* ed. G. Strecker, Tübingen 1975, 299—315.

[2] Chapters 1, 2, and 10 were articles in *NTS* 17 (1970—71), 437—452; 20 (1973—74), 128—144; 2 (1955—56), 127—133. Chapters 11 and 14 appeared, respectively, in *EQ* 29 (1957), 23—28, and in *JBL* 76 (1957), 53—56. Chapter 13 was published in a revised German translation in *ZNTW* 62 (1971), 94—104.

[3] Chapter 7 was written for the Oxford Congress of Biblical Studies, 1965, and appeared in *TU* 102 (1968), 390—399; chapter 9 for a Tyndale Fellowship symposium on *New Testament Interpretation* (ed. I. H. Marshall, Exeter 1977).

the message of God mediated through faithful prophets. It is hoped therefore that, in addition to advancing historical scholarship, they may offer further insight into the prophetic word that initiated and interpreted the earliest Christian proclamation and that continues to enlighten and to guide Christ's church today.

The publication of the volume is largely due to the Alexander von Humboldt-Stiftung, which provided a scholarship for the sabbatical in Göttingen and has partially underwritten the printing costs of the book. For these and many other kindnesses of the Stiftung I am profoundly grateful.

I wish to express my deep appreciation also to Professors Martin Hengel and Otto Michel of Tübingen and Joachim Jeremias of Göttingen, who accepted the volume for publication in the series, *Wissenschaftliche Untersuchungen zum Neuen Testament*. Many years ago Professors Michel and Jeremias introduced me to the strange new world of German theology, and Martin Hengel has been a gracious host during my current sabbatical year. My thanks go as well to the publisher and the editors for their excellent work in dressing the manuscript, to my student, Daniel Meeter, *stud. theol.*, for preparing the indices and to Institutum Judaicum of the University of Tübingen for the generous assistance and provision of facilities that enabled me, amid other pressing commitments, to bring this work to completion.

The volume is dedicated to Professor Oscar Cullmann, whose writings have been a source of stimulation and inspiration through the years.

Tübingen
Lent 1976   E. Earle Ellis

CONTENTS

LIST OF ABBREVIATIONS

BOOKS OF THE BIBLE

Old Testament

Gen	Jud	1 Chr	Ps	La	Ob	Hg
Ex	Ru	2 Chr	Pr	Ez	Jon	Zc
Lev	1 Sam	Ezr	Eccl	Dn	Mi	Mal
Nu	2 Sam	Ne	SS	Hos	Na	
Dtn	1 Ki	Est	Is	Jl	Hab	
Jos	2 Ki	Job	Je	Am	Zeph	

New Testament

Mt	Acts	Gal	1 Th	Tit	1 Petr	3 Joh
Mk	Rom	Eph	2 Th	Phm	2 Petr	Jude
Lk	1 Cor	Phil	1 Tim	Hebr	1 Joh	Rev
Joh	2 Cor	Col	2 Tim	Jas	2 Joh	

Apocrypha

1 Esd	Tob	Ad Est	Sir	S 3 Ch	Bel	1 Macc
2 Esd	Jdt	Wis	Bar	Sus	Man	2 Macc
(= 4 Ezra)			Ep Jer			

Dead Sea Scrolls

1QIs^a	First Isaiah Scroll
1QIs^b	Second Isaiah Scroll
1QLevi	Second Testament of Levi
1QpHab	Habakkuk Commentary
1QS	Rule of the Community (Manual of Discipline)

1QSa (= 1Q28a)	Rule of the Community (Appendix)
1QSb (= 1Q28b)	Collection of Benedictions
1QM	War of the Sons of Light against the Sons of Darkness
1QH	Hymns of Thanksgiving
4QFlor	Florilegium, Cave 4
4Qtest	Messianic Testimonia, Cave 4
4Qpatr	Patriarchal Blessing, Cave 4
4QSi	Songs of the Sabbath Sacrifices, Cave 4
CD	Fragments of a Zadokite work (Damascus Document)

Babylonian Talmud Tractates

Aboth	Aboth	Meg.	Megillah	Shab.	Shabbath
B.B.	Baba Bathra	Naz.	Nazir	Shek.	Shekalim
B.K.	Baba Kamma	Ned.	Nedarim	Suk.	Sukkah
Ber.	Berakoth	Nid.	Niddah	Ta.	Ta'anith
Edu.	Eduyoth	Peah	Peah	Tamid	Tamid
Hag.	Hagigah	Pes.	Pesahim	Yeb.	Yebamoth
Kid.	Kiddushin	Sanh.	Sanhedrin	Yoma	Yoma

Other Abbreviations

BJRL	*Bulletin of the John Rylands Library*
Blass-Debrunner	F. Blass–A. Debrunner, *A Greek Grammar*, ed. R. W. R. W. Funk, Chicago 1961
BT	*The Bible Translator*
BTB	*Biblical Theology Bulletin*
BZ	*Biblische Zeitschrift*
Billerbeck = SB	H. L. Strack und P. Billerbeck, *Kommentar zum Neuen Testament*
BC	*The Beginnings of Christianity*, ed. F. J. F. Jackson and K. Lake
CAP	R. M. Charles, *Apocrypha and Pseudepigrapha*, 2 vols. Oxford 1913
CBQ	*Catholic Biblical Quarterly*
Ct.	Contra, Contrast
DBS	*Dictionnaire de la Bible Supplément*, ed. L. Pirot
DSS	Dead Sea Scrolls
En	I Enoch

ET	English Text
EvTh	*Evangelische Theologie*
ExpT	*Expository Times*
EQ	*Evangelical Quarterly*
Eus*HE*	Eusebius, *Ecclesiastical History*
FT	French Text
GT	German Text
HE	See Eus
HTR	*Harvard Theological Review*
HUCA	*Hebrew Union College Annual*
j	Jerusalem Talmud
JBL	*Journal of Biblical Literature*
JCP	*Journal of Classical and Sacred Philology*
JE	*The Jewish Encyclopedia*, ed. I. Singer
JGC	*Jews, Greeks and Christians*, ed. R. Hamerton-Kelly
Jos	Josephus
JQR	*Jewish Quarterly Review*
JR	*Journal of Religion*
JSJ	*Journal for the Study of Judaism*
JSS	*Journal of Semitic Studies*
JTS	*Journal of Theological Studies*
Jubil	Jubilees
LXX	Septuagint
Mek	The Mekilta
MT	Massoretic Text
n	note, footnote
NEB	New English Bible
NovT	*Novum Testamentum*
NT	New Testament
NTS	*New Testament Studies*
OT	Old Testament
RSR	*Recherches de Science Religieuse*
Rab	Midrash Rabbah
RB	*Revue Biblique*
RevSciRel	*Revue des Sciences Religieuses*
RGG	*Religion in Geschichte und Gegenwart*
RHPR	*Revue d'Histoire et de Philosophie Religieuses*
RQ	*Revue de Qumran*
SB	see Billerbeck

SBL	Society of Biblical Literature
SEÅ	*Svensk Exegetisk Årsbok*
SJT	*Scottish Journal of Theology*
ST	*Studia Theologica*
TB	*Tyndale Bulletin*
TDNT	*Theological Dictionary of the New Testament,* ed. G. Kittel
Test	Testaments of the Twelve Patriarchs
TLZ	*Theologische Literaturzeitung*
TS	*Theological Studies*
TSota	Tosefta, Sota
TU	*Texte und Untersuchungen*
TWNT	see *TDNT*
TynB	see *TB*
VF	*Verkündigung und Forschung*
VT	*Vetus Testamentum*
Weymouth	R. F. Weymouth, *The NT in Modern Speech*
Wycliffe-Purvey	J. Wycliffe and J. Purvey, *The NT in English*
ZNTW	*Zeitschrift für die Neutestamentliche Wissenschaft*
ZTK	*Zeitschrift für Theologie und Kirche*

INTRODUCTION

The mission-praxis of the early church provides an important key to its theology, and this is nowhere more true than in the letters of Paul[1]. Of particular significance for the Pauline mission-praxis is the role of the teaching-leadership, i.e. the way in which it perceives and carries out its task. In the first part of the present volume this issue is addressed.

The first chapter finds that Paul's co-workers constituted recognized leadership groups who, on the basis of their charisms and sometimes of their appointment, had certain responsibilities toward the community and, in turn, were entitled to the community's esteem and support. They were on occasion the recipients as well as the co-senders of Paul's letters. Whether they also had a role in creating certain pericopes within the letters is a question that is taken up again in the second part of the book.

The co-workers who are engaged in preaching and teaching continue to be the subject of discussion in the following two chapters. Such persons have gifts of inspired speech and discernment, 'spiritual' gifts that in the Old Testament are associated with the prophets and the wise men and in the Pauline letters with persons designated pneumatics. The pneumatics, who have prophetic-type gifts, apparently receive their name from the special association of the holy Spirit, the *pneuma,* with the prophets. Like the prophets in the Old Testament and the 'wise teachers' at Qumran, they receive their visions and revelations via angelic powers, who are 'the spirits of the prophets' (I Cor 14:32). From this background, and not from Gnostic mythology as some scholars have contended, the concepts of wisdom and knowledge in I Corinthians are best explained. In the writings and experiences of the apocalyptic writers these concepts are given a per-

---

[1] Cf. M. Hengel, 'Die Ursprünge der christlichen Mission', *NTS* 18 (1971–72), 18: 'the Sitz im Leben of the Pauline theology is the mission of the Apostle'.

spective and definition that provide a most important antecedent for Paul's understanding of the terms.

The pneumatics lead the church's worship and direct its teaching, yet certain of them in the Corinthian church have misused their gifts and are attracted and increasingly attached to Paul's opponents. They provoke a strong response from the Apostle, who sees in their ethics and in their teaching a departure from the rule of Scripture and from the Christocentric model for Christian ministry. They have put their faith in human wisdom and, failing to recognize their gifts as a manifestation of grace, they have become boastful (cf. I Cor 2:5; 4:6f.; 12:3). In a word they have lost the essential focus of Christian faith that, in the language of the Reformation, is *solus Christus, sola gratia, sola fides, sola Scriptura*. In Paul's response to the Corinthians, discussed in chapters 4 and 5, he expresses most clearly his own understanding of wisdom and knowledge by relating the concepts to the risen Christ, who in his exaltation remains 'Christ crucified'.

The opponents of Paul, who also are pneumatics, have gone even further. In his view they have perverted their gifts and now subvert his churches, serving Satan rather than Christ (II Cor 11:13ff.). In the history of the research, sketched out in chapter 6, they were identified as Gnostics (Hammond, Mosheim, Burton, Schenkel), as Judaizers (Tittmann, Baur), or as Gnostics in one place and Judaizers in another (Lightfoot, Lütgert). For the above scholars the Gnostic opponents were carefully distinguished from the second-century Gnostic systems. But in the 'history of religions' school of the early twentieth century (Bousset, Reitzenstein), whose method is open to serious criticism, the opponents of Paul were virtually identified with the views of the later Gnosticism.

In the light of the earlier research the opponents are here evaluated with reference to their theological viewpoint, their role in the church's mission and their origin. As pneumatics they offer a knowledge (γνῶσις) of God based upon the prophet's discernment of God's purpose, e.g. by visions and revelations and by inspired expositions of Scripture. They are not isolated teachers but are a part of a counter-mission that is dangerously active from Syria to Rome. Although they may vary their emphasis somewhat to suit the occasion, they appear to combine libertine sympathies or practices and a boastful, self-confident attitude with ritual strictness and judaizing sentiments. In some respects they are remarkably similar to the false teachers in the letter of Jude who are investigated in chapter 16. One type throughout the Pauline letters, they are adherents of — and deviants from — the circumcision party, the ritually strict wing of the Jerusalem/Palestinian church. Their place within the broader context of the Christian mission is considered in chapter 7.

The problem with the circumcision party in the Pauline churches is part of a larger problem within the total Christian mission. In Acts 6 two groups within the primitive Jerusalem church, the Hebrews and the Hellenists, are in dispute. From this and other texts it becomes clear that, contrary to much scholarly opinion, the names do not primarily designate linguistic differences[2]. For, although some Hebrews may have spoken Aramaic or have been bilingual, others of that party spoke and wrote Greek (Acts 15:22 f.). In so far as they participated in the diaspora mission of the church, they would of necessity have used Greek. In the seventh chapter of the present volume it is argued that the Hebrews in Acts 6, II Cor 11 and Phil 3 are Jews and/or Jewish Christians with a strict, ritualist attitude toward the cultus and that 'those of the circumcision' or the circumcision party is an equivalent designation for the same group[3]. The Hellenists, on the other hand, are those Jews and Jewish Christians characterized by a lax attitude toward the ritual law. Because of their differences the Christian Hellenists and Hebrews pursue separate missions in the diaspora. While the Hebrews as they are led by James of Jerusalem maintain a co-operative fellowship with the Hellenists, others are factious and form a persistent and theologically perverse opposition to the mission of the Hellenists, including that of Paul.

At the close of the first part of the volume the Christian prophet, as he is represented in the book of Acts, is the subject of further inquiry. In Acts the prophets reveal two features that are similar to the role of the pneumatics in the Pauline literature: They engage in ministries of teaching and exhortation (14:22; 15:32; cf. I Th 3:2), and they give Christological expositions of Scripture (13:1, 16—41; cf. I Cor 2:6—16). The latter ministry leads to the theme of the second

---

[2] Martin Hengel (*Judaism and Hellenism*, 2 vols., Philadelphia 1974, I, 58) may be right when he states that the word ἑλληνίζειν primarily meant 'speak Greek correctly' and only secondarily 'adopt a Greek style of life'. However, the question in Acts is not whether the Hellenists could speak Greek but whether it is that characteristic which distinguishes the Hellenists from the Hebrews in the context of first-century Judaism and of the early Christian mission.

[3] E.g. in Acts 10:45; 11:2; Gal 2:12; Col 4:11; Tit 1:10.

part of the book where the biblical hermeneutic of the New Testament writers, and other pneumatics cited by them, is examined in detail.

Prophetic exposition and application of Scripture is one way in which the early Christian pneumatics exercise their ministry. Introducing the essays concerned with this aspect of their task, chapter 9 gives an overview of issues that will be developed more specifically in the subsequent chapters. After a survey of formulas employed to introduce quotations and of testimony-texts that sum up the early church's understanding of its Bible, this essay describes a number of commentary-forms and techniques that are found in the New Testament. It suggests that the testimony-texts and other independent citations often have been derived from earlier commentary (midrash), commentary that established the Christological meaning of the texts by exegetical methods used in contemporary Judaism. The essay also considers the theological presuppositions of New Testament usage, including its conception of salvation history, its typological interpretation of the Old Testament, its corporate view of man and its conviction that the meaning of Scripture is not to be ascertained by 'method' or by human wisdom, but through a charismatic exegesis that becomes a part of the divine revelation itself.

The following four chapters elaborate certain elements of the initial essay. The first provides examples of Paul's use of the Qumran *pesher* technique, that is, the quotation of Old Testament passages in which the wording of the cited text is altered to fit it to the Apostle's present-time, eschatological application. The second detects, in quotations including the formula λέγει κύριος and utilizing the *pesher* method, characteristic marks of the work of prophets. Chapter 12 raises the problem of the definition of biblical commentary (midrash) and paraphrastic translation (targum) and of their relationship to one another; and it gives examples to support the thesis, mentioned above, that certain *testimonia* have been extracted from earlier commentary-contexts. The essay on midrashic features in Acts (e.g. 2:16—36; 13:16—41) investigates further a number of such commentary-contexts.

Exploring the background of Paul's exegesis, the note on I Cor 10:4 (chapter 14) analyses a parallel reference in Paul and a Jewish targum to the rock that followed the Israelites in the wilderness. It concludes that Paul and the targum may draw upon a common tradition about the rock originating in interpretations of the Exodus in Isaiah and the Psalms.

The last three chapters consider the influence of expository patterns on the literary form of the Pauline letters, the letter of Jude and the Gospel traditions. 'Exegetical patterns in I Corinthians and Romans' reveal that commentary-forms are employed not only to present biblical expositions but also to create, in part, the structure of the Pauline letter itself. Similarly, the letter of Jude is nothing other than a commentary on sacred texts set within the framework of a letter. Composed by the prophet of that name who appears in Acts 15, it represents a Scriptural judgment on the same group of false teachers that Paul opposed in his letters.

The final chapter offers a critique of the older form criticism of the Gospels, particularly its asumptions of a sharp discontinuity between Jesus and the post-resurrection church and of an exclusively 'oral period' of transmission of the traditions. Reviewing several recent contributions that signal new directions for the discipline, it calls attention to the role of exegetical forms in the transmission of the teachings of Jesus. Returning to themes discussed above, it makes the following suggestions: (1) Since a considerable number of Jesus' followers were undoubtedly Hellenists and therefore Greek-speaking, some (written) teachings of Jesus were probably being transmitted in Greek already during his earthly ministry. (2) Some independent parables and independent dominical citations of the Old Testament probably represent a secondary stage in which the text and commentary of more original midrashim, i.e. expository units, have been separated for thematic and other reasons.

It is hoped that the two themes of the volume, the role of the pneumatics in the missionary enterprise of the early church and in the formation of a Christian theology of the Old Testament, not only will contribute to a better understanding of New Testament teachings but also will shed new light on those prophetic personalities who did so much to shape the mission and the message of the church.

I. THE PNEUMATICS AND THE EARLY CHRISTIAN MISSION

1. PAUL AND HIS CO-WORKERS

Although St Paul had no disciples, no μαθηταί[1], he did have many associates. These persons present something of a puzzle to the student of Christian origins, both in the titles and functions that are ascribed to them and, more generally, in the precise relationship that they had to Paul. A clarification of their role may serve to illuminate the structure of the early Christian mission as well as a number of problems within the Pauline letters.

In the book of Acts and the canonical literature ascribed to Paul some 100 names[2], often coupled with a score of assorted titles, are associated with the Apostle. Most of these persons are colleagues, co-workers in the Christian mission, whose designations or 'titles', using the term loosely, reflect that fact. If one eliminates those with a general[3] or no designation and those who appear only in Acts[4], there remain thirty-six persons associated with Paul under nine designations[5]. To select from this group those who evidence a

---

[1] The term does not occur in the Pauline letters. The closest approximation is τέκνον, an appellation given to Onesimus (Phlm 10), Timothy (1Cor 4,17; 1Tim 1,2; cf. Phil 2,22) and Titus (1,4) and, in the plural, to the Galatian and Corinthian Christians (Gal 4,19; 1Cor 4,14; 2Cor 6,13). In rabbinic writings a teacher often addresses his disciples as 'my children' (H. L. Strack and P. Billerbeck, *Kommentar zum Neuen Testament*, München, 1922–8, II, 559, 765 f.; cf. Aboda Zarah 2,5); however, the connotation for Paul is 'converts' or partners in work (1Cor 4,17; Phil 1,19 ff.) rather than 'disciples'. See below, 4 f. Acts 9,25 does speak of 'his [Paul's] disciples'.

[2] An annotated list given in E. B. Redlich, *S. Paul and his Companions*, London 1913, 200—86; cf. W. M. Ramsay, *St Paul the Traveller*, London 1900, 397 (42 names).

[3] E. g. ἀγαπητός *(passim)*, ἀδελφή (Phlm 2), ξένος (Rom 16,23), συγγενής (Rom 16,7,11,21). On οἱ ἐκ περιτομῆς see below, 116–128 and note 53.

[4] E. g. Lucius of Cyrene, Manaen, Simeon Niger (Acts 13,1), Gaius of Macedonia (Acts 19,29), Philip the Evangelist (Acts 21,8). On Erastus see note 7.

[5] See the chart in *NTS* 17 (1970–71), 438. The designations, προφήτης, διδάσκαλος, συνέκδημος, are given to specified colleagues only in Acts (e. g. 13,1; 15,32; 19,29). Ποιμήν (1Cor 9,7; cf. Eph. 4,11) is only implied; εὐαγγελιστής (2Tim 4,5;

long-term relationship with the Apostle is a more difficult task, for it raises a number of disputed questions concerning the authenticity of certain letters and the reliability of the data and chronological structure in Acts. However, with a minimal synchronization of Paul's letters with Acts[6] one may in any case date the association of Mark and Titus from the Antiochian period, of Timothy, Prisca, Aquila, Aristarchus, and probably Luke and Erastus from the mission to Greece or 'the second missionary journey'. Demas, Epaphras, Tychicus and Trophimus join Paul at the latest during the mission based at Rome[7]. However, they may be associated with the earlier Ephesian ministry by inference or on the supposition of an Ephesian provenance for Colossians and Philemon. If one grants the historicity of the notices in 2 Timothy 4[8], nine of these co-workers[9] continue in rather close association with the Apostle, though probably not without interruptions, to the end of his life[10]. Five of them — Erastus, Mark, Timothy, Titus, and

---

cf. Eph 4,11; Acts 21,8), λειτουργός (Phil 2,25; cf. Rom 15,16), οἰκονόμος (1Cor 4,1 f.; cf. Tit 1,7), πρεσβύτης (= ambassador, Phlm 9; cf. 2Cor 5,20; Eph 6,20; 2Macc 12,34), and ὑπηρέτης (1Cor 4,1; cf. Lk 1,2; Acts 13,5) are singular occurrences. On ἀπαρχή and λειτουργός see below, note 77.

[6] Without Acts it is doubtful that any chronology of Paul's ministry is possible. For the most thoroughgoing, but highly conjectural, attempt cf. J. Knox, *Chapters in the Life of Paul*, London 1954, 47—88; cf. also, on a more limited scale, J. C. Hurd, *The Origin of I Corinthians*, New Haven and London 1965, 260 f., 289 ff., 295 f.

[7] The identity of Erastus in Rom 16,23 and 2Tim 4,20 with the 'helper' in Acts 19,22 is uncertain; in favour of this is the continuing connection with Timothy and with Corinth. If Luke is not identified with the diarist in Acts (16,10 ff.; 'we'), his contact with Paul can be dated only from the ministry in Ephesus or in Rome. On Tychicus and Trophimus cf. Acts 20,4.

[8] One may do so without accepting the authenticity of the letter. Cf. P. N. Harrison, *The Problem of The Pastoral Epistles*, Oxford 1921, 93—102. However, its composition by an amanuensis or by a colleague during Paul's life and under his eye appears to be the most probable answer to the historical and literary problems. So, recently, C. F. D. Moule, *The Problem of the Pastoral Epistles: A Reappraisal* (*BJRL* XLVII), Manchester 1965; J. N. D. Kelly, *The Pastoral Epistles*, London 1963, 27—34. Cf. A. Strobel in *NTS* XV (1968—9), 191—210; J. A. T. Robinson, *Redating the New Testament*, London 1976, 67—85.

[9] Excepting Demas, who apparently abandoned his ministry (2Tim 4,10), Aristarchus and Epaphras, who are last mentioned in Phlm 23 f.; Col 4,10,12. If the evidence in Colossians and Ephesians is disallowed, the number of persons is reduced by one: Tychicus.

[10] With the exception of Erastus, Trophimus, and Tychicus all are identified as συνεργοί.

Tychicus — stand in an explicit subordination to Paul, serving him or being subject to his instructions[11].

Barnabas, Silas, and Apollos present an interesting variation. Although they are co-workers and on cordial terms with one another, Paul and Apollos always appear to work independently, admittedly with some mutual colleagues[12]. Similarly, Barnabas and Silas, who join Paul on specific missions, go their own way later[13]. None of these persons, at least in Paul's letters, is presented as being under Paul's authority, and it may be significant that all of them are termed apostles[14]. Perhaps Prisca and Aquila also should be included among those who, though in friendly association with the Apostle, for the most part work in relative independence of him.

In summary, the picture that emerges is that of a missionary with a large number of associates. Indeed, Paul is scarcely ever found without companions. Yet few of them are included in his immediate and subordinate working circle, still fewer work with him on a continuing, long-term basis.

I.

When the designations given to Paul's associates are collated, one is struck by the absence of certain terms, not only those later to become traditional for leaders in the Church but also many terms identified with the spiritual gifts or charisms specified by Paul. In his letters no colleague is called prophet, teacher or pas-

---

[11] Acts 19,22; 2Tim 4,11; Phil 2,19; Col 4,8. Apart from the letter addressed to him, the case of Titus is uncertain. In 2Cor 12,18 he is 'urged' to go, apparently in contrast to 'the brothers' who are 'sent'. Cf. Tit 3,12; C. K. Barrett, 'Titus', *Neotestamentica et Semitica*, ed. E. E. Ellis and M. Wilcox, Edinburgh 1969, 11: Titus differs from the brothers in that he is on Paul's staff (κοινωνός).

[12] Cf. 1Cor 3,9. Paul can 'urge' Apollos to go (but not 'send' him) to Corinth with a party of 'the brothers' (1Cor 16,11 f.; cf. Tit 3,13).

[13] After the mission to Greece Silas disappears from view unless he is identified with the 'brother' and amanuensis in 1Petr 5,12. Apparently Barnabas, like Paul, continues his work (independently) in the Aegean area (cf. 1Cor 9,6; Col 4,10).

[14] 1Cor 4,9; 9,5 f. (cf. Acts 14,4,14); 1Thess 2,7. In his letters Paul also does not 'send' or instruct them. However in Acts (17,15) the travel companions receive a command (ἐντολή) for Silas to come to Paul.

tor, let alone elder or bishop. The most used designations are, in descending frequency, συνεργός, ἀδελφός, διάκονος, and ἀπόστολος. Interpreted within their Pauline context, they give an insight into the function of Paul's associates and, consequently, into the form and strategy of his mission.

Not used of believers in general[15], συνεργός like its cognate ἐργά-της often refers to itinerant workers[16]. Co-workers may be describ-ed as equal to one another, as are Paul and Apollos in 1Cor 3,8 f., but this is not implicit in the term. For example, with reference to the plagues on Egypt, Philo can call the insects God's συνεργοί[17]. There is, therefore, no objection, to interpreting συνεργοὶ θεοῦ in 1Cor 3,9 as co-workers 'with God'[18]. That is, Paul views himself and Apollos to be working 'with God' in God's work even though they work as God's paid servants: each to receive 'his reward ac-cording to his toil'[19]. Later in 1 Corinthians Paul associates the 'reward' for 'working' with the right of support from the congre-

---

[15] They are co-workers 'with God' (1Cor 3,9; 1Thess 3,2) 'in Christ' (Rom 16,3.9; cf. 1Thess 3,2), of Paul (Rom 16,21; Phil 2,25; Phlm 24), and for the Christian community (2Cor 8,23; cf. 1 Cor 3,9; 2Cor 1,24). See below, note 26. These qualifiers indicate, respectively, whose work it is, the sphere and com-pany in which it is done, and those who receive its benefits. In 1Cor 3,9; 2Cor 1,24; 8,23 the co-workers are implicitly distinguished from the congregation. Cf. 3Joh 8: those who support the missionaries, viz. 'the brothers', become 'co-workers'. C. K. Barrett, *The Epistle to the Romans*, London 1957, 283 f., dis-tinguishes the church-worker who 'toiled for you' from those 'who toiled in the Lord', i. e. worked as Christians (Rom 16,6.12).

[16] However, this does not appear to be necessarily or always the case. Cf. Phil 4,3; Phlm 1. See note 32.

[17] Philo, *de vita Mosis*, 1,110; in creating and governing the universe the heavenly Potencies (δυνάμεις) are God's 'co-workers' (*de opif. mun.* 75 and *de confus.* 172 ff. on Genesis 1,26; 11,7). Similarly in the DSS, e. g. 1QM 13,10, the angels are 'helpers' (עזר = ? συνεργός) of the congregation. Cf. G. Bertram, *TWNT* VII (1964), 871. The term is functional, and the question of status is not an issue one way or the other. Thus, if συνεργός is equivalent to the rab-binic חבר, it is only in the general sense of 'partner' without the technical con-notation of an unordained or junior colleague (so, Billerbeck, *op. cit.* II, 653; III, 318).

[18] So, on 1Thess 3,2, A. von Harnack, 'ΚΟΠΟΣ', *ZNTW* XXVII (1928), 7. Cf. 2Cor 6,1. C. K. Barrett, *First Epistle to the Corinthians*, London 1968, 86, recognizes that this is 'consistent with Paul's thought' although in 1Cor 3,9 he prefers, on contextual grounds, the translation 'in the service of God'. Similarly, V. P. Furnish, *JBL* LXXX (1961), 369. Cf. Mk 16,20; Rom 8,28.

[19] Cf. 1Cor 3,8 (κόπος) with 3,14 (ἔργον).

gation. This is buttressed[20] *inter alia* by an appeal in 1Cor 9,14 to a saying of the Lord, probably the same as or one similar to that explicitly cited in 1Tim 5,18. This saying, 'the worker (ἐργάτης)[21] is worthy of his reward', is in 1Tim (5,17; cf. 2Tim 2,6) applied to 'those who toil (οἱ κοπιῶντες) in word and teaching'. In the undisputed Pauline letters there is a similar equation of the co-workers and the toilers. Thus, the addressees in 1Cor 16,16,18 are exhorted to be subject παντὶ τῷ συνεργοῦντι καὶ κοπιῶντι[22] and to give recognition to them. Allowing for variations in nuance, the two terms appear to be equivalent expressions for a class of Christian workers[23]. Harnack investigated the latter term with special reference to 1Thess 5,12. He showed, convincingly in my judgement, that those who 'toil, govern and admonish' the 'brothers' are a specific, i. e. an appointed group[24]. Although their function had no legal, contractual character and stood or fell with their charisms, their work entitled them to the community's esteem.

The close relationship of διάκονος to these terms is most clearly observed in 1Cor 3,5,9 and 2Cor 6,1,4 where the word occurs in

---

[20] Cf. 1Cor 9,1,13 f.,17. On 1Cor 9,17 cf. A. Robertson and A. Plummer, *First Epistle of St Paul to the Corinthians*, Edinburgh 1911, 189 f.

[21] The term is used for opponents in 2Cor 11,13 and Phil 3,2, for co-workers in 1Tim 5,18; 2Tim 2,15.

[22] Note the one article bracketing both participles. Cf. also the synonymous use of κόπος and ἔργον in 1Cor 3,8,13 ff. Almost certainly one class of persons is in view. G. Bertram (*TWNT* VII, 1964, 872 f.) thinks that the words correspond to equivalent Hebrew terms עמל and עבד and calls attention to Isaiah 43,24 where God serves (עבד) and toils (יגע) for man's salvation. Less convincingly, he concludes that from such presuppositions and from the imagery of δοῦλος/ἐργάτης in the parables of Jesus, e. g. Mt 13,24–30; 20,1–16, Paul derives his self-description as δοῦλος. See note 38.

[23] Some distinction may be present in 1Thess 1,3.

[24] Harnack, 'ΚΟΠΟΣ', 1–10. So, F. Hauck *TDNT* III (1966/1938), 829: in 1Thess 5,12f. 'the reference is to office bearers of the congregation'. Harnack thinks it very probable that recognized charisms and the laying on of hands (presumably as an 'appointment') were united from the beginning. Against the views of Dibelius and von Dobschütz, reference to 'their work' and to keeping peace 'with them' (𝔓 30ℵ D) presupposes a recognized group; their 'governing' (προϊστάμενους, cf. the similar order: 'helpers', 'administrators', in 1Cor 12,28) apparently implies an official capacity. The fact that 'admonishing' (1Thess 5,14) may be carried out also by a broader group of 'brothers' is no objection to Harnack's exegesis (otherwise: E. Schweizer, *Church Order in the New Testament*, London, 1961, 191 = 23 c). J. B. Lightfoot, *Notes on the Epistles of Paul*, London 1904, 79, calls attention to the verbal parallels between this passage and 1Tim 5,17 and concludes that the same 'office' is in view.

tandem with 'co-worker'. With reference to his opponents Paul apparently equates the *diakonos* with the 'worker' (ἐργάτης) and defines the *diakonos* of Christ in terms of toil (κόπος) and suffering in the service of the gospel[25]. Similarly in 1Cor 16,15 f., 'the co-workers and toilers' are those who have devoted themselves to the *diakonia* of the saints[26]. From such references it is tempting simply to equate *diakonos* with 'church worker'. But several considerations suggest that it has a more restricted meaning. As Professor Georgi has pointed out, the term is used of 'preachers' or with reference to preaching activity both in secular sources and in the New Testament[27]. In contrast to their opponents in Corinth Paul and his companions, *diakonoi* of the new covenant, did not 'peddle' or 'falsify' the word of God (2Cor 2,17; 4,2), but rather accepted pay (ὀψώνιον) from other churches 'for *diakonia* to you', i. e. to preach the gospel to them (2Cor 11,8,7).

A closely related connotation of *diakonos* is that of teacher, i. e. one who has been entrusted with and is, therefore, to communicate the 'mysteries of God'. Thus, as ὑπηρέται of Christ (1Cor 4,1), a term essentially equivalent to *diakonos*[28], Paul and Apollos are stewards of the mysteries of God. Both functions of the *diakonos*,

---

[25] 2Cor 11,23–9; cf. 11,13 (ἐργάται) with 11,15 (διάκονοι). The collection for Jerusalem, which is termed a *diakonia* (2Cor 9,1; cf. Rom 15,25), also falls within this meaning even if its description as a λειτουργία (2Cor 9,12; cf. Rom. 15,27) is taken in a non-cultic sense (so, H. Strathmann, *TDNT* IV (1967/ 1942), 227; but see below, note 77.). For it is viewed not only implicitly as a response to a *diakonia* of the gospel from Jerusalem to them (Rom 15,27) but also explicitly as a religious 'work' bringing God's reward (2Cor 9,6–15). It may have other theological implications as well (cf. J. Munck, *Paul and the Salvation of Mankind*, London 1959, 303–5).

[26] According to Eph 4,11 f. Christ gives to the Church 'apostles, prophets, evangelists, shepherds and teachers' for the 'work of ministry' (ἔργον διακονίας). One may be a *diakonos* of God (2Cor 6,4), of Christ (2Cor 11,23;· Col 1,7), of the gospel (Col 1,23; Eph 3,7; cf. 1Thess 3,2) or to a local congregation (Rom 16,1: obj. gen.; Phil 1,1). See above, note 15. Both Phoebe (Rom 16,1 f.) and Stephanas' house (1Cor 16,15 ff.) are not just those who use their wealth for the benefit of missionaries (Hort) but are themselves involved in ministry. Cf. F. J. A. Hort, *The Christian Ecclesia*, London 1897, 204 ff.

[27] D. Georgi, *Die Gegner des Paulus im 2. Korintherbrief*, Neukirchen 1964, 32–6.

[28] Cf. K. H. Rengstorf, *TWNT* VIII (1969), 543, cf. 533: the καί in 1Cor 4,1 is epexegetical and there is no tension (Spannung) between ὑπηρέτης there and *diakonos* in 1Cor 3,5; the latter term only lays more emphasis on the 'wage' involved in the service. Cf. 1Petr 4,10 f.

preaching[29] and teaching, are elaborated, with special attention to the communication of the mystery, in Colossians/Ephesians[30] and in the Pastorals[31].

In short the *diakonoi* appear to be a special class of co-workers, those who are active in preaching and teaching. They appear in Paul's circle not only as itinerant workers (Georgi) but also as workers in local congregations, such as Phoebe (Rom 16,1) and the

---

[29] According to Eph 3,7 f. Paul was made a *diakonos* according to the gift of grace, i. e. the grace to 'preach the gospel to the Gentiles' (e. g. T. K. Abbott, *The Epistles to the Ephesians and to the Colossians*, Edinburgh 1897, 86). Similarly, Col 1,23. In contrast to false 'teachers', Timothy is to endure suffering, do the work (ἔργον) of an evangelist and (thus) fulfil his *diakonia* (2Tim 4,3 ff.); here the term appears to include preaching and teaching (διδαχῇ, 4,2) generally. Cf. 2Tim 4,11. The references in 1Tim 3,8,12; 4,6 are the same and should not, any more than the others, be read from the presuppositions of later ecclesiastical usage. The English translation 'deacon' (also in Phil 1,1) is, therefore, quite misleading.

[30] Eph 3,5 ff.,7−10: the mystery is divinely revealed to the 'holy apostles and prophets' (5 ff.); the function of the *diakonos* is to enlighten (φωτίσαι) men to it (9 f.). According to Col 1,24−9 Paul as a *diakonos* has a stewardship (οἰκονομία), viz. to make fully known 'the mystery' (25 f.); this he does by preaching and teaching (νουθετοῦντες καὶ διδάσκοντες), activities in which he toils (κοπιάω) to present every man mature in Christ (28 f.). Paul here describes himself in accordance with the particular function of a *diakonos* and does not, of course, exclude himself from other functions, for example, of apostle and prophet. In Eph 4,11 f. (see above, note 26) 'shepherds and teachers' probably refer to two aspects of one group (cf. Abbott, *op. cit.* 118; Lightfoot, *op. cit.* 79) and may represent differing functions of *diakonoi*. But, then, so may the other charisms since *diakonia* is the effect of all of them. In this connection Rom 12,6 f., in which the gift of *diakonia* apparently is distinguished from that of teaching, poses an interesting exegetical question. 'The one who teaches ... the one who exhorts' could be, and in the light of Paul's usage perhaps should be, read in apposition with *diakonia*: 'whether prophecy, in proportion to his faith, or *diakonia*, in his *diakonia* (whether the teacher in his teaching or the exhorter in his exhortation)'. The shift in construction indicates that specific persons are in view. But see C. E. B. Cranfield in *Service in Christ*, ed. J. I. McCord, London 1966, 38 f.

[31] See above, n. 29. By putting Paul's teaching before 'the brothers', Timothy will be a good *diakonos* of Christ (1Tim 4,6). The congregational *diakonoi* are not to be 'double talkers' (διλόγους) and are to hold the 'mystery of the faith' with a clear conscience (1Tim 3,8 f.; cf. Polyc 5,2) − the latter almost certainly refers to a teaching function. The ἐπίσκοποι are explicit stated to be teachers (1Tim 3,2; cf. Tit 1,9) but, as Kelly remarks, 'the functions of deacons covered much the same ground as *episcopoi*' (Kelly, *op. cit.* 80). Cf. also Didache 15,1: the overseers and *diakonoi* perform the same service (λειτουργία) as the prophets and teachers; Ignatius, Phila 11,1: 'Philo, the *diakonos* ... now ministers (ὑπηρετεῖ) with me in the word of God', i. e. assists in teaching. See note 53.

ministers in the church at Philippi (Phil 1,1)[32]. For the essential factor seems to have been ministry not movement, the charismatic function without any peripatetic implications. Their teaching function is of special interest, for it is this type of Christian worker (ὁ κατηχῶν) that in Gal 6,6 is specifically singled out as deserving pay[33].

The right to remuneration is evident not only from such passages as Gal 6 but also from Paul's almost obsessive attention to the question. On the one hand he firmly asserts, on biblical and dominical authority, the right of the 'worker', i. e. preacher[34], to his wage. On the other hand it is his boast that he does not exercise this right[35], and he urges certain persons in Thessalonica to 'imitate us' in this matter[36]. Furthermore, he scathingly denounces

---

[32] Georgi (*op. cit.* 35—8) rightly calls attention to the 'missionary' character of many *diakonoi*, e. g. in Ignatius (Eph 2,1; Phila 10,1; 11,1), and this apparently is also true of Phoebe. But the function precedes and is not necessarily related to travelling. That connection is due in part to the false dichotomy made by Harnack between local and universal ministries. Cf. H. Conzelmann, *Der erste Brief an die Korinther*, Göttingen 1969, 253 (ET: 215). In the light of the above usage, the *diakonoi* in Phil 1,1 refer almost certainly to local ministers (cf. G. Delling, *Worship in the New Testament*, London 1962, 157; Georgi, *op. cit.* 34) who served in an official, i. e. a recognized and designated capacity in the community. See note 16.

[33] E. Schweizer (*op. cit.* 103 = 7 *n*) recognizes in this and other passages a congregational support of some members in acknowledgement of services rendered. For the form of ministry in these churches, however, this issue has greater implications than he appears to be prepared to admit. E. D. Burton, *The Epistle to the Galatians*, Edinburgh 1921, 335, rightly concludes that 'a class of paid teachers' is in view, a class to be observed also in 1Thess 5,12; 1Cor 12,28; Eph 4,11; 1Tim 5,17.

[34] 1Cor 9,3—18,13 (ἐργαζόμενοι), 14 (καταγγέλλουσιν), 16 (εὐαγγελίσωμαι). The right is not limited to apostles, for the fourfold 'proof' (9,7—14) is more broadly based than the 'case' (9,3—6; cf. 3,8) for which it is used. The occurrence of similar proofs elsewhere suggests that some, at least, are a traditional rationale for the support of workers in the Christian mission: Luke 10,7 par.; 1Tim 5,17 f.; 2Tim 2,6; Did 13,1; cf. Rom 15,27.

[35] 1Cor 9,15—18; 1Thess 2,5. This itself is an indication that the practice of remuneration was widespread: it is no grounds for boasting that one gets out of bed in the morning. Also, it is only because Paul's attitude was exceptional that he could be calumniated by his opponents for it. Cf. 2Cor 11,7; A. Plummer, *The Second Epistle of St. Paul to the Corinthians*, Edinburgh 1915, 302, who cites the practice among Greek philosophers. But see also H. D. Betz, *Lukian von Samosata*, Berlin 1961, 114; H. Windisch, *TDNT* III (1966/ 1938), 603—5 (καπηλεύω). On the rabbinic practice, e. g. the payment of the Levites, cf. Billerbeck, *op. cit.* III, 401. Cf. Ket. 106 *a*: teachers who instruct priests in the laws of the temple are to receive fees.

[36] 2Thess 3,7—9. In 1Thess 2,9; 4,11, the charge, 'to work with your hands',

the motives of his opponents who 'serve not the Lord but their own belly'[37]. All in all, Paul recognizes that *diakonoi*, or some of them at least, should be supported by the congregation; and his writings show that this is a widespread, if sometimes corrupting custom even in his own churches. He can himself gratefully accept, for example from the Philippians (4,15—19), voluntary contributions[38] and encourage, as he does in Gal 6,6, the same attitude toward teachers in the several churches.

But if this estimate of the historical situation is granted, it is difficult to avoid the conclusion of Harnack (on 1Thess 5) and of Burton (on Gal 6) that there was from the beginning in Paul's

is stated in a rather general context with the persons in view left unspecified. In 2Thess 3,6—13 their 'idleness' is explicitly contrasted with Paul's toils and labours, both in ministry and to earn his bread. This analogy seems to require a reference to persons who are similarly occupied. 2Thess 3,2 refers, then, to some of them who are not engaged seriously in ministry (and in earning bread) but who, at the same time, are supported by the community. Similarly, cf. Did 11,6; 12,3 f. with 13,1 ff.; Barn 19,10: 'seek out the persons of the saints, either toiling by word and going to exhort and meditating to save a soul by the word; or you shall work with your hands'. On 'the brothers' in Thessalonica see below, 19 ff.

[37] Rom 16,17 f.; cf. 2Cor 2,17; Phil 3,19. In the term δουλεύω, apparently with reference to false teaching (cf. διδαχή, Rom 16,17), there is a touch of irony: in contrast to the *diakonos* the *doulos* did not receive payment. See the following note. It is probable that they are the same opponents who, in Tit 1,11 f. are 'lazy gluttons' and who 'teach for base gain'. See below, 113 f.

[38] In this attitude may lie, in part, the distinctiveness of δοῦλος, a term that Paul applied to himself and to Timothy and, in Colossians, to Epaphras and Tychicus. Unlike the (more inclusive) term *diakonos*, the *doulos* had no right to a 'wage' (cf. K. H. Rengstorf, *TDNT* VIII, 1969, 533); these colleagues may have emulated Paul in forgoing such rights. Perhaps more important is the Old Testament background in which the *doulos* of God signified a special fidelity to Yahweh (G. Sass, *ZNTW* XL, 1941, 24—32) or was a special designation for the prophets. The former meaning probably is present in such references to Abraham and Moses in Jewish writings. The term is used in Amos 3,7 with reference to God's revelation of his 'mystery' to 'his servants the prophets'. This connotation is present both in Qumran (1QpHab 7,3 ff.; 2,1 ff., 8 f.; cf. 1QS 11,15f.; 1QH 13,18; 17,25) and in Revelation (10,7; 11,18; cf. 6,11; 22,6,9; otherwise: A. Satake, *Die Gemeindeordnung in der Johannesapokalypse*, Neukirchen 1966, 87—96). Cf. F. F. Bruce in *Neotestamentica et Semitica*, ed. E. E. Ellis and M. Wilcox, Edinburgh 1969, 225—9. Paul's usage probably is related to that of other Christian writings, e. g. James 1,1; 2Peter 1,1; Jude 1; Rev 1,1. The close association with *diakonos* = teacher of the word of God may be inferred from 2Cor 3,6; 4,1,2,5; cf. preceding note; 2Tim 2,24. And the connotation 'prophet' may be present in Gal 1,10 ff.; cf. Acts 2,18. Cf. Rev 2,19 f.; 10,7 (μυστήριον); IgnEph 2,1; Magn 2,2; Sym 12,1 f.; Phila 11,1. See notes 22, 63.

churches as well as among his missionary colleagues, a class of persons who by virtue of their work were entitled to esteem, and some at least to financial support[39]. Such a group must have been *ipso facto* visible and distinguishable from the congregation. And it must have had a certain measure of continuity. As Professor Schweizer has emphasized, this ministry, like any other, always arose from and depended upon a charismatic authorization[40]. But these *diakonoi* also constituted a professional 'class' (Burton) with a recognizable form, however varied or imprecise the vocabulary by which they were identified[41].

Just as *diakonoi* were a special class of workers, so 'apostles' probably were regarded by Paul as a special class of *diakonoi*. Accordingly, they do the same work, preaching and teaching, as the *diakonoi*, and Paul can, with reference to his apostolic labours, refer to himself as a *diakonos*[42]. An important distinction of

---

'Slave of Christ' is applied also to Christians generally (1Cor 7,22; Eph 6,6; cf. Acts 2,18; 1Petr 2,16), a usage for which Deissmann finds a parallel in the sacred manumission of slaves, e. g. at Delphi. A. Deissmann, *Light from the Ancient East*, London 1927, 319—27. More inclusively, Josephus and Philo use 'slaves of God' of any pious Jew (*Ant.* 11,101; *de mut. nom.* 46; *de migr. Abr.* 45) or the whole world (cf. *de vita Mosis* 1,201).

[39] See notes 24, 33.

[40] Schweizer, *op. cit.* But his words, 'all order is an "afterwards"' (102 f. = 7 m), can be misleading since a recognizable, probably appointed leadership is present from the first weeks (1Thess 5,12; see above, 7). The same 'order' that could appoint missionary representatives in 2Cor 8,19 (cf. Phil 2,25; 4,18) could, and apparently did, appoint local leadership. Charism and appointment (by imposition of hands?), concurrently or in immediate succession, are less explicit but apparently no more mutually exclusive in the earlier Pauline letters than they are in the Pastorals (1Tim 4,14; 5,22; 2Tim 1,6; Tit 1,5,9; cf. 1Tim 2,7 and 2Tim 1,11 with 1Cor 12,28) or in Acts (cf. 6,3,6; 13,2 f.; 14,23 with 20,28). Cf. M. Goguel, *The Primitive Church*, London 1964 (1947), 117 ff.: as 'the second generation succeeded to the first, the organization was not transformed, the character of the ministries did not undergo a sharp change, nor was one system replaced by another. The emphasis in the conception of ministry merely shifted somewhat' (119 f.).

[41] Cf. Burton, *op. cit.* 335. See above, 10.

[42] 1Cor 3,5; Col 1,23,25. Cf. 1Cor 4,9—15 *(apostoloi)* with 2Cor 6,4—10 *(diakonoi)*; Eph 3,7 with 3,5; 1,1. Also 'apostles' in 1Cor 4,9 includes Apollos who, with Paul, is termed *diakonos* in the same context (1Cor 3,5). From Acts 18,24 f.; 19,1—5 it is clear only that Apollos worked independently of the Jerusalem church and perhaps knew only a Galilean tradition of Christianity (cf. F. F. Bruce, *The Acts of the Apostles*, London 1951, 351). The appellation in 1Cor 4,9 suggests that in Paul's view he was commissioned by Jesus, perhaps in the pre-resurrection mission in the style of those in Luke 9,59; 10,1. For

apostles, their dominical commission[43], may explain their absence from Paul's on-going working circle. Apparently each apostle carried out his own commission in relative independence and developed his own group of co-workers[44].

II.

More important for understanding the structure of the Pauline mission are those associates known as 'the brothers'. Like δοῦλοι, the term ἀδελφοί may refer to Christians generally. But there is

Paul the Twelve are qualified by apostleship (1Cor 15,5), but apostleship is not qualified by the Twelve. Nor do the Twelve appear to form any original or central core of apostleship (otherwise: A. Harnack, *The Mission and Expansion of Christianity*, London 1908, I, 323 f.). On the functional emphasis in the Pauline concept of apostle cf. Georgi, *op. cit.* 43—9. For Acts see below, 143 n.

[43] 1Cor 9,1; 15,3—10; Gal 1; but see also 2Cor 11,5 f. (γνῶσις); 12,12 (σημεῖα ×. τ. λ.). This does not exclude the possibility and the fact of false apostles (2Cor 11,13). It is not entirely certain whether they were originally commissioned by Jesus and, like Judas, later were found to be ἀδόκιμοι or whether they are unauthorized impostors, transforming themselves (μετασχηματιζόμενοι, 2Cor 11,13) into apostles of Christ. But the former is probable since Paul does not contest their apostolic claim and he recognizes elsewhere the possibility of deception as well as of self-deception (1Cor 10,6—10; 2Cor 13,5), even in himself (1Cor 9,27). Cf. also 1Cor 14,37 f.; 1Thess 5,20 f.; G. W. H. Lampe, 'Church Discipline and . . . Corinthians', *Christian History and Interpretation: Studies presented to J. Knox*, ed. W. R. Farmer, Cambridge 1967, 360. The origin of the Christian usage of *apostolos* in the 'sending' by Jesus (Mark 6,30; Luke 9,10 par.; so, Hengel) does not exclude its relationship to the concept of the Jewish *shaliah* (cf. Goguel, Rengstorf). The broader connotation of 'authorized representative' or 'envoy' in 2Cor 8,23 and Phil 2,25 shows that the meaning is still fluid and determined by its (implicit or explicit) modifier: 'apostle of Christ', 'apostles of the churches', 'your apostle'. Cf. M. Hengel, *Nachfolge und Charisma*, Berlin 1968, 92; K. H. Rengstorf, *TDNT* I (1964/1933), 435, 445. Further on (fourth century) Jewish *apostoloi* cf. Harnack, *Mission*, I, 328 ff.; K. Lake and H. J. Cadbury (eds.), *Beginnings of Christianity*, London 1920—33, 5, 46—50. The context is traditional, and it is unlikely that the Jews borrowed the terminology from the Christians (so, Goguel, *op. cit.* 95—8).

[44] Cf. Goguel, *op. cit.* 98 f.; see above, 5. Some, like Mark, might work with Paul and then, for example, with Barnabas. Whether Mark and Silvanus in 1Peter 5,12 f. are to be indentified with Paul's colleagues is not at all certain. The 'schools' of St Matthew and St John suggest a similar clustering around an apostle or, at least, around his name. Cf. K. Stendahl, *The School of St Matthew*, Lund ²1969; E. C. Selwyn, *The Christian Prophets*, London 1900, 240—4 (on the Muratorian fragment on the Fourth Gospel see B. F. Westcott, *The Canon of the New Testament*, London 1889, 523 f.).

some evidence that it also carries a more restricted meaning[45]. At first blush one might suppose that such phrases as 'Sosthenes the brother', 'Timothy the brother', 'Titus my brother' signify only fellow believers[46]. However, when Paul speaks of sending 'the brothers', i. e. missionaries and appointed apostles of the churches, or of expecting Timothy to come with 'the brothers', or of urging 'Apollos the brother' to come 'with the brothers'[47], the suspicion grows that something more is involved in the term. It is strengthened by texts in which οἱ ἀδελφοί appears to be used alongside of and in distinction from the church as a whole:

The churches of Asia greet you, Aquila and Prisca with *the church* in their house greet you, all *the brothers* greet you (1Cor 16,19 f.)[48].

Peace to *the brothers* ... Grace be with *all* those loving our Lord Jesus Christ (Eph 6,23 f.)[49].

The brothers with me greet you, all *the saints* greet you, especially those of Caesar's house (Phil. 4,21 f.)[50].

Greet *the brothers* of Laodicea and Nympha and *the church* in their (her) house (Col 4,15)[51].

---

[45] The observation is not novel and was made over a century ago, for example by W. Smith, *Dictionary of the Bible*, New York 1868, 329.

[46] 1Cor 1,1; 2Cor 1,1; 2,13 *et passim*. Similarly 'Quartus the brother' (Rom 16,23). On 1Thess 3,2 see B. Rigaux, *Les Épitres aux Thessaloniciens*, Paris 1956, 467: 'brother', not in the sense of 'Christian' but as a colleague and co-worker. Cf. C. H. Dodd in *BT* 27 (1976), 310 f.

[47] 2Cor 8,18 f.,23; cf. 9,3,5; 11,9; 12,18; 1Cor 16,10 ff.

[48] Most commentators identify the brothers with the Christian community. C. K. Barrett, *Corinthians* 396, who sees the problem, conjectures that they perhaps are Corinthian Christians in Ephesus.

[49] B. F. Westcott, *The Epistle to the Ephesians*, London 1906, 99: Paul first addresses the specific society and then all who love the Lord Jesus. J. A. Robinson, *Epistle to the Ephesians: An Exposition*, London 1909, 190 f.: the concluding greeting (23) is supplemented by Paul's greeting in his own hand.

[50] J. B. Lightfoot, *The Epistle to the Philippians*, London 1879, 167: Paul's personal companions and fellow travellers, as distinguished from the resident Christians, the saints; so, G. Friedrich in *Die kleineren Briefe des Apostels Paulus*, Göttingen 1962, 130. P. Bonnard, *Aux Philippiens*, Neuchâtel 1950, 82, identifies the brothers either as Paul's co-workers or ministers of the local church. Cf. Rom 15,14 f.

[51] J. B. Lightfoot, *Epistle to the Colossians*, London 1875, 243: the brothers are perhaps a Colossian family resident in Laodicea; 'their' represents οἱ περὶ Νύμφας. C. Masson, *Aux Colossiens*, Neuchâtel 1950, *in loc.*: the verse is not clear. H. A. W. Meyer, *Philippians and Colossians*, Edinburgh 1875, 477: the brothers are a church distinct from the Laodicean church but in filial relation with it and meeting in the same house. Cf. E. Lohse, *An die Kolosser*, Göttingen 1969, 245.

These greetings are not of equal force, but the two in 1Cor 16 and Phil 4 clearly imply that 'the brothers' are a more restricted group than 'the Christians', i. e. οἱ ἅγιοι, αἱ ἐκκλησίαι. Similarly, the salutation in Gal 1,2, 'Paul and all the brothers with me' probably refers to the Apostle and his co-workers since in Phil 4,21 the same phrase is distinguished from the saints generally, and elsewhere in his letters co-senders are fellow workers[52]. In Phil 1,14 'the brothers' refers to preachers: 'most of the brothers have been made confident by my chains and are much more bold to speak the word of God without fear'[53].

From such passages one may regard it as probable that, when used in the plural with an article, 'the brothers' in Pauline literature fairly consistently[54] refers to a relatively limited group of workers, some of whom have the Christian mission and/or ministry as their primary occupation[55]. The use of this term elsewhere in the New Testament often suggests the same interpretation. Acts, like Corinthians, presents 'the brothers' as travel companions and sometimes distinguishes them from disciples generally. For example,

At Jerusalem Paul 'attempted to join *the disciples* ... Barnabas brought him to *the apostles* ... And *the brothers* brought him down to Caesarea and sent him off to Tarsus' (Acts 9, 26 f., 30)[56].

From Rome '*the brothers* came to meet us as far as the Forum of Appius', i. e. some forty miles south of Rome (Acts 28,15).

---

[52] Burton *op. cit.* 8. So, for example, J. B. Lightfoot, *Epistle to the Galatians*, London 1890, 72; A. Oepke, *Der Brief des Paulus an die Galater*, Leipzig 1937, 14; D. Guthrie, *Galatians*, London 1969, 58. Otherwise: H. Schlier, *Der Brief an die Galater*, Göttingen 1962, 29: the brothers are the one Christian brotherhood which Paul represents.

[53] On the idiom, 'to speak the Word of God', cf. Acts 4,29,31; 11,19, 13,5,46; 15,6; Hebr 2,2; 18,7; G. Kittel, *TDNT* IV (1967/1942), 115: 'early missionary preaching'. The context (Phil 1,15—18) shows that two groups of preachers are in view. N. B. κηρύσσω, καταγγέλλω. One group, probably of 'the Hebrews' = 'the circumcision party', is antagonistic; but they are apparently 'brothers' and not the 'evil workers' in Phil 3,2. See below, 108 f., 120; Col 4,11.

[54] There are exceptions: Rom 9,3 (the Jews); 1Cor 8,11 f. (weaker brothers); 9,5 (brothers of the Lord); cf. 1Thess 4,10. Also, a specific group may be indicated without an article (2Cor 8,23; 2Thess 3,6; see note 81).

[55] This is clear in the case of those appointed by the churches to accompany Paul (2Cor 8,18 f.; Phil 2,25; cf. Acts 19,29) although some probably were 'helpers' and not engaged in preaching or teaching. See note 84.

[56] Acts 17,15 is ambiguous; probably it is 'brothers' (17,14) who accompany Paul to Athens, but note the similar idiom in Acts 9,30. Also in Acts 21,16 it is

Also like 2Cor 8,18,23, Acts 28,21 identifies the letter-bearing envoys to the Jewish community in Rome as 'the brothers'[57]. Somewhat different, but no less in accord with Pauline usage, are texts that apparently distinguish the brothers in local churches from the general body of believers and, at times, associate them with the church's leadership.

When Apollos 'wished to cross to Achaia, *the brothers* ... wrote to *the disciples* to receive him'[58].

Timothy, 'a certain *disciple* ... was well spoken of by *the brothers* in Lystra and Iconium'[59].

After his escape Peter requests the Christians meeting at the house of Mark's mother to 'tell James and *the brothers*'[60].

At Antioch Paul and Silas are 'commended to the grace of the Lord by *the brothers*', who are none other than *the prophets and teachers* by whom Paul and Barnabas earlier 'had been commended to the grace of God'[61].

'disciples' who are the travel companions. In Acts 10,23; 11,12 'some of the brothers from Joppa accompanied' Peter to Caesarea and then to Jerusalem: in Acts 10,45 they are called simply οἱ ἐκ περιτομῆς πιστοί, apparently to couple Acts 10,23 to 11,2,12. Cf. Acts 11,2 D. See note 53.

[57] Ἀπήγγειλεν (Acts 28,21) refers to an official communication and is hardly to be distinguished from the γράμματα in the same verse. Lake and Cadbury (*op. cit.* IV, 346; cf. V, 48 ff.) think that one 'might' identify such brothers with Jewish 'apostles'. See notes 43, 60.

[58] Acts 18,27. However, in Acts 22,5 Paul receives letters to 'the brothers' in Damascus, i. e. presumably the leadership (οἱ πρῶτοι) of the Jewish community (cf. Acts 28,17,21). On commendatory letters cf. Rom 16,1 f.; 1Cor 16,3; 2Cor 8,23 f.; Phlm 17; ?2Thess 2,2. On 2Cor 3,1, cf. Plummer, *op. cit.* 77 f.

[59] Acts 16,1 f. The movement of 'the brothers' (or of Timothy) between the two cities is implied. In Acts 18,18,22,23 the usage is more ambiguous. Cf. Acts 14,28–15,1; 'they remained ... with *the disciples,* and certain men came down from Judea and began to teach *the brothers*'. It is possible that here the two terms are synonymous. But in Acts 21,17 '*the brothers* received' Paul and his company; later James and the elders tell Paul that *the believers* who are zealous for the Lord *will* hear that he has come. See note 62.

[60] Acts 12,17; cf. 11,1: 'the apostles and the brothers'; 15,23: 'the apostles and the elders, brothers, to the brothers ...'. 'The brothers' in Acts 14,2 apparently are the apostles, Paul and Barnabas (14,4). The 500 'brothers' in 1Cor 15,6 also are probably to be counted as apostles: (1) they are included in a list of apostolic witnesses, and (2) Paul equates or intimately associates an appearance of the risen Lord with an apostolic commission (1Cor 9,1) In the Gospels also appearances are never merely to impress or to satisfy curiosity but always to commission witnesses. Luke 24, 31 and John 20,26–9 are only apparent exceptions to this rule.

[61] Acts 15,40; 14,26. Note the similarity of idiom. Cf. 13,3. The term παραδίδωμι and perhaps also ἀπολύω (Acts 13,3; 15,33) may have a technical, if not sacramental significance. Cf. E. Haenchen, *Acts*, Philadelphia 1971, 437 (on Acts 14,26).

Luke's terminology admittedly is ambiguous, and 'brother' means only 'fellow believer' in some passages[62]. One might argue that the term carries no further implications elsewhere, however exclusive the group to which it is applied. But the probabilities weigh against that understanding of the matter. In all likelihood a technical connotation is present in some passages although Luke is not concerned to make it explicit: there is no need to stress the obvious. The Johannine literature offers clearer parallels. Like 2 Corinthians, 3 John presents the brothers as a circle of travelling workers, probably preachers or teachers associated with or led by the elder. In Revelation the phrase, 'your brothers the prophets' has the ring of a fixed idiom[63]. Also at Qumran[64] and in the rabbinic writings[65] the term 'brothers' occasionally designates a religious order, the priests and/or Levites[66].

Such parallels support the view that 'the brothers' in the Pauline letters often refers to colleagues in the Christian mission. On the basis of this conclusion, one further matter may now be raised, the correspondence addressed to or received by such persons. The Pastorals and Philemon come immediately to mind. Other letters, for example Colossians and 2 Thessalonians, also may fall within the same category[67]. In investigating this possibility it is necessary

---

[62] Cf. Lake and Cadbury, *op. cit.* V, 378 f. The very ambiguity gives added force to the conclusion of K. G. Kuhn (*TDNT* VI, 1968/1959, 727) that 'the depiction of Paul's missionary work in Acts is always in exact agreement with the current situation. Since it is so true to life, there is no reason to doubt its historicity'.

[63] Rev 22,9; note the related expression σύνδουλος and see note 38. Cf. R. H. Charles, *The Revelation of St John*, Edinburgh 1920, I, 177 (on Rev. 6,11): 'the σύνδουλοι and the ἀδελφοί are the same persons viewed under different aspects'. Cf. also John 21,23; Luke 22,32. In John 20,17 f. 'brothers' is equated with 'disciples'. The context of Mt 23,8—10 reflects (or envisions) a situation in which Christian teachers are warned against titles of eminence. In the later church cf. Eus 4,26,13 citing episcopal correspondence of Melito, *Extracts:* 'Melito to his brother Onesimus'. Further cf. G. W. H. Lampe, *A Patristic Lexicon*, Oxford 1961, 30.

[64] 1QM 13,1; 15,4; cf. 15,7; 1QSa 1,18.

[65] SSRab 3,6,6; Yoma 38 *b*; jShek 5,1(2). See note 57.

[66] In the second century B. C. the term is used also of a select group within a pagan religious community. A. Peyron, *Papyri Graeci ... Aegypti*, I, Turin 1826, cited in G. A. Deissmann, *Bible Studies*, Edinburgh 1901, 142.

[67] In this regard Rom 16 and the salutation in Phil 1,1 (cf. 4,2 f.) also are suggestive, as well as certain passages, for example, in Hebrews (3,1; 4,10; 5, 11 f.; 6,10; 13,5,23 f.), Jude (3 f.,22 f.) and Revelation (22,6,9; 1,1,20: ἄγγελοι;

to observe two cautions. First, the formal addressee may not indicate clearly the addressee of consequence, as the letter 'to Philemon, Apphia, Archippus, and the church in your house' illustrates. Second, in most of Paul's letters the audience addressed oscillates within the letter itself[68], shifting from one segment of the church to another, then to an individual or to the whole community[69]. Thus, if local co-workers are the recipients of a letter, very likely some of its contents would be directed to them and some, through them, to the total community. This practice may be expressly indicated in Col 1,2 if with most commentators one translates, 'to the saints and faithful brothers'. If one reads with Professor Moule, perhaps with more probability, 'to the holy and faithful brothers', the letter still may include matter intended for the whole church[70]. However, apart from the salutation, at least one other passage suggests that the immediate recipients of the letter are a group of co-workers. Col 4,16 presupposes that the recipients are in contact with 'the brothers' in Laodicea and are responsible to see that the letter is read (later) to the congregations of both churches. That is, the recipients are a group distinct from the community as a whole, and probably a group with some say in the conduct of worship[71].

---

cf. Justin, *Dial.* 75). The (possibly) composite character of certain letters (e. g. Romans and 2Corinthians) may find an explanation along the same lines, i. e. one segment addressed to a special group within the community. Greetings to the (local) brothers are present in some letters (Rom 16; 1Cor 16,20; Eph 6,23; 1Thess 5,26) but absent in 2Corinthians, Galatians, Philippians, Colossians, 2Thessalonians, 1Timothy, Titus and Philemon; but the reasons for this probably are varied. See below, 235 n.

[68] In the Pastorals, where one person is addressed, this is not ordinarily the case. Even traditional paraenesis is mediated through the addressee (e. g. 1Tim 6,17; Titus 2,1 f.; 3,1) although some is inserted impersonally *en bloc* with only an introductory or subsequent 'charge' clause relating it to the addressee (e. g. 1Tim 3,1–13,14 f.; 4,1–5,6).

[69] E. g. Rom 7,1; 11,13; 14; 1Cor 11,20 ff.; Phil 4,2 f.

[70] Cf. C. F. D. Moule, *The Epistles to the Colossians and to Philemon*, Cambridge 1957, 25 f. Cf. Hebr 3,1: 'holy brothers'.

[71] Ἀναγινώσκω refers to public reading in church (cf. *TDNT* I, 1964/ 1933, 343; W. Bauer–W. Arndt–F. Gingrich, *A Greek–English Lexicon*, Chicago 1957): 'when you have had this letter read in your church, see that the Laodiceans have it read in their church too' (Phillips). Ὅταν implies a later reading. The recipients also are competent to relay an admonition to Archippus. All this fits the role of 'the brothers' as letter-bearers (cf. 1Cor 16,11 f.; 2Cor 8,18,22; Barrett, 'Titus', 11) and exhorters (1Thess 3,2; 2Thess 3,15; cf. 1Cor 16,12). Also, a group of preachers and teachers suits most appropriately the references to 'teaching and admonishing one another in all wisdom' (Col

The authenticity of 2 Thessalonians has been questioned by some scholars because of its peculiar relationship to the first letter, in some respects so close and in other ways removed and distant[72]. Harnack solved the problem by positing different recipients for 2 Thessalonians, viz. a minority group of Jewish-Christians within the congregation. His discernment of a different audience in 2 Thessalonians was a brilliant piece of detection, and for the most part his points are well taken[73]. However, they would be equally or more fittingly applied to Paul's Thessalonian co-workers, 'the brothers'. Decisive for such an interpretation are two further observations, the command regarding the idlers in 2Thess 3,6–15 and the identification of the recipients as God's select 'first fruits' (ἀπαρχή). 'The first fruits' is a concept deeply embedded in the Old Testament cultus as the portion dedicated to God and that which sanctifies the whole. Paul makes direct allusion to it in Rom 11,16: 'if the first portion is holy, so is the whole lump'[74]. The same thought is present in 1Cor 15,20,23: Christ is not merely the first (πρῶτος, cf. Acts 26,23) but the first fruits, the dedicated portion in which the consecration and acceptance of the whole (οἱ τοῦ Χρισ-

---

3,16; cf. 1,28; Eph 5,19) and to their 'word' enabling them to give an 'answer' (Col 4,6). Cf. E. Lohmeyer, *Die Briefe an die Kolosser und an Philemon*, Göttingen 1930, 163 f. Of course, this message to a special group could be included in a letter sent to the whole community. But the probabilities point in a different direction. Long ago, J. B. Lightfoot, *Biblical Essays*, London 1893, 395 f., suggested that Ephesians stands to Colossians (and Romans to Galatians) as a systematic exposition stands to an immediate response to a specific situation and problem. *Mutatis mutandis* Ephesians may be viewed as a general development for the whole community of themes addressed in Colossians to a group of colleagues who then mediated the letter, probably with appropriate exposition, to the congregational meeting. Similarly, on the relation of 1Thessalonians to 2Thessalonians see below.

[72] E. g. W. Wrede, *TU* XXIV (1903), 28–36; cf. A. v. Harnack, 'Das Problem des zweiten Thessalonicherbriefs', *Sitzungsberichte der ... Akademie der Wissenschaften*, Berlin 1910, XXXI, 560 f. Cf. W. G. Kümmel, *Introduction to the New Testament*, rev. ed. London 1975, 264–269.

[73] Harnack, 'Problem', 562 f.: 1 Thessalonians, with virtually no references to the Old Testament, presupposes a gentile congregation (2,14: 'your'). In friendly personal terms Paul addresses the local community (cf. 5,26 f.), considering also the rights and obligations of the leaders (5,12–22). 2 Thessalonians is somewhat strict (2,15; 3,6–15), is coloured by and assumes the readers' knowledge of the Old Testament, and says little new. Cf. B. Rigaux, *Aux Thessaloniciens*, Paris 1956, 605.

[74] Cf. Numbers 15,20 f.

τοῦ) is implicit[75]. The same implication very likely is present in the identification of Stephanas (1Cor 16,15) and of the Thessalonian brothers (2Thess 2,13) as first fruits[76]. They are the consecrated first-born who, like the Levites, are set apart for the work of God[77].

Who are the idlers? The general allusions to them in 1 Thessalonians (4,11 f.; 5,14) become a strong admonition in 2 Thessalonians 3,6–15[78]. The latter passage concerns persons who are commanded to imitate Paul in one specific respect, that is, in forgoing the Christian workers' right to unqualified support[79]. Equally clear is the inference in 2Thess 3,10 that these persons are receiving financial support or, at least, communal meals[80]. Together, these facts point

---

[75] Robertson and Plummer, *op. cit.* 351 f. On the term in Revelation 14,4 cf. H. B. Swete, *The Apocalypse of St John*, London 1906, 177; on James 1,18 cf. J. B. Mayor, *The Epistle of St James*, London 1892, 59 f.

[76] Surprisingly, Harnack ('Problem', 575 ff.) overlooks this and takes ἀπαρχή to refer to the 'first converts', i. e. Jewish Christians. But 'first converts' (so, RSV mg. *et al.*), which suggests only the (possibly correct) temporal sequence, completely misses the significant allusion within the term. Cf. also Rom 16,5 where, in a list of greetings to co-workers, Epaenetus is called 'an ἀπαρχή of Asia for Christ'. In 1Cor 16,15 the term is associated with Stephanas' *diakonia*; in 2Thess 2,13,17, with Christ's work in the brothers by 'work and word', a phrase that Paul uses elsewhere of his own ministry (Rom 15,18; cf. 2Cor 10,11) and that of the 'teachers', i. e. co-workers in Colossae (Col 3,16 f.). This usage, in turn, supports the reading ἀπαρχή against the variant (found also at Rom 16,5) ἀπ' ἀρχῆς.

[77] Cf. Exodus 13,2; 22,28(29) with Numbers 3,11 ff. בכור (= ἀπαρχή; Exodus 22,29 LXX) is used for 'first fruits' or first-born. This frame of reference also may underlie Paul's conviction about the workers' right to payment (1Cor 9, 13 f.; see above, 10) and his use of λειτουργός and its cognates for Christian workers (Rom 15,16; Phil 2,25) and for ministry (Phil 2,17,30; cf. Acts 13,2), especially the collection (Rom 15,27; 2Cor 9,12).

[78] Since ἄτακτος and its cognates occur in the New Testament only in 1Thess 5,14 and 2Thess 3, the passages in all likelihood refer to the same situation. Note also the several words common to 1Thess 4,11 f., and 2Thess 3,11 f. Cf. M. Dibelius, *An die Thessalonicher*, Tübingen 1925, 48: if 1Thess 4,11 f.; 5,14 alludes to the situation in 2Thess 3,6 ff. and does so in anticipation of the latter passage, it is probable that 2 Thessalonians is addressed to a group that the situation directly concerns. Cf. also 1Thess 4,6 with 2Cor 12,16 f. (πλεονεκτέω).

[79] 2Thess 3,8 f.; see above, 10. Paul often asks his converts to imitate him, but never elsewhere in this respect.

[80] Neither of these situations, if addressed to the whole congregation, makes sense unless under the unlikely assumption that the whole congregation is following a communal life-style. One other possible allusion to a communal life among the workers is Col 4,15. If one reads 'the church in their house', Nymphas and the brothers appear to be sharing a dwelling (cf. 1Cor 16,19). He (or

to a group of Christian workers as the recipients of 2 Thessalonians[81].

As a designation for colleagues in religious work the term 'brothers' is occasionally found in first-century Judaism. From there or from the Old Testament[82] Jesus appropriates it, in emphasizing the demands and priorities of his mission, as a designation for his disciples[83]. This background, or something very much like it, accounts for the wide and unexplained currency of the term in the early church, apparently from the beginning. In Paul this designation is closely related, if not an equivalent to 'co-workers'[84]. Paul and his colleagues are not called 'teacher' or 'leader' although some of them do teach and lead. For they have one teacher, the Messiah, and they are all brothers. Probably in response to their Lord's command, they eschew titles of eminence[85]. With reference to their task they are the workers, the servants, the special messengers; with reference to one another they are the brothers. In the mushrooming Christian mission of the pre-70 period the technical significance of such terms was self-evident. But soon there-

she) may be a member of the circle (but contrast the word-order in Rom 16, 14 f.; 2 Tim 4,21), or perhaps he is a patron.

[81] Admittedly, 2 Thessalonians, like 1 Thessalonians, uses 'brothers' without the article (see above, 15 f.). But in the vocative this is inevitable. The command in 1 Thess 5,27 to read the letter to 'the brothers' is in accord with the hypothesis presented here. For the workers, especially those evangelizing a neighbouring area, might not hear a letter sent to the congregation and yet might have need of its teachings for their own work. Masson suggests that if 'the brothers' in 1 Thess 5,27 means 'the Christians', the recipients may be the leading brothers (5,12) who then are commanded to read the letter to all. Cf. C. Masson, *Aux Thessaloniciens*, Neuchâtel 1957, 79.

[82] Cf. Psalm 22,23; Hebrews 2,12; see above, 17.

[83] Mark 3,33 f. parr.; Mt 5,22 ff.,47; 7,3 ff.; 18,15,21,35; 25,40; 28,10; Luke 22, 32; John 20,17.

[84] It is probable that 'the brothers' has a somewhat broader connotation, including συνέκδημοι, amanuenses, and other helpers not engaged in 'religious' functions, e. g. evangelizing and teaching. Cf. 2 Cor 11,9; Acts 19,29; 1 Peter 5,12.

[85] Mt 23,8—12 is clearly an inserted commentary, applying to the Church's leaders the warnings of Jesus to the Jewish churchmen. Whether it is a pre-resurrection saying, a *pesher*-ed version of such a saying, or an oracle from the risen Lord, it was probably known outside Matthean circles. It, or a similar injunction, may well explain the absence of the titles 'prophet and teacher' among Paul and his colleagues. The reluctance to claim such titles also appears later in Barnabas (1,8; 4,9; but cf. 9,9) and in Ignatius (Eph 3,1). Cf. Harnack, *Mission*, I, 354 ff.

after the title 'the brothers', like 'the workers', was displaced by other designations and gradually disappeared from view.

At least from the time of his labours in Antioch Paul had associates-in-mission. Some, whose names are better known to us, accompanied him in his missionary travels. Some, like Epaphras and Epaphroditus, were workers in local congregations who were sent (or left) to join the Apostle's mission elsewhere. It is most likely that in founding a church, no less than in undertaking a missionary journey, Paul appointed co-workers, local converts who participated in the local mission and continued it after the Apostle moved on. For these workers also charism doubtless preceded religious function. But did unstructured function always precede the structured, i. e. appointed role? The above considerations have led me, rather reluctantly at times, to conclude that it did not. From the beginning charism and appointment sometimes went together[86]. But the appointment was, in the most literal sense, to be a worker and a servant. As long as this conception of role continued, structure and authority in an official, worldly sense remained subordinated and contingent[87].

Paul's associates also may have had a literary role. In what measure, for example, did the co-senders of his letters participate in framing their content? Are the signs of 'school activity' in some Pauline exegeses, to which Professor Conzelmann[88] has recently called our attention, to be explained in terms of a Pauline circle or circles similar to the one that appears briefly in Acts 13,1–3? Do any of the pre-formed traditional pieces scattered through Paul's letters find their origin in the co-operative enterprise of Paul and his colleagues? Such questions will be explored below. And they do deserve attention, not least for the better understanding of Paul's associates that they may give. For it does not detract from his greatness to bring into greater prominence those with whom he served, those whom he was glad to praise and pleased to call his co-workers.

---

[86] See above, 11 f. Cf. G. Bornkamm, *TDNT* VI (1969/1958), 664: although there was no absence of organization and offices in the Pauline congregations, Paul rarely gives titles to local office-bearers and mostly refers to them in terms of function.

[87] This is evident, for example, in Paul's own relationship to the Corinthian church.

[88] H. Conzelmann, *NTS* XII (1965—6), 231—44.

2. 'SPIRITUAL' GIFTS IN THE PAULINE COMMUNITY

In the previous chapter we saw that the role of St. Paul's co-workers may be inferred in some measure from the designations or 'titles' given to them. When used of colleagues in the Christian mission, the term 'brothers' often means preachers although it may include travelling companions (συνέκδημοι) and others who are not necessarily engaged in 'religious' functions[1]. 'Co-worker' (συνεργός) also appears to have a rather broad connotation. But it refers most frequently to teachers and preachers, those who are deserving of esteem and of financial support. The designation διάκονος ('minister') emphasizes these functions even more[2]. Some of the terms or their cognates — ἀπόστολος, διακονία — are specifically mentioned by Paul as charisms, gifts from the risen Christ[3]. In brief, Paul's co-workers were charismatically endowed persons. This kind of authorization was, of course, the presupposition of leadership in the early church quite apart from the meaning of the 'titles'[4]. However, with reference to the co-workers engaged in preaching and teaching, one may be more specific. They appear to belong to a category that the Apostle calls πνευματικοί, spiritual ones.

The following remarks propose (1) to show that the terms πνευματικά/πνευματικοί denote, respectively, gifts of inspired utterance or discernment and men who exercise such gifts; (2) to define more clearly Paul's understanding of the origin and nature of this inspiration; (3) to determine the significance of the πνευματικά/πνευματικοί in Paul's churches and among his associates.

[1] See above, 13–17. In Revelation (1,9; 4,11; 12,10; 19,10; 22,9) ἀδελφός always means prophet.

[2] See above, 7–13.

[3] In Eph 4,12 the work of ministry (ἔργον διακονίας) is one purpose for which the gifts are bestowed.

[4] Cf. E. Schweizer, *Church Order in the New Testament*, London 1961, 184 f = 22 e f.

The Pneumatic Gifts of Inspired Speech

Paul uses the term πνευματικά along with χαρίσματα[5] to refer to gifts, i. e. charisms or empowerments, given to the Church from God (1Cor 12,28; 2Tim 1,6 f.) or from the risen Lord (Eph 4,7,11, cf. 1Cor 2,16; 14,37). In this usage the two terms have sometimes been equated[6]. That this is a mistake is evident from Rom 1,11 where πνευματικόν qualifies χάρισμα. Paul desires to go to Rome 'that I may impart some spiritual charism'. The kind of qualification represented by 'spiritual' (πνευματικόν) becomes clear from Paul's usage. That is, χάρισμα can be used of any or all of the gifts[7] while πνευματικόν appears to be restricted to gifts of inspired perception, verbal proclamation and/or its interpretation. Thus, in 1Cor 9,11 the 'spiritual things' that Paul 'sowed' among the Corinthians are defined in the following context as the gospel message[8]. Similarly, in 1Cor 12,1 the 'spiritual' gifts (or persons) are connected directly with 'speaking' ἐν πνεύματι; when, in 1Cor 12,4 ff., other charisms come into consideration, the expression broadens[9].

The same is true of the discussion of spiritual gifts in 1Cor 14. The πνευματικά of 1Cor 14,1 may be identified with the 'greater charisms' of 1Cor 12,31. In any case they are concerned with in-

---

[5] The New Testament usage is almost all Pauline, πνευματικά some twenty times and twice in 1Petr 2,5; χαρίσματα sixteen times and once in 1Petr 4,10. Pneumatikos is not in the LXX. Against a hellenistic derivation cf. W. D. Davies, Paul and Rabbinic Judaism, London ²1955, 191—200; J. Dupont, Gnosis, Paris 1949, 178—80. See note 26.

[6] E. g. R. Bultmann, Theology of the New Testament, London 1952, I, 156; H. Conzelmann, Erste Korintherbrief, Göttingen 1969, 245 (on 1Cor 12,4). The Spirit also may be the source of the charisms (1Cor 12,11). Cf. 1Cor 12,4—6: πνεῦμα, κύριος, θεός.

[7] Rom 12,6; 1Cor 1,7; 7,7; 12,4,28—31.

[8] 1Cor 9,14,15,18; cf. Rom 15,27; 'sowing' in Mk 4,14 and John 4,35—8. Cf. Ign, Eph. 8,2.

[9] 1Cor 12,4—11 may be a traditional piece that Paul incorporates and then, in 1Cor 12,12—27, applies to the Corinthians. It is a self-contained and carefully framed unity with a number of uncharacteristic expressions. Note the hapaxes, both New Testament (διαίρεσις, 4—6; ἐνέργημα, 10) and Pauline (διαιρέω, 11). Also unusual are the phrases ἡ φανέρωσις τοῦ πνεύματος (7), cf. 1Cor 2,4; λόγος σοφίας (8), cf. 1Cor 1,17; 2,1; Col 2,23; 3,16; Eph 1,17; λόγος γνώσεως (8), cf. 2Cor 8,7; 11,6; διακρίσεις πνευμάτων (10), cf. 1Cor 14, 28 f.; τὸ ἓν καὶ τὸ αὐτὸ πνεῦμα (11), cf. 1Cor 11,5; ἰδίᾳ ἑκάστῳ (11), cf. the usage in Rom 14,5; 1Cor 3,8; 7,2 (7,7); 15,23(38); Gal 6,5.

spired speech — a hymn, a teaching (διδαχήν), a revelation, a tongue, an interpretation (1Cor 14,26). The first three, those that are comprehensible, are connected with prophecy or, at least, with the manifestations of a prophet[10]. The prophet also has the power to test (διακρίνειν, 29) a prophetic message and to recognize (ἐπι-γινώσκειν, 37) whether it is 'from the Lord'. But, as Professor Schweizer has rightly observed, πνευματικός is the broader concept of which προφήτης is a special type[11]. The 'spiritual ones' or pneumatics include not only those who pray and sing in strange tongues but also those who interpret the *glossolalia*. Such persons, like the prophets, also are able to discern the origin of a prophetic message[12].

The prophetic character of the pneumatics is confirmed in the striking passage, 1Cor 2,6—16. As they are in 1Cor 14, the pneumatics here (1) are distinguished from the believers generally[13]. (2) They are both the recipients and the mediators of revelation, 'the wisdom of God in a mystery', wisdom that had been hidden[14]. Such knowledge is regarded elsewhere by Paul as an attribute of those who 'have prophecy'[15]. In addition, (3) 1Cor 2,6—16, which has the literary form of a midrash[16] or exposition of Scripture,

---

[10] Cf. 1Cor 14,15 (ψαλῶ), 19 (κατηχήσω) with 14,3 ff.; 14,30 f. (ἀποκαλύπτω, προφητεύω, μανθάνω). In 1Cor 14,6 (cf. Rom 12,6) προφητεία apparently represents a particular kind of prophetic, i. e. 'in the spirit', utterance.

[11] E. Schweizer, *TDNT* VI (1968/1959), 423. Cf. 1Cor 14,1: 'especially that you may prophesy'. Otherwise: H. Leisegang, *Pneuma Hagion*, Leipzig 1922, 114 ff., who contrasts the *pneumatika* with prophecy.

[12] Cf. 1Cor 14,37 ('a prophet or a pneumatic') with 1Cor 14,29 (διακρίνω); 12,10; 2,15 (ἀνακρίνω). In 1Cor 14,37 Paul speaks as a prophet (cf. E. Käsemann, *New Testament Questions of Today*, London 1969, 74). On the role of discerning or testing a prophetic message cf. Ign., Eph 8,2—9,1. Did 11,7 ff is not necessarily contrary to Paul (*pace* Conzelmann, *Korintherbrief*, 289 n.) but only prohibits the judgment (διακρίνω) of a prophet by *the congregation*. Cf. 1Cor 2,15; 6,5 (σοφός). 1Cor 14,29 concerns the judgment of a prophetic message by (a circle of) pneumatics.

[13] Cf. 1Cor 3,1. Ἔχειν πνεῦμα (Rom 8,9) does not mean εἶναι πνευματικός.

[14] 1Cor 2,7.

[15] 1Cor 13,2. 'To have prophecy' apparently is to be constituted a prophet and signifies more than merely 'to prophesy'. See below, 138 f. Cf. Rom 16,25—7; Eph 3,3—5,9: the mystery 'has now been revealed to his holy apostles and prophets by the Spirit' (3,5). Contrast 'to have a demon' (John 8,48; 10,20) or 'to have a spirit of an unclean demon' (Luke 4,33 f.) or 'of divination' (Acts 16,16).

[16] Note the sequence: theme (6 ff.) + Scripture quotation (9) + commen-

probably was created within a (Pauline) group of pneumatics prior to its use in 1Cor 2[17]. This kind of inspired, eschatological exposition appears elsewhere in the New Testament with the signature of prophets and/or inspired teachers[18]; it appears here with the signature of pneumatics ('we').

In this connection we may return to Paul's comment in Rom 1,11 f.:

> I long to see you, that I may impart to you some spiritual charism to strengthen (στηριχθῆναι) you, that is, to experience mutual exhortation (συμπαρακληθῆναι) among you through one another's faith, both yours and mine.

The terms παρακαλέω and στηρίζω are used together elsewhere in Paul only in Thessalonians, once describing the ministry of Paul's co-worker, Timothy (1Thess 3,2), and once of the work of God himself (2Thess 2,17). In Acts (14,22; 15,32, with the cognate ἐπιστηρίζω) they are connected with the activity of Christian prophets. Similarly in 1Cor 14,2 f. παράκλησις is a 'part of the work of prophesying'[19]; that is, one way in which the prophet accomplishes his ministry of οἰκοδομή. The same thought probably is not absent from Rom 1,11 f.

These passages[20] — Rom 1,11 f., 1Cor 2,6—16, and 1Cor 14 — give us a glimpse into the functioning of a certain class of charismatics, the pneumatics with their 'spiritual' gifts[21]. Such persons

---

tary (10—16) with verbal allusions to the preceding (ἄνθρωπος 9,11) and concluding (γινώσκω, 8,11,14,16) quotation (16). On the affinities of this form with Jewish and Christian midrash of the period cf. P. Borgen, *Bread from Heaven*, Leiden 1965, 51—8; see below, 213—217.

[17] Note, for example, (1) the shift from the singular (in 2,1—5 and 3,1 f.) to the plural with the 'we', i. e. the pneumatics as the subject (2,7,10,12 f.,16); (2) the unity of the section independent of its context; and (3) the considerable number of phrases not found elsewhere in the Pauline literature: 'rulers of this age' (6), 'before the ages' (7), 'the spirit of the cosmos' (12), 'the spirit that is from God' (12). However, there is only one Pauline hapax: διδάκτος.

[18] See below, 131—138, 149, 153, 160 f.

[19] G. Stählin, *TDNT* V (1967/1954), 822. Cf. Rom 16,4 f.; 2Cor 5,20. In Rom 12,8, where *prophēteia* is used in a more restricted sense, *paraklēsis* is distinct from it. See note 10.

[20] Gal 6,1 also may be included. On Rom 1,11 f. cf. Barn 1,2—8: '... if I am concerned to impart (μεταδοῦναι) to you some portion of that which I received, it shall turn to my reward for having ministered to such spirits' (5).

[21] Although 1Cor 14,26—36 is addressed to one community, it is clear from verses 33 ('in all the churches') and 37 ('a command of the Lord') that the instructions are not given *ad hoc* but represent a standard operating procedure within the Pauline circle.

were empowered to speak τῷ πνεύματι — whether in prophecy, teaching, speaking in tongues or interpretation. And it is not without significance that the charismatics that Paul placed first in the Church — apostles, prophets, teachers (1Cor 12,28) — are all characterized by pneumatic gifts. These gifts apparently were employed in a prominent way at the worship service of the Churches[22]. On the analogy of the worshiping prophets and teachers in Acts 13,1 f., they probably also were widely cultivated in smaller sessions of pneumatics, who in varying degree were active as a teaching cadre in the Church[23]. This best explains, for example, the comment in 1Cor 2,6—16, 'we speak wisdom among the τέλειοι' (2,6), 'interpreting spiritual things to spiritual men' (2,13)[24]. Likewise, the instructions in 1Cor 11,5 on praying and prophesying probably reflect the procedures used within the prayer sessions of the pneumatics[25].

At this point it is necessary to raise two further questions. First, what is the significance of the appellation πνευματικοί as it is applied to charismatic persons with gifts of inspired speech? Were not all charisms from the Spirit? Secondly, what precisely was Paul's understanding of the inspiration that was operative among the πνευματικοί? To these questions we may now turn.

The divine Spirit in the Old Testament and in inter-testamental Judaism is associated in a special way with the prophet. The spirit of Yahweh is the source of the prophet's inspiration and, conse-

---

[22] E. g. 1Cor 14; 1Thess 5,19—22. On the role of the pneumatics in the worship service cf. Schweizer, *Church Order*, pp. 220—3; M. Goguel, *The Primitive Church*, London 1964, 263—70.

[23] See above, 11 ff.

[24] *Pneumatikoi* ideally should be *teleioi*, i. e. understanding and mature Christians, but the terms are not synonymous. Paul's concern is, through his ministry, 'to present every man *teleion* in Christ' (Col 1,28; cf. 4,12); similarly, through the spiritual gifts granted to some the whole Church should be brought to 'mature manhood' (ἄνδρα τέλειον, Eph 4,11—13). 1Cor 3,1 expresses an irony: some who are *pneumatikoi* in terms of charisms are not yet so in terms of discernment and maturity. Cf. 1Cor 8,1—3,10 (τέλειον); R. Scroggs, *NTS* XIV (1967—8), 38—40; G. Delling, *TDNT* VIII (1972), 67—78.

[25] This could explain the different attitude in this passage, *vis-à-vis* 1Cor 14,33—6, toward the participation of wives in the worship service. Cf. J. Lindblom, *Gesichte und Offenbarungen*, Lund 1968, 140 f. The suggestion that 1Cor 14,33—6 is a non-Pauline interpolation is textually unjustified and overlooks the catch-word connection between verses 28, 30, 34 (σιγάω). Other explanations cannot be discussed here.

quently, the basis for his identification as 'man of the Spirit'[26]. So strong was this identification that later, for example in the Targums, the spirit of Yahweh (or the Holy Spirit) could be identified as the spirit of prophecy[27]. Similarly, at Qumran (IQS 8, 16), the prophets are said to have given their revelations 'in his Holy Spirit'. In the Wisdom of Solomon wisdom is identified with the divine Spirit and makes its recipients 'friends of God and prophets'[28]. In addition, *glossolalia* or speaking in tongues, which figures prominently among the spiritual gifts of Corinth, also may have been exercised by the Old Testament prophets[29].

In the light of this Old Testament — Jewish background, which for Paul's thought and experience is the decisive background, the origin of the Apostle's use of the terms πνευματικά/πνευματικοί becomes clear. The usage arises from the special and deeply rooted association of the Spirit — the πνεῦμα — with prophecy, an association that continues in early Christianity. Note the parallelism in 1Thess 5,19:

The Spirit do not quench
Prophecies do not despise

According to 1Petr 1,10 f. it was the 'spirit of Christ' who spoke in the prophets. Oracles of Christian prophets often are introduced or concluded with a formula including the words, 'the Spirit says'[30].

---

[26] Hos 9,7. The 'spirit of the holy gods' (רוח אלהים) gives Daniel (4,5 f. = 4,8 f.) understanding in God's mysteries. Remarkably, the Spirit is not otherwise associated with Daniel's visions. On the similar absence of the Spirit in the major prophets cf. J. Lindblom, *Prophecy in Ancient Israel*, Oxford 1962, 177–9. In origin *pneumatikos* may be connected with Hos 9,7, cf. Num 11,25.

[27] E. g. the Targum on Judges 3,10; 1Sam 10,6; Isa 63,10. Cf. H. L. Strack and P. Billerbeck, *Kommentar zum Neuen Testament*, München 1924, II, 129; Lindblom, *Prophecy*, 175–9. Similarly, Tosefta Sota 13,2 equates the cessation of prophecy with the departure of the Holy Spirit (Billerbeck, I, 127); cf. W. D. Davies in *Christian History and Interpretation*, ed. W. R. Farmer, Cambridge 1967, 133.

[28] Wis 7,27; cf. 9,17; 7,22 where wisdom is associated or equated with 'your holy spirit'; Eph 1,17: 'a spirit of wisdom'. Cf. J. C. Rylaarsdam, *Revelation in Jewish Wisdom Literature*, Chicago 1946, 99–118; W. Bieder, *TDNT* VI (1968/1959), 371.

[29] 2Kings 9,11; cf. Isa 28,10; Dupont, *Gnosis*, 209 n. Re pagan prophets in the hellenistic world cf. J. Behm, *TDNT* I (1964/1933), 722, 724.

[30] Acts 13,2; 21,11; Rev 2,7. Cf. H. B. Swete, *The Holy Spirit in the New Testament*, London 1910, *passim*; G. Johnston, *The Spirit-Paraclete in the Gospel*

The pneumatics in Pauline usage are, broadly speaking, prophets. Or more precisely, they exercise prophetic gifts since the terms προφήτης and προφητεία have for Paul a more restricted currency[31]. One might leave the matter at that, but one puzzling feature invites further inquiry: Paul associates the pneumatics not only with the *Spirit* but also with 'the *spirits*'. What is the meaning of the plural? To answer this question let us begin with 1Cor 12,3:

> No one speaking in the Spirit [or a spirit] of God says, 'Jesus be cursed'. And no one can say, 'Jesus is Lord', except in the Holy Spirit [or a holy spirit].

Both assertions refer to pneumatic, i. e., 'prophetic' utterances and apparently presuppose that a pneumatic person may give voice to at least two kinds of spirits, evil and good. The charism of 'discernment (διακρίσις) of spirits', which is mentioned a few verses later (1Cor 12,10), probably is to be understood within this context. That is, the plural refers (at least) to a good and an evil spirit. This interpretation finds a measure of support in Thessalonians where, with reference to manifestations of the Spirit, Paul instructs his readers to test all things (πάντα δοκιμάζετε, 1Thess 5, 21) and to disregard any prophecy through a spirit (διὰ πνεύματος) that the day of the Lord has come (2Thess 2,2)[32].

Compare also 1Cor 2,12:

We did not receive the spirit of the world
(τὸ πνεῦμα τοῦ κόσμου)
but the Spirit that is from God
(τὸ πνεῦμα τὸ ἐκ τοῦ θεοῦ).

Possibly 'the spirit of the world' means the dynamic of natural life[33]. However, earlier in this pericope Paul contrasts the wisdom imparted by the Spirit of God with the wisdom of 'the rulers of

---

of John, Cambridge 1970, 137 ff.; below, 149 f., 185, 224 n. In Rev 11,8 πνευματικῶς means 'in prophetic rather than ordinary speech' (E. Schweizer, *TDNT* VI (1968/1959), 449). In the patristic writings the Spirit of God can be described as 'the prophetic spirit' (Justin, *1Apol* 6), and a prophet as one who has 'the divine spirit' (Hermas, *Man* 11,7 ff.) or who speaks ἐν πνεύματι (Did 11, 7 ff.; Barn 10,2).

[31] *Prophētēs* is similarly restricted in Acts. See above, note 15.

[32] Cf. J. E. Frame, *Epistles of St Paul to the Thessalonians*, Edinburgh 1912, 203 f., 206 f., 246: 'In the light of 1Thess 5,19 πνεῦμα [in 2Thess 2,2] clearly refers to the operation of the Spirit in the charisma of prophecy.'

[33] So, F. Godet, *First Epistle to the Corinthians*, Edinburgh 1886, I, 151; J.

this age' (1Cor 2,6,10), who almost certainly represent demonic powers. Very likely 'the spirit of the world', that can impart only human wisdom, likewise refers to an evil, extra-natural power[34].

From these texts — and others might be cited — one observes that the Apostle, in common with other New Testament writers[35] and with apocalyptic Judaism generally[36], both reflects and expressly affirms a world-view that involves a (qualified) ethical dualism. Moreover, he teaches that both the Holy Spirit and 'the spirit of the world' (1Cor 2,6,12) — that is, in the words of Ephesians (2,2), the spirit that now is working in the sons of disobedience — are manifested especially among the pneumatics, the inspired speakers in the Church. For such persons include not only Paul's co-workers[37] but also his opponents, who appear in 2 Corinthians as pseudo-apostles, bearers of 'a different spirit', who boast of their spiritual gifts — visions and revelations[38].

The Angelic 'Spirits' of the Prophets

The simple dualism of a good and an evil spirit does not explain, however, the plural use of 'spirits' in some Pauline texts. 1Cor 14, 12, for example, describes the Corinthians as 'zealots for spirits' (πνευμάτων). Since this follows Paul's exhortation to be zealous

B. Lightfoot, *Notes on the Epistles of St Paul*, London 1904, 180; A. Robertson and A. Plummer, *The First Epistle to the Corinthians*, Edinburgh 1911, 45.

[34] So, H. A. W. Meyer, *Epistles to the Corinthians*, Edinburgh 1879, I, 69: The spirit of the world is 'the spirit proceeding forth from the devil, under whose power the κόσμος lies and whose sphere of action it is'. Cf. John 12,31; 1John 4,3; J. Weiss, *Der erste Korintherbrief*, Göttingen 1970/1910, 63; G. Delling, 'ἄρχων', *TDNT* I (1964/1933), 488 f. Possible: C. K. Barrett, *The First Epistle to the Corinthians*, London 1968, 75; H. Conzelmann, *Korintherbrief*, 85. Contrast 'spirit of man' (1Cor 2,11). Paul elsewhere refers to Satan as 'the god of this age [who] blinded the minds (νοήματα) of the unbelievers' (2Cor 4,4; cf. 1Cor 2,16) and 'the spirit that now works in the sons of disobedience' (Eph 2,2; cf. 4,11 f.), whose servants receive 'a different spirit' (2Cor 11,4,15).

[35] Especially, the Synoptic teachings of Jesus (e. g. Mark 5,1–13; Luke 4, 1–13, 10,18, 22,53) and the Johannine writings (cf. John 12,31; 1John 4,1–6; Revelation, *passim*).

[36] For example, as seen in the Pseudepigrapha and in the Dead Sea Scrolls.

[37] See below, 38.

[38] 2Cor 11,4,13 ff.; 12,1,11; cf. Did 11,8. Cf. D. Georgi, *Die Gegner des Paulus im 2. Korintherbrief*, Neukirchen 1964, 298 ff. See below, 104 f.

for spiritual gifts (πνευματικά, 1Cor 14,1), the two terms have been equated[39]. More probably, the πνευματικά are viewed as the effectual and visible consequence of the empowering πνεύματα[40]. The Corinthians' zeal for 'spirits' would be, then, not a desire simply for specific charismatic manifestations but, more significantly, an interest in the powers that lie behind and attend those manifestations.

A similar instance occurs in 1Cor 14,32: 'The spirits of the prophets subject themselves to the prophets.' Some exegetes[41] explain 'spirits' as the natural faculties of the prophets, their human psyche. Against this is the regular Old Testament identification of the prophetic spirit with the Spirit of Yahweh or from Yahweh, as J. Lindblom has shown[42]. Paul continues the same line of thought: the pneumatics have received the Spirit that is from God, ἐκ θεοῦ (1Cor 2,12). An alternative explanation supposes that the plural 'spirits' reflects the variety of charisms. But this falls into the same confusion of πνεύματα with πνευματικά mentioned above. In both 1Cor 14,12 and 1Cor 14,32, then, a plurality of *good spirits* must be inferred. This conclusion is supported by two other New Testament passages, 1John 4,1—3 and Rev 22,6[43].

The expression, 'the God of the spirits of the prophets' in Rev 22,6 is reminiscent of 1Cor 14,32 and is probably to be similarly interpreted. 1John 4 offers a significant commentary on the Co-

---

[39] So, Conzelmann, *Korintherbrief*, 279; Robertson-Plummer, *I Corinthians*, 311; M. Dibelius, *Die Geisterwelt im Glauben des Paulus*, Göttingen 1909, 76 (on 1Cor 14,32).

[40] Admittedly, the two are closely associated, and in Eph 6,12 the effect may be identified with the cause: 'spiritual hosts (πνευματικά) of evil'. Better, perhaps, is 'spiritual manifestations of wickedness in the heavenly warfare' (cf. Weymouth, Wycliffe-Purvey).

[41] E. g. Meyer, *Corinthians*, II, 29; R. H. Charles, *The Revelation of St. John*, Edinburgh 1920, II, 218; H. B. Swete, *The Apocalypse*, London 1906, 299 (on 22,6). Otherwise and rightly, Godet, *Corinthians*, II, 307: the plural denotes 'the particular impulses and revelations'. However, 'divine inspiration differs from diabolical in the fact that the latter takes man from himself — it is a possession — whereas the former restores him to himself. The present ὑποτάσσεται signifies, not *are subject*, but subject themselves, and that at the very moment when the prophet wills it.'

[42] Lindblom, *Prophecy*, 175—8. Cf. IgnPhld 7,1 (ἀπὸ θεοῦ).

[43] 1Thess 5,21 ('test all things') may have the same meaning. Cf. 1John 4,1: 'test the spirits' = ? the prophets; 1Tim 3,10: 'let the ministers (*diakonoi*) be tested first'; Did 11,11: 'every prophet who has been tested'; 12,1, 15,1. Appar-

rinthian passages. John's readers are urged to test the spirits (δοκι-μάζετε; cf. 1Thess 5,21). Because there are many false prophets,

> by this you know the spirit of God (τὸ πνεῦμα τοῦ θεοῦ): every spirit (πᾶν πνεῦμα) that confesses that Jesus Christ has come in the flesh is from God (ἐκ τοῦ θεοῦ), and every spirit that does not confess Jesus is not from God.

As in Corinthians, there is an oscillation between the singular and plural (cf. 1Cor 12,10 f.) and a subtle distinction between 'the Spirit of God' and 'every spirit... from God'. The dualism is verbalized differently in 1John — that is, as the Spirit of God and the spirit of antichrist or the spirit of truth and the spirit of error[44]. However, both passages similarly distinguish those who are 'from God' and those who are 'from the world' (ἐκ τοῦ κόσμου)[45].

How is one to explain the 'spirits' that Paul associates with Christian prophets and prophecy? Usually in the New Testament the plural 'spirits' refers to demons[46]. The exceptional usage in Paul and John may find an explanation in an Old Testament citation in Hebrews (1,7). This letter, which may have originated in a Pauline or Pauline-associated circle, also describes good angels as spirits:

> God makes his angels spirits and his ministers (λειτουργούς) a flame of fire[47].

The writer then comments (Heb 1,14):

---

ently, the spirit working through the pneumatic becomes so identified with him, or he with the spirit, that pneumatics can be called 'spirits'. See note 55.

[44] 1John 4,3 b,6. 1John 4,2 b–3 a has the marks of a traditional formula that is followed (3 b–6) by John's commentary. In 1Tim 4,1 Paul cites (ὅτι), a prophetic oracle that refers to 'spirits of error'. Cf. TestJud 20,1; Hermas, *Man* 3.

[45] 1John 4,4–6; 1Cor 2,12; cf. John 8,23; 14,17 ('the spirit of truth which the world cannot receive'); 15,19 with 1Cor 2,12; also, cf. John 12,31; 14,30 ('prince of the world') with 2Cor 4,4; Eph 2,2. See H. Windisch, *Der zweite Korintherbrief*, Göttingen 1970/1924, 135 (on 2Cor 4,4): the dualism need not be understood as gnostic but may be derived out of the general primitive Christian conviction that the devil rules 'this world'. Cf. Luke 4,6; Rev 12,9.

[46] Over a dozen times, sometimes (Luke 10,20; 11,26; 1Petr 3,19) without qualification. The term, spirits, also refers less frequently to both good and evil (1Cor 12,10; 1John 4,1) and to good (1Cor 14,12; Hebr 1,7,14; 12,9; Rev 1,4) angelic beings. Similarly, Jub 15,31 f. A close relationship, but not an identification, of spirit and angel appears in Acts 23,8 f. Cf. W. Foerster, δαίμων, *TWNT* II (1935), 17 f. On Beezeboul = Satan = the devil (cf. Mt 4,8,10) as the prince of demons and as an angel cf. Luke 11,17–23; Mt 25,41; 2Cor 11,14.

[47] Ps. 104,4. Cf. Jub 2,2: 'the spirits who minister (τὰ λειτουργοῦντα) before [God]' (cited in Migne, *P. G.* XLIII, 276); Enoch 37, 4: 'Lord of Spirits'.

Are not all [the angels] serving spirits (λειτουργικὰ πνεύματα) sent out for ministry (διακονίαν) for the sake of those who are about to inherit salvation?

The designation of angels as 'spirits' is widespread in apocalyptic Judaism. It is given elaborate expression at Qumran[48], where the spirit of truth appears to be identified with (or to emanate from) God's holy Spirit[49]. Compare the following texts:

God will pour out on man 'the spirit of truth ... in order to instruct (להבין) the upright in the knowledge (דעת) of the highest and in the wisdom (חכמה) of the sons of heaven and [in order to] make wise (להשכיל) the perfect ones in the way. [IQS 4,21 f.]

As one of the wise (משכיל) I have knowledge of you, my God, by (ב) the Spirit that you gave to me. I have faithfully heard your wonderful counsel (סוד). By (ב) your holy spirit you opened to me knowledge (דעת) in the mystery of your wisdom (שכל). [IQH 12,11 ff.]

At the same time the spirit of truth apparently is identified with the angel of truth or light[50], leading angelic hosts who themselves are called 'holy spirits'[51], or spirits 'of truth'[52] or 'of knowledge'[53]. They fight against Belial, the spirit of perversity or angel of darkness, and against his 'spirits', who are 'angels of destruction'[54]. In connection with their role as participants in the battle of angelic powers, men (or certain men) can themselves be described as spirits[55]:

The twisted spirit you cleansed ... to stand with the hosts of holy ones, to enter fellowship with the congregation of the sons of heaven. You [gave over] to man an eternal lot with the spirits of knowledge (רוחי דעת) [IQH 3,21–3; cf. 1,21 ff.]

You made known to your elect the counsel of your truth. In your marvellous mysteries you made them wise (שכל) ... [You cleansed them] from a spirit of perversity ... to stand in array before you with the eternal hosts and with the spirits [of knowledge]. [IQH 11,9 f., 13].

---

[48] On angelology at Qumran cf. Y. Yadin, *The Scroll of the War*, Oxford 1962, 229–42; M. Mansoor, *The Thanksgiving Hymns*, Leiden 1961, 77–84; E. Schweizer, *TDNT* VI (1968/1959), 389–392, 443 ff.

[49] Otherwise, O. Betz, *Der Paraklet*, Leiden 1963, 165, 169, who apparently draws too sharp a dichotomy between the 'monism' of the Old Testament and the dualistic (Persian) origins of the spirit of truth. See note 92.

[50] Perhaps IQS 3,18–25 refers to Michael (cf. *CD* 5,18 with IQM 17,6). So, Betz, *Paraklet*, 66 f.

[51] IQH 8,11 f.   [53] IQH 3,22 f.; 4QSi 40 24,2,6.

[52] IQM 13,10.   [54] IQM 13,10.

[55] Cf. also IQH 1,21–3: 'you open my ears to wonderful mysteries (רזי פלא). But I [am] ... a spirit of error and perversity (רוח התועה ונעוה) without understanding (בינה).' IQH 2,15: 'I have become a spirit of zeal against all seekers of smooth things.' IQH 17,25: 'a spirit of flesh is your servant'. In Wis 7,23,27

The holy Spirit or holy spirits have a special relation to 'the wise' (משכילים), i. e. the teachers[56] at Qumran. One of this group, the author of the Hymns of Thanksgiving[57], speaks both of the holy Spirit and of the holy spirits (רוחות) that God has put within him (1QH 12,11 f.; 17,17,25). This endowment gives him 'knowledge in the mysteries of [God's] wisdom'[58] and participation with the angelic spirits of knowledge (1QH 3,21 ff.) in the heavenly council (סוד) of God (1QH 11,9—13). Probably it is this that constitutes him 'an interpreter of knowledge', מליץ דעת, [59] who is to test (לבחון)[60] the men of truth (1QH 2,13 f.). The same role is given to the *maskilim* as a group: they are to instruct the members of the community 'with regard to all the kinds of spirits

---

those who receive wisdom and are made 'friends of God and prophets' also may be termed πνεύματα (so W. Bieder, *TDNT* VI (1968), 371. The epistle of Barnabas addresses as 'spirits' (1,5) fellow pneumatics (1,8; 4,6,9) who manifest 'the spiritual gift' (ἡ δωρεὰ πνευματική) and to whom he wishes to impart 'perfect gnosis', which is to be found in a proper understanding of Scripture (1,5; 2,1—4). Correspondingly, false teachers, the 'wise' (חכם) of the world, also may be termed 'spirits' by the psalmist of IQH 3,14 f.,18: 'spirits of vipers' (or 'of illusion'). Cf. Mt 3,7; Eph 6,12; Mansoor, *Hymns*, 115 n.

[56] Cf. A. R. C. Leaney, *The Rule of Qumran*, London 1966, 72 f., 230; F. F. Bruce in *Neotestamentica et Semitica*, ed. E. E. Ellis and M. Wilcox, Edinburgh 1969, 228 f.

[57] Mansoor (*Hymns*, 106 n.) and J. P. Hyatt (*NTS* II (1955—6), 277) and others rightly identify him as a teacher or *the* Teacher of Righteousness. Cf. IQH 12,11 f. with IQpHab 7,4 f.

[58] IQH 12,12f.; cf 7,5—7: 'a distorted spirit (רוחעויים) confounded me . . . I thank you, Lord, for you strengthened me by (ב) your power. And your holy spirit you poured out on me that I might not stumble.'

[59] At Qumran מליץ, found primarily in the *Hymns*, refers to the *maskil* (IQH 2,13) and to the opposing demonic-led teachers, the 'interpreters of lies' (IQH 2,31; 4,7,9 f.; cf. 2,14) and, perhaps, to angelic interpreters (IQH 6,13). Although the idea of intercessor, intermediary, or other kind of interpreter may be indicated by the context, it is adjectival (otherwise: Mansoor, *Hymns*, 143 n.). The basic meaning of *mēliṣ* is interpreter, and this appears to be the case also in the Old Testament usage, whether specifying a translator (Gen 42,23), envoy (2Chr 32,31), prophets (?Isa 43,27), or angelic spokesmen or intercessors (Job 33,23; cf. 16,20). From Job 33,23, interpreted in the targum as פרקליטא , G. Johnston, *Spirit-Paraclete*, 101 f.; 120 f., following S. Mowinckel and N. Johansson, infers a connection between the Johannine paraclete (=spirit of truth = Holy Spirit) and an angelic *mēliṣ*. But, unlike O. Betz, he does not identify them. Cf. R. E. Brown, *The Gospel According to John*, Garden City 1970, II, 1138 f.

[60] The word is translated in the Septuagint by διακρίνω and δοκιμάζω. The former term is used in 1Cor 14,29 of the testing by pneumatics of prophetic speakers; the latter is used similarly in 1John 4,1. See above, note 12.

they possess (לכול מיני רוחותם , 1QS 3,14), and they are to distinguish (להבדיל) and to discern (לשקול) the sons of righteousness
'each according to his spirit' (1QS 9,14,17; cf. C D 20,24).

As recipients and transmitters of mysteries, possessors of wisdom, discerners of spirits, and interpreters (מליצים), 'the wise' at
Qumran bear a striking resemblance to the pneumatics in the Pauline community[61]. These similarities underscore the parallel between the angelic spirits given to the wise at Qumran and the
'spirits' sought by the Corinthian pneumatics (1Cor 14,12,32).
They indicate also that the same general conceptual framework
was common to both groups[62].

This view of the matter is supported by a few early Christian
or Christian-influenced writings that speak of the angel 'of the
prophetic spirit' or 'of the holy Spirit'[63]. Similar angelic connotations may be present in the 'seven spirits' of Revelation (1,4)[64],

---

[61] Cf. 1Cor 2,7,13 f.; 14,29; Eph 3. Cf. Eph 4,12 f.; Col 1,26—8; 2,2 with
IQS 4,21 f.

[62] The force of the parallels should not be minimized in deference to a now
somewhat discredited theory of a theological dichotomy between Palestinian
and diaspora Judaism or Christianity. Traditional emphases were present in
the diaspora and syncretistic emphases in Palestine. Also, a religious group
might be strictly traditionalist in one respect (e. g. cultic practice) and syncre-
tizing in another respect (e. g. theology). See below, 91 ff., 125 f.

[63] Hermas, Mandates 11,9; AscenIsa 3,16; 9,36,40; 11,33. Cf. Justin, 1 Apol 6
with 61; Barn 9,2 ('the spirit of the Lord prophesies') with 9,4 ('an evil angel
taught [the Jews] cleverness'); 18,1 f.: 'there are two ways of teaching and
of authority (ἐξουσίας), one of light and the other of darkness... On the one
are arrayed the light-giving angels of God, on the other the angels of Satan.
The [leader of] one is the Lord from everlasting to everlasting, the [leader
of] the other is the ruler of the present season of lawlessness.' According to
Hippolytus (Ref. 6,19 = 6,14) Simon Magus taught 'that the prophets spoke prophecies, inspired by the world-creating angels' (ἀπὸ τῶν κοσμοποιῶν ἀγγέλων
ἐμπνευσθέντας). In Epistula Apos. Jesus sends his power (δύναμις) in the form
of an angel (15,5 = 8,5), and he himself takes the form (μορφή) of an angel
(14,7 = 7,7). Cf. TestJob 43—50.

[64] So Charles, Revelation, I, 11—13 (on Rev 1,4). Cf. Rev 4,5; 5,6; 8,2; Isa
11,2. On 'seven angels' in Jewish tradition cf. Ez 9,2 f.; Tobit 12,15; Enoch 20;
90,21; TLevi 8. According to H. B. Swete (Apocalypse, 310) the Spirit in the
Apocalypse refers generally to the spirit of prophecy. 'The Spirit and the
bride' (Rev 20,17) is practically equivalent to 'the prophets and the saints'
(Rev. 16,6; 18,24). Cf. Charles, Revelation, II, 179. In Rev 12,10, cf. 19,10; 22,9
it is probably the martyr-prophets who are called 'our brothers' by the angelic
voice (so W. Bousset, Die Offenbarung Johannis, Göttingen 1906, 342; cf. Charles,
Revelation, I, 327 f.). On the prophet as martyr in primitive Christianity cf.
G. Friedrich in TDNT VI (1968), 834 f.; O. Michel, Prophet und Märtyrer,
Gütersloh 1932, 25—53.

the 'Father of spirits' in Hebrews (12,9)[65], and the Johannine spirit of truth[66].

Angels and Pneumatics in Paul's Letters

In Paul's writings angels are specifically associated with the activities of the pneumatics. The 'tongues of angels' are included in manifestations of *glossolalia* (1Cor 13,1). And the presence of angels requires the veiling of women[67] in prayer sessions of pneumatics[68]. More significantly, the Apostle reckons with the co-activity of angels in the preaching of his opponents. They are 'pneumatics'[69] who impart 'a different spirit' and serve a pretended 'angel of light'[70]. Probably with reference to them[71] Paul writes:

If ... an angel from heaven should preach to you a gospel contrary to that which we preached to you, let him be accursed[72].

---

[65] So H. Alford, *The Greek Testament*, London 1861, IV, 243; J. Bonsirven cited in C. Spicq, *L'Epître aux Hebreux*, Paris 1953, II, 394; cf. B. F. Westcott, *The Epistle to the Hebrews*, London 1889, 401 f. The phrase is not parallel to 'fathers of *our* flesh'. Most commentators, however, prefer an anthropological interpretation.

[66] The spirit of truth has characteristics similar to the spirit of prophecy. In 1John 4,1,6 there is a direct association, if not an identification, of the spirit of truth and error with true and false prophecy. Cf. 1Tim 4,1; see notes 45, 46, 59.

[67] 1Cor 11,4—10. On the suggested reasons for this practice cf. A. Jaubert, *NTS* XVIII (1971—2), 427 f.; J. A. Fitzmyer in *Paul and Qumran*, ed. J. Murphy-O'Connor, London 1968, 31—47 (= *NTS* IV, 1957—8, 48—58 + postscript). Fitzmyer rightly argues that good angels are in view (40—4). The same is true of Col 2,18 since the angels are distinguished from the opposing principalities and powers (Col 2,15). Also the invocation or worship of demons by the Colossians, unlikely in the nature of the case, would have evoked a far different response from Paul. For the view that κατακαλύπτεσθαι, 'to be covered,' means 'to wear long hair' cf. W. J. Martin in *Apostolic History and the Gospel... presented to F. F. Bruce*, ed. W. W. Gasque, Exeter and Grand Rapids, 1970, 231—41.

[68] 1Cor 11,4,10. See note 25.

[69] See above, 30.

[70] 2Cor 11,3 f.,14 f. See note 38. Note the comparison of their teaching to the serpent's tempting Eve to get 'knowledge' (cf. Gen. 3,5 with 2Cor 11,5). Cf. CD 12,2 f: 'every man over whom the spirits of Belial rule so that he preaches apostasy (סרה)...'.

[71] Paul's opponents in 2Corinthians, Galatians and Colossians belong essentially to the same group, a faction within the Church's Hebraist, i. e. circumcision party. See below, 103—114, 120—126.

[72] Gal 1,8. In the light of 1Cor 14,3,12,32; 2Cor 11,4,14; 2Thess 2,2 this is not

The worship or invocation (θρησκεία) of angels by the Colossian errorists probably reflects the same situation although perhaps at a more advanced stage[73]. Finally, the harassing 'angel of Satan' in 2Cor 12,7 may be mentioned. Although it has a different role, reminiscent of the book of Job, it comes to Paul in connection with an extraordinary pneumatic experience, probably understood as his participation in the heavenly council of God[74].

Both the background of Paul's thought and the evidence of his writings support the conclusion that in his view the spirits of the pneumatics, the inspired speakers, are in fact angelic powers. In the words of Hebrews (1,14), with which Paul would probably not disagree, they are 'serving spirits sent out for ministry' (διακονία). And they fulfil their ministry especially as co-workers of the prophets[75] and as bearers and/or facilitators of the 'spiritual gifts' from the risen Lord[76]. At the same time satanic powers are at work in the opposition. Like their earlier counterparts at Qumran, the pneumatics in the Pauline mission are, in their view, major participants in a battle of cosmic dimensions[77]:

---

rhetorical flourish but rather a sober recognition of the opponents' possible appeal to angelic revelation, whose factual character Paul implicitly accepts. Cf. Gal 3,19 where Paul presupposes the tradition of angelic involvement in the divine disclosure of the Law.

[73] Col 2,18. See note 67. Note the connection with 'visions.' There is a similar worship of good angels in Rev 19,10; 22,8. Cf. Irenaeus, *Against Heresies*, 2, 32, 5: Swete, *Apocalypse*, 248; E. O. Percy, *Die Probleme der Kolosser und Epheserbriefe*, Lund 1946, 149—55. Some scholars, recently E. Lohse, *Colossians and Philemon*, Philadelphia 1971, 177—83 (G. T., 249—57), argue that Colossians and Ephesians exhibit sharp differences from Paul's theology and are, therefore, non-Pauline. Even if the arguments are accepted (and some of them seem to me to be questionable), the differences in style and thought from the other Pauline letters probably are better explained by Paul's use of preformed traditions and/or by the contribution of Paul's circle (or of an amanuensis) writing during Paul's mission and under his eye. One must, I think, resist the temptation simply to equate theological difference with chronological distance. In any case the present thesis does not depend upon the use of these letters.

[74] 2Cor 12,1—9. See notes 104, 105.

[75] 1Cor 14,32. Cf. Rev 12,10; 19,10 where the angels are described as 'brothers', i. e. co-workers and as 'fellow slaves' of the prophets. See above, 13—17.

[76] 1Cor 12,5. Cf. Eph 4,8 where the gifts are ascribed explicitly to Christ and include only the gifts of inspired speech.

[77] Cf. K. Lake and H. J. Cadbury in *The Beginnings of Christianity*, ed. F. J. F. Jackson and K. Lake, 5 vols., London 1920—33, IV, 130: 'Few things are more necessary for an understanding of early Christianity than a perception of the fact that it was essentially a prophetic movement.' O. Everling, *Die pauli-*

For our struggle is not against flesh and blood, but against principalities, against the powers, against the cosmic rulers of this darkness, against the spiritual manifestations of evil (τὰ πνευματικὰ τῆς πονηρίας)[78].

Within the Pauline churches it is Paul's co-workers who are *par excellence* the pneumatics, i. e. the persons with prophetic gifts. This becomes evident in a number of ways. (1) The co-workers are sometimes designated ἀπόστολοι and διάκονοι, charisms that include the function of inspired speaking; sometimes they are called συνεργοί and ἀδελφοί[79], terms that may imply the same role. (2) In Colossians they are probably the recipients of the letter[80] and exercise as a group the same gifts as the pneumatics do in 1Cor 14. Also, (3) they form (or are part of) a pneumatic community of teaching and prayer that is presupposed in a number of passages: Paul and Titus 'walk in the same spirit . . . the same footprints' (2Cor 12,18); Timothy will teach 'just as . . . I teach' (1Cor 4,17). When Paul writes, 'We pray for you[81], he is probably referring *inter alia* to prayer sessions with co-workers and/or co-senders of the letter[82]. These and other considerations suggest that the co-workers were the original subjects of the regulations on teaching and prayer that Paul applies to the Corinthian pneumatics in 1Cor 11,3–12; 14,26–35[83].

---

nische Angelologie und Dämonologie, Göttingen 1888, 43 f., identified the 'spirits of the prophets' as angels who must be distinguished from the other (demonic) spirits (1Cor 12,10). His acute analysis came to my attention only after the present essay was substantially completed and, therefore, offers an independent corroboration of it. See note 78.

[78] Eph 6,12. Cf. 2,6; see note 40. Note the oscillation between the singular (6,11) and the plural (6,12). Cf. H. A. Hahn, *Die Theologie des Neuen Testaments*, Leipzig 1854, I, 30, on 1Cor 14,32 (cited in Everling, *Angelologie*, 40): 'the one spirit of God is thought of as a multiplicity of spirits that are all included (beschlossen) in Him'. Hahn also identified the spirits as angels.

[79] For example, the *sunergoi* (1Cor 3,9) are 'stewards of the mysteries of God' (1Cor 4,1), a function earlier identified with the activity of the *pneumatikoi* (1Cor 2,7,13). Cf. 2Tim 2,15; 1Tim 5,18 *(kopiaō)*; Did 13,1. In Gal 6,1 the *adelphoi* are identified as *pneumatikoi*. See above, 5–13, 16 n.

[80] See above, 17 f.

[81] Col 1,3; cf. 4,12; 1Thess 1,2; 3,10; 2Thess 1,3; cf. Eph 6,18 f.; 2Thess 3,1 f.

[82] Cf. Acts 13,1 f. Such notices remind us that we cannot understand the mission of Paul apart from the mission praxis that underlies it. On the association of prayer and prophecy cf. G. Friedrich, *TDNT* VI (1968), 852 f.

[83] The regulations appear to be traditional (1Cor 11,2 f.; 14,33) and paradigmatic. Cf. also 1Cor 2,6–16, which reflects the activity of a session of pneumatics in which Paul is implicitly included ('we'). See notes 17,21.

The Background of Paul's Thought

The rationale for the role given to angelic powers in the Pauline writings appears to lie both in the Apostle's religious heritage and in his personal experience. Apocalyptic Judaism offers the most immediate antecedent for his thought[84]. To what degree its terminology and/or concepts depend on Iranian sources is a complex question. The influence sometimes has been exaggerated, and it is in any case secondary[85]. The Hebrew Scriptures themselves provide the decisive key to Paul's thought in at least three respects.

(1) Like the Pauline pneumatics, the Old Testament prophets receive their messages through angels and fulfil a role similar to that of angels. For example, in 1Kings 13,18 a prophet in Bethel tests his 'brother' (13,30) prophet with the words,

I also am a prophet as you are, and an angel spoke to me by the word of the Lord, saying...

This casual and unexplained comment indicates that angelic mediation of Yahweh's word was a recognized form of prophetic experience[86]. Both the angel and the prophet communicate God's word to men, interpret the mind of God[87], and discern good and evil[88]. In Judges 13,6,8 the angel appears in the prophet's role and

---

[84] As mentioned above, the most elaborate parallels appear to be in the Qumran writings.

[85] Cf. H. Ringgren, *The Faith of Qumran*, Philadelphia, 1963, 79 f.; Leaney, *Rule*, 43—7; H. Conzelmann, 'σκότος', *TDNT* VII (1971), 432. Otherwise: E. Kamlah, *Die Form der katalogischen Paränese im Neuen Testament*, Tübingen 1964, 49, 163—8; M. J. Suggs, 'The Christian Two Ways Tradition', *Studies in New Testament ... in honor of A. P. Wikgren*, ed. D. E. Aune, Leiden 1972, 64—7.

[86] That is, the prophet apparently 'sees' the messenger as well as 'hears' the message (cf. Lindblom, *Prophecy*, 55 f.).

[87] Cf. Job 33,23 with Isa 43,27 (מליץ). See note 59.

[88] I. e. possess divine wisdom: 2Sam 14,20; Dan 5,16. Cf. Gen 3,4.22. Traditionally the roles of the 'wise man' and the 'prophet' were separate and distinct. But they approximate one another in David (cf. 2Sam 14,20 with 2Chr 8,14), in Ahithophel (2Sam 16,23) and in Isaiah and Jeremiah. In the person of Daniel they are identified. Apparently from the usage in Daniel the prophetic character of (true) wisdom continues in the thought of some apocalyptic and Qumran literature and in the New Testament. See above, 28 f., 34 ff. Cf. J. Lindblom, 'Wisdom in the Old Testament Prophets', *Wisdom in Israel and in the Near East*, ed. M. Noth, Leiden 1955, 192—204; W. McKane, *Prophets and Wise Men*, London 1965, 114—18. See below, 52—59.

is called by the prophet's name, 'man of God'[89]. Conversely, prophets are included in heavenly councils[90], conducted by interpreting angels[91], and guarded by angelic armies[92]. Although the term is not used, the impression is given that prophets and angels are co-workers in a common task.

(2) The activity of evil angels or spirits also has an Old Testament background in the adversary role given to Satan and to the lying spirits[93]. In later apocalyptic thought the conflict escalates into a kind of cosmic war, but the ethical and conceptual framework is essentially unaltered. The devil remains God's devil, used for God's purposes and fully under God's control. Like Job, Paul is 'given' by God an 'angel of Satan' to afflict him[94]. As the prophets in 1Kings 22,19—23 are inspired by lying spirits, so the 'man of lawlessness', the false prophet in 2Thess 2, deceives by the power of Satan (ἐνέργειαν τοῦ σατανᾶ, 2,9). In both cases it is God who sends the power of error (ἐνέργειαν πλάνης, 2,11) to make the wicked hearers believe 'the lie'. It is characteristic of Jewish apocalyptic writings, including the New Testament, to present the battle of spirit-powers within the context of an overarching divine sovereignty[95].

---

[89] Cf. Gen 18,2.9 f.; 19,1; Zech 3,6 f. On the other hand the prophet Haggai (1,13) can be called 'angel,' i. e. 'messenger of the Lord'. Perhaps the angel in Rev 2,1.8.12 is a prophet. Otherwise: G. Kittel, 'ἄγγελος', TDNT I (1964/1933), 86 f.

[90] 1King 22,19—22; Jer 23,18 (וירא וישמע) ; Zech 3; cf. Isa 6; Amos 3,7; Psalm 89,8(7); Job 15,8 (חכמה, שמע).Cf. R. N. Whybray, *The Heavenly Counsellor in Isa 40,13—14*, Cambridge 1971, 49—53.

[91] Dan 10; Zech 4—6; Ez 40—48; cf. 8,3. On the *angelus interpres* in early Christianity cf. Revelation, *passim*; AscIsa 10,6.8; 11,1; Hermas, *Vis* 3; 5; ParalJer 4,12.

[92] In 2Kings 6,16 ff. 'those with us' (16) refers to angels. Cf. Isa 31,3. The experiences related by the prophets provide in part the background for the references to angels in the Psalms. Cf. Ps 34,7; 91,11 with 2Kings 6,17; 19,35; Hab 3; Ps 29,1 f.; 89,6 f.; 148,2 with 1Kings 22,19; Is 6,1—8; Ez 1,22—8.

[93] Job 1; 2; 1Kings 22,19—23; Zech 3,1—4; cf. 13,2 f. Cf. G. von Rad, TDNT II (1964/1935), 75.

[94] 2Cor 12,7. The passive (ἐδόθη), veils a reference to 'the Lord', as is clear from Paul's prayer (12,8 f.). When Paul (cf. 1Cor 2,12; John 16,11; 1John 4, 1—6) contrasts the spirit ἐκ τοῦ θεοῦ with the spirit of the world (τοῦ κόσμου) or terms Satan 'the god of this age' (2Cor 4,4), no dualism is implied, as though Satan were an independent power. Similarly, at Qumran, cf. IQH 4,38; IQM 13,10 f.; Leaney, *Rule*, 45, 53 f.

[95] Paul also can deliver persons to Satan 'in the name of the Lord Jesus' (1Cor 5,4 f.; cf. 1Tim 1,20). According to the Qumran literature God created

(3) Paul identifies the power at work in the pneumatics both as the holy Spirit (e. g. 1Cor 12,11) and as angelic spirits (e. g. 1Cor 14,12,32). This oscillating pattern of thought probably is best explained by the Old Testament conception of 'the one and the many'. In the words of A. R. Johnson, Yahweh is thought of 'as possessing an indefinable extension of personality' by which he is actually present, e. g. in his angelic messengers[96]. In all likelihood Paul shares this conceptual framework and incorporates it into his teaching.

However, for him, no less than for the letter to the Hebrews (1. 2), Jesus represents the presence of God on a level qualitatively different from the angels. This accounts for the reticence with which Paul mentions the activity of angels, especially of good angels: he does not want anything to displace the centrality of Christ Jesus[97]. As Corinthians suggests and Colossians confirms, there was already a tendency to wrongly exalt and/or to misuse the angelic powers[98].

Although Paul perceives and resists this tendency, the (subordinate) role of the angels remains deeply rooted in his consciousness. It is difficult to explain solely in terms of his religious background, and in all likelihood it arises also out of his experience as a prophet. For the Israelite prophets traditional mythological imagery of divine messengers may have formed a background for their visions and made the visions conceptually more meaningful. At the

---

the spirit of deceit = the angel of darkness and determines the time of his activity and of his destruction (1QS 3,18—21; 4,18 f.; cf. 1QM 13,11; 1QH 1,8 f.). Cf. H. Ringgren, *The Faith of Qumran*, Philadelphia 1963, 52—5. Cf. 1Chr 21,1 with 1Sam 24,1.

[96] A. R. Johnson, *The One and the Many in the Israelite Conception of God*, Cardiff 1942, 28 f.; cf. 17 ff., 26—41: In Ps 34,8(7) the 'angel of the Lord' can be viewed as a collective unit (35). Cf. Gen 32,2; 18—19; Hos 12,3f.

[97] 1Cor 2,2; Gal 6,14; Col 2,2 f.,9 f.; 2Tim 2,8. Cf. also the emphasis in 1Cor 12,3 f.,11 upon the one Spirit of God who is the source of all the gifts. Somewhat differently, Leaney, *Rule*, 50. See below, 71.

[98] 1Cor 14,12; Col 2,18. Cf. Jude 8; Hebr 1;2; Rev 19,10. Note the connection with visions in Col 2,18; see above, 37. The letter to the Galatians reflects the same problem if the στοιχεῖα ('elemental spirits', RSV; NEB) of Gal 4,3,9 are identified or associated with angelic, i. e. spiritual beings. So, for example, Everling, *Angelologie*, pp. 70 ff.; F. F. Bruce, *BJRL* 53 (1971), 268 f.; B. Reicke, *JBL* LXX (1951), 261—3. But see G. Delling, *TDNT* VII (1971), 683—7; A. J. Bandstra, *The Law and the Elements of the World*, Kampen 1964, 57—9, and especially his survey of interpretations, 5—30. See below, 111 n., 232.

same time the prophets record encounters with angels, in visional and/or physical reality[99]. Their first-hand accounts are in some instances quite definite; and it is unlikely that second-hand accounts 'would have emerged if visions of angels . . . had not sometimes really occurred'[100]. Such experiences would, for the prophets, have effectively 'demythologized' the stories about divine messengers. For them the myth was 'broken'[101], i. e. brought into the realm of their historical experience.

Such is Paul's testimony in 2Cor 12. His 'visions and revelations of the Lord'[102], include a transposition to 'the third heaven', to 'Paradise'. The imagery implies that, like the Old Testament prophets, Paul was caught up — whether in body or in vision[103] he does not know — into the presence of the angels of God[104], probably into the heavenly council of Yahweh[105]. In the heavenly ses-

---

[99] In the Pauline churches it is implied in such references as Gal 1,8 and Col 2,18; cf. 2Thess 2,2. The *angelus interpres* also may be presupposed in the visions of Acts 12,7—11 and in Acts 27,23.

[100] Lindblom, *Prophecy*, 56.

[101] Cf. B. S. Childs, *Myth and Reality in the Old Testament*, London 1960, 49—57, who develops the theme of the 'broken myth' along somewhat different lines.

[102] Probably a genitive of origin. So, the Jerusalem Bible.

[103] In the light of 1Cor 6,18 ἐκτὸς τοῦ σώματος probably refers to a vision and does not reflect an anthropological dualism.

[104] In Jewish apocalyptic texts paradise and the third heaven (cf. AscIsa 7,24) are sometimes identified (2Enoch 8; 42,3; ApcMos 37,5; 40,2) and/or are associated with the angelic presence (Enoch 20,7) and with the presence of God (cf. 2Enoch 8,2; ApcMos 22,3 f.; cf. Rev 12,7—10; 21—22; Enoch 24—25). Cf. H. Traub, *TDNT* V (1967), 535: 'paradise and the throne of God are in [the third heaven] or in close proximity to it'.

[105] Favouring this is the audition (2Cor 12,4; cf. Jer 23,18), the reference to the third heaven, to the time (2Cor 12,1), and to Satan or his angel (cf. 1Cor 8,5; Eph 6,12; 1Kings 22,21 f.; Job 1;2; Zech 3; see below, note 106). To be meaningful the 'angel of Satan' (2Cor 12,7) must have been announced or given, as the context indicates, at the time of the revelation: the 'exaltation beyond measure' would hardly have begun six months later. In some contemporary writings the third heaven is the locale of God's angelic court (see above, note 104). J. W. Bowker (*JSS* XVI [1971], 157—73; cf. Windisch, *Der zweite Korintherbrief*, 375 f.) suggests that the visions in 2Cor 12 (and Acts 9,3) arose out of *merkabah* contemplation (e. g. on Ez 1.2; cf. Hag 14 b) current among some rabbinic visionaries: (1) both refer to a 'third category' in heaven; (2) both may allude to the divine name 'that man may not utter'; (3) Paul was a highly trained rabbi to whom visions are ascribed and who may, therefore, have practised *merkabah* contemplation. None of these rather general points carry us very far toward Bowker's conclusion. Against Bowker is the context of the visions in Acts: four are night visions (16,8 f.; 18,9; 23,11; 27,23) and two occur

sion he received in his flesh a thorn, an angel of Satan that continued to afflict him in his subsequent ministry[106].

However Paul's strange testimony is evaluated, it shows that personal experiences rather than traditional or mythical stories underlie his conviction about the spirits, i. e. their reality *extra se* and their influence on men[107]. Some expositors have explained Paul's visions psychologically, as internal and subjective phenomena detached from the external world[108]. But, as H. J. Schoeps has seen[109], this is only an easy 'explaining away', an attempt to accommodate Paul's witness to a different confessional viewpoint. Unlike certain philosophers of his day — and of our own as well — Paul could not accept a one-dimensional view of the world, a world 'immune from the interference of supernatural powers'[110].

---

during prayer (9,12; 22,17). Only the Damascus road vision (26,19) is suitable to a context of meditation on Scripture, and neither that nor the visions reported in the letters (cf. Gal 1,12; Eph 3,3) suggest such a context. 2Cor 12 finds its best analogy, rather, in the ancient prophetic experience of being privy to God's secret purposes (Amos 3,7) as that experience is later expressed in Jewish and Christian apocalyptic (e. g. Dan 12,4; IQH 12,11 f.; Mk 9,9; Rev 10,4). H. D. Betz, *Der Apostel Paulus*, Tübingen 1972, 70—73, 84 ('2Kor 12,2—4 ist die Parodie eines Himmelfahrtsberichtes') offers a doubtful alternative.

[106] 2Cor 12,7. Without deciding among the myriad interpretations of the 'thorn' one sees that it is clearly ascribed to satanic power within the context of an 'extra-natural' experience (see above, note 105) that, nevertheless, has its effects in 'natural' physical or psychological symptoms. See below, note 107. Cf. Acts of Petr 32 = MartPetr 3, where the false teacher Simon Magus is termed 'the angel of the devil', with Paul's similar characterization of his opponents in 2Cor 11,14 f.

[107] E. g. 1Cor 5,3—5; 10,20; 11,29 f.; 2Cor 12,12; Col 2,15; 1Thess 2,18; 1Tim 1,20 (Rom 8,38). Cf. Acts 13,10 f.; 16,18; 22,6—16.

[108] E. g. C. Holsten, *Zum Evangelium des Paulus und des Petrus*, Rostock 1868, 87: the thorn is a physical weakness (2Cor 12,7,9), 'the painful exhaustion that is an immediate attendant and successor of intense ecstasy'. H. Weinel, *St Paul*, London 1906, 81 f.: the Damascus road experience, and 2Cor 12 is no different, is 'the inward experience of the apostle'; Paul's blindness is understandable since the 'eye may be disorganized by a psychical commotion'. F. C. Baur (*Paul*, 2 vols., London 1875, I, 68—73,77 f.), along with D. F. Strauss and C. Holsten, marked the transition from an earlier rationalism in which, for example, the blinding light at Paul's conversion had been interpreted as a flash of lightning. Baur took it as an internal impression and Paul's blindness as symbolic. Out of that 'spiritual' experience grew the myth in which 'figurative expressions came to be interpreted strictly and literally' (73).

[109] H. J. Schoeps, *Paul*, London 1959, 54 f. Cf. A. Richardson, *History Sacred and Profane*, London 1964, 201 f.

[110] The phrase is R. Bultmann's in *Kerygma and Myth*, ed. H.-W. Bartsch, London 1960, 7. Bultmann thinks that such a world view is a necessary pre-

The reason, apparently, was not just that he had a different theory about the world but much more that he had a different experience of the world that, in turn, shaped his total world view.

World views, of course, are confessional affirmations, notoriously difficult to prove. And Paul makes no attempt to prove his. But his proclamation of Jesus as Lord had its origin in a 'heavenly vision' (1Cor 9,1; 15,8; cf. Acts 26,19) and found its continuing meaning in the context of a warfare of spirits in which he himself participated. The reality of his proclamation can hardly be divorced from the context that gave it meaning, even by those who find Paul's experiences foreign to their own. Moreover, Paul's witness in this area is important for a Church that again is manifesting a considerable measure of pneumatic phenomena. For it may help the Church avoid not only philosophical misconceptions about the powers at work within it but also an uncritical misuse of them. Today, no less than in the time of the Apostle, the second problem may prove to be greater than the first.

---

supposition for 'the historical method' (*Existence and Faith*, New York 1960, 291). But see Richardson, *History*, 184—94. On the similar rejection in the Greco-Roman world of 'supernatural' causes for historical phenomena cf. R. M. Grant, *Miracle and Natural Law*, Amsterdam 1952, 55 f., 206 (Lucretius, Plotinus).

3. 'WISDOM' AND 'KNOWLEDGE' IN
I CORINTHIANS

Two of the spiritual gifts discussed in the preceding chapter, 'a word of wisdom ... and a word of knowledge' (1Cor 12,8), and the concepts expressed by them, require a closer look. To explain the concepts of wisdom (σοφία) and knowledge (γνῶσις) in 1 Corinthians two general approaches have received considerable scholarly support. One derives St Paul's usage from a nonmythological understanding of the concepts in the Old Testament and later Judaism. The other discerns the influence of mythological origins that may or may not have been mediated through Judaism. The latter view owes its importance in the present century to the 'comparative religions' studies of W. Bousset (1907)[1] and R. Reitzenstein (1910)[2]. It was applied most influentially to New Testament studies by Professor R. Bultmann[3] who, with reference to Corinthians[4], argued that Paul opposed a movement of Gnostic pneumatics and in the process was himself influenced by Gnostic mytholog-

---

[1] W. Bousset, *Hauptprobleme der Gnosis*, Göttingen 1907; *cf. Kyrios Christos*, Nashville 1970 (1913), 164—172, 181—187; J. Doresse, *The Secret Books of the Egyptian Gnostics*, London 1960, 2 ff.

[2] R. Reitzenstein, *Die hellenistischen Mysterienreligionen*, Stuttgart 1966, 127.

[3] *Cf.* R. Bultmann, 'Hintergrund des Prologs zum Johannesevangelium', ΕΥΧΑΡΙΣΤΗΡΙΟΝ *H. Gunkel zum 60. Geburtstage*, Göttingen 1923, II, 3—26; 'Die Bedeutung der... mandäischen und manichäischen Quellen für Verständnis des Johannesevangeliums,' *ZNTW* 24 (1925) 100—146 = *Exegetica*, Tübingen 1967, 10—35, 55—104. But see E. M. Yamauchi, *Gnostic Ethics and Mandaean Origins*, Cambridge, Mass. 1970, 80—89.

[4] R. Bultmann, 'γινώσκω,' *TDNT* I (1966/1933) 708 ff.; *cf. Exegetische Probleme des Zweiten Korintherbriefes*, Uppsala 1947, 4 f., 23—30 = *Exegetica* (see note 3) 298 ff., 315—321. Bultmann offers the following criteria to justify identifying the Corinthian attitudes as Gnostic: the struggle for speculative wisdom (1Cor 1,17 ff.), an insistence on *gnosis* and on the *exousia* that it gave the possessor (1Cor 6,12—18; 8,1—9), pneumatic manifestations, tendencies toward asceticism, a denial of the resurrection. None of these are specifically Gnostic characteristics, and whether they are to be so interpreted in 1Corinthians depends on other considerations.

ical ideas. This orientation supplied the framework for the interpretation of other early Christian literature by Bultmann's pupils[5] and, in the present generation, again for the interpretation of 1 Corinthians by Professors Schmithals and Wilckens[6].

While these two writers make useful and significant contributions[7], their basic thesis represents an elaboration of Bultmann's ideas. The thesis has encountered two critical questions. (1) Is there sufficient evidence in 1 Corinthians to classify the recipients or their mentors as 'opponents' and, thereby, to interpret Paul's teachings in terms of an adversary theology, i. e. a theology incorporating ideas of his opponents that are modified and redirected against them? From 2 Corinthians 10—13, Philippians (1 and) 3; Galatians 1—2; 5; Romans 16,17 f.; Titus 1,10—16 one may observe Paul's response to opponents. In 1 Corinthians, quite in contrast, Paul speaks as a father (4,15). When he differs, he does so by concession and qualification (7,1 f.; 8,1—13) or by a reasoned or apostolic appeal (1Cor 1—4; 11,13—16; 14,37; 15). There is no invective. Apollos and Cephas are his co-workers (3,6; 3,22—4,1; 9,5). The Corinthians who wish to 'examine' or 'judge' (4,3 f.; 9,3, ἀνακρίνειν) Paul do not represent an opposition but, as the context in 1 Corinthians 2,6—16 shows, only wish to subject Paul to the testing usually given to a fellow pneumatic. If at a future time some Corinthians emerge as Paul's opponents, in this letter they appear to be only somewhat confused children[8].

---

[5] E. g. G. Bornkamm, Mythos und Legende in den apokryphen Thomasakten, Göttingen 1933; E. Käsemann, Das wandernde Gottesvolk, Göttingen 1939; H. Schlier, Christus und die Kirche im Epheserbrief, Tübingen 1930.

[6] W. Schmithals, Gnosticism in Corinth, Nashville 1971 (1956); U. Wilckens, Weisheit und Torheit, Tübingen 1959; 'σοφία,' TDNT 7 (1971) 519—523. The books of Schmithals and Wilckens were dissertations written, respectively, under Professors R. Bultmann and G. Bornkamm.

[7] Notably, Schmithals (Gnosticism, 36—86) conjectures and seeks to establish a pre-Christian Jewish 'Christ gnosticism;' Wilckens ('σοφία,' 508 f.) sharply distinguishes sophia from gnosis and postulates a 'sophia' myth' with roots in Jewish wisdom and apocalyptic literature. Both give more attention to interpreting the mythology in terms of Jewish backgrounds; both give more weight to interpreting 1Corinthians in terms of an adversary theology.

[8] Cf. J. C. Hurd, Jr., The Origin of 1Corinthians, London 1965, 108—113; J. Munck, Paul and the Salvation of Mankind, Richmond 1959, 161—167. In 1Corinthians the pneumatics are said to 'discern' or 'judge' all things purporting to be inspired or revelatory knowledge (2,15). This includes, apparently, discerning (ἀνακρίνειν) a person's true state before God (14,24) or discerning (διακρίνειν) the measure of divine truth in another prophet's message (14,29;

Is there sufficient evidence from the total context of Paul's letter to warrant the supposition that he is interacting with or influenced by a mythological *gnosis*? For those affirming this, a major difficulty is the absence of first century evidence for such a developed myth[9]. Even if first century parallels were available, of course, they might not be the parallels most relevant to explain Paul's thought or situation. Alternative influences and reconstruc-

---

cf. Rom 12,6). Paul rejects the Corinthians' testing him in this way, apparently (1) because he regards them not as truly pneumatic (3,1,4) but only as a 'human court' (4,3) and (2) because he has an apostolic exemption from such judgments (9,3; *cf.* 14,37 f.). That is, as an apostle Paul will not allow his message to be treated as simply that of another pneumatic. On this reading of the situation 1Cor 9,3 is the conclusion of the preceding section.

In identifying the 'parties' of 1Cor 1,12 with 'opponents' of Paul *at the time of 1Corinthians* F. C. Baur appears to have given a faulty landmark to subsequent scholars ('Die Christuspartei' [1831], *Ausgewählte Werke*, Stuttgart 1963, I, 1—76). 1Corinthians does not speak of parties, but rather of individual preferences or tendencies: ἕκαστος (1,12), μηδείς (3,21). Only in 2Corinthians does a *group* of opponents appear, and they are outsiders. See below, 103 f.

[9] Schmithals (*Gnosticism*, 79) admits the absence of extant literary evidence from the first century for his *Christusgnosis* but believes, nevertheless, that the presence of the phenomenon can be inferred. Wilckens ('σοφία,' 498—503, 507—509) finds a *sophia* myth in first century Judaism and earlier. But he appears to take the second and third century Gnostic expression of the myth as the norm by which he interprets the earlier passages. For example, he gives no adequate reason why the earlier material should be defined in terms of myth rather than of poetic personification and/or a hypostasis of a divine attribute. Cf. R. N. Whybray, *Wisdom in Proverbs*, London (1965) 83: 'wisdom in Proverbs is fundamentally a divine attribute which in the process of personification has been endowed with secondary mythological characteristics;' H. Ringgren, *Word and Wisdom*, Lund (1947) 131 f.: 'mythological assumptions do not explain how personal Wisdom originated [or] how a great goddess has become a relatively unimportant divine being with an abstract name.' H. Windisch, 'Die göttliche Weisheit der Juden und die paulinische Christologie,' *Neutestamentliche Studien für G. Heinrici*, ed. A. Deissman, Leipzig (1914) 220—234, 222: Paul's idea of wisdom must originate in the hypostasis teaching that finds literary expression in Sirach (1,4,9; 24,9). Against this interpretation of such texts Wilckens (508) suggests only that they 'can be better understood as the adaption of alien myths...' Similarly H. Conzelmann, with qualifications and more extensive argument, in *The Future of our Religious Past*, ed. J. M. Robinson, New York (1971) 234—243. Like Bultmann (see above, note 3), Wilckens (*Weisheit*, 160—190) gives a number of 'Gnostic' traits of *sophia* in later Judaism, e. g. it is sent from heaven as revealer. But they become Gnostic only when Wilckens reads them through the glasses of the later Gnostic systems. Schmithals seems to exhibit a similar weakness in method. For a perceptive critique of Wilckens *cf.* R. Scroggs, 'Paul: ΣΟΦΟΣ and ΠΝΕΥΜΑΤΙΚΟΣ', *NTS* 14 (1967—68) 33—35. *Contra* Schmithals *cf.* J. Munck in *Current Issues in New Testament Interpretation*, ed. W. Klassen, New York (1962) 224—238.

tions, such as the one offered below, still would have to be considered and compared. The lack of first century evidence, however, gives to the 'Gnostic' hypothesis the flavour of uncertainty from the start. It is compounded by the lack of independent second or third century evidence, *i. e.* relevant Gnostic texts that are clearly independent of the influence of Pauline or other early Christian writings[10]. At this point the reconstruction of Bultmann and of those building upon it fully warrants the criticism made by A. D. Nock: 'It is an unsound proceeding to take Manichaean and other texts, full of echoes of the New Testament, and reconstruct from them something supposedly lying back of the New Testament.'[11]

Outside the Bultmannian school scholars generally have been less attracted to a mythological interpretation[12] of wisdom and knowledge in 1 Corinthians[13]. With reference to 'wisdom' earlier

---

[10] If such texts should appear, Pauline dependence could not thereby be assumed as R. McL. Wilson has rightly observed (see below, note 13). It is also possible that Simon Magus (*cf.* Acts 8; Justin, *1Apol* 26) constructed a 'Gnostic System' in the mid-first century. So, W. F. Albright, *From the Stone Age to Christianity*, Garden City ([2]1957) 367—371; G. Lüdemann, *Untersuchungen zur Gnosis*, Göttingen (1975); *contra* K. Beyschlag, *Simon Magus*, Tübingen (1974). But, if so, how developed was it? See below, 82 n.

[11] A. D. Nock, *Essays on Religion and the Ancient World*, Oxford (1971) II, 958 = *HTR* 57 (1964) 278, who adds that 'with the rarest exceptions, it was the emergence of Jesus and of the belief that he was a supernatural being who had appeared on earth which precipitated elements previously suspended in solution'. Unlike R. M. Grant, Nock does not think that the 'waning of the eschatological expectation was a principle factor in the emergence of Gnosticism, for the raw materials were all there before AD 70...' (953). *Cf.* R. M. Grant, *Gnosticism and Early Christianity*, New York (1966) 27—38. The Church Fathers also represent Gnosticism to be derivative from early Christianity even though it would have been in their interest to identify it with pagan origins.

[12] In German theology the attraction to myth as a hermeneutical key has, no doubt, a complex background. But it is not unrelated to developments in post-Kantian Idealism in which the locus of truth is the idea (*cf.* D. F. Strauss) or the existential decision (*cf.* R. Bultmann), i. e. in either case the non-historical and/or mythical realm. On the existential dimension of Platonic Idealism *cf.* P. Friedlander, *Plato: an Introduction*, London (1958) 229, 230—235; W. F. Albright, *History Archaeology and Christian Humanism*, London (1965) 279. Alternatively, *cf.* N. Thulstrup, *Kierkegaards Verhältnis zu Hegel*, Stuttgart (1969) 201: although Kierkegaard was not Hegelian he must be understood within the tradition of German Idealism — against which he protested in various respects but with which he had essential elements in common.

[13] *E. g.* N. A. Dahl, 'Paul and the Church at Corinth...,' *Christian History and Interpretation*, ed. W. R. Farmer, Cambridge (1967) 313—335; Hurd, *Ori-*

writers, *e. g.* H. Windisch and J. R. Harris, sought to understand Paul's Christology in terms of the role of divine wisdom in the Old Testament and later Judaism[14]. Windisch associated wisdom also with Pauline 'mysticism' in which Christians correspond to the wise in whom Wisdom enters and speaks[15]. Professor W. D. Davies, taking a less direct route, found the background of Paul's thought in later Judaism's identification of wisdom with God's Law or Torah[16]: since Paul saw in Jesus' (preresurrection) teachings a new Torah, he was able to identify Jesus as the wisdom of God[17]. While Davies established an important connecting link in Paul's thought, one must ask whether he defined Torah too much in terms of a past revelation and, consequently, gave insufficient attention to Paul's association of wisdom with the teaching of the exalted Jesus through his apostles and prophets[18].

With reference to 'knowledge' Dom J. Dupont has provided the most thorough and one of the most perceptive studies of *gnosis* in the Pauline literature. In contrast to the studies of Norden and

---

gin 105, 147, 277; J. Munck, *Paul* 135–167; Grant, *Gnosticism* 157–159; R. M. Wilson *Gnosis and the New Testament*, Philadelphia (1968) 52–55; in *Judeo-Christianisme*, ed. J. Moingt (= *RSR* 60), Paris (1972) 267: it may well be that 'it was not a case of the Gnostics borrowing from the "orthodox", or the New Testament from a vaguely defined "gnosis", but that both orthodox and Gnostics (in the narrower sense) were drawing upon the same older tradition. . . .' Otherwise: E. R. Goodenough, *By Light, Light,* New Haven (1935) 282: with Aristobulus (*c.* 160 BC), an Alexandrian Jew, the Jewish doctrine of Wisdom had begun to be transformed into a Sophia mystery.

[14] C. F. Burney, 'Christ as the ΑΡΧΗ of Creation,' *JTS* 27 (1926) 160–177 (on Col 1,15–18); Windisch, 'Weisheit,' 220–225, 226–229: from his use of Proverbs and his knowledge of ideas of a hypostatic Wisdom (*cf.* Sir 1,4,9; 24,7; Wis 7,27) Paul, following Jewish antecedents associating Messiah with Wisdom, may have been stimulated to read Ps 109 (110), 3 LXX in the light of Pr 8 and to clothe Jesus with the *Gestalt* of divine wisdom. The wisdom with which Paul in 1Cor 1,24,30 identifies Christ, however, is not a wisdom 'myth' (1Enoch 42) 'but rather the divine knowledge and plan (*e. g.* Job 28) . . . the embodiment of all apocalyptic mysteries' (226; *cf.* Eph. 1,9 f.,17–21). But see W. D. Davies, *Paul and Rabbinic Judaism*, London (²1955) 158–162.

[15] Windisch, 'Weisheit,' 226n.; 1Cor 2,6–16; *cf.* Pr 8,6 f.; Sir 39,1,6; Wis 7, 27 f.; 8,2 ff.

[16] *E. g.* Sir 24,8,23; 1Baruch 3,36 f.; 4,1; 4Macc 1,16 f.

[17] Davies, *Paul,* 144 f., 147, 150–175. But see further M. E. Thrall, 'The Origin of Pauline Christology', *Apostolic History and the Gospel,* ed. W. W. Gasque, Grand Rapids (1970) 310–312. On wisdom Christology in Pauline thought *cf.* A. Feuillet, *Le Christ Sagesse de Dieu,* Paris (1966).

[18] See below, 65 f.; see above, 33 ff.

Bultmann he concludes that the Corinthian *gnosis* is not indebted in any significant way to Hellenism[19]. It is basically a charismatic phenomenon with roots in the experiences of the primitive Christian community, a Christian appropriation and transposition into apocalyptic categories of a privilege claimed by the Jewish teachers of the law. The conclusions of Davies and Dupont set the stage for further research into the use of wisdom and knowledge in 1 Corinthians.

I.

As we saw above, in the Pauline letters, and especially in 1 Corinthians (2,12—14), certain believers have gifts of inspired speech and discernment. They are called pneumatics and, broadly speaking, they exercise the role of prophets. Among other manifestations they are said to speak 'wisdom of God' (2,7,13) or to be 'wise' (3,18; 6,5; *cf.* 14,29 διακρίνειν) or to have 'a word of wisdom' (12,8) and to speak 'in knowledge' or to 'have knowledge' or 'a word of knowledge' (8,10; 12,8; 14,6)[20]. The terms, wisdom and knowledge, are used of pneumatic gifts in other parts of the Pauline literature[21] and occasionally they appear in tandem, both in Paul[22] and elsewhere[23]. With some justification, then, they may be examined together even though in previous research the concepts have generally been treated independently. The present chapter will (1) attempt to define more clearly the employment of the two terms and their relation to one another, (2) suggest the origin

---

[19] J. Dupont, *Gnosis. La Connaissance Religieuse dans les Epitres de Saint Paul*, Paris (1949, ²1960) 531—534, 537 ff., *passim. Cf.* E. Norden, *Agnostos Theos*, Darmstadt (1956, 1912) 287; Bultmann, 'γινώσκω', 708 ff. Writing before the publication of the Dead Sea Scrolls, Dupont found no use of the term *gnosis* in Jewish apocalyptic comparable to that in Corinth. In this matter, therefore, he postulated the influence of Hellenistic usage, perhaps via Alexandrian Judaism (524, 534).

[20] See above, 23—45; 1Cor 14,37; Rom 1,11 f.; Gal 6,1.

[21] Of some 50 New Testament occurences of *sophia* 28 are Pauline and 17 are in 1Corinthians; of some 30 occurrences of *gnosis* 23 are Pauline and 10 are in 1Corinthians.

[22] 1Cor 12,8; Rom 11,33; Col 2,3; *cf.* 1,17.

[23] Lk 11,49,52; *cf.* 7,30,35; Barn 2,3—6; 21,4 f.; Is 11,2 f.

of Paul's usage and (3) specify its context within the Pauline theology and mission praxis.

The term wisdom (σοφία) appears in 1 Corinthians almost exclusively in 1,18—4,21, a section that has the literary form of an elaborate commentary or midrash contrasting 'the wisdom of this age' (3,19; *cf.* 1,20; 2,6) or 'of men' (2,5) with the wisdom of God (2,7; *cf.* 1,24,30)[24]. In 1 Corinthians 2,6—16, a preformed and probably non-Pauline midrash[25], Paul sets forth his teaching on the character of God's wisdom. It is a wisdom, hidden 'in a mystery' (2,7), revealed through the Spirit (2,10) and shared only among mature Christians (τέλειοι, 2,6). It is imparted by *pneumatikoi* 'who interpret (or *pesher:* συγκρίνοντες) the spirit-manifestations (πνευματικά) to spiritual men'[26], 'in order that we may know (εἰδῶμεν) the things given to us by God' (2,13,12). It has to do with God's plan of salvation, 'a wisdom foreordained for our glorification' and 'things God has prepared for those who love him' (2,7,9). The wisdom of God is contrasted to human wisdom in two ways. (1) Since it is 'hidden', it is comprehended neither by natural man and his wisdom (2,13 f.; *cf.* 1,21) nor by the demonic 'rulers of this age' (2,8) under whose sway natural man and his wisdom ultimately stand[27]. (2) Since it is 'wisdom among the mature', it presupposes, as 1 Corinthians 3,1—3 makes clear, not only understanding but also the ethical fruit of the Spirit, a mind that is being renewed to do the will of God (*cf.* Rom 12,2)[28]. 'Jealousy and strife', then, signal the presence of human,

---

[24] *Cf.* W. Wuellner, 'Haggadic Homily Genre in 1Corinthians 1—3,' *JBL* 89 (1970) 199—204.

[25] See above, 25; see below, 213.

[26] On συγκρίνειν as 'interpret' *cf.* Gn 40,8; Dn 5,11 f. (Th.): 'astuteness and understanding (γρηγόρησις καὶ σύνεσις/ שכל וחכמה) like the wisdom (חכמה) of the gods were found in him..., an excellent spirit and knowledge (מנדע) and understanding (שכל) to interpret (פשר) ...'

[27] One need not here decide whether 'the rulers (ἄρχοντες) of this age' refers only to demonic powers (Kümmel) or (also) to political leaders as 'the effective tools of the invisible powers' (Cullmann). H. Lietzmann—W. G. Kümmel, *Korinther I—II*, Tübingen (1949) 12, 170. O. Cullmann, *The State in the New Testament*, London (1957) 63.

[28] The *psychikos* man, who is limited to 'human wisdom' (2,13 f.), is none other than the *sarkikos* man (3,1,3) or the *palaios* man (Rom 6,6,11 f.; Col 3,9; Eph 4,21—24) that continues to dominate the ethic of immature believers and, thus, to prevent or to distort their perception of God's wisdom. See below, 69.

'fleshly' wisdom (2,13 f.; 3,3; 2Cor 1,12) and the absence of the wisdom of God.

In 1 Corinthians 13,2 Paul speaks somewhat differently:

> If I have prophecy, that is, know (εἰδῶ) all mysteries and all knowledge, ... but do not have love I am nothing[29].

Here the Apostle apparently equates knowing 'all mysteries' with knowing 'the wisdom of God in a mystery' (2,6,12: εἰδῶμεν)[30]. He recognizes the reality of the Spirit's gift and asserts only that without the fruit of love the gift does not profit the recipient. By this, however, he does not essentially alter his understanding of the wisdom of God that he has set forth in 1 Corinthians 1—2[31].

II.

In the Old Testament and especially in the apocalyptic literature of later Judaism wisdom and knowledge appear with connotations similar to those noted above in Paul[32]. In the later strata of the Old Testament they are clearly viewed as God's gifts, and in Israel they probably always were so viewed[33]. David is said to be

---

[29] 'To have prophecy' is something more than 'to prophesy' (*cf.* 14,24; H. B. Swete, *The Holy Spirit in the New Testament*, London (1910) 377) and here includes the perception of mysteries, *i. e.* the wisdom of God revealed to pneumatics. *Cf.* J. Weiss, *Der erste Korintherbrief*, Göttingen (1970, 1910) 313 f.; H. Conzelmann, *Der erste Brief an die Korinther*, Göttingen (1969) 262 f. Probably 'mysteries' and 'knowledge' are appositional to 'having prophecy'.

[30] So, J. Calvin, *1Corinthians*, Grand Rapids (1968, 1546) 275: knowledge of mysteries may be used here (1Cor 13,2) instead of wisdom and may be 'added to prophecy by way of explanation'. Similarly, Weiss, Conzelmann (see above, note 29).

[31] 1Cor 1,17; 2,4; 4,19,10 (φρόνιμοι). See below, 76. Paul does recognize among the Corinthians the charism of *gnosis* (1,5) and reckons with the possibility that it may be misused so as to have a detrimental effect not only on the recipient but also on the Christian community (8,1,10 f.). See below, 60 f.

[32] *Ḥokmah*, usually translated by *sophia*, occurs about one hundred times, mostly in Job, Proverbs and Ecclesiastes. The close synonyms, בינה and שכל occur 37 and 16 times, respectively, and are variously translated by the Septuagint. The Hebrew word *ḥokmah* 'has no precedence among the various terms; it is only one amongst others' (G. von Rad, *Wisdom in Israel*, London (1972) 53.

[33] So, von Rad, *Wisdom*, 55, 68. Otherwise: W. McKane, *Prophets and Wise Men*, London (1965) 48—54, who supposes that the older wisdom represented a 'disciplined empiricism' without religious presuppositions. But can one assume such a dichotomy between the 'real' world and religion among ancient

wise 'according to the wisdom of an angel of God to know (לדעת)
all things,' and 'to discern (שמע) good and evil (2Sam 14,20,17).
Likewise, his adviser Ahithophel is said to give counsel (עצה) 'as
though one inquired concerning the word (דבר) of God', i. e. from
a prophet (2Sam 16,23). After Solomon's prayer for a heart 'to
discern and judge (שפט/διακρίνειν) your people', to 'discern (בין/
συνιεῖν) between good and evil', he is said to have the wisdom of
God 'so as to render justice משפט; 1Ki 3,9,12,28)[34].

In these and similar passages God mediates his truth to his people in two ways, the word of the prophet (or of the angel through
the prophet)[35] and the counsel or discernment of the wise man.
With some exceptions the 'word' was thought to be a relatively
clearer revelation than 'discernment'. But both were equally God's
gifts to a privileged few for the instruction and benefit of the
many. Likewise, for God to take away either the word from the
prophet or wisdom from the wise was to bring judgement on the
nation (e. g. Is 29,10,14; cf. 3,2).

The affinity of wisdom with prophecy appears in other ways as
well. A few passages speak of wisdom as a charismatic experience.
Thus, Joseph is 'understanding and wise' to interpret dreams because 'the Spirit of God is in him' (Gen 41,38 f.). Joshua is said
to be 'full of the spirit of wisdom' because Moses had laid his
hands on him (Dtn 34,9). Even the makers of priestly garments
are 'filled with the spirit of wisdom'[36] by God for their seemingly
mundane task. David is said to have the Spirit of the Lord might-
ily upon him from the time of his anointing by Samuel (1Sam
16,13). This probably is to be related to his wisdom (2Sam 14,20)
as much as to his prophecies (2Sam 23,2). This association of the
Spirit with wisdom is not unlike the association of the Spirit with
prophecy[37].

---

peoples? *Cf.* von Rad, *Wisdom* 68n., 61: ... 'for Israel there was only one
world of experience ... in which rational perceptions and religious perceptions
were not differentiated.' It was the same for the older 'wisdom' and for the
prophets.

[34] Compare the parallel in 2Chr 1,10 ff.; wisdom and knowledge (מדע/σύνε-
σις) to judge.

[35] *E. g.* 1Ki 13,18. See above, 39 f.

[36] Perhaps to 'discern' the significance of the symbols (Ex 28,3)? But see
Ex 35,26.

[37] *Cf.* von Rad, *Wisdom*, 296: in later Israel wisdom was 'basically some-

Alternatively the prophets sometimes manifest characteristics that are usually related to the 'wise'. Samuel the prophet judges Israel in a manner that, in Solomon, is credited to the wisdom of God (1Sam 7,15–17; 1Ki 3,9,28). Nathan the prophet gives counsel (עצה) to Bathsheba about the succession of Solomon (1Ki 1,12). Both Isaiah and Amos show, in the opinion of a number of scholars[38], both literary[39] and theological[40] traits usually associated with the wisdom literature.

Admittedly, the prophets criticize those who are 'wise in their own eyes' (Is 5,21). But they mean not the wise men as such but those who reject the voice of Yahweh through the prophet[41]. They make the same criticism of other (pseudo-) prophets (Jer 23,32; Ez 13,9) As late as Jeremiah (18,18) the prophets and the wise may be distinguished as separate classes within Israel:

The law shall not perish from the priest
nor counsel from the wise
nor the word from the prophet.

But, as J. Lindblom has noted[42], the two groups have certain common features in teaching and style. Probably they have been distinguished too rigidly in the past[43].

---

thing like a charismatic gift which was not available to everyone. (Thus the late wisdom teachers were not so wrong when they interpreted wisdom as a charisma...).' *Cf.* Dn 5,11 f.

[38] *Cf.* J. Lindblom, 'Wisdom in the Old Testament Prophets', *Wisdom in Israel and in the Ancient Near East [for] H. H. Rowley*, ed. M. Noth, Leiden (1955) 193–204; S. Terrien, 'Amos and Wisdom,' *Israel's Prophetic Heritage*, ed. B. W. Anderson, New York (1962) 108–115; J. Fichtner, 'Jesaja unter den Weisen', *TLZ* 74 (1949) 75–80; J. W. Whedbee, *Isaiah and Wisdom*, Nashville (1971) 151: 'our study confirms Fichtner's original thesis of a vital connection between Isaiah and wisdom, though we demur with respect to Fichtner's explanation of Isaiah as a former wise man become prophet.'

[39] Literary forms such as parable, proverb (Lindblom, Whedbee), numerals (Terrien), and woe-oracles (Whedbee).

[40] Yahweh's power over Sheol (Amos 9,2); the ascription of wisdom to Yahweh (Is 28,25–29; 31,2) and to Messiah (Is 11,2); the reference to God's wisdom in creation and to the problem of individual judgment (Lindblom, Terrien).

[41] *E. g.* Is 8,9; *cf.* Lindblom, 'Wisdom' 195 f., 204. This kind of wisdom, independent of God and disregarding the word of God, is condemned by Paul as 'the wisdom of men' (1Cor 2,5).

[42] Lindblom, 'Wisdom' 202 ff.

[43] O. S. Rankin, *Israel's Wisdom Literature*, Edinburgh (1936) 14, 70–74; *cf.* J. L. Crenshaw in *JBL* 88 (1969) 142n. On the presence of wisdom themes in Pauline references to prophetic literature *cf.* Feuillet, *Sagesse* 53–55.

In the later Old Testament writings and in wisdom and apocalyptic literature wisdom and prophecy manifest an increasing affinity. For example, wisdom is said to reside in the 'holy prophet'
Moses and, even more, to make men prophets (Wis 7,27; 11,1);
Daniel the wise man is regarded as a prophet (4Qflor 2,3). One
important reason for this trend is the growing association, and
even identification, of both wisdom and prophecy with Israel's
Scriptures[44]. Because wisdom is derived from God (*cf.* Is 33,6), it
is to be found especially in doing God's law: 'that will be your
wisdom and your understanding' (Dtn 4,6). In the later wisdom
literature, in which the principles of Torah are applied to the life
of the people, wisdom is explicitly so described:

Your testimonies are my delight
They are the men of my counsel (עצה).

Ps 119,24

Teach me good judgement and knowledge (דעת/γνῶσις)
For I have believed your commandments

Ps 119,66

All these [expressions of wisdom] are the
book of the covenant of the most high God.

Sirach 24,23

Wisdom is divine knowledge (γνῶσις) and human practice . . .
She is instruction (παιδία) in the law . . .

4Macc 1,16 f.

The prophetic literature witnesses to a similar development.
From the earliest time the prophets are represented as having a
privileged knowledge of God that is associated with their prophetic word[45].

The oracle of Balaam . . . who *hears* the words (אמר/λογία) of God and
knows the knowledge (דעת/ἐπιστήμην) of the Most High, who *sees* the vision
of the Almighty, falling and having his eyes opened (גלה/ἀποκαλύπτειν).

Nu 24,15 f.

---

[44] This attitude does not preclude the recognition of contemporary prophecy,
however, even in the first century. *Cf.* R. Meyer, 'προφήτης,' *TDNT* 6 (1969)
812—828, 821: in Alexandrian theology 'basically everyone who possesses true
wisdom is a prophet'. *Cf.* M. Hengel, *Judaism and Hellenism*, 2 vols., Philadelphia 1974, I, 135 f.
[45] *Cf.* Dupont, *Gnosis* 220—225. As a synonym of wisdom (חכמה), knowledge (דעת) is also the possession of the wise. *Cf.* Pr 22,17,20 f.; 30,3.

Similarly, God says to Moses:

[There] I shall *meet* (יעד/γινώσκεσθαι) you so as to *speak* to you.

Ex 29,42; *cf.* 25,22

Samuel did not yet *know* (ידע) the Lord, and the word of the Lord had not yet been revealed (גלה/ἀποκαλύπτειν).

1Sam 3,7

This prophetic 'word of knowledge' is later understood to reside in the Scriptures, *i. e.* the Law

Because you (Israel) have rejected *knowledge,* I reject you... Because you have forgotten the *law* of your God, I also will forget your children.

Hos 4,6

The lips of the priest should guard *knowledge*
And men should seek *Torah* from his mouth.

Mal 2,7

I will put my *law* within them ...
For they shall all *know* me.

Je 31 (38),33 f.

God found out the way of *knowledge* (ἐπιστήμη) and gave it to Israel his servant... It is the book of the *commandments* of God and the *law* that abides forever.

1Bar 3,36 f.; 4,1

The same conclusion is to be inferred from the later prophets' practice of giving prophecies in terms of the revelations in earlier Scriptures and from their probable role as expositors of Scripture[46].

In both wisdom and prophetic literature, then, an increasing emphasis appears to be placed upon the *discernment* of God's wisdom or knowledge in the law of God. Among the rabbis this emphasis has its own unique development[47]. In the apocalyptic writers (and in their experiences) it is given a perspective and definition that provide a most important antecedent for the apostle Paul's understanding of wisdom and knowledge.

---

[46] See below, 133—138. *Cf.* the Creation and Exodus motifs in Is 40—66. Specifically, *cf.* Is 2,2—4; 26,21; 58,1 with Mi 4,1—4; 1,3; 3,8; Is 19,16; 24,1; 47,1—3, 9; 52,7 with Na 3,13; 7,11(10); 3,4 f.; 2,1(1,15); Is 41,7; 44,12—15; 46,7 with Je 10,1—16; Is 66,20 with Zeph 3,10.

[47] *Cf.* L. Blau, 'Bat Kol', *JE* 2, 589 ff.; Meyer (see above, note 44), 816—819.

III.

The apocalyptic seers combine the prophetic *vision and word of knowledge* and the *wise discernment* of its meaning within the context of a revelation of final and cosmic dimension. While they reflect features of the (earlier) prophet and wisdom teacher, they cannot be identified exclusively with either. If wisdom is the mother of apocalyptic (von Rad), prophecy has an equal claim to be the father (*cf.* von der Osten-Sacken, Hanson)[48].

As forerunners of Pauline thought, the apocalyptic writers are best represented in the book of Daniel and in the Qumran scrolls. In Daniel the divine gifts of wisdom (שכל, חכמה) and knowledge (מדע, 1,4,17; 2,21 f.) enable the seer to understand (בין) visions, dreams and sacred writings and to interpret or *pesher* them (1,17; 2,27–30; 5,12: פשר συγκρίνειν), that is, 'to make known the mystery' למגלא רזא 2,47)[49]. Moreover, they enable him to understand (בין) Scripture, *viz.* Jeremiah's prophecy (9,2,22 f.). By implication these divine gifts will, in the future, enable the ('wise' משכילים) to understand Daniel's prophecy as well (12,9 f.).

As professor F. F. Bruce has shown, the wise teachers (משכילים) at Qumran[50] understand their own role from the perspective of

---

[48] The precise relationship remains unclear. *Cf.* Meyer (see above, note 44), 819; G. von Rad, *Wisdom* 278n.; *Theology of the Old Testament*, Edinburgh (1962, 1965) II, 306 ff.; P. von der Osten-Sacken, *Die Apokalyptik in ihrem Verhältnis zu Prophetie und Weisheit*, München (1969) 63: 'apocalyptic is a legitimate, if late and peculiar child of prophecy.' For von Rad the wisdom element is primary; for P. Vielhauer, the eschatological (*cf. Hennecke's New Testament Apocrypha*, ed. W. Schneemelcher, London (1964) II, 597 f.). But these factors should not be placed in separate cubbyholes as though they were isolated developments. Cf. P. Hanson, *Dawn of Apocalyptic*, Philadelphia 1975, 7 ff.

[49] *Cf.* Amos 3,7: 'Surely the Lord God does nothing without revealing (גלה) his secret (סוד) to his servants the prophets.' Je 23,18: 'Who among them has stood in the council (סוד) of the Lord to perceive (ירא) and to hear his word...?' Sir 4,18; 14,21: 'The man who meditates on the ways [of wisdom]... shall have knowledge (νοεῖν/בין) in her secrets' (ἀποκρύφοις/תבונה). *Cf.* Dn 5,16.

[50] This seems to be the best translation of *maskilim* (see above, 33 ff.) although it has been taken to be an honorific title for every full member of the sect (*cf.* P. von der Osten-Sacken, *Gott und Belial*, Göttingen (1969) 163–165). In Ne 8,8 the 'wisdom' (שכל) is the interpretation of the Scripture: 'The Levites read from the book of the law of God clearly and gave the interpretation (שכל) and caused the people to understand (בין) in the reading. Cf. Rev 13,18; 17,9. Similarly, 1Chr 22,12: 'The Lord grant you discretion and understanding (שכל

the book of Daniel[51]. The Teacher of Righteousness, as an interpreter of Scripture, is described as one 'to whom God has revealed
all the mysteries (דעת)of his servants the prophets'[52]. Similarly, the author of the Thanksgiving Hymns writes,

> As one of the wise (משכיל) I have knowledge of you, my God, by the spirit
> that you gave to me. I have faithfully heard your wonderful counsel (סוד). By
> your Holy Spirit you opened to me knowledge (דעת) in the mystery of your
> wisdom (שכל).
>
> 1QH 12,11 ff.
>
> You made me a sign (נס) for the chosen of righteousness and an interpreter
> of knowledge (מליץ דעת) in wonderful mysteries in order to test (לבחן = LXX
> διακρίνειν, δοκιμάζειν) the men of truth and to try (נסה = LXX πειράζειν)
> those who love [correction]. To the interpreters (למליצי) of error I have be-
> come a man of controversy.   1QH 2,13—14

According to the *Manual of Discipline* the *maskilim* are 'to
guide [the members] with knowledge (דעת) and wisdom (שכל) in
the mysteries (רזין) ... so that they may walk maturely' (תמים =
LXX τέλειοι, 9,12,18 f.). They are to distinguish (להבדיל , *cf.* διακρίνειν) and to discern (לשקול) the sons of righteousness 'each according to his spirit' (1QS 9,14,18; *cf. CD* 20,24; 1Cor 4,7; 12,10; 14,
29). Or the process may be described thus:

> [God will] purge a part of mankind ... so that the upright ones may achieve
> insight (להבין) in the knowledge of the Most High and in the wisdom of the sons
> of heaven and that the mature (תמים) in the way become wise (להשכיל).
>
> 1QS 4,20,22

Those in the sect who are to be given leadership, *i. e.* in the council (עצה) of the community, are the wise (חכמה), the understanding
(בינה) and the mature in the way (תמימי הדרך; 1QSa 1,27 ff.).

In sum, the *maskilim* at Qumran are recipients and transmitters
of divine mysteries, possessors of wisdom, interpreters of knowledge, guides to a mature life, and discerners of spirits. As such, they
not only reflect their kinship with the earlier prophets but also

---

ובינה)... that you may keep the law of the Lord...' 2Chr 30,22: 'The Levites
taught the good wisdom (שכל) of the Lord.' Ezr 8,16,18: 'Then I sent for...
men of insight (בין),... [and] they brought us a man of wisdom'(שכל). In
this literature *sql* and *binh* are paired as *ḥkmh* and *binh* are elsewhere.

[51] F. F. Bruce, 'The Book of Daniel and the Qumran Community', *Neotestamentica et Semitica [for] Principal M. Black*, ed. E. E. Ellis and M. Wilcox,
Edinburgh (1969) 221—235.

[52] 1QpHab 7,4 f.

bear a striking resemblance to the pneumatics in the Pauline community.

IV.

In 1 Corinthians 'wisdom' is used almost exclusively in the exposition of 1 Corinthians 1—4[53]. There it is Christ who is identified with the wisdom of God (1,24,30). In the light of the background sketched above it appears that Christ is portrayed as God's wisdom in two ways. (1) The work of Christ, *i. e.* his crucifixion, is the content and meaning of God's secret plan of redemption, and (2) the exalted Christ presently mediates God's hidden wisdom to his people. Both ideas are present in the midrash at 1 Corinthians 2,6—16. The opening verses (2,7 f.) declare that the demonic 'rulers of this age' crucified the Lord of glory because they did not know that 'wisdom hidden in a mystery'. That is, they were privy neither to God's secret counsel (סוד) nor to the wise understanding (בינה) of God's plan that was 'revealed' to the pneumatics 'though the Spirit' (2,10). The closing verse of the passage more clearly specifies the source of the revelation: 'we have the mind of Christ' (2,16). As the connection with 2,10 indicates, it is here a question not so much of Christ being identified with Torah (Davies) as of Christ being identified with the Spirit that gave both the Torah and its inspired, prophetic interpretations and that continues to mediate God's revelation through the oracles and inspired exposition of the pneumatics[54].

This understanding of wisdom is confirmed elsewhere in the Pauline letters. In Romans 11,33—36 Paul concludes his exposition on the election and destiny of Israel with the words,

O the depth of the riches and wisdom and knowledge of God. How unsearchable his judgments and inscrutable his ways. For who has known the mind of the Lord. . . .

Unlike 1 Corinthians 2,6—16 the passage in Romans does not give an explicit answer. But the reference clearly points to the preced-

---

[53] See above, 51.

[54] See above, 17—22 and notes 17, 18. E. Lohse, *Colossians and Philemon*, Philadelphia (1971) 24—27.

ing exposition, the 'mystery' of God's plan for Israel that Paul has discerned and has disclosed from the Scriptures (Rom 11,25 ff.). The relationship of this conception to 1 Corinthians 2 is unmistakable.

Colossians 2,3 and Ephesians 1,8 f.; 3,9 f. only restate exegetical conclusions that are found in their more original commentary forms in 1 Corinthians 1—4 and Romans 11. Elsewhere in Colossians and Ephesians wisdom is presented, as it is in 1 Corinthians 2, as the prerogative of the pneumatics (including Paul) and as the product of their teaching[55].

The use of 'knowledge' in 1 Corinthians is more ambiguous, an ambiguity that appears to be rooted in the Jewish background. On the one hand the term occurs, at least in its verb form, simply as a synonym of wisdom: 'no one knows (ἔγνωκεν) the things of God,' i. e. 'the wisdom of God in a mystery,' because they are discerned (ἀνακρίνειν) spiritually (πνευματικῶς)[56]; but we pneumatics have 'received the spirit that is from God in order that we might know' (εἰδῶμεν) these things[57]. To know is to have wisdom.

On the other hand knowledge is (1) a pneumatic gift that has affinities with the knowledge of a prophet, and (2) it is also the accurate perception of Christian truth. The Corinthian pneumatics, who lack wisdom, are said to have been enriched 'in every word and all knowledge' (1,5; cf. 2Cor 8,7). Apparently they are gifted to speak, as Paul puts it in 1 Corinthians 14,6, 'in revelation or in knowledge or in prophecy or teaching.' The precise relationship of these forms of inspired speech is not altogether clear. But in 1 Corinthians 13 knowledge 'in part' is related to 'seeing' in a faulty mirror. Dupont[58] may be right in understanding this

---

[55] There are similarities in the mission of Jesus. In Mark 6 the synagogue exposition of Jesus is characterized as 'wisdom', and his teaching elsewhere is perceived and received by those who are called 'children of wisdom' (Lk 7,35). Jesus' promise to give his persecuted and arraigned followers 'a mouth and wisdom' is regarded by Luke (21,15) to be fulfilled *inter alia* in the inspired (?synagogue) exposition of Stephen whose 'wisdom' could not be withstood (Acts 6,10; cf. 7,1—53). In Revelation (e. g. 17,9) 'the mind that has wisdom' is one that can rightly interpret the prophet's revelation.

[56] *I. e.* via the prophetic spirit. Cf. Rev. 11,8; E. Schweizer, πνεῦμα, *TDNT* 6 (1968), 449.

[57] 1Cor 2,11,7 f.,14,12.   [58] Dupont, *Gnosis*, 142—148, 252.

to be knowledge received by visions, visions that have an uncertain meaning.

In 1 Corinthians 8 knowledge (γνῶσις) denotes an accurate perception of a particular Christian truth, *i. e.* regarding the nature of idols and of food offered to them. Yet such knowledge tends to puff one up. Thus, if knowledge produces a 'knowing' attitude, that is itself evidence that the knowledge is partial (8,1 f.). The gift of knowledge, apparently, has to do with particulars. Only when it is accompanied by a broad understanding and by the fruit of love does it witness to a yet more significant knowledge: 'if one loves God, one is known by him' (8,3).

Among the Corinthian pneumatics 'knowledge', a charism of the Spirit (1,8), has been manifested apart from the fruit of the Spirit (13,2), and, thus, has become distorted. It has not issued in divine wisdom, a true perception and manifestation of the mind of Christ (2,16). Rather, in its distortion it has been coupled to human dialectics (διαλογισμοί, 3,20) and has produced only a 'fleshly wisdom,' a 'wisdom of this age' (1,20; 3,18 f.; *cf.* 2Cor 1,12)[59]. Therefore, Paul concludes his exposition in 1 Corinthians 1—4 with a warning to the Corinthians 'not to go beyond what is written' (4,6), *i. e.* in the Scriptures that he has just expounded to them. As their factiousness shows, they have 'gone beyond' and have fallen under the judgment of Scripture, *i. e.* the judgment of God upon human wisdom[60].

Nevertheless, in Paul's eyes 'knowledge' is highly esteemed, both as a pneumatic 'word' and as an accurate perception of Christian truth (*cf.* 2Cor 11,6). When it is exercised properly, the gift enables one to function in the community as a teacher. Thus Paul writes to the Romans (15,14):

I myself am satisfied about you, my brothers, that you yourselves are full of goodness, filled with all knowledge and able to instruct (νουθετεῖν) one another.

---

[59] See above, 29 f.; see below, 69. Paul probably regards human wisdom to be subjected to and/or distorted by the demonic 'rulers of this age' (1Cor 2,6.10). The person who manifests it may, thereby, have come under the danger of their control (1Cor 12,3). *Cf.* O. Betz, 'Die Proselytentaufe in der Qumransekte und im Neuen Testament', *RQ* 1 (1958) 223 (on 1QH 3,12—17): by 'viper creatures' the sect refers primarily to the false teachers to whom the 'wise of the world' belong.

[60] On 1Cor 4,6 *cf.* A. Robertson—A. Plummer, *First ... Corinthians*, Edinburgh 1953 (1914), 81.

In 1 Corinthians Paul expresses most fully his understanding of wisdom and knowledge by the way in which he associates the concepts with Christ and with his own ministry. He identifies wisdom and the source of wisdom with Christ (1,24,30). He identifies knowledge as one of Christ's gifts (12,5), one that is to be earnestly sought (14,1). He views himself as one who 'has prophecy' (14, 37; *cf.* 13,2) and as a steward of the mysteries of God (4,1), *i. e.* one who stands with the prophets and seers to discern and then to reveal God's purposes in Christ.

The roles of the prophet and of the wise man which, as we have seen above, were increasingly associated in later Judaism find their unified expression in the Pauline community in the person of the pneumatic, or more precisely, in those pneumatics who — like Paul — manifest the requisite gifts and fruit of the Spirit. The role of such persons is summed up most concisely, perhaps, in the words of Colossians 1,25—28:

I became a minister... to make the Word of God fully known, the mystery hidden for ages and generations but now made manifest to his saints. To them God chose to make known how great among the Gentiles are the riches of the glory of this mystery, which is Christ in you, the hope of glory. Him we proclaim warning every man and teaching (νουθετεῖν) every man in all wisdom that we may present every man mature (τέλειος) in Christ.

4. CHRIST AND SPIRIT IN 1 CORINTHIANS

The meaning of πνεῦμα in Pauline thought and the relationship of πνεῦμα to Christ have stimulated much discussion and raised a number of issues that cannot be pursued here[1]. It may be helpful, however, to indicate the perspective from which the present chapter is written. With W. D. Davies, I. Hermann and others this writer regards the decisive influence on Paul's understanding of Spirit, apart from his personal experiences, to be his heritage from the Old Testament and Judaism[2]. The Spirit apparently is identified with the Old Testament spirit of Yahweh, at least in so far as the latter is understood as the spirit of prophecy (1Cor 7,40; cf. Eph 1,13 f.). Within this context it is probably to be understood primarily as power rather than substance though for Paul the distinction may not have been meaningful. Although its manifestations may not always appear to be so, the Spirit is personal: it 'bears witness', 'intercedes', 'comprehends', 'teaches', 'dwells', 'wills', 'gives life', and 'speaks'[3]. Also, in Paul's usage, no discernible difference appears between the (divine) Spirit, Spirit of God = Spirit of Christ (Rom 8,9), Spirit of the Lord and the holy Spirit.

I.

The meaning of πνεῦμα, particularly within 1 Corinthians, may be seen more clearly by observing (1) its connection with the close-

---

[1] Most of the significant literature is given in E. Schweizer, 'πνεῦμα', *TDNT* VI (1968), 334, 415–37; I. Hermann, *Kyrios und Pneuma*, München 1961; and A. Wikenhauser, *Pauline Mysticism*, Edinburgh 1960. Some representative works are: H. Gunkel, *Die Wirkungen des Heiligen Geistes*, Göttingen 1888; A. Deissmann, *Paul*, New York 1957/1912, 138–44; W. Bousset, *Kyrios Christos*, Nashville 1970/1913; R. B. Hoyle, *The Holy Spirit in St Paul*, London 1927; J. Weiss, *Earliest Christianity*, New York 1959/1914, II, 463–71; W. D. Davies, *St Paul and Rabbinic Judaism*, London 1948.

[2] Davies, *op. cit.*, pp. 177–226; Hermann, *op. cit.*, 123–31.

[3] Rom 8,16,26; 1Cor 2,11,13; 3,16; 12,11; 2Cor 3,6; cf. Rom 8,11; 1Tim 4,1.

ly related concept δύναμις, (2) its function within the charisms, and (3) the infrequent but significant plural use of the term. Πνεῦμα and δύναμις sometimes appear together as parallel terms:

It is sown in dishonor, it is raised in glory:
It is sown in weakness, it is raised in *power:*
It is sown a natural body, it is raised a spiritual body.
... The first man Adam became a living being.
The eschatological Adam became a life-giving *spirit.*

(1Cor 15,43–5)

The combined use of the terms in Rom 1,3 f. reflects the same meaning, the miraculous power of God manifested in the resurrection of Christ[4]:

... (God's) Son: who was from the seed of David
according to the flesh,
Designated Son of God in *power* by the resurrection from the dead
according to the *spirit* of holiness.

As an eschatological reality present in the Christian community, 'the concept of power is linked indissolubly with that of Spirit'[5]. In some passages, however, Paul draws a distinction between 'spirit' and 'power' in which πνεῦμα appears to be connected especially with 'inspired speech' and δύναμις with (other) miraculous acts. This is most clearly expressed by the chiastic pattern in Rom 15,18 f.[6]:

... Christ wrought through me ... by word and work,
By the *power of signs and wonders,* by the *power of the Spirit.*

That is, the δύναμις of God, which is here the more inclusive concept, may be expressed as the Spirit-carried 'word' or as a miraculous 'work'. In a somewhat different verse-pattern the same distinction is present in 1Cor 2,4:

(My kerygma was) not in persuasive words of (human) wisdom,
But in demonstration of *Spirit and power:*
That your faith might not rest in the wisdom of men,
But in the *power of God.*

---

[4] Cf. Eph 1,17–20; compare 1Cor 6,14 ('through his power') with Rom 8,11 ('through his Spirit').
[5] W. Grundmann, 'δύναμις', *TDNT* II (1964/1935), 312.
[6] *Ibid.,* 311.

In this passage Origen apparently was the first to identify 'spirit' with (Old Testament) prophecy and 'power' with miracles[7]. His interpretation is supported by the literary pattern, by Paul's comment in 2Cor 12,12 that his ministry to the Corinthians did include miraculous 'powers'[8], and by the similar contrast of 'spirit' and 'power' elsewhere.

Two other Pauline passages may be mentioned[9]. In 1Thess 1,5 Paul and his co-workers write, 'our gospel did not come to you in word only but also in *power* and in *holy Spirit* and much assurance' (πληροφορία). 'Assurance', a word that is closely coupled to 'spirit', can mean the conviction that accompanies prophetic understanding and proclamation[10]. It appears to be used similarly here[11] and, if so, serves to qualify 'spirit' in that way. Although it is not clearly defined, the same distinction probably is present in Gal 3,5: 'the one who supplies the *Spirit* to you and works miracles (δυνάμεις) among you'.

In these texts God's δύναμις, manifested in the resurrection of Christ, is operative through the exalted Christ in two distinct ways: in the Spirit (inspired perception and speech) and in power (miracles). This interpretation is strengthened by a few traditions in the Gospels and in Acts. In Acts 6,8,10, Stephen is represented thus: ... 'full of grace and *power* he did great wonders and signs ... And they were not able to withstand the *spirit* and wisdom with which he spoke.' 'Spirit and wisdom' are probably a hendiadys. In such a combination 'spirit' is usually the more inclusive term with wisdom as a gift of the Spirit or one expression of the Spirit's work, i. e. in prophetic perception (1Cor 12,8; cf. Col 1,9) or teaching[12]. Thus, Sirach (24,1,23 ff.) identifies wisdom as

---

[7] Origen, *Contra Celsum* 1, 2.

[8] Cf. W. Bousset, 'Der erste Brief an die Korinther', *Die Schriften des Neuen Testaments* II, Göttingen 1917, 83.

[9] But cf. also Eph 3,5—7,16; Hebr 6,5.

[10] Cf. C. F. D. Moule, *Colossians and ... Philemon*, Cambridge 1958, 86 (on Col 2,2): 'the conviction is the result of insight, of understanding'. According to 1Clem 42,3 the apostles, having been 'assured' by the resurrection, were then confirmed 'in the word of God with full assurance of the Holy Spirit' (πληροφορίας πνεύματος ἁγίου).

[11] Cf. L. Morris, *Epistles to the Thessalonians*, Grand Rapids 1959, 57: '... the primary meaning is the assurance the Spirit gave to the preachers'.

[12] The 'wise' (*maskilim*) at Qumran are those prophetic persons who by God's Spirit are given understanding in the Scriptures. Cf. 1QS 9,17—19; 1QH

Torah, i. e. as the prophetic teaching that flows from the (divine) 'spirit of understanding' (cf. 39,6). Not essentially different, Wis 7,22—7; 9,17 virtually equates 'wisdom' with 'your holy spirit', whose coming makes men 'prophets'[13]. Mark 6,2 may be understood in the light of this background: 'what is the *wisdom* given to this one, and what sort of *miracles* (δυνάμεις) are being done by his hands?'

With these passages in mind we may return to 1 Corinthians. In 1Cor 1,18—31 the 'word of the cross' effecting salvation is identified as δύναμις θεοῦ (1,18), and is then specified in terms of Christ (crucified), 'the power of God and the wisdom of God' (1,24). The idea is very similar to 1Cor 2,4 in which Paul's kerygma 'in the power of God' is specified in terms of 'spirit and power'. 1Cor 2,1—5 is a bridge passage between the two expository pieces, 1Cor 1,18—31 and 1Cor 2,6—16[14]. The latter is concerned with the role of the pneumatics, those endowed with the 'spiritual' gifts of inspired perception and speech. In the former, *viz.* 1Cor 1,24, Christ is identified with the power of God in the community, both as miraculous act (δύναμις) and as prophetic word (σοφία). Via the 'bridge' in 1Cor 2,4 (δύναμις/πνεῦμα) we may infer that he is identified also with τὸ πνεῦμα τὸ ἐκ τοῦ θεοῦ in 1Cor 2,12. In both cases the nature of that identification remains unstated, and it may be clarified by an examination of the role of Christ and the Spirit in Paul's discussion of charisms in 1Cor 12—14.

II.

The Spirit appears in 1Cor 12,4—6, in parallel with the Lord (Christ) and God, as the source of the charisms, those gifts of the

---

12,11 f.; E. Lohse, *Colossians and Philemon*, Philadelphia 1971, 25, 27 (on Col 1,9); see below, 134; above, 34 f., 57 f.

[13] Cf. W. Bieder, 'πνεῦμα', *TDNT* VI (1968), 371; U. Wilckens, 'σοφία', *TDNT* VII (1971), 501 f.; J. Lindblom, *Prophecy in Ancient Israel*, Oxford 1962, 175—9. Cf. Sirach 24,33; Luke 11,49; Philo, *QuaesExod* II,29; *de gig.* 47,54 ff.

[14] Note the 'proem midrash' pattern: theme and proem text (1Cor 1,18 f.) + exposition (1,20—30: σοφία/μωρία) + concluding text (1,31). Similarly in 1Cor 2,6—9,10—15 (ἄνθρωπος/πνεῦμα, εἴδον), 16. See below, 155 f., 213—217.

eschatological age that create and empower the Christian community. In the following verses (12,7—13) the Spirit alone is the source: 'the one and the same Spirit' distributes all the charisms 'as he wills' (11). Clearly the Spirit is not just 'the spirit of prophecy'; he is the source of other gifts, including the miracle of the new life itself (13). The inclusive meaning of Spirit and its use in parallel with Christ are similar to 1Cor 15,45 and 1Cor 6,17. All three passages identify the Spirit, in the words of E. Schweizer, 'with the exalted Lord, once this Lord is considered not in himself but in his work toward the community'[15].

Elsewhere, however, Paul in a similar fashion identifies the Spirit with God. As Professor Moule's perceptive essay has shown[16], he probably does so in 2Cor 3,16 f. ('the Lord is the Spirit') even if christological connotations also are involved. He clearly does so in 1Cor 3,16 f. by the equation of 'the temple of God' with the indwelling of the holy Spirit[17]. Also, the far-ranging parallelism between Christ and Spirit, noted by Deissmann[18], is found on a more limited scale between God and the Spirit:

You must consider yourselves to be dead indeed to sin
but living τῷ θεῷ in Christ Jesus.

(Rom 6,11)

You have died and your life is hid with Christ ἐν τῷ θεῷ.

(Col 3,3)

Through the law I died to the law that I might live θεῷ . . .
I have been crucified with Christ; but I live,
no longer I, but *Christ lives in me.*

(Gal 2,19 f.)

Such parallels suggest the essential equivalence of the varying expressions denoting the resurrection life: 'with reference to God' or 'in God', 'Christ in me' or 'in Christ', 'in the Spirit' or 'ac-

---

[15] Schweizer, *op. cit.*, 433. Cf. Eph 4,4—6 (Spirit, Lord, God), 7—11 (Christ alone is the source).

[16] C. F. D. Moule, '2Cor 3,18b', *Neues Testament und Geschichte, Oscar Cullmann zum 70. Geburtstag*, Tübingen 1972, 235 f. One should perhaps compare this passage with the exposition in Eph 4,8—11 in which ascriptions to God (Ps. 68) are given an eschatological application to Messiah.

[17] Hermann, *op. cit.*, 133 f.: what is said in 2Cor 3,17 of the Lord (Christ) and his Spirit is said in 1Cor 3,16 of God and the Spirit.

[18] Deissmann, *op. cit.*, 138 ff.

cording to the Spirit' (Rom 8,5,9). Similar instances are the phrases, the mind of Yahweh, the mind of Christ (1Cor 2,16), the mind of the Spirit (Rom 8,6) and, returning to 1Cor 12,4—6, the ascription of the charisms to the Spirit, to Christ (cf. Eph 4,7 f.) and to God.

At the same time things are said of Christ (or God) that cannot be said of the Spirit[19]. The relationship, therefore, includes distinction as well as identity, and the oscillation in terminology is reminiscent of that between Yahweh and the Spirit of Yahweh in the Old Testament[20]. The distinction is perhaps best expressed in Gal 4,6: 'God sent the spirit of his Son into our hearts.' The spirit of God in its eschatological role is (solely) at the disposal of the Son, the resurrected Lord, who as the Spirit lives and works among his people[21].

Πνεῦμα is used in 1Cor 12,1—3 and 1Cor 14 in the more restricted sense of 'the spirit of prophecy'[22]. This meaning was present in the Old Testament and Judaism[23], and it continues in early Christianity[24]. It is given there a special christological orientation that is most explicit in Rev 19,10: 'the spirit of prophecy is the witness to Jesus.' 1Cor 12,1—3 makes the 'witness to Jesus' the hall-mark of a (prophetic) utterance in 'holy Spirit' or in 'the Spirit (or a spirit) of God'. The passage serves to clarify the relation of Christ and Spirit in 1Cor 2: 'the spirit that is from God' (2,12) not only manifests the 'mind of Christ' (2,16) but also gives the 'witness of God' (2,1, ℵ° BD), which is the witness to 'Jesus Christ . . . crucified' (2,1; cf. 1,18).

Πνευματικά is used similarly in these passages of 'prophetic' gifts of inspired speech and discernment — a hymn, a teaching, a revelation, a tongue, an interpretation(14,24). The term is not equivalent to the more general χαρίσματα, although it may be identi-

---

[19] Cf. A. Wikenhauser, *Pauline Mysticism*, Edinburgh 1960, 80—91.

[20] Cf. A. R. Johnson, *The One and the Many in the Israelite Conception of God*, Cardiff 1961, 15 f. But see also Hermann, *op. cit.*, 82 f.

[21] Hermann, *op. cit.*, 65 f., 105. Cf. C. F. D. Moule, 'The Holy Spirit in the Scriptures', *The Church Quarterly* III (1970—1), 285 f.

[22] See above, 27—30, 64 ff.

[23] Hos 9,7; cf. 1QS 8,16. Cf. the Targum on Judg 3,10; 1Sam 10,6; Isa 63,10; Philo, *de fuga* 186; *vita Mosis* II, 40.

[24] E. g. 1Thess 5,19; 1Petr 1,10 f.; Acts 13,2; 21,11; Rev 2,7; cf. 11,8; *Did* 11,7 ff.

fied with the 'greater charisms'[25]. Likewise, the pneumatics (πνευματικοί), those who manifest the gifts of inspired speech, are closely associated with the 'prophet' (14,37). As Professor Schweizer
has observed, πνευματικός is probably the broader concept of
which προφήτης is a special type[26]. Apparently πνευματικός/πνευ-
ματικά, used both in the general meaning of resurrection life (1Cor
15,44) and in the more restricted meaning of 'prophetic' persons
or powers, are of Christian coinage. In both meanings they represent a development of the same twofold use of πνεῦμα. Like
πνεῦμα they are inseparable from the exalted Christ, who is the
'life-giving Spirit' and the 'wisdom of God'.

III.

One further question may be raised: what was there in the Corinthian situation that caused Paul to underscore the unity of the
Spirit with the exalted Christ specifically with reference to the
prophetic gifts of inspired speech and discernment? Two answers
may be suggested. First, as 1Cor 1—4 reveals, some of the 'philo-
sophic' Corinthians have displayed an attitude of factious rivalry
and have viewed it (proudly) as a manifestation of wisdom (cf. 3,
18). They have displayed it not only in an intellectual dialectic of
'persuasive words of wisdom' but also in ethical attitudes, 'jeal-
ously and strife', a boasting 'in men', and arrogance (3,3; 4,6—8,
18 f.)[27]. In short they have reflected a 'fleshly wisdom', a 'wisdom of this age' (1,20; 3,18 f.; cf. 2Cor 1,12). In contrast to it
Paul, in the context of an 'eschatological' exposition of scripture,
sets forth a wisdom that consists in and is imparted by the crucified and exalted Christ (1,23 f.,30) speaking through the pneumatics (2,13). He and Apollos have conformed their life-style to that
wisdom (2,5—9; 4,1), and he urges the Corinthians also to forgo
boastful 'dialectics' and to live 'according to scripture' (3,20; 4,6
RSV; see below, 72—79).

The plural use of 'spirits' in 1Cor 14 may supply a second answer to our question: the Corinthians are described as 'zealots for

---

[25] Cf. Rom 1,11; 1Cor 14,1 with 1Cor 12,31. See above, 24—27.

[26] Schweizer, *op. cit.*, 423; cf. 1Cor 14,1.

[27] Cf. H. Conzelmann, *1 Corinthians*, Philadelphia 1975, 42.

spirits' (πνεύματα, 14,12), and must be reminded that 'the spirits of the prophets subject themselves to the prophets' (14,32). The πνεύματα here are not to be equated with the πνευματικά, nor do they represent simply the variety of spiritual charisms. They are probably to be understood rather as the angelic beings that, under Christ, mediate the πνευματικά and minister with and through the pneumatics[28].

The evidence for this interpretation has been detailed above. In brief, one may say that in the Old Testament the angelic mediation of Yahweh's word was a recognized form of prophetic experience[29] and that the prophets were included in heavenly (angelic) councils[30], were conducted by interpreting angels and guarded by angelic armies[31].

In apocalyptic Judaism the role of angels, often designated 'spirits'[32], is given elaborate expression. At Qumran 'the spirit of truth' appears to be identified with both God's holy Spirit and with the angel of truth or light[33]; conversely, angels can themselves be called 'holy spirits' or spirits 'of truth' or 'of knowledge'[34]. The holy Spirit or holy spirits have a special relationship to 'the wise' (משכילים), i. e. the teachers[35], who are represented as recipients and transmitters of mysteries, possessors of wisdom, discerners of spirits and interpreters (מליצים)[36]. As such, they bear a striking resemblance to the pneumatics in the Pauline community[37]. These similarities lend weight to the parallel between the angelic spirits given to the wise at Qumran and the 'spirits' sought by the Corinthian pneumatics.

---

[28] Rightly, O. Everling, *Die paulinische Angelologie und Dämonologie*, Göttingen 1888, 11–48, 43 f. Otherwise: M. Dibelius, *Die Geisterwelt im Glauben des Paulus*, Göttingen 1909, 74. See above, 30–38.

[29] E. g. 1Kings 13,18.

[30] Cf. 1Kings 22,19; Isa 6,1–8; Jer 23,18; R. N. Whybray, *The Heavenly Counsellor in Isaiah 40,13–14*, Cambridge 1971, 52.

[31] Ez 40,3; Zech 1,9, *passim;* 2Kings 6,16 f. ('with us').

[32] Cf. Jub 2,2; 1Enoch 15,6 ff.

[33] Cf. 1QS 4,21 f. with 1QH 12,11 f.; 1QS 3,18–25.

[34] 1QH 8,11 f.; 1QM 13,10; 1QH 3,21 ff.; cf. 11,9–13.

[35] See above, 34, 57 ff.

[36] See above, note 35. Further, 1QH 12,12 f.; 2,13 f.; 1QS 3,13 f.; 9,14,17.

[37] Cf. 1Cor 2,7,13 f.; 12,10; 14,29; Eph 3. Cf. Eph 4,12 f.; Col 1,26–8; 2,2 with 1QS 4,21 f.

Paul himself[38], as well as other New Testament writers[39], also associates angelic (and demonic) spirits with prophets and/or 'spiritual' gifts. His usage, together with the parallels in Judaism and early Christianity, strongly supports the interpretation of the 'spirits of the prophets' given above. The apostle identifies the power at work in the pneumatics both as the holy Spirit (1Cor 12, 3,11) and as angelic spirits (1Cor 14,12,32). The oscillation, like that between Christ and the Spirit, probably reflects the Old Testament conception of 'the one and the many' in which God may be present 'in person' in his angelic messengers[40].

If Paul recognizes the role of angels in the pneumatic gifts, why does he mention it only in the passing references in 1Cor 12—14? First, he may regard the 'pneumatic' Corinthians' zeal 'for spirits' (14,12) as an erroneous tendency, clearly evident in other churches, towards a veneration of angels[41]. Second, this tendency may have facilitated their indiscriminate acceptance of ecstatic phenomena even of demonic origin (12,3). Paul reckons with such activity of (evil) angels in the preaching of his opponents, pneumatics who impart 'a different spirit', serve a pretended 'angel of light', and boast of visions and revelations[42]. These factors also give Paul adequate reason to avoid any emphasis on angelic spirits, and to stress instead the Spirit's unity with Christ, its witness to him and its role in edifying his body (12,4—6,3,25—8). By this emphasis the Apostle calls his readers back to the centrality of Jesus Christ, the indelible mark of the Pauline gospel.

---

[38] 1Cor 13,1; 11,4,10.

[39] Rev 12,10; 19,10; 22,6; Hebr 1,14 (διακονία); 1John 4,1—3.

[40] Johnson, *op. cit.*, 28—32. See above, 32 f., 38 n., 67 f.

[41] Cf. Col 2,18; Rev 19,10; G. Johnston, *The Spirit-Paraclete in the Gospel of John*, Cambridge 1970, 119—26: the Spirit-Paraclete doctrine is part of a polemic against an incipient angel cult and has affinities with Qumran.

[42] 2Cor 11,4,13—15; 12,1,11; Gal 1,8; Col 2,18; 2Thess 2,2. See above, 36 ff.; below, 107—114.

5. 'CHRIST CRUCIFIED'

Outside of the gospels the words 'cross' and 'crucify' appear in the New Testament almost exclusively in the Pauline literature[1]. There, the latter term is found only in Corinthians and Galatians, the former additionally in Philippians, Colossians, and Ephesians. They are used primarily as theological concepts[2]. This is not to say that the historical event of the crucifixion has become less important, much less that the theological concept has displaced it. In accordance with Paul's thought generally the theological meaning arises out of and remains united with the historical occurrence, the 'salvation history', to which it refers. Nevertheless, the meaning is more specifically determined by Paul's historical situation and by a somewhat unusual expression, χριστὸς ἐσταυρωμένος.

I.

The phrase 'Christ crucified' is found in two Pauline passages, 1Cor 1—4 and Gal 3. In 1 Corinthians, the concern of this essay, it appears initially in 1Cor 1,18—31, a set piece of exposition[3]:

For Jews seek signs and Greeks seek wisdom (σοφία)
But we proclaim Christ crucified
To Jews an offense (σκάνδαλον)
and to Gentiles foolishness (μωρία)
But to those who are called — Jews and Greeks —
Christ, God's power and God's wisdom (σοφία)

1,22—24

---

[1] Elsewhere, they occur only with a literal sense: Hebr 12,2 ('cross') and Acts 2,36; 4,10; Rev 11,8 ('crucified').

[2] The theological meaning also occurs in the Gospels, e. g., Mt 10,38; Lk 9,23 ('daily').

[3] That is, theme and proem text (1,18 f.) + exposition + concluding text (1,31). Cf. W. Wuellner, 'Haggadic Homily Genre in 1 Corinthians 1—3', *JBL* 89 (1970), 199—204. See below, 155 f., 213—217.

The phrase occurs once more in the application of the exposition to Paul's Corinthian mission:

> ... I did not come in excellence of word or of wisdom (σοφία)
> when I proclaimed to you the testimony of God
> For I decided to know nothing among you
> except Jesus Christ, that is (καί), him as the crucified one[4].
> ... And my word and proclamation
> were not in persuasive words of wisdom
> but in a demonstration of spirit and power
> in order that your faith might not rest in the wisdom of men
> but in the power of God

2,1–5

The phrase 'Christ crucified' is clarified in a number of ways by the context. It appears to be an elaboration or explanation of the earlier phrase, 'the word of the cross' (1,18), that opens the section. Like that expression it is equated with God's power. Specifically, it represents the present mediation of God's power in two ways, in prophetic wisdom and in miracle (δύναμις, 1,24), both of which have been manifested at Corinth in Paul's inspired utterance and miraculous works (πνεύματος καὶ δυνάμεως, 2,4)[5]. It is the former, 'God's wisdom', that is the primary concern in 1Cor 1—4. As such, 'Christ crucified' is set in opposition to the 'wisdom of the world' (1,20; cf. 3,18) or 'of men' (2,5) or 'of word' (1,17; 2,4). It is not just a concept nor, as it is for unbelievers, just a past reference to a crucified person. It refers primarily to the exalted Lord who, in his exaltation, remains the crucified one. This contextual understanding is confirmed grammatically by the use of the perfect participle, ἐσταυρωμένος[6].

In sum, 'Christ crucified' is not only the message or 'word' of Paul's proclamation but also the one who speaks through and in that 'word', not only the historical content of the message but also the 'wisdom' that is active in it. That is, the term expresses the perspective from which the risen Christ presently works and,

---

[4] Cf. H. Conzelmann, *1 Corinthians*, Philadelphia 1975, 53. On the explanatory καί with οὗτος cf. Blass-Debrunner, 229 (§ 442, 9).

[5] For this interpretation of 1Cor 1,24; 2,4; see above, 66. Cf. Rom 15,18 f.; 2Cor 12,12.

[6] Rightly, W. C. Robinson, Jr., 'Word and Power,' *Soli Deo Gloria, Essays for W. C. Robinson*, ed. J. M. Richards, Richmond 1968, 71.

thus, the perspective from which 'God's wisdom' is presently manifested.

II.

1Cor 1—4 begins with a thanksgiving for the Corinthians' rich charismatic endowment, especially in the pneumatic gifts of inspired speech and discernment (1,5—7)[7]. It then appeals to the Corinthians to put an end to their dissensions and to 'be united in the same mind and in the same judgment' (1,10). The relation of the two motifs is confirmed by the subsequent expository section (1,18—4,21) in which wisdom, one of the pneumatic gifts[8], is a governing motif. The exposition presents a contrast between human wisdom and the wisdom that is 'from God' (1,30; cf. 2,12) and leads to the conclusion that the Corinthians not go beyond 'what stands written' (4,6), that is, in the Scriptures that Paul has expounded to them[9]. On the one hand the exposition is an attack on human wisdom, not merely on wisdom as a way of salvation[10] but on the inherent structure of 'the wisdom of men' as such. As he shows in Romans (1,22) Paul regards human thought and human conduct to be not only bound together but also under sin and

---

[7] See above, 24—30.   [8] Cf. 1Cor 2,6—16; 12,8.

[9] Otherwise: M. D. Hooker, '"Beyond the things which are written"...', *NTS* 10 (1963/64), 127—32.

[10] Otherwise: Robinson, *op. cit.*, 74 f. The parallel with Galatians, which Robinson invokes, is attractive. (1) In both Corinthians (1,23) and Galatians (5,11) 'Christ crucified', or the cross, is the indispensable *skandalon* of the Christian message. (2) In both it is associated with charismatic workings of the Spirit in the Church (1Cor 1,26; 2,4; Gal 3,5). (3) In both it is set over against the 'fleshly' attempt to become mature Christians by human achievement, either by the wisdom of men (1Cor 3,1 ff., 18 f.) or by the works of the law (Gal 3,2 f.). (4) In both Paul condemns the attempt because it nullifies the 'cross' of Christ (1Cor 1,17; Gal 2,21). And in both he does so by a biblical exposition that is similar to the midrashic patterns of Philonic and rabbinic exegesis. Cf. 1Cor 1,18—31; 2,6—16; Gal 3,6—29; P. Borgen, *Bread from Heaven*, Leiden 1965, 47 ff.; see note 33. (5) In both Paul appears to identify or associate the 'spirit' active in the two aberrations, *viz.* 'the spirit of the world' and 'the elemental spirits', with demonic powers (1Cor 2,6.12; Gal 4,9). Nevertheless, even if there are important parallels, the problems addressed are different. In Galatians it is a question of the wrong use of something that is good (the law of God). In Corinthians it is the confusion of something that is good (the wisdom of God) with something that is at root perverse (the wisdom of men).

innately warped. For this reason Paul can infer that, since the Corinthians' claim to 'wisdom' (cf. 3,18) is accompanied by 'fleshly' ethical aberrations, their wisdom proceeds not from a wisdom 'taught by the spirit' but only from words 'taught by human wisdom' (2,13; 3,1 ff.).

The wisdom from God is 'not fleshly (σαρκική) wisdom but God's gift' (2Cor 1,12). Furthermore, it has a cruciform manifestation, for it proceeds from the one who as the exalted Lord remains 'Christ crucified'. Thus it appears both as 'power' and as 'cross' in Paul and Apollos, the stewards of God's mysteries (2,7; 4,1). By perceptive teaching such men 'build' God's temple (3,9 f., ἐποικοδομεῖ) but also, like Christ, they manifest this wisdom of God in weakness and

when reviled, we bless
when persecuted, we endure
when slandered, we try to conciliate[11].

Such conduct is the ethical corollary, and indeed the proof, of the wisdom 'that is from God'.

The basic problems in the Corinthian church manifest themselves in ethical attitudes: divisiveness (σχίσματα), strife, envy and, especially, conceit (φυσίωσις; cf. 1,10 f.; 3,3; 4,6,18 f.; 5,2; 8,1; 2Cor 12,20). Such problems are specifically in the foreground in 1Cor 1—4. In responding to this deplorable situation, Paul is not content merely with exhortation[12]. He will not allow a separation of ethics and theology[13]. For he perceives theological ignorance and even misunderstanding to be an underlying cause of the unethical practices: faulty ethics reflect poor theological perception, even as bad theology corrupts good moral habits[14]. Therefore, Paul addresses the ethical problems with theological instruction.

---

[11] 1Cor 4,12 f. Cf. 1Petr 2,23.

[12] Paul knows, of course, that in its concrete expression the Church is a *corpus mixtum*, containing both elect and reprobate, and that dissension and factionalism are in some measure inevitable 'in order that those who are genuine among you might be recognized' (1Cor 11,18 f.). Cf. 2Cor 13,5; Gal 4,11.

[13] Cf. V. Furnish, *Theology and Ethics in Paul*, Nashville 1968, 224—27.

[14] Cf. 1Cor 15,33; Rom 1,21 ff.,24 with 1Cor 3,20 (διαλογισμός). Paul does not use the Johannine idiom 'to do the truth' (1Joh 1,6), but the same implicit bond between thought and conduct is reflected in the phrase 'obey the truth' (Rom 2,8; Gal 5,7).

III.

What is the theological error in 1Cor 1–4 that Paul discerns beneath the faulty ethics of the Corinthians? Its general character, a wrong kind of 'wisdom' (1,17; 2,4; 3,18), may be inferred from the theme of the section. But what, precisely, was its content? (1) According to some recent studies the Christians at Corinth espoused a 'wisdom of men' that denied any soteriological significance to Christ's crucifixion; in the face of such teaching Paul set forth the message of the cross[15]. If the above analysis is correct, this view of the situation is mistaken in interpreting 'the word of the cross' and 'Christ crucified' primarily of the past fact of the crucifixion. Also, it is inconsistent with 1Cor 1,13 (cf. 1Cor 15,3) which presupposes that the Corinthians have, in fact, a positive view of the crucifixion. In the perceptive comment of W. C. Robinson, Jr., 'Paul would hardly have sabotaged his whole argument by beginning it with the statement that [the Corinthians] would ridicule'[16].

(2) Is the Corinthians' error perhaps 'a misunderstanding of the mode of possessing God's gifts'[17]? The opening thanksgiving (1,5) and the later section on the pneumatic gifts, 1Cor 12–14, lend some support to that interpretation. The gifts, including, 'the word of wisdom' (12,8), should be used above all for 'edification' (οἰκοδομή, 14,26) so that there might be 'no dissension (σχίσμα) in the body' (12,25). In the 'hymn to love' that is a 'hymn to Christ'[18] the gifts, including 'knowledge' (γνῶσις), are declared to be of no effect if they are not manifested in the context of a love that is not envious (ζηλόω) or conceited (φυσιόω)[19]. In 1Cor 12–14 the wrong attitudes apparently are occasioned by a lack of understanding about spiritual gifts (12,1). They bear a striking similarity to the attitudes condemned in 1Cor 1–4, and it is probable that the underlying causes are not unrelated. However, Paul's different response to the symptoms in 1Cor 1–4 suggests that something more is involved than just a misunderstanding or misuse of the gifts.

---

[15] U. Wilckens, *Weisheit und Torheit*, Tübingen 1959, 20, 214.
[16] Robinson, *op. cit.* 72.   [17] So, Robinson, *ibid.*, 75.
[18] 1Cor 13; cf. N. Johansson, '1Cor 13 and 1Cor 14', *NTS* 10 (1963/64), 386 f.
[19] 1Cor 13,1,2,4.

(3) It has been suggested by a number of scholars that the Corinthians reflect 'an over-realized eschatology'. They suppose that the victory over sin and death has been consummated[20]:

Already you have been filled
Already you are rich
Without us you have reigned.

This is the other side of the same coin that has been examined above: if the Corinthians have not discounted the crucifixion, they at least think that it is totally in the past. It remains for them only to share Christ's 'reign'. Indeed, according to this view they can in 1Cor 15 even deny a future resurrection because, like Hymenaeus, they think that 'the resurrection is past already' (2Tim 2,18)[21].

There are, however, certain problems with this understanding of the situation in 1Cor 1—4. First, the error in 1Cor 15 offers doubtful support for an eschatological interpretation of 1Cor 4,8. Even if it is a precursor of the teaching of Hymenaeus, it probably reflects more a Platonic anthropology than a 'realized' eschatology: the immortal soul, released to eternal life at death, has no need of resurrection[22]. Secondly, in Paul's own teaching — and very likely in his teaching at Corinth — the Christian already has been (corporately) raised with Christ to resurrection life. Having come 'alive to God in Christ Jesus', he is to 'walk in newness of life'[23]. As 2Cor 13,4 shows, because Paul himself 'shares in Christ's resurrection life, he also shares in the power which is manifest in that life'[24]. It is unlikely, then, that he would criticize the Corin-

---

[20] E. g. F. F. Bruce, *1 and 2 Corinthians*, London 1971, 49 f.; J. Munck, *Paul and the Salvation of Mankind*, Richmond 1959, 165; E. Käsemann, *Essays on New Testament Themes*, London 1964, 171.

[21] This view appears later in Gnostic theology. Cf. Tert., *de res.* 22 (perhaps alluding to 1Cor 4,8); Iren., *Against Heresies* 1, 23, 5 (re Menander).

[22] This also is part of later Gnostic thought. Cf. W. Schmithals, *Gnosticism in Corinth*, Nashville 1971, 157 f.; Justin, *Dial.* 80.

[23] Rom 6,4,11,13; cf. Gal. 2,19 f.; 2Cor 6,9; 13,4. The expression 'raised with Christ' (Col 3,1; cf. 2,13; Eph. 2,6) is essentially no different, for this conception is presupposed in the phrase 'to walk in newness of life' (cf. R. Tannehill, *Dying and Rising with Christ*, Berlin 1967, 11). Cf. E. E. Ellis, *Eschatology in Luke*, Philadelphia 1972, 15 n.; W. D. Davies, "The Moral Teaching of. the Early Church", *The Use of the Old Testament in the New*, ed. J. M. Efird (Durham (N. C.), 1972), 318 n. Otherwise: E. Lohse, *Colossians and Philemon*, Philadelphia 1971, 180.

thians merely for appropriating an eschatological perspective that he himself has taught and, indeed, has earlier applied to them: 'in Christ you have been made rich' (1Cor 1,5).

Nevertheless, a mistaken eschatological perspective may well be involved in the false wisdom of the Corinthians. But the error is not in affirming the *reality* of a present participation in Christ's resurrection life and power, but rather in misconceiving the *way* in which that reality is presently to be manifested. In Paul's teaching Christ's followers have in the past been (corporately) 'crucified with' him and 'raised with' him[25]. And they are destined to actualize individually this corporate reality. But they will actualize the 'resurrection with Christ' only at the parousia when, having been 'found in him', they shall 'attain to the resurrection from the dead' and shall 'put on immortality'[26]. In the present life they are called to actualize the 'crucifixion with Christ'. As imitators of Paul[27] they are to seek not their own benefit but that of others[28], to endure suffering

as sorrowful, yet always rejoicing
as poor, yet making many rich
as having nothing, yet possessing all things[29].

In imitating Paul they are, in fact, imitating Christ[30], completing 'what is lacking in Christ's afflictions for the sake of his body, that is, the Church'[31].

This *imitatio Christi* is, moreover, the context in which Christ's resurrection power is presently manifested. For Christ's 'power is made perfect in weakness'[32]. The Corinthians have not followed this path. They have engaged in competitive wrangling[33]. Having

---

[24] Tannehill, *op. cit.*, 99.

[25] Gal 2,19 f.; Rom 6,4; Col 3,1; cf. E. E. Ellis, *Paul and His Recent Interpreters*, Grand Rapids 1961, 37—40 (= *NTS* 6 (1959/60), 212—16).

[26] Phil 3,9,11; 1Cor 15,53; cf. 2Cor 5,3 f. There is, of course, a present *ethical* imperative 'to walk in newness of life' that is related to the Christian's identification with Christ's resurrection.

[27] Cf. 1Cor 4,16; 11,1; Gal 4,12 f.; 1Thess 1,6; 2Thess 3,9.

[28] 1Cor 10,33 f.; cf. 15,31; Rom 12,1.

[29] 2Cor 6,10.

[30] 1Cor 11,1; 1Thess 1,6. On the primacy of the Christological motif in Paul's ethic cf. Davies, *op. cit.*, 314—32.

[31] Col 1,24; cf. 1 Cor 3,9—17; Gal 2,19 f. (συνεσταύρωμαι!).

[32] 2Cor 12,9 f.

[33] Perhaps along the lines of the Jewish practice of 'discussions with asso-

'been made rich' in Christ's gifts of word and knowledge, they 'boast' as though the gifts were their own attainment[34]. Having been endowed in order to 'build' God's temple, they are instead destroying it by their boasting, envy, strife, and dissension. In consequence their cherished wisdom, in a subtle transformation that even they have not discerned, has become mere cleverness, a manifestation of human words rather than of divine power[35]. And apparently they have failed to distinguish the resulting 'wisdom of this age' from 'the wisdom from above'[36]. The apostle wishes to call them back from this disastrous course. To do so, he invokes among other things an image of Christ that he has used earlier in his letter to the Galatians. In a word he reminds them that the Christ who manifests God's wisdom and God's power is the one who in his exaltation remains 'Christ crucified', the serving and the sacrificing one. And this exalted Christ manifests these divine gifts among his followers only under the sign of the cross.

---

ciates [and] argument with disciples' (Pirke Aboth 6,6) about the meaning of Scripture. So, Wuellner, op. cit., 203, who follows D. Daube and S. Liebermann in identifying λόγος σοφίας (1Cor 2,4) with the debar ḥokmah in rabbinic discussions. Cf. Rom 2,17—24; Acts 18,15; 1Clem 45,1. See above, note 3.

[34] 1Cor 1,5; 4,7. Since this attitude would be equally wrong after the parousia, 1Cor 4,8 cannot refer merely to a mistaken eschatological perspective. It is primarily an ethical aberration that Paul addresses.

[35] 1Cor 3,18 ff.; 4,19 f.

[36] Cf. Jas 3,13—15,17, where the same kind of critique of 'wisdom' is made.

6. PAUL AND HIS OPPONENTS

Trends in the Research

I.

Among the Protestant reformers John Calvin distinguished between the 'different gospel' of Paul's adversaries in 2Cor 11,4 and the 'different gospel' mentioned in Gal 1,6—8. In the Pastorals also he discerned two groups of heretics: there were Jewish legalists (Tit 1,14) and — in the prophecy at 1Tim 4,3 — Encratites and Montanists who, though not imposing a law on Christians, attached 'overmuch importance on superstitious observances like avoiding marriage and not eating flesh.' However, most early Protestant expositors seem to have been content to identify the false teachers in the Pauline letters rather generally with representatives of Jewish (Christian) legalism[1].

Henry Hammond of Oxford apparently marks the first thoroughgoing break with this tradition. In his essay, *de Antichristo.* published in 1651, he discerned behind Paul's reference to the 'mystery of lawlessness' (ἀνομία; 2Thess 2,7) an allusion to Gnosticism[2]. In that[3] and a subsequent work[4], he went on to identify as Gnostics certain other false teachers and/or libertines referred or alluded to in Romans, Corinthians, Galatians, Ephesians, Phi-

---

[1] J. Calvin, *2 Corinthians, Timothy, Titus, Philemon*, Edinburgh 1964 (1550), 42, 238 f., 365; cf. M. Luther, *Galatians*, London 1953 (1535) 70.

[2] Henrico Hammond, 'de Antichristo,' *Dissertationes Quatuor*, London 1651, 1—51, referring to such texts as Rom 12,9; 2Cor 11,13; Eph 3,19; Phil 3,2; 2Thess 2,10; 1Tim 3,6; 2Tim 3,3 f.; 4,3; cf. Rom 13,11. The false teachers in the Johannine epistles, 2 Peter, Jude and Revelation also are identified as Gnostics (5). See below, 230 ff.

[3] *Ibid.*, 11—28.

[4] H. Hammond, *A Paraphrase and annotations upon . . . the New Testament*, 4 vols., Oxford 1845 (1653, ²1659), IV, 89, 200, 517 f.

lippians, Thessalonians and the Pastoral letters. For example, when in 1Cor 8,1 f. the *gift of knowledge* results in puffing men up, Paul uses γνῶσις with reference to those who call themselves γνωστικοί. Earlier, in 1Cor 6 the Apostle speaks against *dissension* in the congregation 'in opposition to the compliances and apostasies of the Gnostics'[5] and in 1Cor 16,22 makes them the object of his anathema. In condemning *libertines* in Rom 16,18; Gal 5,15,20 f.; Eph 5,3—6; Phil. 3,18 f. he has the Gnostics in view. Hammond refers to most of the texts that are adduced by subsequent works and also foreshadows some later scholarship in ascribing to the Gnostics virtually all of the false teaching alluded to in Paul's letters. Indeed, he was apparently so obsessed with the subject that (Archbishop) James Ussher and other colleagues were apprehensive of meeting him 'lest they should again be troubled with this eternal mention of the Gnostics'[6]. However, Hammond treated the texts rather briefly and did not develop a comprehensive thesis[7].

In the following century J. L. von Mosheim of Göttingen joined a more cautious expression of Hammond's thesis to the Reformation tradition about the opponents of Paul[8]. He saw two heretical tendencies in first century Christianity, one that molded Christian doctrines into conformity with philosophical γνῶσις and another that combined Christianity with Jewish opinions. The former appeared in Col 2,8; 1Tim 1,3 f.; 6,20; 2Tim 2,16. The Judaizers were less significant and, as a schismatic movement, a second century manifestation (the Ebionites). The Gnostics, how-

---

[5] *Ibid.*, 164.

[6] E. Burton, *An Enquiry into the Heresies of the Apostolic Age*, Oxford 1829, XXVI.

[7] Hammond's views were soon discussed in Germany as is evident in the thoroughly documented survey of early (mainly second century) heresies by Thomas Ittigius, *De heresiarchis aevi Apostolici & Apostolico proximi*, Lipsiae 1690, 166. The increasing interest in this aspect of early Christianity is also reflected in M. de Beausobre, *Histoire critique de Manichée et du Manichéisme*, 2 vols., Amsterdam 1734, 1739.

[8] J. L. von Mosheim, *Institutes of Ecclesiastical History*, 4 vols., London 1845 (1755), I, 115—129; *Historical Commentaries*, 2 vols., New York 1852 (1753), I, 214—221, 228—235: Hammond applies 'several passages in the New Testament to the Gnostics, on no other ground, as it should seem, than that of a very slight accordance in terms. There are, however, many observations of his from which it would be inconsistent with candour to withhold our assent' (229).

ever, 'went out from us' (1Joh 2,19), that is, formed separate societies already in the apostolic period. According to the Fathers these heretics were a novelty, arising only in the time of Hadrian (Hegesippus, in Eusebius, *HE* 3,32,7 f.; Clem. Al., *Strom* 7,17; Tert. *de Praes.* 29 f.). But in fact — writes Mosheim — though small in number until the second century, they were infecting the Church already in the time of Paul. They drew their tenets from a pre-Christian 'Oriental philosophy,' not from Platonism as the Fathers, knowing only Greek philosophies, mistakenly thought (e. g. Tert., *de Praes.* 7).

In 1773 C. C. Tittmann responded that 'no traces of the Gnostics are to be found in the New Testament'[9] and offered an alternative thesis. Gnosticism originated in second century Egypt, the background of most of the heresiarchs mentioned in the ancient Christian writings. It drew its doctrines from three sources, Greek philosophy, Jewish cabalistic theology, and certain re-interpreted Christian doctrines (393—399). If in the first century Philo agreed with the Gnostics in certain views (301 f.) and if some Christians, influenced by Jewish allegorical interpretations of Scripture, denied the resurrection (395 f.; 1Cor 15,12; 2Tim 2,17 f.) and even if Simon Magus had gnostic elements in his teachings (Epiph. *Panarion* 21; 27), they are not thereby made Gnostics. The heresy of Gnosticism emerged from obscurity in the early second century. Had it existed from the beginning of the Church, it could not have been successfully opposed as a novelty. And the term Gnostic could not have continued to be used by Clement of Alexandria for any learned Christian teacher.

Of those who saw Gnosticism in the New Testament, and some even in the Old Testament, Tittmann had further criticisms. Hammond, he concluded, was simply 'blinded by attachment to [his] own preconceived opinion' (318). Against Mosheim he offers not only the testimony of the Fathers but also of Josephus who, when treating the Jewish sects, never mentions any Oriental or Gnostic philosophy — nor does Philo. How can Mosheim identify this philosophy with the Essenes[10] when they, unlike the Gnostics, are faithful adherents of the law (395 f.)?

---

[9] C. C. Tittmann, *Essays and Dissertations*, New York 1829, Leipzig 1773, I, 275—399.

Tittmann contended that New Testament texts that are alleged to reflect Gnosticism (e. g. Col 2,8; 1Tim 6,20) are better explained as judaizing tendencies (317—393). In Colossians Paul is concerned to show 'the excellence of Gospel doctrine above the Jewish law' (324) which, having been deformed, can be termed a 'philosophy' or 'elements of the world' or (with regard to its regulations of abstinence) a 'worship of angels' (Col 2,18; cf. Gal 3,19; Lk 20,36). Indeed, everything in Colossians 'is to be understood as relating to the ceremonial law and its zealous supporters' (344). One must not jump to the conclusion that terms later used by the Gnostics (e. g. πλήρωμα, γνῶσις) had, therefore, a Gnostic connotation in the New Testament. The 'falsely-named γνῶσις' in 1Tim 6,20 is associated with 'teachers of the law' (1Tim 1,7) and 'Jewish myths' (Tit 1,14) and must refer, therefore, to 'contentions of the Jews respecting the ceremonial law and religious subjects in general' (351)[11].

Mosheim and Tittmann are representative of viewpoints that in a number of ways set the course of subsequent studies of Paul's opponents. (1) They identified two mutually exclusive heretical tendencies in early Christianity, judaizing and gnosticizing, and chose between them for the most likely explanation of the false teaching attacked in the Pauline letters, *viz.* Colossians and the Pastorals. (2) They raised the question of the relationship of the Essenes to Gnosticism. (3) Tittmann, particularly, posed the problem of the definition and the chronological context of the terms and concepts used. Both writers also revealed weaknesses in their reconstructions, Mosheim in not being able to establish the existence of a pre-Christian Oriental Gnostic philosophy and Tittmann in making — rather too easily — a sharp distinction between (first century) gnostic teachings and the (second century) Gnostic heresy.

The British scholar, Nathaniel Lardner, provides a contrast to Mosheim and Tittmann. Writing about the same time, he ascribed to the apostolic period the 'seedling' teachings of both gnosticizing (cf. 1Cor 15,12; Gal 4,9; Col 2,18; 1Tim 1,4; 2Tim 2,23) and juda-

---

[10] Cf. also J. D. Michaelis, *Introduction to the New Testament*, London 1802, IV, 82.

[11] Following Tertullian, *de Praes.* 33 f.

izing (Gal 5,2; 1Tim 4,3) heresies[12]. However, Lardner concerned himself almost altogether with the second century situation.

II.

In the Bampton Lectures for 1829 Edward Burton, the Regius Professor of Divinity at Oxford, offered a masterly and comprehensive analysis of 'the heresies of the apostolic age'[13]. He viewed these heresies essentially as varieties of Gnosticism. Admittedly, he rejected (174 f.) the statement of Epiphanius (*Panarion* 28,2,3 f.) that it was the Gnostic Cerinthus who 'seduced the Galatians to Judaism,' and formed the opposition to Peter and Paul in Acts 11,2; 15,1; 21,27 f. On the other hand he apparently regarded judaizing in the heretical sense to be of little significance in the first century (165). Like Mosheim, he located this movement in the second century among the Nazarenes 'whose faith had gradually become corrupted' (518) and the Ebionites, who themselves were Gnostics with origins perhaps among the Essenes (501—519).

Although the name was applied only later, Gnosticism originated in the Platonic school of Alexandria in pre-Christian times (contra Tittmann). It was not a distinct Oriental philosophy, as Mosheim thought, but rather a combination of Platonic ideas, Jewish mysticism (Cabala) and the Iranian 'two principles' of good and evil (68—78, 111, 263). Probably this mixture was first joined with Christian ideas and terminology by Simon Magus, a student in Alexandria (*Clem. Homil.* 2,22), who in this sense is to be regarded as the father of all Gnostic heresies (88 ff.)[14]. In Ephesus and Corinth Gnostic doctrines may have been preached by Simon, together with the name of Christ, before Paul's arrival there[15].

---

[12] N. Lardner, *Historie of the Heretics*, ed. J. Hogg, London 1788 (c. 1765), 17—19. His work apparently was influenced in considerable measure by M. de Beausobre (above, n. 7).

[13] Burton, *op. cit.* To the eight lectures (1—253) were appended 103 special notes (255—594) elucidating particular points. The introduction includes a valuable survey of previous studies.

[14] Cf. Irenaeus, *adv. Haer.*, 1, 23, 2; cf. Epiphanius, *Panarion*, 21, 7, 2; 27, 2,1. In another work, *Ecclesiastical History of the First Century*, Oxford 1831, 75 to 82, 206, 310, Burton discusses the important adversary role in earliest Christianity that he gives to Simon Magus. See above, 35 n., 48 n.

[15] *Ibid.*, 176 f.

According to Acts 19,19 Ephesus, at any rate, 'seems to have been particularly infected with Gnostic doctrines' (103). Only if Simon's apostasy were widespread (94) would Luke tell of its origin (Acts 8) and later writers of its presence in Rome in the reign of Claudius (Justin, *1Apol* 26).

Paul's letters, then, might be expected to reflect the battle with Gnosticism (80—85, 113 ff.). The γνῶσις of 1Cor 8,1; 1Tim 6,20 and the genealogies and contentions about the Law in 1Tim 1, 4—7; Tit 3,9 f. are so applied by the Fathers, and certain other references to γνῶσις (2Cor 10,5; 11,6) and to false teachers motivated by greed may have Gnostics in view (Acts 20,29; Rom 16, 18; 2Cor 2,17; 1Thess 2,5; Tit 1,11; Jude 16). The denial of the resurrection in 2Tim 2,14—18 is to be similarly interpreted. But in 1Cor 15 it is the product of philosophical speculation though, as Paul knew, once denied, the resurrection might in the future be explained away 'by the allegorical subtleties of the Gnostics' (133)[16]. 2Thess 2 and 1Tim 4,1 likewise have in view the future dangers of Gnosticism to the congregation. In Col 1,16 *(Christus creator)*, Col 2,3,18 (θησαυροί, ἄγγελοι) and Eph 3,18 f.; 4,13 (πλήρωμα) Paul had in mind 'notions of the Gnostics' which he reapplied 'to a higher and holier sense' (83 f.). By this re-application 'the system of the Gnostics was totally subverted' (113, cf. 416 ff.). 1Cor 1—2, however, probably is alluding to 'ordinary disputes of Grecian philosophers' (416) and can be traced to the Gnostics only at the risk 'of indulging our fancy' (85). Likewise, the Galatians, who evidently had 'a fondness for Judaism' seem to have suffered 'merely from Jewish teachers' (120 f.; Gal 4,9). However, Gal 5,13,19 f. may refer to the Gnostic danger (102, 143n.), and it is possible that the ecclectic Gnostics 'made a boast of observing [Mosaic] ordinances' in order to win the Jews (120).

Standing in succession to Hammond and Mosheim, Burton offered the most thoroughgoing presentation of their thesis: Paul's opponents were, with insignificant exceptions, the devotees of Gnosticism. More than those before him, he sought an historical explanation for Christian Gnosticism by underscoring the role of Alexandrian Platonism and of Simon Magus. He apparently was

---

[16] In his *History* (214) Burton changes his mind and inclines to attribute the error in 1Cor 15 as well as the Corinthians' sexual attitudes in 1Cor 6—7 to Gnostic influences.

the first to identify the views of the false teachers, on a large scale, by interpreting the Apostle's statements as adversary theology, i. e. the employment and re-application of his opponents' terms and concepts. On the negative side, Burton also falls under Tittmann's criticism of Hammond and Mosheim. At times he too easily accepted the later Gnostic understanding of a term or concept as a key to its (adversary) use in the Pauline letter, and he too easily transferred the Fathers' anti-Gnostic application of a Pauline passage to the intention of Paul himself. One must add, however, that in such instances Burton usually expressed himself with cautious and qualified judgements.

In the early nineteenth century two continental writers[17] signaled important developments in the research, Augustus Neander of Berlin and F. C. Baur of Tübingen. Through J. B. Lightfoot, Neander influenced later British and American scholarship; Baur was a dominant factor in German studies for the rest of the century. Accepting an earlier interpretation that the dissensions of 1Cor 1,12 reflected general sectarian divisions within the Church — parties 'of Paul,' 'of Apollos,' 'of Cephas,' 'of Christ,' Baur made this passage, in the words of Professor Käsemann[18], the Archimedean point from which the history of early Christianity was to be pried open. 'Die Christuspartei' (1831)[19] was not, however, neutral nonsectarian Christians (Eichhorn) nor wisdom-seeking Gentiles who, rejecting Paul's authority, appealed solely to Jesus' teachings (Neander). Nor was it Sadducean Christians (Grotius), for the opponents in 1Cor 15 who denied the resurrection were Gentiles, influenced by materialistic Greek philosophies (19). Following J. E. C. Schmidt, Baur recognized in 1Cor 1,12 only two

---

[17] Cf. also M. J. Matter, *Histoire critique du Gnosticisme*, 3 vols., Paris 1843 (1828), I, 187—216, who gives brief attention to the Pauline texts and concludes that Paul's adversaries in Corinth, Ephesus and elsewhere generally manifest 'the germs of Gnosticism' and may be regarded as 'the precursors of the Gnostics' (200); M. Schneckenburger, *Über das Alter der jüdischen Proselyten-Taufe und . . . die Irrlehrer zu Colossä*, Berlin 1828, 189—234; C. E. Scharling, *De Paulo Apostolo ejusque Adversariis*, Havniae 1836. Schneckenburger, elaborating Mosheim's view, showed the affinity of the Colossian false teachers with the Essenes, e. g. their astrological interest and attitude to angels.

[18] In F. C. Baur, *Ausgewählte Werke*, 4 vols., Stuttgart 1963—1970, I, IX.

[19] *Ibid.*, I, 1—76, 14—24. For a summary of the German discussion of the 'parties' cf. H. A. W. Meyer, *Epistles to the Corinthians*, New York 1884, 19—24 (on 1Cor 1,12).

opposing parties, the Pauline-Apollonine and the Petrine-Christine. The opponents of Paul were the latter group (24), Judaizers who adhered to Peter as the first of the original apostles and claimed, thereby, to have a more direct relation to Christ: οἱ τοῦ Χριστοῦ of 1Cor 1,12 are those professing Χριστοῦ εἶναι in 2Cor 10,7.

From this adversary dialectic Baur developed a critique, along the lines of Hegelian philosophy, of the whole course of Paul's ministry and writings[20]. In his work on *Paul* (1845)[21] he sets this forth in clearest fashion. 'Judaizing opponents' of Paul, Jews or Jewish Christians who in Galatians sought to impose circumcision on the Gentile Christians, later appear in Corinthians. Since 'the conflict has entered on another stage' (I, 253, 256) they no longer raise the issue of circumcision but rather attack Paul's apostolic authority. These ψευδαπόστολοι (2Cor 11,13), who now appeal to the authority of Peter, thus reveal their relation to the Jerusalem apostles and probably are their 'disciples and delegates.' The ὑπερλίαν ἀπόστολοι (2Cor 11,5) are either the opponents or (like the στῦλοι in Gal 2,9) James, Peter and John as they are regarded by their party (I, 277). But did Baur have adequate reasons to tie 'the Christ party' (1Cor 1,12) to Peter or to the opponents in 2Cor 10—13? And did the professed pedigree of the opponents — apostles of Christ, Hebraioi, Israelites, seed of Abraham, ministers of Christ (2Cor 11,13,22 f.) — point to the Jerusalem apostles or at most to the Palestinian church?

In the more systematic and conciliating presentation of Paul's teaching in Romans the opponents are only alluded to; the Judaizing false teachers in Rom 16,17—20 are a non-Pauline addition (I, 365). The kind of opposition that appears in Colossians, Philippians and the Pastorals, as well as the presence of Gnostic terms and concepts, witness to the post-Pauline origin of these letters. In Colossians the adversaries are best identified with Ebionites rather than with the earlier Judaizers (II, 28); this is made clear by the polemic against the regulations of food and days, the exaltation of angels, and circumcision (Col 2,11—21). The 'Jewish opponents' in Philippians (3,2,18) appear to be a rather vague imitation of

---

[20] And of early Christian history as a whole. Cf. W. G. Kümmel, *The New Testament: ... Investigation of its Problems,* Nashville 1972, 127—143.

[21] F. C. Baur, *Paul,* 2 vols., London ²1876 (1845).

those in 2 Corinthians (II, 55). In the Pastorals the opposition is clearly second century Gnosticism since, as Hegesippus (Eusebius, *HE* 3,32) witnesses, that heresy had hardly appeared in Paul's time (II, 21,98—101). What then of Simon Magus? He is a fiction, a personification of heathenism read back into the apostolic period by the second century author of Acts (I, 219 ff.)[22].

Baur, very much like Burton, understood Gnosticism as a pre-Christian complex of Hellenistic (and Oriental) speculation[23]. However, in restricting the influence of Gnosticism on Christianity to the second century and in identifying Paul's opponents virtually exclusively as Judaizers, he stands in succession to Tittmann. Baur was the first to make Paul's opponents a decisive key to the whole of the Apostle's writings[24]. In this lay both the strength and the weakness of his presentation. With his key Baur brought the whole of Paul's ministry into a unified historical presentation of unusual power and appeal. But outside Germany he gave most scholars the impression that, in substantial measure at least, his exegesis had become too much the servant of his theory.

Within German-speaking scholarship a further question was raised: did Baur's identification of Paul's opponents provide the right key? Supported by his teacher, W. M. L. de Wette of Basel[25], Daniel Schenkel[26] argued that Paul's Corinthian opponents, the

---

[22] Cf. F. C. Baur, *The Church History of the First Three Centuries*, 2 vols., London 1878 (1853), I, 93; *Die christliche Gnosis*, Tübingen 1835, 310 n., which was published the same year as his essay on the Pastoral epistles. In it Baur pointed to the Gnostic opponents as an objection to the origin of the Pastorals in the Pauline period. See above, 48 n.

[23] Baur, *Gnosis*, 52.

[24] His views are elaborated, with minor modifications, by O. Pfleiderer, *Paulinism*, 2 vols., London 1877, II, 3 f., 95—99, 194 f. Cf. also A. Stap, 'L'apôtre Paul et les Judéo-Chrétiens,' *Origines du Christianisme*, Paris 1864, 39 to 115. On the heavy impact of Baur's views in the German discussion cf. C. Machalet, 'Paulus und seine Gegner. Eine Untersuchung zu den Korintherbriefen,' *Theokratia* 2 (1970—1972), 184 f. Unavailable to me were H. Lisco, *Paulus Antipaulinus*, Berlin 1894 (on 1Cor 1—4) and *Judaismus Triumphatus*, Berlin 1896 (on 2Cor 10—13); F. Mejan, *L'Apôtre Paul et les Judéo-Chrétiens ... aux Galates*, 1892.

[25] W. M. L. de Wette, *Briefe an die Corinther*, Leipzig 1855 (1840), 256 (on 2Cor 10,7): 'probably the leaders of the Christ party boasted that they stood in a mysterious, immediate relationship with Christ through visions.'

[26] D. Schenkel, *de ecclesia Corinthia*, Basel 1838, as discussed in de Wette (*Corinther*, 3—6), Baur (*Paul*, I, 286—290) and A. Neander (*Planting and Train-*

Christ party, were Jewish Christian libertines who rejected all apostolic authority and claimed a special wisdom and γνῶσις based on visions and revelations (2Cor 12,11). These pneumatics or Gnostics, whose gnosis probably was of a Jewish-Alexandrian sort, were similar to the false teachers at Colossae and probably came with letters of recommendation from a congregation in Asia Minor. The party 'of Cephas' was Jewish-Christian 'weaker brothers' (1Cor 8—10) and allies of Paul who, in their opposition to the Christ party, appealed to Peter to decide the question.

A. Neander[27] also discerned in Corinthians, in addition to the Judaizers, 'the germ of that Gnosis which sprung up in the soil of Alexandria' (230). It appeared among the followers of Apollos, 'wisdom seeking Greeks' (232, 241) who, appealing to their γνῶσις and ἐξουσία, disregarded the weaker brothers, abused their Christian freedom, engaged in immoral excess, and (together with the Christ party) perhaps believed only in a spiritual resurrection (238, 253). This group contained the seed of 'a later pseudo-Pauline Gnostic tendency' (244), even as the similar Colossian false teachers were the forerunners of a judaizing Gnosticism (319 to 328). In the face of Baur's continuing influence these views did not receive immediate success in German scholarship. But in the next century Schenkel's opinions were revived by Wilhelm Lütgert, and Neander exercised a considerable influence on the British scholar and bishop, Joseph Barbour Lightfoot.

In the English-speaking world of the later nineteenth century the most influential Pauline commentator was J. B. Lightfoot of Cambridge and Durham. Like F. C. Baur, Lightfoot placed the controversies of Paul within the context of the whole of early Christian history. In a brilliant monograph on 'St. Paul and the Three,' appended to his commentary on Galatians (1865), he set forth his reconstruction and provided, in the process, a devastating critique of the views of Baur[28]. From his first battle at Antioch, Lightfoot

---

ing of the Christian Church, 2 vols., London ³1880 (1832), I, 237—240). Schenkel's work was unavailable to me.

[27] Neander, *Planting*, I, 220—253, 319—328.

[28] J. B. Lightfoot, *Epistle to the Galatians*, London 1892 (1865), 292—374. This monograph (and his other work) largely accounts for the failure of Baur's Tübingen School ever to gain a sizable following among English speaking scholars, as E. Haenchen (*Acts*, Philadelphia 1971, 22) has rightly noted. It remains instructive today, especially for a generation that 'knew not Joseph'

writes, 'St. Paul's career was one life-long conflict with judaizing antagonists,' Pharisaic Judaizers and Gnostic Judaizers (311). Although among the Galatians (5,13), 'as in the Corinthian Church, a party opposed to the Judaizers had [perhaps] shown a tendency to Antinomian excess' (208), the significant error in Galatia was Pharisaic judaizing. In Corinthians also the Pharisaic party is present, although 'party' may be 'too strong to describe what was rather a sentiment than an organization.'[29] It is the Christ party (1Cor 1,12), extreme Judaizers, whom Paul opposes in 2Cor 10–11. The party of Cephas, on the other hand, is simply Jewish Christians of rather strict ritual observance, predecessors of the later (orthodox) Nazarenes (372 f., cf. 317 to 321)[30].

In his work on Philippians (1868)[31] Lightfoot identified Paul's opponents in Phil 1,15–17; 3,2 also as Pharisaic Judaizers not, to be sure, within the Philippian church but within Paul's own situation at Rome (88 ff., 144). However, in Phil 3,12–19 'the persons denounced are not the judaizing teachers, but the Antinomian reactionists' (155). They appear 'to belong to the same party' to which Rom 6,1–23; 14,1–15,6 is chiefly addressed and who in 1 Corinthians (1,17; 4,18 f.; 8,1 f.; 10,15) make a claim to 'wisdom.' Some of them are condemned in Rom 16,17–19 in language similar to that used in Phil 3,17–20 (155). They 'professed

---

and is attracted to the views of a more recent Bauer on *Orthodoxy and Heresy in earliest Christianity*, Philadelphia 1971.

[29] Influenced perhaps by H. Alford, *The Greek Testament*, 4 vols., London 1849–1861, II (⁴1861), 476: the designations in 1Cor 1,12 'are not used as pointing to actual parties formed and subsisting among them but representing the spirit with which they contended with one another, being the sayings of individuals and not of parties' (ἔκαστος). This is confirmed by 1Cor 4,6 where two leaders can be samples to show a proper attitude toward *any* leaders. Against this is only 'the determination of the Germans' to regard their 'parties' as historical facts (499). Alford viewed the opponents to have evolved from one group, Judaizers in the earlier letters who in Colossians (2,16) add various Essene-like superstitions, in Philippians (3,13) reflect doubts about the resurrection and in the Pastorals reflect a heresy intermediate between the Judaizers and the later Gnostics (III, *Prol.* 75–77).

[30] Lightfoot appears to be influenced here by W. J. Conybeare and J. S. Howson, *The Life and Epistles of St. Paul*, 2 vols., London 1852, I, 476–492, a remarkable work that went through countless printings and continues to be published today. It views the Paul party as tending toward licentiousness and as paving the way for the Gnostic heresy, an exegesis to be elaborated in the next century by W. Lütgert.

[31] J. B. Lightfoot, *Epistle to the Philippians*, London 1888 (1868).

the Apostle's doctrine but did not follow his example [and] avail-
ed themselves of his opposition to Judaism to justify the licentiousness of Heathenism' (70). Such licentious speculators are at first
Epicurean in their denial of a resurrection (1Cor 15,12), but afterward they spiritualize it by applying it to the present new birth
of believers (2Tim 2,18). Their immoral practices are reflected in
the Pastorals (2Tim 3,2—7), in Rev 2,6,14 f.,20,24 and, later, in
the antinomian Gnosticism condemned in the Epistle of Poly-
carp 7[32].

Following Neander[33], Lightfoot views 'the Colossian heresy'
(1875)[34] as the product of a pre-Christian Oriental theosophy that
had found expression in Judaism among 'the Essenes'[35] and Essene types and, through them, among some Jewish Christians
(91 ff.). In *The Jewish War* Josephus, who was for a time a member of a group of Essenes (*Vita* 2), describes the sect as strict legalists, exceeding even the Pharisees in regard for the sabbath, reverence for Moses, observance of kosher food requirements (*War* 2,
143 f.) (According to Hippolytus the same is true of their zeal for
circumcision)[36]. In addition they were ascetics, some renouncing
marriage (2, 120) and some (the closely allied Therapeutae) re-
fraining from wine and meat, and fasting in the pursuit of wisdom
(σοφία)[37]. They were also speculators, reverencing the names of
angels and some rejecting a belief in resurrection for philosophical
notions of immortality (2, 128—158; cf. Eusebius, *HE* 2, 23).

---

[32] J. B. Lightfoot, *The Apostolic Fathers*, 3 vols. London 1889, II, I, 586 f.

[33] Cf. also F. Godet of Neuchatel, disciple of Neander: the same ascetic
Judeo-Christianity that appears in Rom 14 ('the weak') and achieves developed form in Colossae arrives at a 'deeper degree of decadence' in the Pastorals (*Introduction to the New Testament: the Epistles of Paul*, Edinburgh 1894,
565 f.; cf. 301, 432.

[34] J. B. Lightfoot, *Epistles to the Colossians and to Philemon*, London 1886
(1875), 71—111.

[35] *Ibid.*, 347—417.

[36] Hippolytus, *Ref.* 9,21: some Essenes threatened to slay Gentiles who engaged in a discussion of the law but refused circumcision. Cf. Josephus, *Ant.* 20,
40—45, where one Jewish missionary to Adiabene counsels a convert not to be
circumcised (for safety's sake) but another insists on it: to read Torah and not
be circumcised is impiety.

[37] Philo, *vita cont.* 34—39, 69—74; cf. Hegesippus in Eusebius, *HE* 2, 23: abstinence from wine and meat also characterized James of Jerusalem. Cf. Lk
1,15.

Lightfoot concludes (85) that 'in the asceticism of the Essene we seem to see the germ of ... Gnostic dualism,' a germ that found its christianized form in the false teachers at Colossae. Like the Essenes, these Gnostic Judaizers manifested an ascetic, speculative, exclusivist tendency and, as Christians, added two new elements to their speculations, the idea of redemption and the person of Christ (78). Although the heresy in Colossae is vague and undeveloped (111) and may have received its name only later (79), it is the forerunner of the full-blown second century (Jewish) Christian Gnosticism (103)[38].

'The heresy combated in the Pastoral epistles' (1865) is one and the same as that in Colossae, although in a 'more advanced and definite' form[39]. Promulgated chiefly by converts from Judaism and rooted in a claim to a superior γνῶσις[40], it engaged in speculative disputations, including a denial of the resurrection (2Tim 2,18) and perhaps a regard for mediating beings (1Tim 1,4; cf. 1, 17; 2,5). For the most part its adherents were ascetics (1Tim 4,3; Tit 1,15), included sorcerers (2Tim 3,13, γόητες) and promoted magical rites (1Tim 4,1) as well as an observance of the law[41]. But unlike the false teachers in Colossae, they included persons who, from the same dualistic principle that matter is evil, followed the opposite extreme of licentious antinomianism (Tit 1,16; 2Tim 3,6). Only in the second century Gnostic systems do the 'ascetic' and 'libertine' forms become clearly distinct and separate, when the libertine Gnosticism broke with Jewish practice completely and became anti-Judaic.

In his later writings Lightfoot recognized the 'germs' of this libertinism 'in the incipient Gnosticism which S. Paul rebukes at Corinth.'[42] Thus, (1) from the dualism that was fundamental to

---

[38] Cf. Lightfoot, *Fathers*, II, I, 373—388: the false teaching attacked by Ignatius appears to be 'a closely allied form of Gnostic Judaism' opposed in the Pastoral epistles (375). Cf. B. Jowett, *The Epistles of St. Paul to the Thessalonians, Galatians, Romans*, 2 vols., London 1855, I, 83: the second century heresies 'would be more correctly regarded not as offshoots of Christianity but as the soil in which it arose.' Lightfoot devoted one of his earliest articles (*JCP*, 1856) to an analysis of this book. Ct. V. Corwin, *St. Ignatius*, New Haven 1960, 52 f.

[39] J. B. Lightfoot, *Biblical Essays*, London 1893, 411—418, 413.

[40] 1Tim 1,4 ff.; 4,7; 6,4,20 f.; 2Tim 2,14 ff., 23; 4,4; Tit. 3,9.

[41] 1Tim 1,7 f.; Tit 1,10,14; 3,9.

[42] Lightfoot, *Fathers*, II, I, 387, 586 f. Cf. 1Cor 6,12—18; 8,1 f.; 15,12.

all Gnostic thinking and (2) from the undeniable unity of a heretical group in the Pastorals (and in Ignatius) that incorporated both ascetic-legalistic and libertine manifestations, Lightfoot was able to find a rationale by which both of these dispositions in certain other Pauline communities could be traced to the one heretical tendency of judaizing Gnosticism[43]. The question about the Essenes raised a century earlier by Tittmann now was answered.

It would be incorrect to say that Lightfoot's views dominated the later nineteenth century[44] since Anglo-American scholarship has been traditionally a rather independent enterprise, less attracted to 'schools' than its German counterpart. For example, F. J. A. Hort of Cambridge[45], Lightfoot's friend and sometime colleague, is of a completely different mind. Skeptical of 'parties' in 1Cor 1,12, he ventures only that the passage indicates a certain partisanship. Judaizing traducers do appear in Corinthians (95—99), as they do in Colossians and in the Pastorals (181 f.). Nowhere, however, is there 'clear evidence of speculative or Gnosticizing tendencies' (146) although it is 'probable enough that a misunderstanding of the language of [Ephesians] contributed to the Pseudo-Gnostical terminology' of the early second century[46]. American writers of the period, although not uninfluenced by Lightfoot's views, likewise take an independent line[47].

---

[43] *Ibid*, II, II, 124 on Ignatius, *Mag.* 8,1; cf. 10,3 (134) where this 'Judaism crossed with Gnosticism' that Paul opposed in Colossae is described as ἰουδαΐζειν, as is the pharisaic judaizing in Gal 2,14. Ct. C. K. Barrett, *JGC*, 240—244.

[44] H. L. Mansel of Oxford, *The Gnostic Heresies of the First and Second Centuries*, London 1875, 48—63, for which Lightfoot wrote a preface, generally followed the views of E. Burton. The Corinthian epistles contain the 'germs' of the later Gnostic teaching (48), and 1Cor 13,8,10; 2Cor 11,6 are best understood 'if we recognize in the Corinthian opponents... the precursors of the Ebionite Gnostics'... (50). In Colossae 'Gnostic speculations were accompanied by a spurious asceticism based on the Jewish law'... (57). The work of J. J. Skeet (1866) on the third chapter of Philippians was unavailable to me.

[45] F. J. A. Hort, *Judaistic Christianity*, Cambridge 1894, 116—146.

[46] F. J. A. Hort, *The Romans and the Ephesians*, London 1895, 120.

[47] A. C. McGiffert of Union, *A History of... the Apostolic Age*, New York 1897: the 'rival factions' in 1Cor 1,12 are due to the converts of Apollos; the Christ party is nonsectarian, the Cephas party Jewish-Christian but not judaizing; in Philippians there are only unbelieving Jews (3,2) and antinomians (3,18) (389—393); the Colossian false teachers, like those in 1Tim 4,3, are not Essene but Alexandrian, 'the first appearance of that syncretism of Oriental theosophy and Christian faith' that characterized a later Gnosticism (369, 502). G. T

Nevertheless, Lightfoot is the most significant and representative figure of the later nineteenth century. (1) In understanding the Pauline controversies within a broad historical context, he marked a clear advance beyond F. C. Baur. 'By a more thorough exegesis and by a more faithful adherence to the actual sources, Lightfoot constructed a picture of the development of the early Church which was plainly more reliable than anything the Tübingen school had been able to produce.'[48] (2) Building upon earlier insights, he showed that the dichotomy between 'judaizing' and 'gnosticizing' (Hilgenfeld) had been wrongly drawn, and he distinguished in the Pauline texts two kinds of judaizing, pharisaic (Galatians, 2 Corinthians, Phil 3,1 f.) and Essene-Gnostic (Colossians, Romans, Phil 3,12—19, 1Corinthians, the Pastorals), the latter expressed both in an ascetic-legalistic and in a licentious-libertine form as the individual or circle might be moved.

Lightfoot's reconstruction of a judaizing Gnosis is strengthened by the fact that he was not seeking to reduce the errors in the Pauline communities to one heresy across the board. At the same time he thereby left other questions unresolved. In addressing the error in Galatians, Paul appears to reckon both with visions of angels (1,4), ascetic ritualism and subjection to the στοιχεῖα (4,9 f.) and perhaps with libertinism (5,13 ff.). The former traits appear in Colossians (2,8,16 ff.) and both kinds appear in the Pastorals. Is the error in Galatians, even with the added element of circumcision, so different then from that in Colossians and in the Pastorals? Even if Galatians shows a relationship with the (pharisaic) Palestinian 'circumcision party,'[49] is the attitude of the Galatian opponents identical with it? As Lightfoot himself had shown, ju-

---

Purves of Princeton, *Christianity in the Apostolic Age*, New York 1900: with the coming of 'Judaistic emissaries' in 2 Corinthians (3,1; 10—13) there appears 'a distinct anti-Pauline party' (222); the heresy at Colossae is 'not the old Judaistic error' but, like the Essenes, 'combines Jewish rites with a mystic theosophy' and is 'the crude beginnings of what afterward became Gnosticism' (243 f.). B. W. Bacon of Yale, *The Story of Paul*, Boston 1904: Gnosticism, as it was later called, was essentially Alexandrian in type and Hellenistic in derivation; it was present already in Paul's day in Ephesus and in the Corinthian church among the converts of Apollos who exaggerated their enlightenment (γνῶσις) (176 ff., 299 f., 315 f.).

[48] J. W. Hunkin in *Beginnings of Christianity*, 5 vols., ed. F. J. Foakes Jackson and K. Lake, London 1920—1932, II, 420.

[49] Gal 2,12; cf. Acts 11,2; 15,5. See below, 121 f.

daizing could not be defined solely in terms of pharisaic Christians. And, apparently, the line of distinction between the attitudes of the Essenes and of the Pharisees was not always entirely clear in first century Judaism[50].

III.

In German studies of the early twentieth century there was an increasing shift away from F. C. Baur's estimate of Paul's opponents. Wilhelm Lütgert of Halle, in a series of clearly written and closely argued essays, poses the sharpest alternative. Although he apparently was unacquainted with the work of Lightfoot, he reaches conclusions that in a number of respects are remarkably similar to those of the English scholar. He is not concerned to identify a heretical system of thought but to demonstrate the presence of a religious 'type' that appears in a variety of forms in the various Pauline churches[51]. Thus, when he identifies the opponents as 'Gnostics' he defines them as pneumatics who view Christianity as a higher knowledge that emancipates one from moral and churchly authorities — whether of Scripture, Jesus or apostles[52]. Such persons have their background in liberal, probably Alexandrian Judaism and teach a Jewish Gnosis in the form of haggadic exposition and expansion of Scripture[53].

As did Baur, Lütgert began with a study of the Corinthian letters[54]. Against Baur's thesis he objects (51–62) that the verbal parallels, 'another gospel' (2Cor 11,4; Gal 1,6) and 'belonging to Christ' (2Cor 10,7; 1Cor 1,12), are not sufficient to identify the opponents in 2 Corinthians with a judaizing Christ party or with the Galatian Judaizers. Indeed, the preaching of 'another spirit' precludes Judaizers since the preaching of the law and the reception of the Spirit are mutually exclusive (Gal 3,2). In 2Cor 5,12

---

[50] Cf. K. Kohler in *The Jewish Encyclopedia*, 12 vols., ed. I. Singer, New York c. 1966 (1901), V, 225.

[51] W. Lütgert, *Die Vollkommenen im Philipperbrief und die Enthusiasten in Thessalonisch*, Gütersloh 1909, VII.

[52] W. Lütgert, *Die Irrlehrer der Pastoralbriefe*, Gütersloh 1909, 91 ff.

[53] *Ibid.*, 21 f., 65, 92 f.

[54] W. Lütgert, *Freiheitspredigt und Schwarmgeister in Korinth*, Gütersloh 1908.

to 16 the opponents are not Judaizers who deny Paul's personal acquaintance with Jesus but pneumatics who deny his spiritual knowledge of Jesus. The opponents are not accused of judaizing tendencies and, on the assumption that they are Judaizers, never reveal any clear image in the text. The self-conception of the opponents also is not established by Schenkel although he had a better insight into the Corinthian situation.

What, then, is the opponents' view of themselves as it appears in 2Cor 10–12 (62–101)? By claiming to give 'the spirit' (11,4), by disparaging Paul's gnosis (11,6) and by attacking him as 'weak' (10,10) and as lacking the miraculous and visionary 'signs of an apostle' (12,11 f.), the opponents present themselves as pneumatics who offer a higher gnosis. But the gnosis of these persons, Paul counters, is separated from obedience to God. Like that which Satan offered to Eve (11,3), it manifests an arrogant presumption that raises itself against the true knowledge of God (10,4 ff.). The opponents, then, are not Judaizers but Gnostics who in claiming to be 'of Christ' (10,7) suppose that they are exempt from obedience to authority. The fact that Paul, too, claims to be 'of Christ' and in his preaching of freedom (Freiheitspredigt) has encouraged believers not to be slaves to men (e. g. 1Cor 7,23) suggests that the opponents represent an excessive, libertine extension of Paul's own viewpoint. This is confirmed by 2Cor 6,14–7,1, which is original to the letter and directed against a sexually immoral libertinism that despises the fear of God (7,1; cf. 5,11).

From this foundation Lütgert proceeds to 1 Corinthians. He assumes the identity of those who claim to be 'of Christ' with the Christ party of 1Cor 1,12 and concludes that in 1 Corinthians it is they who scorn the weakness of the cross (1,18), pursue a false, hellenistic, philosophical wisdom (1,17; 3,18), by dissension destroy God's temple (3,16 f.), ignore the authority of Scripture (4, 6 ff.), engage in immoral practice (6,9,20) and deny the resurrection (15,12). With its dualism of spirit and nature this libertinism can also incorporate an asceticism that is inwardly bound together with it (102–135).

This indeed occurs among 'the false teachers of the Pastoral epistles' (1909)[55], who represent the same Gnostic libertinism

---

[55] Lütgert, *Pastoralbriefe*. Although he regards the Pastorals as Pauline, Lüt-

'veiled' by a cloak of asceticism (36 ff., 92). Their 'other teaching' (1Tim 1,3, ἑτεροδιδασκαλεῖν), reminiscent of the term 'another gospel' in Gal 1,6; 2Cor 11,4, is not a denial of Paul's gospel but a going beyond it. To pharisaic Judaizers Paul teaches, as he does in Galatians, freedom from the law; to antinomians Paul stresses that the law still has significance for the Christian community when sin is found in it (1Tim 1,8—11). So is it in the Pastorals (11 f.). Like the opponents in Corinthians, these false teachers question Paul's apostleship (1Tim 2,7), appeal to a false gnosis (1Tim 6,20), deny the resurrection (2Tim 2,18), misuse the Scripture (Tit 1,14) and accent an emancipation from authority characterized by immoral sexual practices (2Tim 3,6 f.). Like 1 John (2,18; 4,3), Paul warns that the false teaching prophesied [? in earlier oracles] for the 'last days' (1Tim 4,1—3; 2Tim 3,1,5) is already active in the present (1Tim 1,6; Tit 1,15 f.; cf. 2Tim 4,10).

Here, as elsewhere, Lütgert may weaken his case at times by excessively reading an adversary theology out of Paul's statements. If Paul must remind them to be obedient (1Tim 2,1 f.; Tit 3,1), that means they were not. If he teaches that God is invisible except in Christ (1Tim 3,16; 6,15 f.), the opponents must have been stressing visions of God. If he underscores Christ's death (2Tim 2,8) or salvation for all (1Tim 2,4), perhaps they — like the later Gnostics — have a docetic Christology and restrict salvation to one class of mankind (54 f., 60 f.).

'The perfect ones in Philippians and the enthusiasts in Thessalonians' (1909)[56] reflect some of the same characteristics. In Phil 3 two groups of opponents are addressed. The first (3,2 ff.) are probably Jews (not judaizing Christians) who persecute the community in Philippi, since Paul proceeds to show 'not why he is not a Judaizer but why he is not a Jew' (7). In brief, Paul exchanged Judaism for a gnosis, a gnosis of Jesus Christ (3,10). Lest this be equated with the views of the libertines or enthusiasts, he proceeds (3,12—21) to distinguish his teaching from theirs. Paul

---

gert seeks to identify the false teachers from the text without prejudging the question, what kind of false teachers could have existed at the time of the letters.

[56] Lütgert, *Die Vollkommenen*, 1—54. Does Paul, however, give up his 'Jewishness' or only his 'confidence' in the law as a way to 'righteousness' (Phil 3,4 ff.)?

taught that by faith the believers already were resurrected with Christ (cf. Gal 2,20; Rom 6,1,13; Col 2,12 f.; 3,1,9 f.). Some misunderstood this to preclude a future resurrection (as some today misunderstand the Gospel of John, e. g. 5,25) and to convey a present perfection in which all is permitted (12—14,31 f.). In consequence they have become 'enemies' of the gospel of the cross and have given way to licentiousness (3,19). In response to such views Paul stresses the future resurrection hope (3,10,21) and denies that he has been 'perfected' (3,12, τετελείωμαι). For Paul, to be 'perfect' (3,15, τέλειος) is not to have reached the goal but to share Christ's sufferings and to strive toward a future goal.

Only in his analysis of 'law and spirit' (1919) in Galatians does Lütgert see evidence of (Christian) pharisaic Judaizers[57]. Following de Wette[58], he regards Paul to be fighting against two 'fronts,' libertines who have perverted Paul's gospel of freedom and a pharisaic legalism that — as in Rom 2 and Mt 5—7 — does not really (6,13) take the law seriously (103). The libertine tendency is clearly present, and not just a hypothetical possibility, in 5,15,21 where dissension and immorality are connected with an emphasis on freedom and the Spirit (cf. 1Cor 3,3; 6,12—20). From the latter emphasis one may infer that the 'pneumatics' (6,1)[59] form a part of the group of 'free spirits' (14—22) who have, like the similar group in Corinth, made accusations against the Apostle: he still preaches circumcision (cf. 5,11), re-establishes the law (cf. 2,18), has his gospel from men (cf. 1,11 f.), yields Christian freedom in the face of pressures from Jerusalem (cf. 2,5). They are those who preach 'another gospel' (1,6) and, in turn, are warned (4,8—20) by Paul that their 'backsliding into paganism' (67—89) places them no less than the Judaizers under the curse of the law. For the 'seasons' and the 'weak and beggarly elements' in Gal 4,9, like the similar passage in Colossians (2,16,20 f.), probably refer to as-

---

[57] W. Lütgert, *Gesetz und Geist. Eine Untersuchung zur Vorgeschichte des Galaterbriefes*, Gütersloh 1919.

[58] *Ibid.*, 14 ff. Cf. W. M. L. de Wette, *An die Galater...*, Leipzig 1864 (1841), 110, on Gal 5,13: apparently the freer Pauline Christians and those tending toward Judaism lay in conflict and the Pauline group acted with arrogance.

[59] Lütgert does not explain how, then, Paul could call upon the pneumatics to restore those who have fallen into such sins.

cetic practices and pagan astrological interests of the free spirits who 'regarded [Christian] participation in pagan cults to be allowed' (80).

Because of such libertine conduct the Galatians, or the Jewish Christians among them, have come under Jewish persecution (4,29; cf. 5,11; 6,12). To avoid it and to come under the state's protection of the Jewish *religio licita*, the judaizing false teachers urge circumcision on the Galatians (96—106). Paul responds that, if they accede to this, they would reject the cross (5,11; 6,12), fall away from grace (5,4), deny the gospel and be obligated to keep the whole law (5,2 f.). Paul, then, stands between the two fronts: he fights for freedom but against licentiousness, for obedience but against legalism (106).

Against the traditional 'Judaizer' interpretation of the Galatian opponents Lütgert scores some impressive points, but he also raises some questions. (1) In inferring an adversary's viewpoint from certain of Paul's statements, he is not always convincing. (2) Although he recognizes the pneumatic (6,1) as a specially gifted Christian, he appears to confuse and thus to connect the term with ζῆν πνεύματι (5,25), a characteristic of all Christians. That is, he apparently fails to distinguish εἶναι πνευματικός (1Cor 14,37) from ἔχειν πνεῦμα (Rom 8,9). This error will re-appear in the studies of subsequent scholars (e. g. Schmithals). (3) The supposition of 'two fronts' of opponents contains an inherent improbability and requires a frequent shift of reference that is not always clear from the text. (4) The question raised above about Lightfoot's view of the Galatian situation applies also to Lütgert: has he defined 'Judaizer' too narrowly? It is quite conceivable that one group might have been both ritually strict (regarding circumcision) and at the same time theologically syncretistic and morally lax.

Lütgert's view of Paul's opponents was shared by K. Lake[60] with respect to 2 Corinthians and by J. H. Ropes[61] with respect to Galatians. With modifications it was followed also by A. Schlat-

---

[60] K. Lake, *The earlier Epistles of St. Paul*, London 1914 (1911), 219—232, 227 f. M. Rauer, *Die 'Schwachen' in Korinth und Rom*, 1923, was unavailable to me.

[61] J. H. Ropes, *The Singular Problem of the Epistle to the Galatians*, Cambridge (Mass.) 1929.

ter[62] and F. Büchsel[63]. But in the subsequent research it was over-shadowed by the views of the *religionsgeschichtliche Schule*.

C. Machalet[64] has rightly remarked that twentieth century studies on Paul's opponents sound like a replay of the same musical scale, reminiscent of the world of Ecclesiastes. His observation may be illustrated by the use of such terms as Gnostic and Gnosticism. For a century scholars — from Neander to Lütgert — who called Paul's opponents Gnostics qualified their usage to distinguish the term from the later, developed second century Gnostic systems. At about the time that Lütgert was writing, however, scholars of the 'history of religions' school began to minimize or discount this distinction. They defined such Pauline concepts as 'pneumatic' and 'gnosis' in terms of a Gnosticism that was found only in post-Christian and/or Christian-influenced sources but that was, nevertheless, asserted to be 'a pre-Christian movement which had its roots in itself.'[65] From this perspective these scholars offered a reconstruction of early Christianity equally as far-reaching as that of F. C. Baur and one that had considerable significance for the present theme. For, when writers who shared these assumptions, such as Professor Bultmann of Marburg[66], spoke of

---

[62] A. Schlatter (*Die korinthische Theologie*, Gütersloh 1914, 94—100, 117 to 125) argued that the opponents were not, however, an extreme extension of Paul's viewpoint but had their origin in anti-pharisaic elements in the Palestinian church. This view was developed further by E. Käsemann, 'Die Legitimität des Apostels,' *Paulusbild*, ed. K. H. Rengstorf, Darmstadt 1969, 475—521 (= *ZNTW* 41, 1942, 33—71): the opponents are pneumatics but not Gnostics since they do not appear to represent a specific mythological and speculative doctrine of salvation (36, 40).

[63] F. Büchsel, *Der Geist Gottes im Neuen Testament*, Gütersloh 1926, 394 f., who supposes that the Judaism of the opponents had gone 'beyond that which is written' (1Cor 4,6) into a syncretistic form through the influence of the ἄνθρωποι θεῖοι of the hellenistic world, a view to be espoused a generation later, e. g., by D. Georgi (*Die Gegner des Paulus im 2. Korintherbrief*, Neukirchen 1964, 220—234); cf. J. F. Collange (*Énigmes de la deuxième épître de Paul aux Corinthiens*, Cambridge 1972, 69—72, 320—324). But was there such a fixed concept of the 'divine man' in the first century hellenistic world? Cf. H. C. Kee in *JBL* 92 (1973), 421 f.; D. L. Tiede, 'The Charismatic Figure as Miracle Worker,' *SBL Dissertation Series* I, Missoula (Mont.), 1972.

[64] C. Machalet, 'Paulus und seine Gegner... [in] den Korintherbriefen,' *Theokratia* II (1970—72), 185.

[65] W. Bousset, *Kyrios Christos*, Nashville 1970 (1913), 245; cf. R. Reitzenstein, *Die hellenistischen Mysterienreligionen*, Stuttgart 1966 (1910), 299 f., 379.

[66] R. Bultmann, *Theology of the New Testament*, London 1952, I, 168—172; 'γνῶσις,' *TDNT* I, 708—711; *Exegetische Probleme des Zweiten Korinther-*

Paul's opponents as pneumatics and Gnostics, they reflected a viewpoint quite different from that of Lightfoot or of Lütgert and more reminiscent of Mosheim's 'Oriental philosophy.' But, also like Mosheim, they were unable to find first century evidence for this (later) Gnosticism and reconstructed their picture of Paul's opponents largely from the concepts and motifs of second and third century sources. Such a method warranted the criticism of A. D. Nock[67] that 'it is an unsound proceeding to take Manichean and other texts, full of echoes of the New Testament, and reconstruct from them something supposedly lying back of the New Testament.' However, in spite of this weakness the approach of the 'history of religions' school became a prominent, if not a dominant factor in the German discussion of Paul's opponents during the third quarter of the twentieth century.

IV.

Since mid-century the interest in Paul's opponents has continued to evoke extensive discussion and to manifest a wide diversity of opinion[68]. While one may call attention to some of the more

---

briefes, Uppsala 1947, 23—30 (= *Exegetica*, Tübingen 1967, 315—321). Cf. G. Bornkamm, 'Die Häresie des Kolosserbriefes,' *Das Ende des Gesetzes*, München 1961 (1948), 139—156; H. Köster, 'Häretiker . . .', *RGG*[3] III (1959), 17—21.

[67] A. D. Nock, 'Gnosticism,' *Essays on Religion and the Ancient World*, 2 vols., Oxford 1972, II, 958 (= *HTR* 57, 1964, 278). Similarly against Reitzenstein, J. G. Machen, *The Origin of Paul's Religion*, Grand Rapids 1947 (1925), 247—250: . . . 'it is very precarious to use the [post-Christian] Gnostic systems in reconstructing pre-Christian paganism in detail — especially where the Gnostic systems differ from admittedly pagan sources and agree with Paul. In reconstructing the origin of Paulinism it is precarious to employ the testimony of those who lived after Paul and actually quoted Paul' (250).

[68] J. J. Gunther (*St. Paul's Opponents and their Background*, Leiden 1973, 1—5) lists from eight (Galatians) to forty-four (Colossians) different opinions on the identity of the false teachers in the Pauline letters. The lists are inflated, however, since a number of his categories represent a distinction without a difference. For the German discussion cf. Machalet, *op. cit.* W. Schmithals, *Gnosticism in Corinth*, Nashville 1971 (1956, ²1965), and *Paul and the Gnostics*, Nashville 1972, contain extensive bibliographies with useful, if partisan discussion. Cf. also D. Guthrie, *New Testament Introduction: the Pauline Epistles*, London 1961, 162—166 (on Colossians): W. G. Kümmel, *Introduction to the New Testament*, Nashville ²1975, *passim*; R. M. Wilson, *Gnosis and the New Testament*, Philadelphia 1968, 1—59.

frequent contributors to the topic such as Professor Barrett of Durham[69] and Professor Schmithals of Berlin[70], it is difficult, standing in the midst of the developments, to delineate any clear trends in the research. The concluding segment of this chapter will, then, seek to present the state of the question as the writer sees it, incorporating and interacting with the various contributions as they bear upon the several matters considered.

Of the various Pauline letters in which opponents or false teachers appear, 2Cor 10—13 presents perhaps the most detailed picture. The section gives both Paul's accusations against the opponents and, in one or two instances, their own perception of their status and mission. It provides, then, the best starting point from which similar persons and groups in other Pauline letters may be compared.

The false teachers are generally recognized to be outsiders (11, 4) of Jewish Christian background (11,22) who represent themselves as 'apostles of Christ' and 'ministers (διάκονοι) of Christ' (11,13,23). On the basis of their pedigree and visionary experiences they apparently boast of a privileged authority that the Co-

---

[69] C. K. Barrett, 'Paul and the Pillar Apostles,' *Studia Paulina*, ed. J. N. Sevenster, Haarlem 1953, 1—19; 'Cephas and Corinth,' *Abraham unser Vater*, ed. O. Betz, Leiden 1963, 1—12; 'Christianity at Corinth,' *BJRL* 46 (1963—64), 269—297; 'Things Sacrificed to Idols,' *NTS* 11 (1965), 138—153; 'Ψευδαπόστολοι (2Cor 11,13)', *Mélanges Bibliques B. Rigaux*, ed. A. Descamps, Gembloux 1970, 377—396; 'Paul's Opponents in 2 Corinthians,' *NTS* 17 (1970—71), 233—254; *Signs of an Apostle*, London 1970, 36—40: 'Such envoys [of the Jerusalem apostles like those in Gal 2,12; Acts 15,22 f.], possibly out of hand and acting *ultra vires*, are probably to be seen in those who were unsettling the Galatian churches (Gal 1,7) and in the false apostles whom Paul condemns in 2Cor 10—13' (40). They are Judaizers even though in Corinth they do not, for their own reasons, emphasize circumcision ('Opponents,' 252 ff.). In 1 Corinthians Paul stands between a Jewish Christian legalism (Peter group) and a Gentile, gnostic rationalism (Christ group) within the Corinthian congregation ('Idols,' 152). In important respects Barrett is reminiscent of Baur.

[70] W. Schmithals, *Gnosticism; Gnostics; Paul and James*, London 1965. Schmithals, elaborating the view of his teacher R. Bultmann, seeks to establish the thesis that Paul's opponents throughout seven letters — Romans, Corinthians, Galatians, Philippians, Thessalonians — were Jewish (Christian) Gnostics (cf. *Gnostics*, 244 f.). His many acute insights on individual points often depend, however, on the validity of the method of the 'history of religions' school. Like it, he appears to define 'Gnostic' in terms of the mythological gnosis found in second and third century systems and to assume, thereupon, that this is the concept and context of the usage in the Pauline letters. See above, note 67.

rinthians accept and Paul rejects, scornfully labeling them 'super apostles' (ὑπερλίαν ἀποστόλων)[71]. Probably they disparage Paul's apostolic credentials and conduct (10,2, 10—12) and, in any case, their behavior has encouraged some of the Corinthians to do so (11,5; 12,11 f., 16).

The principal questions about the opponents appear to be these. What is their precise teaching? Do they come from the Jerusalem church (Schlatter, Käsemann, Dupont) or from the diaspora Christian mission (Bultmann, Georgi)? Are they pharisaic Judaizers (Barrett), pneumatics (Käsemann) or second-century-type Gnostics (Bultmann, Schmithals)? What is their relationship to the intruders in 2Cor 1—9, to the dissidents in 1 Corinthians and to the opponents and false teachers in other Pauline letters?

The intruders in 2Cor 1—9 who 'huckster the word of God' (2,17; cf. 11,7), present 'letters of recommendation' (3,1; cf. 10, 12,18) and 'boast in appearance' (5,12; cf. 11,18) are not to be distinguished from the opponents in 2Cor 10—13, even if the latter section was originally a separate letter. In 1 Corinthians, on the other hand, there are individual dissensions (1,12, ἕκαστος) and erring children but no opponents nor, in the strict sense, false teachers[72]. For, (1) in contrast to 2Cor 10—13 Paul speaks as a father (4,15), differs by concession and qualification (7,1 f.) and engages in no invective. The desire to 'examine' (4,3; 9,3; ἀνακρίνειν) Paul is not an exception but apparently represents only the Corinthians' attempt, that Paul will not allow, to 'test' Paul's apostolic message as they would that of any other pneumatic (cf. 14,29,37)[73]. Also, (2) the so-called 'Christ party' (1,12) can hardly

---

[71] 2Cor 11,4 f.,20; 12,11. Following Baur and Käsemann, Barrett ('Christianity,' 294 f.) translates ὑπερλίαν ἀπόστολοι ironically as 'greatest apostles' and identifies them with the pillar apostles (cf. Gal 2,2,9) of Jerusalem. But this is precluded by the fact that the 'super apostles' were those relating their visions to the Corinthians and, thereby, forcing Paul to relate his (2Cor 12,11). The 'super apostles' are identical with the false teachers. So, Bultmann, *Probleme*, 27 ff., and the commentaries of Windisch, Plummer, and Lietzmann-Kümmel.

[72] The ἄλλοι (1Cor 9,2) are possibly an exception since they may be the same opponents that (later) appear in 2 Corinthians. But there is apparently no indication that they are already present in Corinth. Probably Paul is alluding to his experience elsewhere.

[73] See above, 46. Cf. J. C. Hurd, *The Origin of 1 Corinthians*, London 1965, 108—113; J. Munck, *Paul and the Salvation of Mankind*, Richmond 1959, 166 f.

be identified with the opponents in 2 Corinthians (10,7) on the uncertain basis of the idiom, 'to be Christ's,' especially since Paul applies the idiom to himself in the same text. But (3) there is some probability that the self-professed 'wise' (4,10, φρόνιμοι) Corinthians who 'boast' of their spiritual status (4,7; cf. 14,36 f.) are the same 'wise' (φρόνιμοι) in 2 Corinthians who are receptive and favorable to the opponents, who also boast in their spiritual status[74]. On the basis of this vaunted status, probably connected with their pneumatic charism of γνῶσις (8,1, φυσιοῦν), these Corinthians have displayed (cf. 4,6,18 f. with 5,2, φυσιοῦν) and may continue to display contentious and licentious practices (2Cor 12,20 f.; cf. 7,1).

The opponents, who find supporters among such Corinthians, probably share their libertine sentiments. (1) 'The secret things of shame,' that Paul has renounced, appear to refer to such practices of the opponents[75] (2) By the description, disguised as 'servants of righteousness' (δικαιοσύνη, 2Cor 11,15), Paul implies that they are actually ἄδικοι (cf. 1Cor 6,9) or ἄνομοι (cf. 2Cor 6,14), terms that he associates with immoral and idolatrous practices. (3) The references to the Church as Christ's 'chaste virgin' being corrupted (φθείρειν) from its purity (ἁγνότητος) may have similar connotations[76]. (4) Lütgert may be right in connecting the opponents with the admonition given at 2Cor 6,14—7,1 (cf. 7,1 with 5,11 f., 'fear of the Lord;' 'boast in outward appearance'). At least Paul suspects that the influence of the false teachers will tend in this direction (2Cor 12,21).

A number of characteristics mentioned in 2 Corinthians identify the opponents' spiritual status (like that of their Corinthian promoters) as pneumatics, i. e. persons with charisms of inspired speech and discernment[77]. This is implicit in their claim to visions and revelations (12,1,11) and to be 'apostles' (a charism that includes such manifestations) and 'ministers' (διάκονοι, a term used of pneumatics)[78]. It is probably to be inferred from Paul's comparison of the opponents' teaching with Satan's temptation of Eve (11,3), i. e. to get 'knowledge' (cf. Gen 2,9, γνωστόν/דעת) apart

---

[74] 2Cor 11,18 f.; cf. 5,12. Cf. Kümmel, *Introduction*, 284 f.

[75] 2Cor 4,2. See below, note 94.

[76] At least an idolatrous disloyalty is to be inferred. Cf. 2Cor 11,4; Jas 3, 15–17; E. E. Ellis, *Paul's Use of the Old Testament*, Edinburgh 1957, 63.

[77] See above, 24—27.   [78] 2Cor 11,13,23; see above, 7—13.

from obedience to God, and from Paul's comment about 'every proud obstacle against the knowledge (γνῶσις) of God' (10,5)[79].

One can, then, speak of the opponents not only as pneumatics but also as gnostics in the sense of offering a gnosis of God based upon the prophet's discernment of Yahweh's purpose, e. g. by inspired exposition of Scripture[80], by oracles and inspired teaching, and by visions and revelations. (In this sense, of course, Paul also is a gnostic, 11,6). But as Käsemann has observed[81], in 2 Corinthians there is nothing of the mythological speculations of the second century Gnostic systems[82].

The claim to be 'apostles of Christ' fixes the origin of the opponents in Palestine. In Paul's usage the term ἀπόστολοι may be used of persons commissioned and sent out by churches (e. g. 2Cor 8,23). But where it is qualified as 'apostle of Jesus Christ,' it means a direct commission from (the risen) Jesus[83]. In all likelihood the

---

[79] That is, if Paul, as one suspects, is implying that the opponents' false gnosis is the obstacle to the true gnosis of God. Cf. 2Cor 2,14,17 where Paul contrasts his preaching of God's gnosis with the many who huckster the Word of God. It is significant that, with the exception of the qualified usage in 1Tim 6,20, Paul does not concede the term γνῶσις to the false teachers but always uses it in a good sense (also in 1Cor 8,1; cf. 2Cor 12,7).

[80] Thus, in the exposition of Exod 34 in 2Cor 3 Paul reads Scripture without a 'veil' (3,15 f.) in the light that the gnosis of God produces (4,6, Plummer) or in the enlightenment that gives the gnosis of God (cf. Windisch). Such exposition is a manifestation of Paul's gnosis. Whether it is adversary theology, i. e. a reworking of what Paul regards as a perverse exposition by the opponents, as Schultz thinks, is less clear to me. Cf. S. Schultz, 'Die Decke des Moses,' *ZNTW* 49 (1958), 1–30; G. Friedrich, 'Die Gegner des Paulus im 2. Korintherbrief,' *Abraham unser Vater*, ed. O. Betz, Leiden 1963, 181–215, 184.

[81] Käsemann, 'Legitimität,' 35, 40 f.: that the opponents were pneumatics in the sense of the hellenistic Gnosis, as Reitzenstein asserted, is anything but certain (40).

[82] For the thesis that the conceptual background of wisdom and gnosis in Corinthians lies in the prophetic and apocalyptic traditions of Judaism, with special affinities with the Qumran literature see the argument above, 45–62. To be avoided in any case is the error of an earlier generation that sharply contrasted 'Palestinian' and 'Hellenistic' as though Palestine and the diaspora were culturally or theologically isolated from one another. Cf. I. H. Marshall, 'Palestinian and Hellenistic Christianity,' *NTS* 19 (1972–73), 271–287; H. J. Schoeps, *Paul*, London 1959, 35; W. D. Davies, *Paul and Rabbinic Judaism*, London ²1955, 1–16; J. N. Sevenster, *Do You Know Greek*, Leiden 1968. See below, 245 ff.

[83] 1Cor 9,1; 15,8 f. It is conceivable that the opponents claim apostleship on the basis of a vision of Christ and that Paul, standing on the same ground,

term is so applied to the opponents and thereby presupposes their personal acquaintance with Jesus[84].

The opponents apparently make no demands about circumcision and the law of Moses. Whether an underlying Judaizing attitude is implied in their superior airs and their boast of being *Hebraioi* (10,22) depends on the significance of that term for their background. When used to distinguish certain Jews from other Jews, *Hebraios* in pre-Christian usage appears to denote a dignity or status associated with traditional Jewish values and customs, perhaps including priestly or religious class, Palestinian background and/or the Hebrew language[85]. The term occurs in three New Testament passages, among which Acts 6,1 appears to be an important key to its usage in early Christianity[86]. Several lines of evidence suggest that the dispute in Acts between the *Hebraioi* and the Hellenists reflects primarily a difference not in language or geographical origin but in attitudes toward the Jewish cultus and customs. (1) The term, Hellenist, rarely found in the literature of the period, probably is connected to the meaning of the verb form, 'to live according to the Greek manner' (Cullmann); the term *Hebraios* would, then, have a connotation correspondent to it. (2) The dispute is over foods and probably is not an isolated event but in Luke's mind is a part of the continuing tension in the Jerusalem church over this issue and the related problem of the temple[87].

---

does not contest it. But Paul speaks of Christ's appearance to him as 'last of all' and as 'an abortion,' i. e. without a prior period of apprenticeship under Jesus. He evidently regards this as unique and knows no other 'apostles of Christ' of this sort. Furthermore, the opponents boast in a way that implies an apostolic relationship to Christ (2Cor 11,13,23) superior to that of Paul. This probably included not only a claim to superior apostolic signs, which Paul can and does contest, but also acquaintance with and commission from the earthly Jesus, which Paul could not and does not contest. Had the opponents claimed only a sometime vision of Christ, would Paul have let that pass and would the Corinthian pneumatics have been so impressed?

[84] So, Kümmel, *Introduction*, 284 f.

[85] Cf. K. G. Kuhn and W. Gutbrot in *TDNT* 3 (1966/1938), 367 ff., 372 to 375. Cf. Josephus, *bell.* 1, 3: 'I Josephus, son of Matthias, by race a *Hebraios*, a priest from Jerusalem' . . .; Philo, *vit. Mos.* II, 31 ff., 36 f.: The high priest sent to Alexandria *Hebraioi*, educated in their ancestral lore and in Greek, to translate the Hebrew Scriptures. Tested in wisdom (σοφία), they accomplished their task under inspiration.

[86] See below, 118 f.; cf. O. Cullmann, '. . . Beginnings of Christianity,' *The Scrolls and the New Testament*, ed. K. Stendahl, New York 1957, 18—32, 26.

[87] Later in Acts Peter is commanded by God to eat unclean food (10,14), is

(3) The episode is connected to the Hellenist Stephen's polemic 'against the holy place and the [ritual] law' (6,13) and 'the customs Moses delivered' (6,13 f.), a polemic that evoked a persecution primarily against Hellenist Christians (8,1; 11,19 f.) led by Paul the *Hebraios* (Phil 3,5). (4) Since strict and lax attitudes toward the cultus and the ritual laws existed in Palestinian as well as in diaspora Jewry, such differences probably were present in the Church from the beginning[88].

When coupled to their claim to be apostles of Christ, the opponents' title *Hebraioi* very likely refers to their association with the ritually strict segment of the primitive Church. Likewise, their pneumatic powers have their (professed) background in the pentecostal manifestations of the Jerusalem church (Schlatter, Dupont), manifestations that included the same pneumatic powers[89]. Like Paul (Gal 1,18; 2,2), the opponents have some connection and stand in continuity with the Palestinian church even if they, also like Paul, pursue their mission in the church of the diaspora[90].

Paul does not deny the distinguished background of the *Hebraioi* opponents in Corinth or their pneumatic powers. He does not make an issue of their 'theology.' But in their arrogance, their huckstering of the word of God (2,17; 4,2), their opposition to his apostleship, their libertine practices or sympathies he discerns a demonic perversion of what may once have been valid gifts of the Spirit. In a word he views them as false prophets and his own role also as a prophet whose struggle, in the words of Ephesians (6,12), 'is not against flesh and blood, but against the principalities,

---

criticized by the circumcision party because he ate with Gentiles (11,2 f.; cf. Gal. 2,12) and recalls the event at the Jerusalem council, a meeting that compromises a problem over circumcision and food laws (15,1, 15–29). Later, James reminds Paul of this agreement in asking him to demonstrate that he is not, as alleged, alienating diaspora Jews from 'Moses,' 'circumcision,' and the 'customs,' doubtless including the food laws (21,20–26). That is, he implies, we made concessions for you, now you do this for us. The attitude toward the temple, circumcision and the food laws is all part of one divisive and continuing problem within the Jewish Christian church.

[88] See below, 119 n., 245 ff.

[89] Cf. Acts 2,4,17; 6,3 f., 8,10,15; 8,13–19; 10,10 f.,44 ff. The author of Acts was acquainted with the Palestinian church (21,17, 'we') and gives important, if partial and episodic disclosures of its piety and practice. Cf. J. Dupont, *Gnosis*, Paris 1949, 261 ff.

[90] See above, note 82.

against the powers, against the world rulers of this present darkness, against the spiritual manifestations (πνευματικά) of wickedness in the heavenly warfare.'

The opponents in 2 Corinthians are not isolated teachers but, as their letters of recommendation (3,1) and their self-designation as 'apostles,' 'ministers,' and 'workers' show, they are part of a larger group of missioners[91]. Their antagonism to Paul and his rather strong opinions about them imply that they are workers in a rival mission that Paul has encountered elsewhere. There is, then, a certain presumption that they are associated or identical with false teachers mentioned in other Pauline letters[92].

The opponents in Phil 3, who probably are one group throughout the chapter[93], are described in terminology strikingly similar to that used of the adversaries at Corinth:

2 Corinthians	*Philippians*
4,2 'hidden things of shame'[94].	3,19 'whose glory is in their shame'.
10,7, 18 'being confident in himself,' 'boast according to the flesh.'	3,3 (unlike them) 'we boast in Christ Jesus and put no confidence in the flesh.'
11,13 'deceitful workers'.	3,2 'evil workers'.
11,22 'Are they *Hebraioi?* So am I.'	3,5 (like them, I am) 'a *Hebraios* born of *Hebraioi*.'

With Lütgert one may draw other, less certain inferences from Paul's teachings in Phil 3, especially if one assumes that the in-

---

[91] Georgi, *Gegner*, 31—38, 49 ff.; see above, 3—11 (on the mission praxis).

[92] Like Burton, Baur and Lütgert, Professor Schmithals (*Gnostics*, 242—245) seeks a comprehensive understanding of the opponents as they appear in the various Pauline letters (during the Aegean mission) and assumes one type of opponent unless the sources require a multiplicity. In this he is methodologically quite justified, however one may judge the success of his efforts.

[93] There is no hint in the chapter of a shift to a different type of false teacher. So, Schmithals (*Gnostics*, 85 f.), H. Köster (*NTS* 8, 1962, 318), and J. Gnilka (*BZ* 9, 1965, 276). Most scholars infer two groups of opponents, Judaizers (3,2 f.) and libertines (3,18 f.), because they suppose that one group could not incorporate both tendencies. A few obtain one group by eliminating one tendency or the other.

[94] 'Αἰσχύνη appears in Paul only here and in the Philippian parallel and apparently refers to some kind of ethical corruption, whether greed (cf. 2,17) or deception (11,2 f.) or immorality. A contrast to the practices of the opponents is implied. So, A. Plummer, *Second Corinthians*, Edinburgh 1951 (1915), 111; H. Windisch, *Zweite Korintherbrief*, Göttingen 1970 (1924), 132.

truders in 2 Corinthians share (or come to share) some of the ideas of their Corinthian supporters. But the above parallels are sufficient to show that in both letters Paul refers to 'workers' who combine libertine attitudes and a boasting in their Jewish pedigree, with its attendant ritual strictness and (in Philippians) judaizing tendencies. It is highly probable that the same type of false teacher, if not precisely the same persons, are in view in both letters[95].

Romans (16,17—19) warns against persons that also are described in terms similar to those used in 2 Corinthians and Philippians and Titus. These persons make dissensions against (Paul's) teaching and deceive by fair and flattering words (cf. Tit 1,9 f.; 2Cor 11,3). They do not serve Christ but their own belly (cf. Phil. 3,19), a term that appears to refer to some ethical corruption or a perverse kind of asceticism[96]. They may promote a wrong kind of 'wisdom,' and the defeat of their teaching or the power behind it is a defeat of Satan (cf. 2Cor 11,15). Since the letter was written from Corinth within a few years of 2 Corinthians, at most, the similar descriptions strongly suggest that the same type of opponent is in view[97].

Galatians and Colossians are more problematic. Both letters have a provenance and destination outside of the Aegean basin, and both may stand chronologically at a somewhat greater distance from Paul's Aegean mission[98]. But the importance of these differences can be overdrawn. The total work of Paul, i. e. during

---

[95] This is true whether Philippians is given a dateline of Rome in the early sixties or of Ephesus (or Caesarea) in the later fifties. In either case the false teachers would be workers in the Aegean area well within one decade, whose apostasy and present activities were known to Paul.

[96] Cf. Col 2,21. It cannot refer merely to the observance of Jewish food laws which for Jewish Christians Paul never opposes, or to an ascetic life-style as such, which Paul allows (Rom 14). Nor do the words 'their own' appear to be appropriate for describing a judaizing attitude.

[97] So E. Käsemann, *An die Römer,* Tübingen 1973, 398: the conclusion suggests itself that there occurs here an early battle with heretics which, as in 2Cor 10—13 and Phil 3, is directed against (libertine) gnosticizing Jewish Christians. His conclusion is strengthened if Rom 16 is destined for Ephesus, as seems likely, but if the destination is Rome (so K. P. Donfried, 'A Short Note on Romans 16,' *JBL* 89, 1970, 441—449), it is not rendered improbable.

[98] I take Galatians to have been written before the Jerusalem meeting of Acts 15 (so, F. F. Bruce, 'Galatian Problems. 4. The Date of the Epistle,' *BJRL* 54, 1971—72, 250—267, 266 f.) and, with less certainty, accept the traditional Roman provenance of Colossians.

the period covered by his letters, occupies less than two decades.
If his opponents represent a mission (or a perversion of a mission)
rooted in an important Hebraist segment of the primitive Jerusalem church, as 2 Corinthians indicates, they would not have begun
their work in the mid-fifties and would hardly have limited their
activities to the Aegean area. Admittedly, in the varied atmosphere of the diaspora they may have altered their emphases or
character in this or that time or place. But they could be expected
to have remained reasonably true to type.

In Galatians the false teachers also are outsiders[99]. They bring
'another gospel' (1,6), perhaps based on or supported by angelic
visions (1,8), and persuade some Galatian Christians to serve the
στοιχεῖα by calendrical observances (4,10), to be circumcised (5,2,
12; 6,12 f.) and, thus, to be justified (5,4). To this end they zeal-
ously court (ζηλοῦν) the Galatians, not for their good but to elicit
their allegience to themselves (4,17) so that the false teachers may
'boast (καυχᾶσθαι) in your flesh' (6,13).

Several of these features resemble the *Hebraioi* opponents described in 2 Corinthians: the 'other gospel,' boasting 'according
to the flesh' (2Cor 11,4,18), appeal to (angelic) visions[100], and dis-
paragement of Paul's apostleship[101]. The Galatian Judaizers probably are a part of or related to the group opposing Paul in Gal 2,
who originate in the Jerusalem church[102]. If so, further parallels
with 2 Corinthians (11,20,22,26) appear in the phrases, 'bring us

---

[99] Note the third person; the second person is used when referring to the
Galatians. E. g. 1,7; 5,10,12; 6,12. Cf. F. F. Bruce, 'Galatian Problems. 3. The
"Other" Gospel,' *BJRL* 53 (1970–71), 259 f.; otherwise, J. B. Tyson, 'Paul's
Opponents in Galatia,' *NovT* 10 (1968), 254.

[100] In chapter two above I have sought to show that Paul identifies the
power at work in the pneumatics with angelic spirits (1Cor 14,12,32), and that
in Corinth (and clearly in Colossians) he detects among the pneumatics a tendency to wrongly exalt or misuse these spirits and a failure to distinguish good
from evil spirits (1Cor 12,3). The intruders in Corinth, who impart a 'different
spirit,' probably belong to the same context of pneumatic experience.

[101] 2Cor 10,10: 'weak'; cf. Gal 1,10 ff.,18 ff.: 'from men.'

[102] Bruce ('Other Gospel,' 270 f.) supposes that Judaizers who visited Antioch (Gal 2,12; Acts 15,1) extended their mission on to Antioch's daughter
churches in Galatia. This is likely although 'those from James' (Gal. 2,12)
probably are not Judaizers but only ritually strict Jewish Christians who do
not wish to offend the Judaizing or segregationist faction in their party (Acts
11,2). See below, note 105.

into bondage' and 'false brothers' (2,4), and in the reference to 'the circumcision party' (2,12, οἱ ἐκ περιτομῆς).

The στοιχεῖα (4,3,9) have been identified with the 'elementary teaching' of legal observances (Lightfoot); with 'the law and the flesh' understood as cosmic forces that, prior to Christ, held Jew and Gentile alike under their sway (Bandstra); and with angelic powers standing behind the cosmic elements and/or planetary bodies that regulated the religious life of both Jew and pagan (Schlier, Bruce)[103]. Favoring the interpretation, 'angelic powers,' are (1) the earlier connection of angels with the giving of the law (3,19) and with the 'other gospel' (1,8) and (2) the use of στοιχεῖα in Col 2,8,20 in close association with the invocation of angels and with the angelic 'principalities and powers.' As Schlier (136n.) rightly observed, the role of the angelic στοιχεῖα distinguishes the opponents from a simply ritually-strict Judaism and associates them more with the practices of apocalyptic Judaism and, indeed, with the Qumran Essenes where strict calendrical observances and a studied emphasis upon the role of the angels go hand in hand[104].

The relation of the Galatian opponents to the Essenes is further strengthened if 'the circumcision party' (Gal 2,12) is an equivalent designation for *Hebraioi*, the ritually strict segment of the primitive Jerusalem church[105]. For there is some evidence that the term

---

[103] Cf. G. Delling, *TDNT* 7 (1971), 670–687; Lightfoot, *Galatians, in loc.*; A. J. Bandstra, *The Law and the Elements of the World*, Kampen 1964, 57–68; Bruce, 'Other Gospel,' 266–270; H. Schlier, *An die Galater*, Göttingen 1951, 133–137; E. Lohse, *Colossians and Philemon*, Philadelphia 1971, 96–99. On the angelic regulation of seasons and years in apocalyptic Judaism cf. 1Enoch 43; 60,11–22; 75,3; 2Enoch 19,4; (3Baruch 9,1–4). On verbal similarities with the role of angels at Qumran cf. Y. Yadin, *The Scroll of the War*, Oxford 1962, 241. Cf. W. H. Brownlee, *NTS* 3 (1956–57), 207. The explicit identification of στοιχεῖα with angelic powers apparently does not occur, however, before the second century. Cf. C. F. D. Moule, *To the Colossians and to Philemon*, Cambridge 1958, 90 ff. See above, 41 n.

[104] The role of the angels in regulating the stars does not appear to be clearly attested in the Qumran literature, but 'the concrete contacts in theology, terminology, calendrical peculiarities, and priestly interests [with] Enoch, Jubilees and the Testaments... are so systematic and detailed that we must place the composition of these works within a single line of tradition' (F. M. Cross, *The Ancient Library of Qumran*, Garden City 1961, 199).

[105] See below, 116–122. The phrase οἱ ἐκ περιτομῆς appears in the New Testament at Acts 10,45; 11,2,18 (ritually strict Jewish Christians, some with Judaizing and/or segregationist tendencies); Rom 4,12 (Jews and Jewish Christians); Gal 2,12 (ritually strict Jewish Christians with segregationist or juda-

Hebraios is associated in early Christianity not only with ritual strictness but also with those interested in exalting angelic powers[106].

While the Galatian opponents apparently do not reveal any libertine tendencies[107], they are sufficiently similar to the adversaries in Paul's (later) Corinthian correspondence to warrant the conclusion that they are of the same type. They are not merely Judaizers (Acts 15,5) but Judaizers that combine circumcision and ritual strictness with an unhealthy attention and subservience to angelic powers. Such teaching points more to an Essene and/or Qumran background. In this context it implies an interest in divine γνῶσις even if the term is not used and the interest is less explicit than in Corinthians and Colossians.

'As J. B. Lightfoot suspected, and recent discoveries have confirmed, the error combated by the epistle to the Colossians appears to be tainted with Essenism. A return to the Mosaic Law by circumcision, rigid observance concerning diet and the calendar, speculations about angelic powers; all this is part and parcel of the doctrines of Qumran.'[108] To these words of Père Benoit, one may add the theme of knowledge and wisdom in God's mysteries[109]. Whether the errors in Colossae are the work of (outside) false teachers, as in 2 Corinthians, or — less likely — the result of tendencies within the church, as in 1 Corinthians[110], the situation has

izing tendencies); Col 4,11 (ritually strict but not judaizing Jewish Christians); Tit 1,10 (gnosticizing Judaizers with ascetic and probably immoral practices). Cf. Justin, *Dial* 1,3: Trypho is an Ἑβραῖος ἐκ περιτομῆς. The 'Gospel of the *Hebraioi*,' which appears in the first half of the second century, reflects a Jewish Gnosticism with an emphasis on angelic powers (cf. P. Vielhauer, *New Testament Apocrypha*, ed. W. Schneemelcher, Philadelphia 1963, II, 158—165). The canonical letter 'to the *Hebraioi*' addresses a ritually strict, Jewish Christian group that may tend to exalt angelic powers (Hebr 1,4, 13 f.; 2,5).

[106] See above, note 105. Cf. M. Black, *The Scrolls and Christian Origins*, London 1961, 79; J. H. Moulton and J. Milligan, *Vocabulary of the New Testament*, Grand Rapids 1950, 178.

[107] The warnings in Gal 5,13—21 seem to have no reference to the Judaizers except in so far as any departure from the Spirit and faith results in a state in which the 'works of the flesh' become manifest.

[108] P. Benoit, 'Qumran and the New Testament,' *Paul and Qumran*, ed. J. Murphy-O'Connor, London 1968, 16 f.

[109] E. g. 1QH 2,13—15; 11,9 f.,13; 12,11 ff.; 1QS 4,20,22. Cf. Col 2,2 ff.; W. D. Davies in *The Scrolls and the New Testament*, ed. K. Stendahl, New York 1957, 166—169; *Conflict at Colossae*, ed. F. O. Francis, Missoula (Mont.) 1973.

[110] So, Morna Hooker ('Were there False Teachers in Colossae?' *Christ and*

features similar to the problem in Corinth. Like some Corinthians, some Colossians are seeking 'wisdom and knowledge' (2,2 ff.,23) apart from the centrality of Christ. They are pursuing desirable manifestations of pneumatic gifts (1,9) both by 'philosophical' wisdom (2,8; cf. 1Cor 3,20) and by experiences of vision and/or ecstacy. In both Corinth and Colossae the latter course has resulted in an improper attention being given to the angelic powers, e. g. that mediate the gifts[111]. The Colossians, like the Galatians, take a judaizing (2,16) road of asceticism and apparent humility. But for Paul that attitude, no less than the boastful assurance of the Corinthians, is caused by or results in a person 'vainly puffed up by the mind of his flesh' and primed for a libertine 'indulgence (πλησμονή) of the flesh' (2,18,23; cf. 1Cor 4,8,10,18 f.; 8,1, φυσιοῦν). Just that type of false teacher surfaces in the Pastoral letters.

The Colossian situation is much less extreme. Since the whole pneumatic context of the Pauline mission had affinities with and — via a Christian 'pentecost' — a part of its background in Essene prophetism[112], it was not always easy for Paul to distinguish a deficient teaching in need of helpful correction from what to him was a perverse heresy demanding excision. The Colossian pneumatics have apparently picked up some unhealthy tendencies but are regarded by Paul as genuine and teachable and without the ethical aberrations present in Corinth. This may account for the relatively mild admonitions in the face of potentially dangerous errors. In several respects these errors reflect the type of false teaching found in the earlier Pauline letters: the (Essene) judaizing character, the displacement of Christ from his proper central role, the tendency to misuse and thus to pervert the Christian pneumatic (prophetic) experiences.

The Pastoral letters probably reflect the state of the Pauline

---

Spirit in the New Testament, in honour of C. F. D. Moule, ed. B. Lindars and S. S. Smalley, Cambridge 1973, 315–331), who thinks that the Colossians are only 'under pressure to conform to the beliefs and practices of their pagan and Jewish neighbours' (329). It seems, however, that the τίς (2,8,16; cf. 2,4,18) alludes to false teachers who already are present or who may soon appear to exploit a weakness in the church. For a more probable case against opponents in Thessalonica cf. E. Best, *Thessalonians*, New York 1972, 16–22.

[111] Col 2,18; cf. 1Cor 14,12 (πνεύματα). See above, 69 ff.

[112] See above, 30–36.

mission in the Aegean basin in the mid-sixties of the first century[113]. Throughout the letters the false teachers represent one
general type of opposition[114]. Some are from 'the circumcision
party' (Tit 1,10; cf. Col 4,11), and others represent a defection
from a Pauline viewpoint. Cf. 1Tim 1,3; 2Tim 1,15 f.; 2,17; cf. 4,
10. Unlike the earlier letters, the opponents appear to include a
considerable number of former co-workers whose apostasy creates
an especially bitter situation.

They are 'teachers of the law' who engage in disputes about it
and, in haggadic fashion, indulge in Jewish 'fables (μῦθοι) and
genealogies.' Cf. 1Tim 1,4,7; 6,4; 2Tim 2,14,23; Tit 1,14; 3,9.
That they are pneumatics is confirmed in the claim to give γνῶσις
and in Paul's application to them of an earlier oracle, i. e. that
their teaching is the product of 'erring spirits and teachings of
demons' that brings one into the 'snare of the devil.' Cf. 1Tim
4,1–3,7 (2Cor 11,4,18); 6,20; 2Tim 2,26; cf. 3,8,13, γόητες; Gal
3,1, βασκαίνειν. They are 'puffed up' (τυφοῦσθαι), motivated by
greed, and promote a perverse asceticism that issues, perhaps, in a
subtle licentiousness. Cf. 1Tim 4,3; 6,4 f.; 2Tim 3,4 ff.; Tit 1,11
(Phil 3,19).

The description of the false teaching differs considerably from
earlier Pauline letters. There are few verbal parallels and no references to (angelic) visions or ecstatic phenomena. The haggadic exposition of Scripture and the opposition of Paul's own converts
and co-workers also is hardly found elsewhere, although intima-
tions of the latter appear in Corinthians and Philippians (3,18).
Nevertheless, the description does conform in some measure to the
type of error encountered in the other letters. The opponents are
pneumatics. Like Colossians, there is an (even more rigid) asceticism reminiscent of some Essenes and, like Corinthians, there is a

---

[113] The non-Pauline literary expression and theological emphases look more
like an amanuensis incorporating traditions of Paul's circle under the Apostle's
eye in the sixties than like a later 'disciple' exercising his second century imagination about Paul's work in the sixties or about Paul's attitude toward issues
in the pseudepigrapher's own time. Cf. J. N. D. Kelly, *The Pastoral Epistles*,
London 1963, 6–10, 30–34; W. Metzger, *Die letzte Reise . . . Paulus*, Stuttgart
1976.

[114] So, Kelly, *Pastoral*, 10 f.; M. Dibelius–H. Conzelmann, *The Pastoral
Epistles*, Philadelphia 1972, 65 ff. Otherwise: W. Lock, *The Pastoral Epistles*,
Edinburgh 1952 (1924), XVII.

licentious tendency and a claim to give γνῶσις whose source Paul believes to be 'another spirit,' an 'erring' demonic spirit.

V.

The Pauline mission was an enterprise of pneumatics, persons who claimed special understanding of the Scripture and who experienced manifestations of inspired, ecstatic speech and of visions and revelations. The primary opposition to that mission arose from within a segment of the ritually strict *Hebraioi* in the Jerusalem church and with variations in nuance continued to pose, sometimes as a counter mission and sometimes as an infiltrating influence, a settled and persistent 'other' gospel. It also laid claim to pneumatic powers and experiences. Each group claimed to be the true voice of Jesus, each claimed to give the true γνῶσις of God and, on occasion, each made its higher appeal to apostolic status. It was, in a word, a battle of prophets, and the congregations were called upon to choose — Paul or his opposition. The dust of their warfare has settled and history has recorded the choice of the churches, at least of the continuing churches. If scholars are still drawn to the ancient debate and to the issues it raised, they are influenced in no small part, one suspects, by the attraction of the one unsilenced voice in the conflict, Paul the Jew of Tarsus, who in his letters continues the battle for his Messiah.

7. THE CIRCUMCISION PARTY AND THE EARLY CHRISTIAN MISSION

In the preceding chapter it was observed that Paul's opponents are sometimes designated *Hebraioi* or Hebrews, sometimes 'those of the circumcision' or the circumcision party. The two terms may now be investigated more closely. If they prove to be parallel or equivalent designations, this fact will shed considerable light not only on the identity and relationship of the opponents but also on the broader structure of the early Christian mission.

I.

Col 4,11 identifies certain of Paul's co-workers as 'those of the circumcision', οἱ ἐκ περιτομῆς. The expression appears six times in the New Testament, always in Acts or the Pauline epistles, including one instance in the Pastorals[1].

The phrase apparently does not occur in the Septuagint nor in the intertestamental literature. A passage in Justin's *Dialogue with Trypho* (1,3) is the earliest parallel in the patristic writings[2]. There Trypho identifies himself as 'a Hebrew of the circumcision', Ἑβραῖος ἐκ περιτομῆς. Cf. Eusebius *HE* 3,4,2.

Turning to the biblical usage, at Acts 10,45; 11,2 the commentaries often identify 'those of the circumcision' simply as Jewish Christians[3]. But it is more likely that Ac 11,2 at least, refers to a particular kind of Jewish believer[4]. For it alludes to a dispute not

---

[1] Acts 10,45; 11,2; Rom 4,12; Gal 2,12; Col 4,11; Tit 1,10.

[2] Eusebius (citing Hegesippus?) later uses phrase for Hebrew believers (ἐξ Ἑβραίων πιστῶν), i. e., orthodox Jewish Christians in the Jerusalem church during A. D. 70—135. Cf. Eusebius, *HistEccl* 3,35; 4,5,2—5; 6,4.

[3] E. g., E. Haenchen, *Acts*, Philadelphia 1971.

[4] So, F. J. Foakes Jackson, *The Acts of the Apostles*, New York 1931, 97;

between Jewish and Gentile Christians but between two groups in the Jerusalem church[5].

The Pauline references are diverse. Rom 4,12 apparently refers to Jews. It names Abraham the father 'of the circumcision' who not only are ἐκ περιτομῆς but also have a faith like Abraham's. In Gal 2,12 and Titus 1,10, where opponents of Paul are in view, those of the circumcision are best understood of a faction of Jewish Christians[6]. In Titus they are gnosticizing Judaizers[7]. In Galatians they no doubt include Judaizers but probably, like those in Acts 21,20 who are 'zealous for the law', they represent a wider group of ritually strict Jewish Christians[8]. A wider definition certainly is required at Col 4,11 where 'those of the circumcision' are Paul's co-workers. In Colossians the expression customarily is taken to refer merely to Jewish Christians[9], but this definition is in no way self-evident. And it does not accord with the meaning of the phrase elsewhere.

In its New Testament usage, then, οἱ ἐκ περιτομῆς presents something of a puzzle. It seems to be a specific, almost technical designation. Yet none of the usual definitions will fit in all instances. The connection that Justin Martyr makes between ἐκ περιτο-

A. Wikenhauser, *Die Apostelgeschichte*, Münster 1951, 101; cf. F. F. Bruce, *The Acts of the Apostles*, London 1951, 229.

[5] The criticism, 'eating' with Gentiles, is raised again in Gal 2,12 by 'those of the circumcision'. But here it is withdrawn; for Luke οἱ ἐκ περιτομῆς apparently are not Judaizers (Acts 11,3,18; cf. 15,5).

[6] Some take Gal 2,12 to refer to Jews. E. g., J. Munck, *Paul and the Salvation of Mankind*, London 1959, 107; W. Schmithals, *Paul and James*, London 1965. Schmithals correctly identifies 'those of the circumcision' with a third party and not with the messengers 'from James'. But probably it is a mistake to view them, following G. Dix (*Jew and Greek*, London 1955, 42 ff.), as hostile Jews. The danger that James fears is Christian schism, not Jewish persecution. (That was present quite apart from this issue; cf. Acts 12,2 f.). Acts 21,17 to 26 points to the nature of his anxiety. Some of 'those of the circumcision', i. e., ritualist Jewish-Christians and not only Judaizers, probably are saying things about Peter in Antioch that they will say later about Paul in Asia.

[7] W. Lock (*The Pastoral Epistles*, Edinburgh 1936, XVII) suggests that the gnosticizing and Judaizing teachers are separate groups. But some connection between them, if not an identification of them, is highly probable (see above, 114).

[8] As J. B. Lightfoot (*Epistle to the Galatians*, London 1905, 114) observed, Gal 2,14 does not accuse Peter (or 'the circumcision party') of being Judaizers. The meaning is only that, if Jewish Christians segregate themselves, the effect will be to force Gentile Christians to judaize in order to maintain the unity of Christian fellowship. So, Schmithals, *op. cit.*, 57.

[9] I noted no exceptions in the literature that I consulted.

μῆς and Ἑβραῖος may offer a clue for a wider New Testament investigation.

Ἑβραῖος appears in three New Testament passages. Ac 6,1 contrasts the Hebrews with the Hellenists. Traditionally these two terms have been identified with Jewish Christians who spoke Aramaic and Greek respectively[10]. Since synagogues 'of the Hebrews' existed among Greek speaking Jews, however, some suppose that the distinctiveness of that group was its Palestinian background and connections rather than its language[11]. But then one must ask whether the diaspora grandchildren, long removed from Palestine, would change the name of the synagogue[12]. Recently O. Cullmann and W. Schmithals have argued that the expressions, Hebrews and Hellenists, point primarily to distinctive attitudes toward the Jewish cultus and customs[13]. This seems to explain best the terminology and the context of Acts, however one may judge their elaborations of this insight. That is, Hebrews designated those Jews with a strict, ritualist, viewpoint; and Hellenists those with a freer

---

[10] This interpretation occurs as early as Chrysostom (Homily 14 on Acts 6,1); cf. Haenchen, *Acts*, 260 n.

[11] Cf. J. Moffatt, *The Epistle to the Hebrews*, Edinburgh 1924, XVII; F. J. Foakes Jackson and K. Lake, *The Beginnings of Christianity*, London 1920 to 1933, V, 62 n (Cadbury); M. Dibelius, *An die Philipper*, Tübingen 1937, 87. H. Lietzmann—W. G. Kümmel, *An die Korinther I, II*, Tübingen 1949, 150, 211: in the diaspora — Rome, Corinth — gravestones written in Greek identify the deceased as a member of the 'synagogue of the Hebrews', i. e., a particular colony of Palestinian Jews. E. Haenchen (*Acts*, 260, 266 f.), combines the two interpretations: Hellenists were diaspora Jews who spoke Greek; Hebrews were Palestinian born Jews who spoke Aramaic.

[12] Cf. Munck, *op. cit.*, 218. While in Acts 6,9 some congregations are organized along 'national' lines, the synagogue of the Libertines suggests a different basis, perhaps including ritual or cultic distinctions.

[13] O. Cullmann, *The Scrolls and the New Testament*, ed. K. Stendahl, New York 1957, 25–28; Schmithals, *op. cit.*, cf. H. J. Schoeps, *Das Judenchristentum*, Bern 1964, 50. For earlier pointers in this direction cf. J. B. Lightfoot, *Epistle to the Philippians*, London 1891, 147 ('Εβραῖος signified one who spoke Hebrew and retained Hebrew customs); Foakes Jackson and Lake, *op. cit.*, IV, 64 (Lake and Cadbury); H. Windisch, *TDNT* II, 508. Similarly, M. Black, *The Scrolls and Christian Origins*, London 1961, 79; D. Georgi, *Die Gegner des Paulus im 2. Korintherbrief*, Neukirchen 1964, 55: the description 'Hebrew' often appears in hellenistic-Jewish apologetic literature 'wo eine *bestimmte Lebensweise* in den Blick genommen ist'. However, following K. G. Kuhn and W. Gutbrot, he ties this together with language and geography (58; cf. *TDNT* III, 368 ff., 374 ff.). His examples do not directly meet the New Testament situation since in them the term apparently is not used to distinguish certain Jews from other Jews. But they do illustrate a part of the background.

attitude toward the Jewish Law and cultus[14]. The hypothesis of the present chapter builds upon this interpretation.

The two other passages, in which the Ἑβραῖοι appear as opponents of Paul, are open to the same interpretation. In 2Cor 11 it is not clear that they are merely Judaizers, as usually has been supposed[15]. But certainly they regard themselves as a special type of

---

[14] Several facts favor this interpretation. 1) Both strict and lax attitudes toward the Law and cultus are known to have existed not only in the diaspora but also in Palestine. Cf. O. Cullmann, *op. cit.*, 19; W. D. Davies, *Paul and Rabbinic Judaism*, London 1948, 5—8; E. R. Goodenough, *Jewish Symbols in the Greco-Roman Period*, New York 1953, I, 53, 111, 115, 264—67; Schmithals, *op. cit.*, H. J. Schoeps, *Paul*, London 1961, 35. 2) Stephen's martyrdom and the following persecution grew out of his words 'against this holy place and the law' (Acts 6,13), and the persecution apparently was principally against (but not limited to) Hellenist Christians (Acts 8,1; 9,31). This is best understood if the Jews interpreted the Hellenist Christian polemic in the context of a known Hellenist laxity toward the cultus. The chief persecutor is Paul 'the Hebrew'. 3) The dispute in Acts 6 probably is not viewed by Luke as an isolated event. It is related to the continuing tension in the Jerusalem church, a tension that clearly concerns the cultus (Acts 11,3—7; 15,5—21; 21,20—26). 4) The substantive, Hellenist, probably has some connection with the meaning of its verb form, i. e., to live as a Greek and not just to speak Greek (Cullmann). However, the question is difficult since, apart from Acts, the substantive does not appear in any pre-Nicene literature. Cf. Foakes Jackson and Lake, *op. cit.*, V, 59 f. (Cadbury). See above, 106 f.; below, 245 f.

[15] E. g., A. Plummer, *Second Epistle of St. Paul to the Corinthians*, Edinburgh 1915, XXXVI—XLI; Lietzmann—Kümmel, *op. cit.*, 1—11, 211. The identification is much disputed. J. Munck (*op. cit.*, 175—87) has shown how easy it is to overestimate their role in Second Corinthians and how difficult it is to identify their doctrinal viewpoint. But it is a mistake (176 ff.) to disassociate these opponents (2Cor 11,5) from false teaching (2Cor 11,4) and from the persons with letters of recommendation (2Cor 3,1). If Paul does not attack their teachings, Munck himself has given a sufficient reason: those teachings are not now at issue between Paul and the Corinthians (186). Likewise, D. Georgi's (*op. cit.*, 148 f.) well ordered arguments against the 'Judaizer' hypothesis show only that those questions were not at issue. Georgi (cf. 245, 249 ff., 303) seeks the background of the opponents in 'hellenistic-Jewish apologetic'. While this is not impossible, the difficulty is to define that term with some precision and then to point out teachings in Second Corinthians that are best interpreted from such a background. The high regard for visions, which also is present in rabbinic Judaism (cf. W. D. Davies, *op. cit.*, 198, 210 ff.), and for Spirit charisms (2Cor 12,1,11 f.), is most immediately located not in Jewish mysticism or legalism but in the eschatological, pentecostal roots of Christianity itself. Cf. Acts 2,17; 7,30 f.; 9,3; 10,10 f.; 18,9; Col 2,18. Also, the glorification of Moses (2Cor 3) and the customs (2Cor 11,22) was from the beginning characteristic of the strict, traditionalist element of Jewish Christianity. Cf. Acts 15,5,21; 21,20 f. If Judaizer is too precise an identification of the opponents, apologists in the tradition of hellenistic Judaism also appears to be a bit wide of the mark. G.

Jewish Christian, superior to the common herd[16]. They have either joined with[17] or are sympathetic to the gnosticizing[18] element that Paul faced in First Corinthians. Likewise, Paul's claim to be 'a Hebrew' in Phil 3,5 probably presupposes a similar claim to superiority by those judaizing opponents[19]. If so, the opposition both in Second Corinthians and in Philippians is characterized as 'Hebrews' who are evil 'workers' and whose boasting is 'in the flesh'[20]. Probably they belong to the same circle although they may not occupy precisely the same part of it[21].

There are a number of similarities also between the heretical Ἑβραῖοι in Second Corinthians and Philippians and the heretical οἱ ἐκ περιτομῆς in Galatians and Titus. Both are persuasive speak-

---

Friedrich's more specific identification of the opponents with the Christian Hellenists of Acts 6—8 removes some but not all of the above objections. Cf. G. Friedrich in: *Abraham unser Vater, Festschrift für O. Michel*, Leiden 1962, 196—215.

[16] 2Cor 11,22. Only on this understanding would the claim to be 'Hebrews' have any weight over against a Jewish missionary like Paul. For the same reason the letters of recommendation probably point to Palestinian, if not Jerusalem, credentials. Cf. Acts 15,22 ff.; Gal 2,1 f. But, of course, they are not necessarily from the apostolic leaders there.

[17] So, Lietzmann—Kümmel, *op. cit.*, 211. H. Windisch (*Der Zweite Korintherbrief*, Göttingen 1924, 25 ff.) thinks that the two groups may have combined even before First Corinthians was written. The Marcionite prologue to First Corinthians gives some support to this. It identifies Paul's opponents as false apostles, 'quidam a philosophiae verbosa eloquentia, alii a secta legis Judaicae inducti' (cited in Lietzmann—Kümmel, *op. cit.*, 221). Cf. Schoeps, *Paul*, 76 n. The same problem is present in the Pastorals (see above, note 7) and in the Ignatian letters. In both it is likely that the judaizing and gnosticizing opponents are the same group. Cf. J. B. Lightfoot, *The Apostolic Fathers, Second Part: St. Ignatius*, London 1889, I, 374—78; see above, 92 f., 108 f.

[18] Cf. Lietzmann-Kümmel, *op. cit.*, 192; J. Moffatt, *The First Epistle of Paul to the Corinthians*, London 1938, 143 f. See above, 103 f.

[19] E. Lohmeyer (*Der Brief an die Philipper . . .*, Göttingen 1954 (1930), 126) identifies the opponents in Phil 3 as Jewish agitators. More likely, however, they are judaizing Christians, perhaps Pharisees (Phil 3,3,5; cf. Acts 15,5) whose error is bound up with cultic practices (λατρεύοντες). Significantly, his status as a 'Hebrew' is one of those gains that Paul counted as loss for the sake of Christ (Phil 3,7); and his affiliation with the Pharisees is mentioned only in this passage.

[20] 2Cor 11,13,18; Phil 3,2 f.; cf. Gal 6,13 f. On the broader issue of Paul's opponents, see above, 80—115.

[21] It is true, of course, that all bad pastors do not necessarily belong to the same group (Georgi). But when a writer in a relatively small and close-knit religious movement describes opponents in the same area at about the same time with similar and distinctive terminology, very likely there is some connection between them. Also, see above, 110—114.

ers (2Cor 11,6; Tit 1,10) who present themselves as advocates of righteousness (2Cor 11,15; Gal 2,21). But in truth they are mutilators (Phil 3,2; Gal 5,12) who for selfish gain (Phil 3,19; Tit 1,11) preach another gospel (2Cor 11,4; Gal 1,6). It is a gospel that for both is tied up with Jewish legalism (Phil 3,2 f.; Gal 3,2 f.). Interestingly, the Hebrews apparently show gnosticizing tendencies (or alliances) in Second Corinthians, less so in Philippians where their judaizing character is in the foreground; those of the circumcision show gnosticizing tendencies in Titus but less so in Galatians where their judaizing character is in the foreground. In Acts both groups are well regarded Jewish Christians, although a particular type of Jewish Christian.

Several writers recently have shown that both strict and lax attitudes toward the Law and the cultus co-existed in pre-Christian Judaism, in Palestine as well as in the diaspora[22]. I suggest that 'the Hebrews' and 'those of the circumcision' were equivalent designations for Jews or, in our case, Jewish Christians with a strict attitude toward the Jewish cultus and customs[23]. In the beginning they belonged to the mainstream of Christianity. Indeed, in their opinion they were the most orthodox, 'zealous for the law' (Acts 21,20). Yet, very quickly the Christian Hebrews divided into factions. Some, like James, accepted Hellenist and Gentile Christians without requiring them to adhere to the Law. Others insisted that all followers of Messiah must obey the Law or, at least, practice

---

[22] See above, note 14.

[23] Apparently they also had ascetic tendencies. This is implied in Rom 14,2, 5,21, where the observance of days is tied to the abstinence from meat and wine. Very likely the persons in view are the strict Jewish element in the Roman church, i. e., 'those of the circumcision' (Rom 4,12) who already are questioning Paul's teaching about justification apart from the Law (Rom 3, 8,31). In Rom 14 (and in 1Cor 8,7 ff.; 9,20; 10,32) Paul urges a regard for the 'weaker' Jewish brother. Nevertheless, the principle has its limits and, in the Pastorals, where 'those of the circumcision' (Tit 1,10) have made asceticism a requirement, Paul condemns it (1Tim 4,3 ff.; cf. Rom 14,14; 1Cor 10,26,29 f.; 1Tim 5,23). The essential identity of the false teachers in First Timothy and in Titus is quite probable; cf. J. N. D. Kelly, *The Pastoral Epistles*, London 1963, 10 f.; Dibelius–Conzelmann, *op. cit.* According to Hegesippus (Eusebius, *Hist-Eccl* 2, 23,5 f.) James of Jerusalem was a non-drinker and a vegetarian. Such tendencies probably are the antecedents of later ascetic practices in Jewish Christianity. Cf. J. Daniélou, *The Theology of Jewish Christianity*, London 1964, 370 ff. On the 'Hebrew' background of such asceticism cf. Black, *op. cit.*, 83—88.

circumcision. Still a more complex, gnosticizing-libertine tendency, comes into view in Paul's letters[24].

II.

Both Hebrews and Hellenists apparently were present in pre-Christian Palestinian Judaism[25]. And we must suppose that from the beginning both groups were represented among the followers of Jesus[26]. Their differences made necessary, also from the beginning, some measure of diversity in the organization and worship of the post-Pentecost Church[27]. This is presupposed in the problem

[24] The development is apparent in Acts 15 where there are three viewpoints, all Jewish Christian. Besides Paul and Barnabas (the Hellenists), James and the moderate Hebrews are set over against some of 'the party of the Pharisees', the judaizing Hebrews. Cf. W. G. Kümmel, *Religion in Geschichte und Gegenwart³*, ed. K. Galling, Tübingen 1959, III, 969; Schoeps, *Paul*, 66—70. This twofold character of the Hebrews is mentioned by Justin (*Dial* 47): some observe circumcision and the other traditions (τὰ ἔννομα) but do not force their views on Gentile Christians; others refuse fellowship to any who do not keep their traditions. The differences among the Hebrews, i. e., those of the circumcision, explain their ambiguous role in Paul's letters. The third tendency apparently represents a libertine development among certain Judaizers in the diaspora mission, a development that found a doctrinal justification and elaboration, e. g. in a denial of the resurrection (1Cor 15,12; cf. 2Tim 2,18), partly in a Platonic-dualistic view of man. See above, 101—115.

[25] The names appear, respectively, in inscriptions and Justin's *Dialogue* (1,3) and in Acts (9,29; cf. 11,20) as non-Christian Jewish groups.

[26] Cf. Cullmann, *op. cit.*, 30. See below, 245 f.

[27] Schmithals (*op. cit.*) rightly recognizes this. But he supposes that the *gesetzesfreie* Christian Hellenists originated in Galilee; the Jerusalem setting of Acts is a Lukan *Tendenz* (28 ff., 36). However, this reconstruction is quite unnecessary in view of Schmithals' (22 f., 29) own evidence of a Hellenist Judaism in Jerusalem. Very likely both groups were native to both places. Cf. Schoeps, *Judenchristentum*, 26. In any case the 'freedom from the Law' of Christian Hellenists, whether Stephen or Paul, did not derive from the cultic attitudes of Jewish Hellenists. It arose from Christian eschatological convictions concerning the meaning of Jesus' resurrection, as W. Manson has shown (*The Epistle to the Hebrews*, London 1951, 29—36). This is no less true even if Christians with a Hellenist background were more disposed to accept such an interpretation. (But Paul, the former Hebrew, provides an outstanding contrary example). Indeed, if there were 'primary' and 'secondary' elements in the Jerusalem church, Hellenists would have the best claim to priority. For their attitude to the Law and the cultus has more in common with Jesus' pre-resurrection teaching than that of the Hebrews. Cf. H. Conzelmann, *Die Apostelgeschichte*, Tübingen 1963, 43; B. Gärtner, *The Temple and the Community in Qumran and in the New Testament*, Cambridge 1965, 120 ff.

of the widows in Acts 6[28]. While the mission to the Gentiles complicated the problem, the tension in the Church between the Hebrews and the Hellenists continued quite apart from the Gentile question. This is evident both in Paul's letters and in Acts 21[29].

The differences in ritual and discipline between the Hebrews and the Hellenists have important implications for the structure of the early Christian mission and for the theological developments and aberrations within it[30]. Given the division in the Jerusalem church, it is not improbable that the mission to the diaspora likewise would have a twofold character. The Hebrews would evangelize the ritually strict congregations. The Hellenists would direct their activities toward the less strict Jewish groups and, of course, the Gentiles.

Several items of evidence give a measure of support to this hypothesis. Paul's debate with the Jerusalem Hellenists (Acts 9,29) may, for Luke, point to the kind of Jews that the Apostle's mission ordinarily will include. Following the Alexandrian reading at Acts 11,20, F. J. A. Hort thought that the Hellenists of Antioch, to whom Paul later ministered, perhaps had a separate organization and were the objects of 'a special mission to them by Cyprians and Cyrenians, themselves Hellenists, as a part of the general evangelisation'[31]. Similarly, synagogues of the Hebrews, known to exist in the diaspora, could have provided a setting for a special evangelization of that group.

---

[28] Conzelmann (*op. cit.*, 43) argues that the structure must have been recognizable to outsiders since (*pace* Munck, *op. cit.*, 225) the persecution of Acts 8 was directed solely against the Hellenist Christians.

[29] Paul regards the Judaizers as a threat not only to Gentile Christians but also to his own liberty in Christ. Cf. 1Cor 10,29; Gal 2,4: 'that they might bring *us* into bondage'; Acts 21,21.

[30] The identification of 'those of the circumcision' argued above also removes the most important support for the view that Luke was a Gentile (Col 4,11.14). Cf. E. E. Ellis, *Luke*, London ²1974, 51 ff.

[31] F. J. A. Hort, *Judaistic Christianity*, London 1904, 59, cf. 58 ff. Hort thought it probable that the 'Ιουδαῖοι in Antioch corresponded to the Hebrews of Acts 6. They, like their Jerusalem counterparts, were set in contrast to the Hellenists in Antioch, who may have included Godfearers. In support of the reading, Hellenist, Hort argued: 1) the manuscript evidence favors it; 2) Luke would represent a turning to the Greeks with a more formal statement (cf. Acts 13,46); 3) the phraseology resembles Acts 9,29 where Paul debates with the Hellenists. Cf. B. F. Westcott and F. J. A. Hort, *The New Testament in the Original Greek: Appendix*, London 1882, 93 f.

The hypothesis of a twofold diaspora mission also clarifies several Pauline texts. Col 4,11 would then reveal, to use a modern term, a venture in ecumenical Christianity. Here, as probably also was the case in Antioch[32], Paul and certain Hebrews were pursuing their distinctive missions in a cooperative fashion[33]. In a negative way Paul's Hebrew opponents in Second Corinthians also fit the picture of a twofold Christian mission. For, as D. Georgi has observed, it is likely that they are not isolated figures but representatives of a large group of missionaries[34]. Unfortunately Acts and the Pauline letters present only one side of the picture, the mission of the Hellenists. Therefore, for the most part, the diaspora mission of the circumcision party comes into view only in its aberrant judaizing and/or gnosticizing form.

It is difficult to estimate the degree to which the diaspora mission kept to a twofold pattern. Probably there was considerable overlapping. But it is clear that differences in ritual and custom were from the beginning a widespread problem and posed very quickly a major threat to the unity of the Church[35]. The problem did not concern just the Pauline churches; for it was present, for example, in Antioch and Rome. And it was not just a problem between Jews and Gentiles, for Paul identifies himself with those who are free from the Law and from the obligations of the Jewish ritual[36].

---

[32] The probability does not arise solely from Acts 11,20 (above). The division of labor between Peter and Paul in Gal 2,7 ff. is usually understood of a Jewish and a Gentile mission. But Paul never regards his mission as limited to Gentiles (1Cor 9,20; 2Cor 11,22 f.; Acts, passim). It is possible, therefore, that 'the circumcision' also is only a special sector of the mission of Peter *and James* and, like Gal 2,12, refers not to Jews in general but to the ritually strict Hebrews.

[33] From Paul's words, 'these alone', it appears that the effort was failing. There is little evidence that travelling missionaries deliberately organized as Hebrew/Hellenist teams although that may be the situation of Paul and Mark earlier (Acts 13,5). See below, 234 ff.   [34] Georgi, *op. cit.*, 218.

[35] The discussion of 'foods' and 'days' in Romans, Corinthians, Galatians, Colossians, the Pastorals, and Hebrews witnesses to the widespread nature of the problem. Cf. Rom 14,1; 1Cor 8—10; Gal 4,10; Col 2,16; 1Tim 4,3 ff.; Hebr 9,9 f.; 13,9. Likewise, the Apostolic Decree in Acts 15 very likely is to be understood of cultic proprieties rather than moral principles. So, recently, C. S. C. Williams, *The Acts of the Apostles*, London 1964, 183. The repetition of the Decree in Acts 21 fits same pattern. There a similar 'ritual' request is asked of the Hellenists (not of the Gentiles) by the Hebrews.

[36] Cf. 1Cor 9,20 f.; 10,29; Rom 14,5,14.

R. H. Strachan, among others, rightly saw a connection between Paul's opponents in Second Corinthians and similar elements in Romans (cf. 3,8; 16,17 f.), Galatians (cf. 4,10) and Colossians (cf. 2,16). He went on to relate this opposition to a Philonic type Judaism that combined devotion to the Law with an interest in speculative philosophy[37]. Such influences cannot be excluded but it is doubtful that they play a large role[38]. The primary and more direct background of such tendencies probably lies within the Christian movement. And it could well have its origin in legalistic, Palestinian circles. Recent studies have shown that the traditional dichotomy between an orthodox Palestinian and a hellenized diaspora Judaism cannot be maintained[39]. Nor is it possible to make a simple equation between first century Jewish legalism and the anti-syncretistic legalism of later rabbinic writings[40]. E. R. Goodenough has called attention to the fact that the Pharisees, who in manners and customs sharply resisted hellenization, were in parts of their theology (e. g., anthropology and eschatology) deeply influenced by hellenistic religious ideas[41]. One receives a similar impression of the Hebrews in Acts and the Pauline letters. Not only are they prone to judaizing[42]. In the diaspora, at least, they are

---

[37] R. H. Strachan, *The Second Epistle of Paul to the Corinthians*, London 1935, XXII—XXVIII; cf. Philo, *De migr. Abr.* 89—94. See above, 50 n., 85, 101—115.

[38] The difficulties surrounding D. Georgi's similar hypothesis also apply here (see above, note 15). In addition, the similarities between Philo and the Sadducees, noted by E. R. Goodenough (*By Light Light*, New Haven 1935, 78—80), do not fit Paul's opponents.

[39] See above, note 14; see below, 245 f.

[40] Rabbinic Judaism itself did not escape the infiltration of Gnostic ideas. Cf. the literature cited in W. D. Davies, *The Setting of the Sermon on the Mount*, Cambridge 1964, 193 n. Like the patristic Church, it was both in reaction against and influenced by Gnostic currents of thought.

[41] Cf. Goodenough, *Light*, 6; E. E. Ellis, *NTS* 10 (1963—64), 277 n.

[42] M. Friedländer (*Die religiösen Bewegungen innerhalb des Judentums im Zeitalter Jesu*, Berlin 1905, 31—34) argued that the proselyting zeal of the Pharisees was not to make converts to Judaism but to make legalists out of persons already won to Judaism. Cf. Josephus, *Ant.* 20, 38—48. Jesus' condemnation in Mt 23,15 is only thus to be understood. So W. C. Allen, *The Gospel according to Matthew*, Edinburgh 1912, 246; P. Bonnard, *L'Évangile selon S. Matthieu*, Paris 1963, 338. The thesis probably is correct although it may be overstated. (Cf. the discussion in the schools of Hillel and Shammai on the baptism of proselytes, e. g., Pes 8,8; Edu 5,2; cf. H. L. Strack—P. Billerbeck, *Kommentar zum Neuen Testament*, München 1922, I, 102—13). One observes, therefore, a certain similarity of method between the Pharisees and the Judaizers

the source or supporters of gnosticizing-libertine tendencies. That is, such syncretistic developments found their earliest and most rapid growth in Christianity not, as has been supposed[43], among the Hellenists but among the Hebrews; not among those who were free with regard to the ritual Law but among those who were most strict in their observance of the Law and who prided themselves in their legitimacy[44]. If valid, this conclusion raises a question about the continued usefulness of such a term as 'hellenistic Jewish-Christian' syncretism.

It would strengthen the hypothesis proposed here if one could find New Testament evidence, apart from Acts and the Pauline letters, for ritually strict and segregated Jewish Christian communities in the diaspora. Two examples may be suggested. Although usually assigned simply to Jewish-Christianity[45], some Matthean traditions and perhaps the Gospel of Matthew itself belong more specifically to ritually strict Jewish Christians[46]. No less than the

---

who preyed on Paul's converts. Cf. also the advice of Trypho the 'Hebrew' to Justin (*Dial* 8): first be circumcised then observe... the Sabbaths and the feasts and the new moons...' The first part of the *Dialogue* largely concerns Jewish Law and customs, and the identification of Trypho as 'a Hebrew' probably signifies something more than just 'a Jew'.

[43] E. g., Cullmann, *op. cit.*, 18—32; cf. Daniélou, *op. cit.*, 72. For a criticism of Cullmann's thesis cf. Haenchen, *op. cit.*, 214. Black (*op. cit.*, 75—81) has shown that the Hebrews provide a more probable link than the Hellenists between the Jerusalem Christians and the 'non-conformist Judaism' represented by Qumran.

[44] This accords with the testimony of patristic writers who connect the origins of Christian Gnosticism with Judaism. Later Jewish Christian heresies likewise continued to reflect combinations of anti-Pauline, legalistic, ascetic and/or Gnostic currents. Cf. Irenaeus, *AdvHaer* 1,26,2; 3,11,1; Origen, *c. Celsum*, V,65; Eusebius, *HistEccl*, 3,27; 4,22,4—7 (Hegesippus); Daniélou, *op. cit.* 55—58, 63, 69 ff. See above 84, 92 n.

[45] E. g., G. D. Kilpatrick, *The Origins of the Gospel according to Matthew*, Oxford 1946, 124; R. Hummel, *Die Auseinandersetzung zwischen Kirche und Judentum im Matthäusevangelium*, München 1963, 26 ff. H. J. Schoeps (*Judentum*, 15) would reserve the name, Jewish Christianity, to the strict, segregating party.

[46] It is not sufficient, of course, to point to linguistic or 'Palestinian' peculiarities although they may be concurrent features. However, Matthew's special traditions give considerable attention to questions relating to the Jewish cultus. Cf. Mt 5,23 f.,33—37; 6,1—8,16—18; 17,24—27; 23,3,16—22; G. Bornkamm, G. Barth, H. J. Held, *Tradition and Interpretation in Matthew*, London 1963, 86 to 92. And as a whole the Gospel reflects both sympathy for and intimate acquaintance with Jewish traditions. Cf. Hummel, *op. cit.*, 53—56, 78—82. At

circumcision party, i. e. the Hebrews of Acts and the Pauline letters, the Church of St. Matthew is deeply concerned with questions of the Jewish cultus and customs[47].

For a second example we may return to the term Ἑβραῖος. Apart from the passages mentioned above, the word appears once more in the New Testament. It is in the title of the letter πρὸς Ἑβραίους. Some years ago my former teacher, William Manson, advanced the thesis that these Jewish Christians were products of the world mission of Stephen and the Hellenists. Later, in reaction against the gospel of freedom from the Law they adopted attitudes similar to the Hebrews of the Jerusalem church. The letter, Manson concluded, seeks to retrieve these Christians from a new en-

---

the same time there is a heightened polemic against the Pharisees. Cf. Kilpatrick, *op. cit.*, 106—23; Allen, *op. cit.* L—LIX.

We may agree with Davies (*Sermon*, 330) that these peculiarities represent not a judaizing or anti-Paulinist element but rather Matthew's loyalty to the traditions of Jesus' ministry. But the question remains: why are these traditions concentrated in Matthew — *and together with* a sympathetic attitude toward the Gentile mission? Possibly the attention given to the Pharisees reflects a post — A. D. 70 situation in which that party (overnight?) became the dominant representative of Judaism (Kilpatrick, *op. cit.*, 120 f.; cf. Davies, *Sermon*, 315). But it may only point to the type of Jewish Christian community, i. e., the Hebrews, that was in sharpest contention with the similarly strict Jewish and judaizing Christian ritualists. On this reading the opponents in Matthew are not those who abandoned the Law but those who perverted it. The Gospel is not just 'the Christian answer to Jamnia' (Davies) but perhaps even more the answer of the 'orthodox' followers of James to the Christian 'Pharisees', the Judaizers. The lack of criticism of the temple cult is not because the question is now, after A. D. 70, a dead issue (Hummel, *op. cit.*, 96) but because the Church of St. Matthew saw no contradiction between Christianity and an observance of the Jewish cultus.

It is interesting to note in this connection that the judaizing faction in Acts 15 belonged to the party of the Pharisees. The same implication may lie behind Paul's (only) use of the term, Pharisee, in Phil 3,5. Hegesippus (Eusebius, *HistEccl* 4, 22,7) lists the 'Pharisees' as a party 'within the circumcision'. M. Simon, 'Les sectes juives d'après les témoignages patristiques,' *Studia Patristica I*, ed. K. Aland and F. L. Cross (*TU* 63, Berlin 1957, 530 ff.) takes this, as well as a similar mention in Justin (*Dial* 80,4), to refer a heretical Christian group. Cf. Black, *op. cit.*, 48—54. If, against the same group, Matthew included an anti-Gnostic polemic (B. W. Bacon, A. Schlatter; *contra:* Davies), the opponents would be quite similar to those in Second Corinthians and Titus. But probably such a motif is not present. Cf. Davies, *Sermon*, 192—208.

[47] This is not the case in the Gospel according to Mark. It may well be that Mark the Hebrew and companion of Paul, is not the same person as Mark the Evangelist and companion of Peter. Cf. Dix, *op. cit.*, 73, 75; *contra:* V. Taylor, *The Gospel according to St. Mark*, London 1953, 27—31.

tanglement in Jewish ritualism, an entanglement that threatens to cut them off from Christ[48].

Manson's thesis has much to commend it. However, if one recognizes that the diaspora mission had a two-pronged thrust, Hellenist *and* Hebraist, a somewhat different picture emerges. The recipients of the letter are not disaffected Hellenists but rather those of the circumcision, the Hebrew element in (Jewish) Christian communities in the diaspora[49]. From the beginning they had the highest concern to relate their faith to the cultic traditions of Israel. But their devotion to the traditions increasingly obscured their vision of the new reality in Christ. The letter is addressed not merely to a local problem and probably not (only) to one congregation. No less than Paul's letter to the Romans, it is a broadly based apologetic directed to a question that has endangered the unity and the faith of the Church from Jerusalem to Rome.

---

[48] Manson, *op. cit.*, 42–44. Cf. F. F. Bruce, *Hebrews*, London 1964, XXVIII ff.

[49] Several scholars have called attention to similarities between the recipients of the letter 'to the Hebrews' and the Qumran sect. As was noted above (note 43) the latter may have some relationship to the Hebrews of Acts 6. Cf. the literature cited by F. F. Bruce, *NTS* 9 (1962–63), 217 f., 232, and H. Montefiore, *The Epistle to the Hebrews*, London 1964, 17. They do not think that the similarities are sufficient to establish a direct or very close connection between the recipients of the letter and Qumran.

8. THE ROLE OF THE CHRISTIAN PROPHET IN ACTS

In several passages in Acts, the phenomenon of prophecy is ascribed to Christian disciples generally. Thus, the Pentecostal experience of tongues, which is identified as prophecy[1], is manifested by the whole Christian community. Likewise, the Ephesian disciples 'began to speak with tongues and prophesy' (Acts 19,6) upon their reception of the Holy Spirit. Ananias, who received a prophetic revelation concerning Paul, also is designated simply as 'a certain disciple' (Acts 9,10). Alongside these texts is the equally significant fact that Luke restricts the term or title προφήτης, as it is used of his contemporaries, to a select number of 'leading men' (cf. Acts 15,22) who exercise considerable influence in the Christian community[2]. Among them are a group from the Jerusalem church visiting Antioch, including Agabus (Acts 11,27 f.; cf. 21, 10); a group resident in Antioch, including Barnabas and Paul (Acts 13,1)[3]; and the two prophets who accompanied the Jerusalem Decree to Antioch, Judas Barsabbas and Silas (Acts 15,22,32). Peter also, who is not called προφήτης, nevertheless has the marks of a prophet, for example, in the knowledge of men's hearts (Acts 5,3; 8,21 ff.; cf. Luke 7,39) and in the experience and proclama-

---

[1] Acts 2,4,11,17 f. Probably the equation of the proclamation in tongues with prophecy arises because the various tongues are, in fact, the native, understood languages of the respective hearers. Similarly, the 'prophecy' in Acts 19,6 probably is an interpretation of the preceding strange 'tongues' (cf. Acts 10,46; 1Cor 14,13). This appears to be preferable to an identification of the two phenomena although that cannot be ruled out (cf. H. Conzelmann, *Die Apostelgeschichte*, Göttingen 1963, 27). In 1Cor 14,5,39 Paul also desires that the whole congregation should prophesy.

[2] Apart from references to Old Testament prophets cf. Lk 4,24; 7,16,39; 9,8, 19; 13,33; 24,19; Acts 3,22 f.; cf. Acts 7,37 (of Jesus) and Acts 11,27; 13,1; 15, 32; 21,10; cf. Lk 11,49 (of Christians). Cf. Lk 1,76; 7,26; 20,6 (of the Baptist). The verb form always in Acts refers to Christians: Acts 2,17 f.; 19,6; 21,9.

[3] It is probable *pace* J. Lindblom that both 'prophets and teachers' describe the whole group. See below, note 45.

tion of revelations in visions and dreams[4]. Among such leaders perhaps should be included the four daughters of Philip 'who prophesied'[5].

In summary, Christian prophecy in Acts is represented as an eschatological power of the Holy Spirit from God (Acts 2,17) or from the risen Jesus (Acts 1,8; 2,17,33; cf. Ps 68,19(18); Eph 4,8). Although prophecy is a possibility for any Christian, it is primarily identified with certain leaders who exercise it as a ministry (see below). The specific 'prophetic' functions of these persons is more difficult to establish. That is, which of their activities are specifically a manifestation of their role as προφήτης? What is the relationship of prophecy to other ministries in Acts? To identify the role of the Christian prophet it is necessary to discover Luke's understanding of what constitutes and what distinguishes prophecy.

I.

Certain functions of the Christian προφήτης are clearly reminiscent of the role of the prophet in the Old Testament. In addition to the marks of the prophet mentioned above, these include the prediction of future events (Acts 11,28; 20,23,25; 27,22), the declaration of divine judgments (Acts 13,11; 28,25–28), and the employment of symbolic actions (Acts 21,11). The prophets in Acts also expound the Scriptures and 'exhort' and 'strengthen' the dis-

---

[4] Acts 10,10; cf. 9,10; 16,9; 18,9; 22,17 ff.; 27,23. Visions and dreams (Joel 3,1 = Acts 2,17) are specific manifestations of prophecy. Cf. Num 12,6; J. Lindblom, *Prophecy in Ancient Israel*, Oxford 1962, 147 f., 201. Apparently miracles were not necessarily or even usually associated with a prophet (*ibid.*, 201 f., 217; cf. Joh 10,41 with Lk 7,26 par.). In Lk 7,16 the disciples and the crowd make an explicit connexion between them; but Lk 7,20 ff. better expresses the Evangelist's view of the significance of miracles. Acts (2,17 f.,43; 5,12–16; 10,34,40; 19,11 f.) distinguishes prophecy from miracle working and, like Paul (2Cor 12,12; cf. Rom 15,19), associates signs and miracles with the 'apostle', but not exclusively so (Acts 6,8; 8,6 f., 13; 1Cor 12,28 f.; 14,22).

[5] Acts 21,9. The patristic references (Eusebius, *Ecclesiastical History* 3, 31,4; 3, 37, 1) suggest that their activity was not an occasional phenomenon but was a distinguished and long-remembered ministry. So, J. Lindblom, *Gesichte und Offenbarungen*, Lund 1968, 179, who distinguishes them as persons who have the prophetic charism as 'a continuing possession'. Cf. Lk 2,36 where Anna is called a prophetess; Rev 2,20.

ciples. Whether these activities also represent for Luke a distinctly prophetic function requires a closer look.

Luke's use of παρακαλέω/παράκλησις with reference to Christian prophets is relatively frequent. The verb is used to describe the proclamation of the Baptist[6] as well as the ministry of those in Acts who are designated prophets[7]. As a description of Peter's preaching, it may be one of the prophetic traits that characterize Luke's presentation of the apostle's ministry[8]. In Acts 15,32 the phrase παρακαλέω καὶ ἐπιστηρίζω ('exhort and strengthen') is specifically connected to the fact that Judas and Silas are prophets[9]. It is found elsewhere in the New Testament only in Acts 14,22, used of the prophets Paul and Barnabas, and (with the cognate στηρίζω) in the Thessalonian letters[10].

The noun παράκλησις, which occurs in the New Testament only in Luke-Acts, Paul and Hebrews, is associated by Luke with the activity of the Holy Spirit[11]. Furthermore, the written παράκλησις of the Jerusalem Decree is set in parallel with the verbal 'exhortation' of the prophets Judas and Silas, and the term 'son of παράκλησις', applied to Barnabas in Acts 4,36, possibly represents, 'son of prophecy'[12]. The understanding of παράκλησις as the specific

---

[6] Lk 3,18; cf. 7,26.

[7] Barnabas (Acts 11,23), Paul and Silas (Acts 16,40), Paul (Acts 20,2). It is noteworthy, however, that the term is not used to describe the ministry of Jesus.

[8] Acts 2,40 (διαμαρτύρομαι καὶ παρακαλέω); cf. 1Thess 2,12; above, note 4. On μαρτυρέω cf. also Acts 10,42 f.; 18,5; 20,21 ff.; Eph 4,17. It appears at times to be virtually a *terminus technicus* for an utterance in the Spirit, i. e., prophecy.

[9] F. J. F. Jackson and K. Lake, *BC*, 4, 182, noting the parallelism between Acts 15,27 and Acts 15,32, translate 'Judas and Silas themselves, being prophets...' and reject the reading, 'who also were themselves prophets', with its allusion to Acts 13,1 f.

[10] 1Thess 3,2; 2Thess 2,17. The former describes the task given to Timothy, their 'fellow-worker', by Paul and Silas. See above, 6.

[11] The church walks 'in the παράκλησις of the Holy Spirit' (Acts 9,31); the prophets Paul and Barnabas are invited to give a 'word of παράκλησις', i. e., an exposition of Scripture (Acts 13,15); the Jerusalem Decree, which is given through the Holy Spirit, is termed a παράκλησις (Acts 15,28,31). Cf. O. Schmitz, *TDNT* 5 (1968), 794—96.

[12] *Bar-nebû'ā* or *bar-nebiyyā*, assuming that παράκλησις in Acts 4,36 means 'exhortation'. So, already commonly a century ago, J. A. Alexander, *The Acts of the Apostles*, New York 1884, 1857, I, 183; cf. H. J. Holtzmann, *Die Apostelgeschichte*, Tübingen 1901, 45; Jackson and Lake, *op. cit.*, 4, 49; F. F. Bruce, *The Acts of the Apostles*, London, ²1952, 130 f. If this interpretation is correct,

ministry of a prophet is supported in the Pauline literature by
1 Corinthians 14,2 f. There the prophets' ministry of 'edification'
is accomplished by means of παράκλησις and παραμυθία[13] which
are, in the words of G. Stählin, 'a part of the work of prophesying'[14]. A similar impression is given in Romans 15,4 f., where
the Scripture or God gives παράκλησις and in 2 Corinthians 5,20
where God 'exhorts' through Paul and Timothy[15]. It is true that
in Paul παράκλησις is not always explicitly identified as a Spirit-
mediated, eschatological reality and, even as a charism, it can be
listed alongside of and distinct from προφητεία (Rom 12,8). Nevertheless, it probably has a special connexion with Christian prophecy, even when that connexion is not explicitly expressed.

To return to Acts 15,32, in the light of the above considerations
it is very likely that the fact that Judas and Silas are prophets is
the basis of their ministry of παράκλησις[16]. The clause should then
be translated, 'since they themselves also were prophets'. It compares their *verbal* exhortation with the written, and also prophetic, παράκλησις of the Jerusalem Decree[17]. In Luke's thought παράκλησις is one way in which the Christian prophets exercise their
ministry and, in this context, is a form of prophecy.

The interpretation of Scripture, usually in the synagogues, is a
key feature of the missions of the prophets Paul and Barnabas,
Paul and Silas, as well as of Peter and other Christian leaders[18].

---

his Christian name like Peter's (Mt 16,18) describes what his distinctive ministry or function in the Christian community was or was to be (cf. Mt 1,21; Acts
13,1). The clause, 'called Barnabas by the apostles', makes improbable the
suggestion that Barnabas was a family designation or surname.

[13] That is, *paraklēsis* and *paramuthia* show or define the nature of the *oiko-
domē*. Similarly, H. D. Wendland, *Die Briefe an die Korinther*, Göttingen 1965,
1936, 109; H. Conzelmann, *1 Corinthians*, Philadelphia 1975, 234 f.; otherwise:
A. Robertson and A. Plummer, *The First Epistle of St. Paul to the Corinthians*,
Edinburgh 1914, 206. Cf. 1Thess 2,12; Phil 2,1 where these two terms are joined
to describe respectively the ministries of Paul, Silas and Timothy and, more
generally, the effects of the Holy Spirit in the congregation.

[14] G. Stählin, *TDNT* 5 (1968), 82. Cf. 1 Cor 14,31.

[15] Cf. also 2Thess 2,16 f.

[16] So E. Haenchen, *Acts*, Philadelphia 1971.

[17] Acts 15,27 f.,31. E. Käsemann. *New Testament Questions of Today*, London 1969, 74, has called attention to the parallel between Acts 15,28 and the
edict of the Spirit reflected in 1Cor 14,37. See below, 137 f., 228 f.

[18] E. g., Acts 2,14–36; 3,12–26; 4,8–12 (Peter); 6,9–11; 7,2–53 (Stephen);
8,30–35 (Philip); 9,20–22; 13,5,16–41; 17,2,10 f.,17(22–31); 18,4; 19,8; 26,22 f.;
28,23 (Paul); 18,24–28 (Apollos).

This manner of teaching is elaborated in Acts 13,16—41 in the form of a synagogue address. It may or may not be significant that the 'prophets' in question also are 'teachers'. (The exposition of Scripture is ascribed to Barnabas [Acts 13,5; 14,1] but not to Silas.) Also this activity in Acts is not described as 'prophecy' nor limited to 'prophets'. In what degree then can it be regarded as 'prophetic' activity?

The interpretation of Scripture as an activity of a prophet was not unknown in the first century since it was explicitly ascribed to Daniel (9,2,24). It may be inferred also from other Old Testament texts in which the prophet uses and reapplies older biblical phraseology and ideas[19]. These phenomena support the views of S. Krauss and others who connect the prophets with the origins of the synagogue and regard them as the first to dispense religious teachings in such assemblies[20]. The rabbinic tradition, reflects a similar picture. According to the Targum on Judges 5,9, Deborah, under prophetic inspiration, 'did not cease to give exposition of the Torah.'[21] The rabbis, moreover, regarded themselves, as the teachers of Israel, to be the successors of the prophets: they sat 'in Moses' seat'[22].

---

[19] For example, cf. Jer 48,45 with Num 21,28; 24,17; Jer 50—51 with Isa 13–14; Zeph 2,15 (zô't = αὕτη) with Isa 47,8. On Dan 11,30 as a reinterpretation of Num 24,24 see F. F. Bruce, 'The Book of Daniel and the Qumran community', *Neotestamentica et Semitica*, ed. E. E. Ellis and M. Wilcox, Edinburgh 1969, 233. See below, 188 n. Cf. 2Chr 13,22.

[20] Cf. L. Zunz, *Die gottesdienstlichen Vorträge der Juden*, Hildesheim 1966, 1892, 37 f.: Already in the Old Testament period older Scriptures were interpreted and in a certain sense changed. Ezra and the Levites appear as interpreters of the laws; the Chronicler makes use of midrash; Daniel is the interpreter of Jeremiah. The schools of the prophets become assemblies of the wise. S. Krauss, *Synagogale Altertümer*, Hildesheim 1966, 1922, 54, sees the incipient synagogue reflected in the 'house of the people' (Jer 39,8) = 'house of assembly' (Ps. 74,8), which began as assemblies in the temple area. I. Elbogen, *Der jüdische Gottesdienst*, Hildesheim 1967, 1931, 235, on the other hand, finds the origin of the synagogue in assemblies in the Exile in which prophets 'strengthened the religious consciousness of the people by readings from the Scriptures followed by teachings of exhortation and consolation'. Cf. *SB* 4, 115. For a different view cf. B. Reicke, *The New Testament Era*, Philadelphia 1968, 119 f.

[21] *SB* 4, 116. Cf. R. Meyer, *TDNT* 6 (1969), 817: According to the rabbis the prophets are 'the oldest expositors of the Law ...'

[22] Mt 23,2; R. Meyer, *op. cit.*, 6, 818 f. 'Since the temple was destroyed prophecy has been taken from the prophets and given to the wise' (Baba Bathra 12a). Haggai, Zechariah and Malachi were viewed as the first members of the

With respect to the interpretation of Scripture, then, there was not a sharp division between the prophet and the teacher. This is perhaps to be most clearly observed in the Qumran community's 'teacher' *(mōreh)* and the wider number functioning as 'instructors' *(maśkīlīm)*. In a perceptive essay Professor Bruce has compared the wisdom possessed by 'Daniel the prophet'[23] and by the 'wise' *(maśkīlīm)* in Daniel 11,12 with that of the 'wise' at Qumran. 'The *maśkīl* here, as in Daniel, is one who, having received from God understanding in his hidden purpose, is thus in a position to impart that understanding to others.'[24] Without identifying themselves as prophets, the teachers at Qumran engage in an interpretation of Scripture that has as its model the activity of Daniel the prophet. This becomes more significant for the present essay when one observes the similarities between the method of biblical interpretation at Qumran and that in Acts 13,16–41[25]. In Acts, however, the interpreter is given the title 'prophet' as well as 'teacher'.

Both terms also are applied to Jesus. It is clear from Luke 7,39 f. that they are not mutually exclusive: the one who is addressed as teacher may also be (the eschatological) prophet. Also, Jesus' teaching 'in their synagogues'[26] often must have included *ipso*

---

chain of rabbinic tradition (Krauss, *op. cit.*, 47 f.) 'Moses received ... and delivered to Joshua, and Joshua to the elders, and the elders to the prophets, and the prophets to the men of the great synagogue' (Aboth 1,1). See also J. Jeremias, *Jerusalem in the Time of Jesus*, London 1969, 233–245.

[23] So identified in 4Qflor 2,3. Cf. Dan 9,22,25.

[24] Bruce, 'Daniel and Qumran', 228 f. Cf. 1QS 9,17–19: the *maśkīl* is to conceal the teaching of the Law from the men of falsehood but to instruct the Community 'in the mysteries *(rāzēy)* of wonder and truth'; 1QH 12,11 f.: 'as a *maśkīl* have I come to know thee, my God, through the spirit that thou hast given me, and by thy Holy Spirit I have faithfully listened to thy marvellous secret counsel *(sôd)*.' Similarly, of the Teacher of Righteousness, 'to whom God made known all the mysteries *(rāzēy)* of the words of his servants the prophets' (1QpHab 7,4 f.).

[25] See below, 198–205; above 57 ff.

[26] For example, Lk 6,6; 13,10; Joh 6,59; 18,20; cf. Mk 1,39 parr. In Mt 4,23; 9,35 it is included in the editorial summaries of Jesus' ministry. Some of the 'teaching in the temple' (ἱερόν; Mk 12,35), which is primarily concerned with the exposition of Scripture, may have its historical setting in a synagogue in the temple enclosure. On the existence and services of such a synagogue compare Elbogen, *op. cit.*, 236; Krauss, *op. cit.*, 66–72, 95; and I. Levy, *The Synagogue*, London 1963, 15 ff. Cf. Yoma 7,1; Sotah 7,7. One of the temple episodes, Mk 12,1–12 parr. (= Is 5,1 f. + parable + Ps 118,22 + Dan 2,34 f., 44 f.) has

facto a midrash or exposition of Scripture[27]. It is less clear, however, to what degree such teaching is the cause of, or attached to, the conviction that Jesus is a prophet.

Two passages that bear upon this question are Mark 1,21 (cf. Lk 4,31) and Mark 6,2 (cf. Lk 4,16; Mt 13,54). In the former text Jesus' exposition, in contrast to that of the Jewish theologians, is characterized by ἐξουσία. Although some commentators interpret ἐξουσία as pointing to the prophetic character of Jesus' teaching[28], this is not as clear as one might wish. For the word is seldom if ever used elsewhere to describe a prophet's teaching[29] although it may, in the New Testament, represent his personal rights in the congregation or his miraculous powers[30]. The prophetic character of Jesus' exposition may perhaps be inferred, however, from its connexion with his miraculous powers, which also are described as a 'teaching' (Mark 1,27)[31].

In Mark 6,1—6 also both Jesus' synagogue teaching and his miraculous powers are the cause of the people's astonishment. Nevertheless, there are two significant differences: his teaching is here described as σοφία, and Jesus compares or identifies his role with that of a prophet[32]. The 'wisdom' (σοφία) that is 'given' to Jesus

the form of an ancient synagogue homily. Cf. *SB* 4, 173 f.: In the oldest form (pre-second century) 'the speaker more or less reproduced the Scripture lesson or parts of it, thereby pointing to the exhortation, warning or consolation included in this or that word in it. Or he illumined the Scripture lesson by means of a parable and strengthened the words that he himself had added by a further Scripture-text' (173). For a different approach to Jesus' teaching cf. M. Hengel, *Nachfolge und Charisma*, Berlin 1968. See above, 60; below, 247—253.

[27] Cf. Lk 4,16—28; Acts 13,14—43; Philo, *Quod Omnis Probus Liber* 81 f.; E. Schürer, *A History of the Jewish People*, Edinburgh c. 1890, II, II, 54 f., 76, 82; Elbogen, *op. cit.*, 194 f.; *SB* 4, 171. A Greek inscription in a first century Jerusalem synagogue states that it was built 'for the reading of the law and the teaching (διδαχή) of the commandments' (E. L. Sukenik, *Ancient Synagogues in Palestine and Greece*, London 1934, 70). *lmd* (= διδάσκω) and its derivatives are used in the oldest rabbinic exegetical literature to couple the text to its exposition (cf. W. Bacher, *Die exegetische Terminologie der jüdischen Traditionsliteratur*, Darmstadt 1965, 1899, I, 94 ff.).

[28] V. Taylor, *The Gospel according to St. Mark*, London 1959, 173, 470; C. E. B. Cranfield, *The Gospel according to St. Mark*, Cambridge 1959, 74; J. Schniewind, *Das Evangelium nach Markus*, Göttingen 1960, 1936, 18.

[29] Cf. C. K. Barrett, *The Holy Spirit and the Gospel Tradition*, London 1947, 96; G. Friedrich, *TDNT* 6 (1969), 843.

[30] 2Thess 3,9: Paul and Silas (cf. Didache 13); Rev 11,6.

[31] Cf. E. Schweizer, *Das Evangelium nach Markus*, Göttingen 1967, 27.

[32] Cf. Lk 13,33. C. K. Barrett, *op. cit.*, 97, objects to taking the proverbial

is recognized by his audience to be an extraordinary pneumatic power; the question is whether it has a divine or demonic origin. In an instructive essay on the concept of σοφία U. Wilckens writes that Mark uses his received picture of Jesus as a Scripture teacher to present him as the archetype of Christian charismatics[33]. Whether such a broad inference may be drawn from this text or not, it is true in any case that Jesus is so regarded in the primitive church[34]. Furthermore, probably no strong dichotomy should be made between the rabbinic 'wisdom' of being learned in the Scriptures — the ordained rabbi[35] — and the 'wisdom' of the knowledge of God's mysteries that is present in the prophets and teachers of Jewish apocalyptic, especially in Daniel and Qumran[36]. The context of the wisdom, that is, the biblical revelation, is the same. The difference in the case of Jesus, however, is not just that he, an unordained person, manifests the bearing and biblical knowledge of an ordained rabbi (so Daube). There is also a qualitative distinction. Like the synagogue teaching of his later follower Stephen, no one 'could withstand the wisdom and the spirit' with which Jesus expounded the Scriptures[37].

---

expression, 'a prophet is not without honour except in his own country' (Mk 6,4), as representing Jesus' literal estimate of his ministry. But even if Jesus is only referring to an (admittedly) common view of himself, 'by not merely adopting the view but also preparing to exemplify it, Jesus numbers himself among the prophets', Friedrich, *op. cit.*, 6, 841; cf. 843 f. Of course, for both Jesus (cf. Lk 7,26) and the Evangelist 'prophet' is not a category exclusive of any other, higher role. Cf. O. Cullmann, *The Christology of the New Testament*, Philadelphia 1959, 44. See above, 66.

[33] U. Wilckens, *TDNT* 7 (1964), 515; cf. P. Bonnard, *L'évangile selon S. Matthieu*, Neuchâtel 1963, 213. The accusations that Jesus was demonically inspired concern not only his miraculous powers (Mk 3,22 parr) but also his teaching (Joh 8,48, 52; 10,19 f.; Mk 3,21; cf. D. E. Nineham, *The Gospel of St. Mark*, Harmondsworth 1963, 123). Also, according to the rabbinic tradition Jesus was condemned because he practised sorcery and enticed Israel to apostasy. The latter charge is couched in the words of Deut 13,8 f., the condemnation of a false prophet (Sanh 43a). Cf. Justin, *Dial* 69; J. L. Martyn, *History and Theology in the Fourth Gospel*, New York 1968, 64—68.

[34] Cf. E. Schweizer, *Church Order in the New Testament*, London 1961, 189 f. (23b). See above, 130.

[35] Wilckens, *op. cit.*, 7, 505f. Daube (*op. cit.* [149n], 207, 216) thinks that the passage represents Jesus to be teaching as though he were an ordained rabbi.

[36] See above, note 24. Cf. Wilckens, *op. cit.*, 7, 503 ff.

[37] Acts 6,9 f.; cf. 6,8 (δύναμις); Lk 2,46 f.,52. Although he did not follow out its implications for the synagogue teaching of Jesus, C. H. Dodd rightly called

While the limited amount of evidence does not allow certainty in the matter, it is probable that not only the miracle-working context but also the manner of Jesus' exposition of Scripture in the synagogue contributed to the conviction that he was a prophet. And it could do so because such exposition was regarded as the proper activity of a prophet. Very likely Luke, at least, views the same kind of exposition of 'prophets and teachers', e. g., in Acts 13 also to be an exercise of a prophetic gift[38]. It is true that this conclusion depends in some measure on Luke's understanding of the relationship of 'teacher' and 'prophet' (see below). But it is supported as well by the mention given to Judas and Silas in connexion with the Jerusalem Decree.

E. Käsemann has noted the similarity of the words in the Decree, 'it seemed good to the Holy Spirit and to us' (Acts 15,28), to the promulgation of eschatological law elsewhere in the New Testament. He thinks that the latter is the work of Christian prophets, and that often 'holy Scripture provided the primitive Christian prophets with the stylistic form in which to clothe their sentences of holy law'[39]. Indeed, the formula λέγει κύριος in Acts 15, 16—18 reflects something more: the *exposition* of Christian prophets[40]. In addition, the theme of the citation, the inclusion of the Gentiles, is specifically the 'mystery' that according to Paul 'has now been revealed to (Christ's) holy apostles and prophets by the

attention to this distinction as an important clue for understanding 'Jesus as Teacher and Prophet' (*Mysterium Christi*, ed. G. K. A. Bell and A. Deissmann, London 1930, 56 ff.).

[38] The eschatological interpretation of Scripture in Acts 2, Acts 7, and elsewhere is no different even when προφήτης is not used and the location is not the synagogue (but cf. Acts 6,9). Cf. Lk 4,22 with Acts 4,13.

[39] E. Käsemann, 'Sentences of Holy Law in the New Testament', *New Testament Questions of Today*, London 1969, 77; cf. 74, 76 ff. The content and style of the Decree itself are admittedly quite different from Käsemann's 'Sentences of Holy Law'. See above, note 17.

[40] Like the texts that Käsemann adduces, the λέγει κύριος quotations also sometimes include the theme of *jus talionis* (Rom 12,19; 14,11; 1Cor 14,21; Hebr 10,30). And they form a distinct class of quotations that are most likely the product of Christian prophets. See below, 182—187; Lindblom, *Gesichte*, 188. It is also worth noting that Acts 15,14,15 ff. follows a recognizable midrashic style, Current Event → Scripture (see below, 200 n., 204 f.; B. Gerhardsson, *Memory and Manuscript*, Uppsala 1961, 252, 260) and that traces of a midrashic literary form are evident elsewhere in James' speech (Acts 15,14—21; cf. J. W. Bowker, *NTS* 14 [1967—68], 107 ff.).

Spirit'[41]. This theme is, in turn, directly related to the 'new temple', a major motif in the λέγει κύριος quotations[42]. Taken together, these facts strongly suggest that the prophets Judas and Silas were not chosen incidentally to accompany the Decree. Probably they were chosen because they had already exercised an influential role in establishing (or proclaiming) the biblical rationale upon which the provisions of the Decree were justified[43].

The foregoing discussion enables us to return to the question raised earlier and to answer it with some measure of confidence. The interpretation of Scripture was indeed regarded, under certain conditions, as prophetic activity[44]. And it is likely that Luke does so regard it, even in such persons as Peter and Stephen who are not given the explicit appellation προφήτης.

II.

The persons in Acts named προφῆται exercise a rather widespread ministry and they do so in a varied fashion — singly or in groups, travelling or in settled congregations. The content of their activity also is varied — prediction (Acts 11,28; 20,23,25,29 f.; 21,11), specific direction of the community in its decisions (Acts 13,1 f.; 15,27) and teaching by exhortation and biblical exposition[45]. Yet, as was noted at the outset, persons who are not termed 'prophets' exercise some of the same functions. This fact raises two questions that must be answered if the role of the prophet in Acts is to be placed in clearer perspective. First, in view of the breadth of the prophetic function, why is the term relatively so restricted? Furthermore, what is the relationship of the prophet to other designated ministries in Acts, specifically the apostle, the teacher, and the elder?

---

[41] Eph 3,3–5; cf. Rom 16,25. Note the use of γνωρίζω and (in Acts) γνωστός.

[42] Eph 2,20; cf. Acts 7,48 ff.; 2Cor 6,16 ff. On Hebr 8,8–12 see below, 183 n.

[43] Similarly, Lindblom, *Gesichte*, 185 n. Significant also is the fact that the Decree is termed a παράκλησις (see above, 131 f.). See below, 228 f.

[44] Cf. E. G. Selwyn, *The First Epistle of St. Peter*, London 1946, 134: 'In the case of Christian prophets... the searching of the Scriptures... was an important part of their task...'

[45] Lindblom, *Gesichte*, 180–88.

Long ago H. B. Swete distinguished between those in the primitive Church who on occasion prophesied and a relatively small number who were known as οἱ προφῆται, 'forming a charismatic order to which a recognized position was given in the Church'[46]. In a recent study J. Lindblom reaches a similar conclusion, apparently independently, and enumerates as such 'berufsmäßige Propheten' Agabus and his companions (Acts 11,27 f.), the Antioch circle (Acts 13,1 ff.), Judas and Silas (Acts 15,32), and the daughters of Philip (Acts 21,9)[47]. This kind of distinction, which is supported by several texts in Paul and in Revelation, may be the best explanation of the matter[48]. E. Schweizer rightly cautions against making a sharp distinction in the earliest period between official or 'ordained' and unordained ministries, and the *caveat* applies to Luke's own time as well[49]. Nevertheless, a special recognition and authoritative status appear to be conferred upon the *persons* of those who have manifested certain charisms in a prominent and/or continuing manner[50].

Except for the twelve apostles (Acts 1,22; 6,2,6) Luke shows little interest in defining the ministries that he names. Even in that case it is 'the twelve' whose ministry is (partly) explained by apostleship, not apostleship by the twelve. This is clear from the fact that Luke can also call them 'disciples' and name other persons apostles[51]. The latter instance presents a further complexity in that 'the apostles Barnabas and Paul' are previously named 'prophets and teachers'. Thus, the triad of gifts in 1 Corinthians 12,28 are clustered around and apparently applied to the same persons in Acts[52]. Also, in Acts 20,17,28 the editorial 'elders' is

---

[46] H. B. Swete, *The Holy Spirit in the New Testament*, London 1910, 377.

[47] Lindblom, *Gesichte*, 179.

[48] There is an apparently recognized group of prophets (in Corinth) whom God 'appointed (τίθημι) in the Church' (1Cor 12,28; cf. 14,29 ff.; Acts 20,28) and who 'have prophecy' (1Cor 13,2). Similarly, Rev 22,9.

[49] Schweizer, *Church Order*, 102 f., 184—87 (5i, 7m, 22efg). See below, n. 65.

[50] For example, in the case of apostleship cf. 1Cor 9,1 ff.; 12,28 f.; 15,9; 2Cor 1,1; 12,11 f.; Gal 1,1,17 ff. Further, H. Greeven, 'Propheten, Lehrer, Vorsteher bei Paulus,' *ZNTW* 44 (1952—53), 1—43: 'by προφῆται (1Cor 14,29) specific, known persons appear to be meant...' (4 f.); teaching also is designated not just as an activity (Rom 12,7) but also with reference to specific persons (16 f.) On ministry in the Pauline church, see above, 3—22.

[51] Lk 9,12,16; 22,14,30,39; Acts 14,4,14; 15,6,13 (?James); cf. Acts 1,25 f.; Gal 1,19; Lk 11,49. Otherwise, Gerhardsson, *op. cit.*, 220. See note 66.

[52] M. Goguel, *The Primitive Church*, London 1964, 1947, 111, shows that the

equivalent to the term 'bishops' in the speech of Paul that follows (cf. Phil 1,1). In part the ambiguous nature of the specified
ministries in Acts is traceable to the differing terminology in
Luke's sources, terminology that he is unconcerned to conform to a
consistent pattern. But the lack of concern itself suggests that for
Luke no less than for his traditions there is a certain ambiguity
and fluidity in the designation of ministries. On the one hand, the
Spirit is itself the gift and to be 'full of the Spirit' implies the em-
powerment to manifest a variety of gifts (Acts 2,33; 6,3,8 ff.). On the
other hand, certain persons may be so identified with a specific
gift as to be recognized and set apart in the community on that
basis. For Paul also certain persons are set apart in terms of a
specific charism (1Cor 12,28)[53]. At the same time one person may
manifest a multiplicity of charisms (1Cor 12,31; 14,1; 2Tim 1,11),
and (some) charisms and charismatics may be grouped in an undif-
ferentiated manner as πνευματικά and πνευματικοί (1Cor 14,1,37;
3,1).

In this context it is not always easy to distinguish the role of the
prophet from that of other ministries. Seeking to do so, G. Friedrich concludes that 'teachers expound Scripture, cherish the tradition about Jesus and explain the fundamentals of the catechism,
the prophets . . . speak to the congregation on the basis of revelations . . .'[54] While this distinction may be true as far as it goes, it
does not give sufficient weight to the teaching role of the early
Christian prophet. Predictive prophecy, of course, presents no
problem. But as the above discussion has shown, there is no clear
division in Judaism or the primitive church between the teaching
of a prophet and of a teacher. Likewise, the false prophets in the
church teach   (1Joh 2,22,26 f.; 4,1 ff.), and the false teachers in

---

triad of gifts in 1Cor 12,28 are embodied in Paul. A fourth-century work, which
may reflect a much earlier textual tradition of Acts 13,1 ff., identifies Barnabas and Paul as 'prophets and teachers', the others as 'prophets'. The text is
given in Bruce, *Acts*, 253; cf. T. Zahn, *Introduction to the New Testament*,
Grand Rapids 1953, 1909, III, 28. On the basis of τε instead of καί before Manaen and Saul (Acts 13,1) W. M. Ramsey, *Saint Paul the Traveller*, London
1896, 65, concluded that they were teachers and the others were prophets. But
this is a slight basis for distinguishing the functions (so Haenchen, *op. cit.*, 338).
Probably both titles apply to all. Cf. E. Fascher, ΠΡΟΦΗΤΗΣ, Giessen 1927,
185; Zahn, *op. cit.*, I, 116; Schweizer, *Church Order*, 72, 183 (5k, 22c). Otherwise,
Lindblom, *Gesichte*, 176 n.

[53] See above, note 50.   [54] Friedrich, *op. cit.*, 6, 854; cf. Gal 1,12.

the church correspond to the false prophets of the Old Covenant (2Petr 2,1). As H. Greeven rightly recognizes, both the prophet and the teacher expound the Scriptures and the sayings of the Lord, and in this area the transition from teaching to prophecy is 'gewiß fließend'[55]. For Paul prophecy apparently is a formal term embracing certain kinds of inspired teaching[56]. The teaching of the prophet appears to overlap that of the teacher and can be distinguished from it only by the manner in which it is given or by the recognized status as 'prophet' of the one who is teaching. In Acts also various kinds of teaching are present in the activities of the prophets. Probably the same relationship between the prophet and the teacher is assumed. But one cannot speak with assurance, especially since διδάσκαλος occurs only in Acts 13,1.

There also is an overlapping of the roles of apostle and prophet. Indeed, E. C. Selwyn argued that 'apostles' were 'prophets on circuit' in contrast to 'prophets in session'[57]. That is, an apostle is simply a prophet who is sent (ἀποστέλλω) as a missionary. In support he cites Didache 11,3—5.

> But concerning the apostles and prophets (τῶν ἀποστόλων καὶ προφητῶν) do according to the ordinance of the gospel. Every apostle who comes to you receive as the Lord ... But if he remains three days he is a false prophet.

The usage is remarkable, and it is one possible explanation why Barnabas and Paul on tour are called apostles (Acts 14,4,14) but are named prophets only while resident in Antioch (Acts 13,1), However, it is more likely that the shift in terminology reflects Luke's use of a different tradition. In any case the explanation hardly accords with the use of the terms elsewhere in Acts where 'apostles' reside in Jerusalem and 'prophets' travel.

To pose the question differently, is there any activity ascribed to the Christian prophet that is not also true of those named apostle? Apparently there is none. The example of the apostle Peter, mentioned above, illustrates that every activity of the prophet —

---

[55] Greeven, *op. cit.*, 29; cf. Fascher, *op. cit.*, 185.

[56] Goguel, *op. cit.*, 265. Neither προφητεία nor διδασκαλία occurs in Luke-Acts; in Acts διδάσκαλος appears only at 13,1.

[57] Cf. E. C. Selwyn, *The Christian Prophets*, London 1900, 24 f.; *Saint Luke the Prophet*, London 1901, 35, 27—32. So also, Fascher, *op. cit.* 185. Selwyn's works contain considerable information and some good insights, but they are marred by an erratic style and by unsupported and extravagant assertions.

including prediction, exhortation and biblical exposition — can also be ascribed by Luke to the apostle[58]. On the other hand, unlike the prophets the apostles do 'many wonders and signs' (2,43), witness to the resurrection of Jesus (1,22; 13,31; cf. 26,16), exercise an authority in the congregations, and impart the Holy Spirit (8,15 ff.; cf. 19,6). It may be significant that it is in connexion with one of these activities, miracle-working, that Barnabas and Paul are named apostles[59]. Likewise, in the Pauline literature the mark of an apostle includes 'signs and wonders and mighty works' (2Cor 12,12; cf. 1Cor 9,1). In summary, the ministries of the apostle and the prophet in Acts may be compared to two concentric circles, in which the circle of the prophet's activity is somewhat smaller.

Christian 'elders' (πρεσβύτεροι) appear in Acts as a leadership group in the congregations of Jerusalem (11,30; 21,18), Galatia (14,23), and Ephesus (20,17). Their function is 'to shepherd' (ποιμαίνειν) the church of God (20,28), a term whose cognate ποιμήν is listed in Ephesians 4,11 among the spiritual gifts. In Acts the elders also are given their task by the Holy Spirit (20,28) even though they may be appointed by a prophet or apostle (14,23)[60]. The description of the prophets Judas and Silas as 'leading men' apparently sets them apart from the 'apostles and elders' in Acts 15,22 (so Haenchen). However, several facts suggest that the elder, like the prophet, had a teaching function in addition to his responsibilities of general oversight of the community.

The Christian use of the term πρεσβύτερος is clearly derived from Judaism where it was used of a group in the Sanhedrin and of the community and/or synagogue leaders[61]. Traditionally the elders

---

[58] See above, note 8. Cf. Friedrich, *op. cit.*, 6, 850.

[59] Acts 14,3 f.,10,14. Their authority over the congregations is indicated in the same chapter (14,23) but its description is perhaps more reminiscent of Acts 13,1 ff. than, for example, of Acts 6,6. It should be added that miraculous signs also are ascribed to Stephen and Philip, persons who are called neither apostles nor prophets. Cf. Acts 6,8; 8,6 f.; Schweizer, *Church Order*, 196 f. (24b).

[60] *Ibid.*, 183 f., 186 (22df). Cf. 1Petr 5,1 f. The term πρεσβύτερος does not appear in the Pauline literature outside the Pastoral Epistles where, like Acts 20,17,28, it is equated with ἐπίσκοπος (Tit 1,5,7; cf. Phil. 1,1).

[61] According to G. Bornkamm, *TDNT* 6 (1969), 662 f., the elders in Acts 11,30; 21,18 resemble a synagogue council; the 'apostles and elders' in Acts 15 reflect a different tradition and, patterned after the Sanhedrin, function 'as a supreme court and normative teaching office for the whole Church'. Similar-

in Judaism were a 'lay nobility', heads of ancient patrician families. In the first century, however, persons who also had been trained as scribes were preferred when community or synagogue leaders were chosen. That is, one who was selected to be elder was likely to be a theologian[62]. For the early Christian community this would correspond to a charismatic person, e. g., a teacher, even though he may have been titled πρεσβύτερος (in conformity with the Jewish custom) or ἐπίσκοπος within the organizational structure.

This view of the matter accords with a number of New Testament texts. (1) As they do in Judaism, the elders in Acts 15 and Acts 20 functions as guardians of the tradition, although the similarity is qualified by the role of the Spirit among the Christians[63]. (2) The Christian elder may exercise a specific ministry of teaching (1Tim 5,17; 3Joh 1)[64]. However, the same kind of ministry may be exercised without reference to any name or title[65]. Although in Acts the elder is a part of the organized expression of the church, he is very likely selected on the basis of certain spiritual gifts[66]. And his ministry itself is doubtless viewed as a mani-

---

ly, Gerhardsson, *op. cit.*, 251. But does this give sufficient weight to the charismatic and prophetic nature of the assembly's actions?

[62] Jeremias, *op. cit.*, 236 f. The Sadducees obtained their scribes from within this lay nobility, i. e., the 'elders', who thus functioned as interpreters and guardians of the tradition (231).

[63] Cf. also, 1Petr 5,1 ff.; Schweizer, *Church Order*, 200 (24i).

[64] Concerning 2, 3 John cf. Bornkamm, *op. cit.*, 6, 671. The elder also may be expected to exercise gifts of healing (Jas 5,14). According to Didache 15 the bishops and deacons 'also perform the service of the prophets and teachers'. 'Bishop' (ἐπίσκοπος) is here equivalent to πρεσβύτερος.

[65] Cf. 1Cor 16,16; 1Thess 5,12 with 1Tim 5,17.

[66] Cf. Acts 6,3; Schweizer, *Church Order*, 184 (22e). The absence of the term in Paul (outside the Pastorals) is remarkable and its use possibly 'represents a later assimilation to Jewish forms' (*ibid.*, 200). But in view of the early necessity of structure (Acts 6) and the Church's identification of itself as the true Israel it is more likely that in some Jewish-Christian communities the term was used in an official way from the beginning. Cf. B. Reicke, 'The Constitution of the Primitive Church,' *The Scrolls and the New Testament*, New York 1957, 143—56. A comparison of Acts 1,20b,25 (ἐπισκοπή, ἀποστολή) with Acts 20, 17,28 (πρεσβύτερος, ἐπίσκοπος) suggests that for Luke the apostle may be a special kind of elder just as the Twelve are a special kind of apostle (cf. 1Tim 3,1; see above, 142). This would place Acts 15 in a different light and clarify its relation both to Acts 11,30; 21,18 and to the readings of Codex Bezae at Acts 15,5,12,41 ('elders'). Cf. E. E. Ellis, *The Gospel of Luke*, London ²1974, 132 to 135, on the relation of 'the apostles' and 'the Twelve'. See note 61.

festation of a charism. Therefore, the role of the prophet may overlap that of the elder as it does that of the apostle and the teacher, especially in certain teaching functions. But unlike the prophet the apostle (in Jerusalem at least) and the elder or 'shepherd' are incorporated into the organizational structure.

III.

At a number of places in Acts the early Christian mission is viewed as a continuation of Jesus' mission and as a contest between conflicting spirit-powers. The former is expressed most clearly as the immediate action of the exalted Lord himself (Acts 1,1 ['began']; 9,5; 10,13; 16,7; 22,18; 23,11). The contest is explicit in the encounter of Peter with Simon Magus (8,9—24) and the encounter of Paul with the false prophet Barjesus (13,6 ff.) and the medium in Philippi (16,16). The same kind of conflict may be inferred from the episode of the Jewish exorcists (19,13—20). The role of the Christian prophet is related to both of these Lukan themes. The prophet is the Lord's instrument, one among several means by which Jesus leads his church. As one who makes known (γνωστός) the meaning of the Scriptures, exhorts and strengthens the congregation, and instructs the community by revelations of the future, the Christian prophet manifests in the power of the Spirit the character of his Lord, who is the Prophet of the end-time (3,22).

II. PROPHECY AS EXEGESIS: EARLY CHRISTIAN HERMENEUTIC

9. HOW THE NEW TESTAMENT USES THE OLD

I. *The Character of New Testament Usage*

1. General

Old Testament phraseology in the New Testament occurs occasionally as the idiom of a writer whose own patterns of expression have been influenced by the Scriptures (1Thess 2,4; 4,5). Most often, however, it appears in the form of citations or intentional allusions or reminiscences. Dr. Hartman suggests three reasons for an author's citation of another: to obtain the support of an authority (Mt 4,14), to call forth a cluster of associations (Mk 12, 1 f.), and to achieve a literary or stylistic effect (Tit 1,12). He rightly observes that an allusion sometimes can be discerned only after the total context of a passage has been taken into account[1].

As might be expected in Greek writings, citations from the Old Testament are frequently in agreement with the LXX, the Greek version commonly used in the first century. But they are not uniformly so, and at times they reflect other Greek versions, Aramaic targums, or independent translations of the Hebrew text[2]. Apart from the use of a different text-form, a citation may diverge from the LXX because of a lapse of memory. However, this explanation is often less probable than has been supposed in the past[3]. More frequently, as will be detailed below, citations diverge from the LXX because of deliberate alteration, i. e. by *ad hoc*

---

[1] L. Hartman, 'Scriptural Exegesis in the Gospel of Matthew and the Problem of Communication,' *L'evangile selon Matthieu*, ed. M. Didier, Gembloux 1972, 131—152, 134.

[2] Cf. E. E. Ellis, *Paul's Use of the Old Testament*, Edinburgh 1957, 11—16, 150—152; R. H. Gundry, *The Use of the Old Testament in St. Matthew's Gospel*, Leiden 1967, 9—150; K. Stendahl, *The School of St. Matthew*, Lund 1969 (1954), 47—156.

[3] Cf. Ellis, *Paul's Use*, 14 f.

translation and elaboration or by the use of a variant textual tradition, to serve the purpose of the New Testament writer. The variations, then, become an important clue to discover not only the writer's interpretation of the individual Old Testament passage but also his perspective on the Old Testament as a whole.

2. Introductory Formulas

Formulas of quotation, which generally employ verbs of 'saying' or 'writing,' correspond to those found in other Jewish writings, e. g. the Old Testament[4], the Qumran scrolls[5], Philo and the rabbis[6]. They locate the citation with reference to the book or writer or, less frequently, the story ('in Elijah,' Rom. 11,2; 'at the bush,' Mk 12,26). At times they specify a particular prophet (Acts 28,25), a specification that on occasion may be important for the New Testament teaching[7]. When one book is named and another cited, the formula may represent an incidental error or, more likely, the cited text may be an interpretation (Mt 27,9)[8] or elaboration (Mk 1,2) of a passage in the book named.

Introductory formulas often underscore the divine authority of the Old Testament, not in the abstract but within the proper interpretation and application of its teaching. Thus, the formula 'Scripture (γραφή) says' can introduce an eschatological, i. e. 'Christianized' summation or elaboration of the Old Testament (Joh 7, 38; Gal 4,30), and γραφή can be contrasted to traditional interpretations (Mt 22,29). That is, it implies that the revelational, 'Word of God' character of Scripture is present within the current interpretation. In the words of Renée Bloch, Scripture 'always

---

[4] E. g. 1Ki 2,27; 2Chr 35,12.

[5] E. g. 1QS 5,15; 8,14; cf. J. A. Fitzmyer in *NTS* 7 (1960–61), 299–305.

[6] E. g. Philo, *de migr.* 118. Cf. Ellis, *Paul's Use*, 48 f.

[7] E. g. Mk 12,36; cf. R. T. France, *Jesus and the Old Testament*, London 1971, 101 f., 163–169.

[8] Cf. J. W. Doeve, *Jewish Hermeneutics in the Synoptic Gospels and Acts* (Assen 1954), 185 f.; Gundry, *Matthew*, 125n.

[9] R. Bloch, 'Midrash,' *Dictionnaire de la Bible: Supplément, V* (Paris 1957), 1266. Cf. B. B. Warfield, *The Inspiration and Authority of the Bible*, Philadelphia 1948, 148: 'Scripture is thought of as the living voice of God speaking in all its parts directly to the reader;' M. Barth, 'The Old Testament in Hebrews,' *Current Issues in New Testament Interpretation*, ed. W. Klassen, New York 1962, 58 ff.

concerns a living word addressed personally to the people of God and to each of its members. . . .'[9] The formula 'it is written' can also have the intended connotation of a specific and right interpretation of Scripture (Rom 9,33; 11,26) even though the connotation may not always be true (Mt 4,6).

Sometimes an explicit distinction between reading Scripture and knowing or hearing Scripture may be drawn. It is present in the story of the Ethiopian eunuch (Acts 8,30) and, implicitly, in Jesus' synagogue exposition at Nazareth (Lk 4,16 f.,21). It may be presupposed, as it is in rabbinical writings, in the formula 'have you not (οὐκ) read?'[10] That is, 'you have read but have not understood.' This formula is found in the New Testament only on the lips of Jesus and usually within a Scriptural debate or exposition[11].

A few formulas are associated with specific circles within the Christian community. The nine λέγει κύριος ('says the Lord') quotations probably reflect the activity of Christian prophets[12]. The ἵνα πληρωθῇ ('that it might be fulfilled') quotations, found especially in the Gospels of Matthew and John, may have a similar origin[13]. Both kinds of quotations contain creatively altered text-forms that facilitate an eschatological re-application of the Old Testament passages, similar to that found in the Qumran scrolls[14], to the experiences and understanding of the early church. This is a kind of activity recognized in first century Judaism to be appropriate to prophets as well as to teachers[15].

Somewhat similar are the πιστὸς ὁ λόγος ('faithful is the word') passages in the Pastoral letters[16]. They appear to be instructions of Christian prophets (cf. 1Tim 4,1,6, τοῖς λόγοις τῆς πίστεως) and/or inspired teachers, used by Paul in the composition of the letters. Although they do not contain Old Testament quotations, some of

---

[10] Cf. D. Daube, *The New Testament and Rabbinic Judaism*, London 1956, 423–436.

[11] Cf. Doeve, *Hermeneutics*, 105 f., 163 f. Cf. Mt 12,3,5; 19,4.

[12] See below, 182–187.

[13] Stendahl, *School*, 163, 200 f.: 'Matthew's formula quotations give evidence of features of text interpretation of an actualizing nature, often closely associated with the context in the gospel.' '(They) seem to us . . . to be a decisive indication that we must postulate a School of Matthew.'

[14] Cf. Ellis, *Paul's Use* 139–47. See notes 48, 49; below, 173–181.

[15] See above, 55–60, 130 ff.

[16] Cf. G. W. Knight, *The Faithful Sayings in the Pastoral Epistles*, Kampen 1968. E. g. 1Tim 1,15; 4,9; 2Tim 2,11.

these 'faithful sayings' may refer to the exposition of the Old Testament[17]. They appear to arise out of a prophetic circle engaged in a ministry of teaching.

3. Forms and Techniques in Quotation

(a) Combined quotations of two or more texts appear frequently in a variety of forms: a chain of passages (Rom 15,9—12), a commentary pattern (Joh 12,38—40; Rom 9—11) and composite or merged citations (Rom 3,10—18; 2Cor 6,16—18). With the exception of the last type these patterns were commonly employed in Judaism[18]. They serve to develop a theme and perhaps exemplify the principle in Dtn 19,15 that two witnesses establish a matter. Sometimes (Rom 10,18—21), in the fashion of the rabbis, they bring together citations from the Law, the Prophets and the Writings. Such combinations usually were formed in conjunction with catchwords important for the theme (e. g. 'stone,' 'chosen' in 1Petr 2,6—9).

(b) Testimonia. Citations 'testifying' to the messiahship of Jesus were of special interest to the early church. Sometimes they appear as combined quotations (Hebr 1), combinations that possibly lie behind other New Testament citations[19]. Such 'testimonies' were primarily thematic combinations for instructional and apologetic purposes and, as the testimonia at Qumran indicate (4Qtest), some may have circulated in written form during the apostolic period. However, the hypothesis that they were collected in a precanonical 'testimony book,' used by the Church in anti-Jewish apologetic[20], is less likely.

The 'testimonies' apparently presuppose a worked-out christological understanding of the particular passages and are not simply proof texts randomly selected. The earliest Christians, like twentieth century Jews, could not, as we do, simply infer from traditional usage the 'Christian' interpretation of a biblical word or

---

[17] Tit 1,9,14; 3,5 f.,8; 1Tim 2,13—15; 3,1a.

[18] For the practice in classical literature cf. F. Johnson, *The Quotations of the New Testament from the Old*, London 1896, 92—102. On merged citations, see below, 152 f.; they are infrequent in rabbinic usage.

[19] Cf. Ellis, *Paul's Use*, 98—107; P. Prigent, *L'épitre de Barnabé I—XVI et ses sources*, Paris 1961.

[20] So J. Rendel Harris, *Testimonies*, 2 vols., Cambridge 1916, 1920.

passage. Proof texts standing alone, therefore, would have appeared to them quite arbitrary if not meaningless.

According to a thesis of C. H. Dodd[21] the 'testimony' quotations were selected from and served as pointers to larger Old Testament contexts that previously and as a whole had been christologically interpreted. For example, Mt 1,23 in citing Is 7,14 probably has in view the total section, Is 6,1—9,7, as the additional phrase 'God with us' (Is 8,8,10 LXX) and the frequent use of Is 6—9 elsewhere in the New Testament indicate. Dodd correctly perceived that the *testimonia* were the result of 'a certain method of biblical study' (126). But what precisely was that method? It may well have included, as Dodd thought, a systematic christological analysis of certain sections of the Old Testament. Beyond this, however, the method probably corresponded to a form and method of scriptural exposition used in contemporary Judaism and known to us as midrash.

4. Quotation and Midrash

(a) The Hebrew term 'midrash' has the meaning 'commentary' (cf. 2Chr 13,22; 24,27), and in the past it has usually been associated with certain rabbinic commentaries on the Old Testament. Recently it has been used more broadly to designate an activity as well as a literary genre, a way of expounding Scripture as well as the resulting exposition[22]. Thus, 'the house of midrash' (Sirach 51,23) was a place where such exposition was carried on (and not a library of commentaries). According to Miss Bloch (*op. cit.*, note 9) the essence of the midrashic procedure was a contemporization of Scripture in order to apply it to or make it meaningful for the current situation. It can be seen, then, in interpretive renderings of the Hebrew text (= implicit midrash), e. g. the Greek LXX[23] and the Aramaic targums, as well as in more formal 'text

---

[21] C. H. Dodd, *According to the Scriptures*, London 1952, 78 f., 107 f., 126.

[22] See below, 188—192; M. P. Miller, 'Targum, Midrash and the Use of the Old Testament in the New Testament,' *Journal for the Study of Judaism* 2 (1970) 29—82.

[23] E. g. in Is 9,11(12) 'Aramaeans and Philistines' becomes in the LXX the contemporary 'Syrians and Greeks.' In agreement with Bloch, G. Vermes (*Scripture and Tradition in Judaism*, Leiden 1961, 179) characterizes the LXX and targums as a 're-writing of the Bible' in which contemporary interpreta-

+ exposition' patterns (= explicit midrash), e. g. the rabbinic commentaries[24]. Both kinds of midrash appear in first-century Judaism in the literature of the Qumran community.

(b) In the use of the Old Testament by the New, implicit midrash appears in double entendre, in interpretive alterations of Old Testament citations and in more elaborate forms. The first type involves a play on words. Thus, Mt 2,23 cites Jesus' residence in Nazareth as a 'fulfilment' of prophecies identifying the Messiah as a Ναζωραῖος (= ?Nazirite, Jud 13,5,7 LXX) or a *netzer* (= branch, Is 11,1; cf. 49,6; 60,21)[25]. Possibly the double meaning of 'lift up' in Joh 3,14; 12,32 ff., i. e. hang and exalt, alludes to an Aramaic rendering *(zᵉkaph)* of Is 52,13, which carries both meanings; the terminology is clarified in the Synoptic Gospels where Jesus prophesies that he is to 'be killed and rise' (Mk 8,31; cf. Lk 18,33)[26]. A similar double entendre may be present in Acts 3,22–26 where 'raise up' apparently is used both of Messiah's pre-resurrection ministry and of his resurrection.

The second type can be seen in Rom 10,11:

> For the Scripture says, 'Everyone (πᾶς) who believes on him shall not be put to shame.'

The word 'everyone' is not in the Old Testament text; it is Paul's interpretation woven into the citation and fitting it better to his argument (10,12 f.). Similarly, in the citation of Gen 21,10 at Gal 4,30 the phrase 'son of the free woman' is substituted for 'my son Isaac' in order to adapt the citation to Paul's application. More elaborate uses of the same principle will be discussed below.

More complex forms of implicit midrash occur (1) in making a merged or composite quotation from various Old Testament texts,

---

tions are woven into the text. He distinguishes two purposes for such midrash, to eliminate obscurities in the biblical text and to justify current beliefs and practices from the Scripture. Cf. his 'Bible and Midrash,' *Cambridge History of the Bible I*, ed. P. R. Ackroyd, Cambridge 1970, 221. On other midrashic elements in the LXX and targums cf. D. W. Gooding in *JTS* 25 (1974) 1–11.

[24] A. G. Wright (*CBQ* 28, 1966, 105–38, 517–57) prefers to restrict the use of the term to explicit midrash. On the continuing problem of defining the relationship of targum and midrash cf. R. Le Déaut in *Biblical Theology Bulletin* 4 (1974), 18–22; see below, 190–191; A. Diez-Macho in *Revue des Sciences Religieuses* 47 (1973), 171–175.

[25] Cf. H. H. Schaeder in *TDNT* 4 (1967/1942), 878 f.; Stendahl, *School*, 198 f.; for the various interpretations, Gundry, *Matthew*, 97–104.

[26] Cf. M. Black in *BJRL* 45 (1963), 315 ff.

altered so as to apply them to the current situation, and (2) in the description of a current event in biblical phraseology in order to connect the event with the Old Testament passages. Contemporized composite quotations appear, for example, in 1Cor 2,9; 2Cor 6,16—18. The use of Scriptural phraseology to describe and thus to explain the meaning of current and future events is more subtle and reflects a different focus: the event appears to be of primary interest and the Old Testament allusions are introduced to illumine or explain it. This kind of midrash occurs, for example, in the Lucan infancy narratives, in Jesus' apocalyptic discourse and his response at his trial and in the Revelation of St. John[27].

In the infancy narratives the Annunciation (Lk 1,26—38) alludes to Is 6,1—9,7 — e. g. 7,13 f. (27, παρθένος, ἐκ οἴκου Δαυίδ); 7,14 (31); 9,6 f. (32,35) — a section that C. H. Dodd has shown to be a primary source for early Christian exegesis[28]. It probably also alludes to Gen 16,11 (31); 2Sam 7,12—16 (32, ?35, υἱὸς Θεοῦ); Dan 7,14 (33b); and Is 4,3; 62,12 (35, ἅγιον κληθήσεται). The Magnificat (1,46—55) and the Benedictus (1,68—79) appear to be formed along the same lines. It is probable that family traditions about the events surrounding Jesus' birth were given this literary formulation by prophets of the primitive Jerusalem church[29].

The response of our Lord at his trial (Mk 14,62 par) is given by the Gospels in the words of Ps 110,1 and Dan 7,13. It probably represents a summary of Jesus' known response, a summary in biblical words whose 'messianic' exegesis either had been worked out in the Christian community or, more likely, had been taught to the disciples by Jesus. That Jesus made use of both Ps. 110,1 and Dan 7,13 in his preresurrection teaching is highly probable[30].

---

[27] In Revelation no formal quotations occur, but almost 70 % of the verses contain allusions to the Old Testament.

[28] See note 21.

[29] See E. E. Ellis, *The Gospel of Luke*, London ²1974, 27 ff., 67 f. Lk 1,5 to 2,40 is a literary unity and reflects a Hebraic source or sources that were composed in part, at least, from the perspective of a narrator in Jerusalem (e. g. 2,38). The evidence for the presence in the Jerusalem church of the Virgin Mary and of the brothers of Jesus (Gal 1,19; Acts 1,14; 12,17; 15,13; 21,18) is not without significance for this matter, even if their presence in diaspora churches also is attested (1Cor 9,5; Epiph, *Panarion* 78, 11, 2).

[30] On the use of Ps 110,1 by Jesus cf. D. M. Hay, *Glory at the Right Hand: Psalm 110 in Early Christianity*, Nashville 1973, 110 (on Mk 12,35—37); France, *Jesus*, 101 ff.

The apocalyptic discourse (Mk 13 par), which also includes the use of Dan 7,13, apparently consists of a midrash of Jesus on certain passages in Daniel, a midrash that has been supplemented by other sayings of the Lord and reshaped by the Evangelists and their predecessors 'into something of a prophetic tract' linked to the Church's experiences. In the course of transmission the midrash 'lost many of its once probably explicit associations with the OT text'[31]. If this reconstruction is correct, it shows not only how teachings of Jesus were contemporized in a manner similar to the midrashic handling of Old Testament texts but also how our Lord's explicit midrash was modified so that the Old Testament references, although not lost, were largely assimilated to the current application. The process is much more thoroughgoing than is the case in the composite quotations cited above.

These examples suggest that implicit midrash sometimes presupposes or develops out of direct commentary on the Old Testament, i. e. explicit midrash. We may now turn to that form of the early Christian usage.

(c) Explicit midrash in the New Testament has affinities both with the *pesher* midrash at Qumran and with certain kinds of midrash found in rabbinic expositions. The ancient expositions of the rabbis are preserved in sources that are dated several centuries after the New Testament writings[32]. However, in their general structure they provide significant parallels for early Christian practice since (1) it is unlikely that the rabbis borrowed their methods of exposition from the Christians and (2) similar patterns may be observed in the first-century Jewish writer, Philo[33]. They probably originated not only as 'sermon' or 'homily' but also as 'commentary,' that is, not only as the complement of the synagogue worship but also as the product of the synagogue school[34]. The

---

[31] So, L. Hartman, *Prophecy Interpreted*, Lund 1966, 235—52, 242, who identifies the original midrash with Mk 13,5b—8,12—16,19—22,24—27. His acute analysis is largely persuasive.

[32] E. g. W. G. Braude, *Pesikta Rabbati*, 2 vols., New Haven 1968. He dates the expositions in this seventh century collection from third and fourth century Palestinian rabbis.

[33] Cf. P. Borgen, *Bread from Heaven*, Leiden 1965, 59—98.

[34] In Judea, apparently, the synagogue served in the pre-destruction period primarily for the study of Scripture and only later as a center of worship. Cf. J. W. Bowker, 'Speeches in Acts,' *NTS* 14 (1967—68), 96—99 and the literature cited there. See below, 199 f.

type of discourse that finds most affinity with New Testament expositions is the 'proem' midrash[35]. As used in the synagogue, it ordinarily had the following form:

The (Pentateuchal) text for the day.
A second text, the proem or 'opening' for the discourse.
Exposition containing additional Old Testament citations, parables or other commentary and linked to the initial texts by catch-words.
A final text, usually repeating or alluding to the text for the day.

The general outline of this pattern, with some variation, occurs rather frequently in the New Testament. Without the text for the day, it appears in Hebr 10,5–39 (see below, 193 n.):

5–7   – Initial text: Ps 40,7–9.
8–36   – Exposition containing additional citations (16 f., 30) and linked to the initial text by catchwords: Θυσία (8, 26), προσφορά (8, 10, 14, 18), περὶ ἁμαρτίας (8, 18, 26), ἁμαρτία (17).
37–39   – Final text and application alluding to the initial text with the verbs ἥκειν and εὐδοκεῖν: Is 26,20; Hab 2,3 f.

The pattern is expressed more specifically in Rom 9,6—29:

6 f.   – Theme and initial text: Gen 21,12.
9   – A second, supplemental text: Gen 18,10.
10–28   – Exposition containing additional citations (13, 15, 17, 25–28) and linked to the initial texts by the catchwords καλεῖν and υἱός (12, 24 ff., 27).
29   – A final text alluding to the initial text with the catchword σπέρμα.

A less complex form occurs in 1Cor 1,18—31. Here the second, supplemental text has been merged with the initial text; and the final text, the only subsequent citation, does not allude to the opening text.

---

[35] Cf. Pesikta Rabbati 33,7: Text (Is 51,12) + Second Text (Hos 6,1) + Exposition (with parable and application, linked verbally to the second text) + Additional Text (La 1,13) + Concluding Text (Is 51,12). Also: Pesikta Rabbati 44,7. For Acts 2 and 13 cf. Bowker ('Speeches,' 96—111) and Doeve (*Hermeneutics*, 168—86); for Joh 6,31—58, Rom 4,1—22, Gal 3,6—29 cf. Borgen (*Bread*, 37—52); for 1Cor 1,18—3,20; Rom 1,17—4,25 see below, 213—220.

18–20   – Theme and initial texts: Is 29,14 and 19,11 f.; cf. 33,18.

20–30   – Exposition linked to the initial and final texts by the catchwords σοφός (26 f.), σοφία (21 f., 30), μωρός (25, 27), μωρία (21, 23), καυχᾶσθαι (29).

31   – Final text. Cf. Jer 9,22 f.

In 1Cor 2,6–16 the initial texts are a composite and highly interpreted quotation:

6–9   – Theme and initial texts. Cf. Is 64,4; 65,16.

10–15   – Exposition linked to the initial and final texts by the catchwords ἄνθρωπος (11, 14; cf. 13), ἰδεῖν (11 f.), γινώσκειν (11, 14).

16   – Final text and application: Is 40,13.

Instead of a composite quotation the initial text of the commentary at Gal 4,21–5,1 is itself a summary of a Genesis passage, an implicit midrash introducing the key word ἐλευθέρα. It is probably Paul's summation, but it might have been drawn from a Genesis midrash similar to Jubilees or to the Qumran Genesis Apocryphon[36].

21 f.   – Introduction and initial text. Cf. Gen 21.

23–29   – Exposition with an additional citation, linked to the initial and final texts by the catchwords ἐλευθέρα (22, 23, 26, 30), παιδίσκη (22, 23, 30, 31) and *ben*/υἱός = τέκνον (22, 25, 27, 28, 30, 31).

30 ff.   – Final text and application, referring to the initial text. Cf. Gen 21,10.

---

[36] See below, 190–191, 224 ff. A somewhat different pattern appears in 1Cor 10: Implicit Midrash (1–5, cf. Ex 13 f.; Num 14,16) + Application (6) + Additional Text (7 = Ex 32,6) + Exposition/Application, alluding to the preceding midrash and other texts (8–31). Such midrashic summaries also appear to form the 'texts' on which the letter of Jude makes its commentary, e. g. Jude 5 (Num 14), 6 (Gen 6), 7 (Gen 19), 14 f. (1 Enoch 1,9; cf. Gen 5,22). This is, in effect, midrash on midrash. One can, thus, understand how Jude and others could use an interpretation of biblical material, e. g. 1 Enoch, as a 'text' without necessarily regarding the book of Enoch *eo ipso* as Scripture. The targums provide an analogy in Jewish practice: they set forth an interpretation of Scripture for the synagogue hearers without themselves being given the status of Scripture.

The pattern in 2 Petr 3,5–13 is similar, although less clear. As in Gal 4, the initial 'text' is a selective summary of a section of Scripture:

5 f.	– Initial text (with eschatological application). Cf. Gen 1.6.
7–12	– Exposition (with an additional citation: 8) linked to the initial and final texts by the catchwords οὐρανός (5, 7, 10, 12), γῆ (5, 7, 10), ἀπόλλυμι (6, 9, cf. 7). Cf. ἡμέρα (7, 8, 10, 12).
13	– Final text and applications.[37] Cf. Is 65,17.

The above examples show how a composite, interpreted citation and an interpretive summary of a larger section of Scripture may serve as the 'text' in a midrash. The use of short, explicit midrashim as 'texts' in a more elaborate commentary-pattern is only an extension of the same practice. One instance of this appears in 1Cor 1,18–3,20[38], which is composed of the following sections, all linked by catchwords, e. g. σοφία, μωρία:

1,18–31	– Initial 'text.'
2,1–5	– Exposition/Application.
2,6–16	– Additional 'text.'
3,1–17	– Exposition/Application.
3,18–20	– Concluding texts: Job 5,13; Ps 94,11.

The synoptic Gospels also display exegetical patterns similar to those in the rabbis[39]. Mt 21,33—44 corresponds to an ancient form of a synagogue address[40]:

33	– Initial text: Is 5,1 f.
34–41	– Exposition by means of a parable, linked to the initial

---

[37] The application following the final quotation, which appears in a number of the examples above, has a parallel in Philo and the rabbis. Cf. Philo, *leg. alleg.* III, 75b–76; *Sacr. Abel.* 87b; Borgen, *Bread*, 53; E. Stein, 'Die homiletische Peroratio...,' *Hebrew Union College Annual* 8–9 (1931–32), 353–71, 368; cf. Pesikta Rabbati 5,4; 9,2; 22,1.

[38] See note 35 and, for the structure of 1Cor 1,18–31; 2,6–16, above 155 f.

[39] See below, 247–252; B. Gerhardsson, *The Testing of God's Son*, Lund 1966 (on Mt 4,1–11). Cf. also J. A. Sanders in *Essays in Old Testament Ethics*, ed. J. L. Crenshaw, New York 1974, 247–271 (on Lk 14); C. Perrot in *Revue des Sciences Religieuses* 47 (1973), 324–340 (on Lk 4,16–30).

[40] So SB IV, 173–8 citing MekExod 19,2 (69b); SifDtn 3,23 (70a). See note 35.

and final texts by a catchword λίθος (42, 44, cf. 35; Is 5,2, *saqal*); cf. οἰκοδομεῖν (33, 42).

42–44   – Concluding texts: Ps 118:22 f.; Dan 2:34 f., 44 f.[41]

In Lk 10,25–37[42] appears a somewhat different pattern, called in the rabbinic writings the *yelammedenu rabbenu* ('let our master teach us'), in which a question or problem is posed and then answered. Apart from the interrogative opening it follows in general the structure of the proem midrash (see above, 155):

25–27   – Dialogue including a question and initial texts: Dt 6,5; Lev 19,18.

28   – A second text: Lev 18,5.

29–36   – Exposition (by means of a parable) linked to the initial texts by the catchwords πλησίον (27, 29, 36) and ποιεῖν (28, 37a, 37b).

37   – Concluding allusion to the second text (ποιεῖν).

Mt 15,1–9 is similar[43]:

1–4   – Dialogue including a question and initial texts: Ex 20,12; 21,17.

5–6   – Exposition/application linked to the text and/or the dialogue by the catchwords τιμεῖν (4, 6, 8), παράδοσις (3, 6), cf. ἐντολή/ἔνταλμα (3, 9).

7–9   – Concluding text: Is 29,13.

---

[41] As Is 5,1 f. appears in the Gospels, the phrase 'cleared it of stones' is lacking; but it was probably in the original form of the midrash. Here the gospel tradition tends to reduce the Old Testament references. Luke curtails them further and the Gospel of Thomas (65 f.) eliminates them altogether. On the dependence of Thomas on canonical Luke (here) see below, 206 = *ZNTW* 62 (1971), 102; (in other sayings) cf. H. Schürmann in *BZ* 7 (1963), 236–260. Otherwise: H. Montefiore and H. E. W. Turner, *Thomas and the Evangelists*, London 1962, 62 ff.

[42] On the original unity of the pericopes, Mt 21,33–44 and Lk 10,25–37, see below, 247–252. Cf. further J. D. M. Derrett, *Law in the New Testament*, London 1970, 208–227 = *NTS* 11 (1964–65), 22–37; B. Gerhardsson, *The Good Samaritan*, Lund 1958, 28.

[43] D. Daube (*The New Testament and Rabbinic Judaism*, London 1956, 143) regards the passage, Mt 15,1–20 as an original unity, 'one whole from the outset,' with a close parallel in structure to GnRabba 8,9 (on Gen 1,26) and Num Rabba 19,8 (on Num 19,2). Even so, Mt 15,1–9 remains an original literary unity, relatively self-contained, and the midrash from which the rest of the passage proceeds.

Compare also Mt 19,3–8:[44]

3–5	– Question, answered by the initial texts: Gen 1,27; 2,24.
6	– Exposition linked to the initial text by the catchwords δύο, σάρξ μία.
7–8a	– Additional citation (Dt 24,1), posing a problem, with exposition.
8b	– Concluding allusion to the (interpolated!) initial text (ἀπ' ἀρχῆς).

As the Gospels uniformly attest, debates with scribes, i. e. theologians, about the meaning of Scripture constituted an important part of Jesus' public ministry. They were certainly more extensive than the Gospel accounts although they may have followed the same general pattern. In any case a *yelammedenu* pattern known and used by the rabbis is the literary form often employed by the Gospel traditioners[45]. In the rabbinical writings the pattern is usually not a dialogue but the Scriptural discourse of one rabbi. In this respect the exegetical structure in Rom 9—11 is closer to the rabbinic model than are the Gospel traditions[46].

Certain differences between rabbinic and New Testament exegesis should also be noted. Unlike the usual rabbinic practice the New Testament midrashim (1) often do not have an initial text from the Pentateuch, i. e. do not employ the sabbath text of the synagogue lectionary cycle. (2) They often lack a second, proem text. (3) They often have a final text that does not correspond or allude to the initial text. (4) They have an eschatological orientation (see below, 163 ff.). Nevertheless, in their general structure they have an affinity with the rabbinic usage that is unmistakable and too close to be coincidental.

(d) A kind of exposition known as the *pesher* midrash appears in the Qumran writings, e. g. the commentary on Habakkuk. It

---

[44] A more complex stating of a problem is found in Mt 22,23–33 = Mk 12, 18–27, the Sadducees' question about the resurrection.

[45] For the Gospels, as the above examples indicate, the forms in Matthew are at times clearer and closer to the Jewish, rabbinical patterns, i. e. presumably more primitive; those in Mark are at times broken and somewhat dissipated. This raises questions about the source criticism of the Gospels that cannot be discussed here.

[46] Cf. the midrash in Rom 9,13,14–23 (see below, 218 f.).

receives its name from the Hebrew word used in the explanatory formula, 'the interpretation *(pesher)* is.' This formula and its apparent equivalent, 'this is' *(hû'h)*, sometimes introduce the Old Testament citation (CD 10,16) or, more characteristically, the commentary following the citation. Both formulas occur in the Old Testament[47], the latter translated in the LXX by the phrase οὗτος (ἐστίν).

Besides the formula, the Qumran *pesher* has other characteristics common to midrashic procedure. Like the midrashim discussed above, it apparently uses or creates variant Old Testament text-forms designed to adapt the text to the interpretation in the commentary. It also links text and commentary by catchwords. It is found, moreover, in various kinds of commentary patterns: anthology (4Qflor), single quotations (CD 4,14) and consecutive commentary on an Old Testament book (1QpHab).

More significantly for New Testament studies, the Qumran *pesher*, unlike rabbinic midrash but very much like early Christian practice, is both charismatic and eschatological. As *eschatological exegesis*, it views the Old Testament as promises and prophecies that have their fulfilment within the writer's own time and community, a community that inaugurates the 'new covenant' of the 'last *('aharit)* days[48],' and constitutes the 'last *('aharôn)* generation' before the coming of Messiah and the inbreaking of the kingdom of God[49].

This characteristic feature, the *pesher* formula combined with an eschatological perspective, appears in a number of New Testament quotations:

'In Isaac shall your seed be called' (Gen 21,12). That is (τοῦτ' ἔστιν)... the children of the promise are reckoned for the seed. For this is (οὗτος) the word of promise. '... for Sarah there shall be a son' (Gen 18,10).

Rom 9,7–9

---

[47] Cf. Is 9,14; Ez 5,5; Zc 1,10; 5,6; Dan 4,21(24); 5,25 f.; at Qumran, 4Qflor 1,2 f.,11 f.,14; 1QpHab 3,1 ff. See below, 201–205. For the use of the formula in the rabbinic literature cf. W. Bacher, *Die Proömien der alten jüdischen Homilie*, Farnborough (Eng.) 1970 (1913), 17; *Exegetische Terminologie der jüdischen Traditionsliteratur*, Darmstadt 1965 (1899, 1905), 173 f., 177 f.

[48] Jer 31,31; 1QpHab 2,3–6; cf. CD 6,19; 8,21; 19,33; 20,12 f.; 1Cor 11,25; Hebr. 8,7–13.

[49] CD 1,12; 1QpHab 2,7; 7,2; 4QpIsaᵃ 8; Mk 13,30; cf. Mt 4,14–17; Acts 2,17; 1Cor 10,11.

Do not say in your heart, 'who shall ascend into heaven' (Dt 30,12), that is (τοῦτ' ἔστιν) to bring Christ down . . .

Rom 10,6—8

'On account of this shall a man leave father and mother and be joined to his wife, and the two shall be one flesh' (Gen 2,24). This is (τοῦτο . . . ἐστίν) a great mystery . . . for Christ and the Church.

Eph 5,31 f.

It is written, 'Abraham had two sons . . .' (cf. Gen 21). These are (αὗται . . . εἰσιν) two covenants . . .

Gal 4,22—24

All our fathers were under the cloud . . . But with many of them God was not pleased, for they were destroyed in the desert (cf. Ex 13 f.; 16 f.; Num 20; 14). These things (ταῦτα) happened as types for us . . .

1Cor 10,1—5,6 f.

They were all filled the Holy Spirit and began to speak in other tongues . . . This is (τοῦτό ἐστιν) what was spoken by the prophet Joel, 'I will pour out my spirit . . .' (Joel 2,28).

Acts 2,4,16 f.

Jesus Christ of Nazareth. . . . This is (οὗτός ἐστιν) 'the stone that was rejected by you builders, which has become the head of the corner' (Ps 118,22).

Acts 4,10 f.

The Qumran *pesher* is regarded by the community as *charismatic exegesis*, the work of inspired persons such as the Teacher of Righteousness and other wise teachers *(maśkīlīm)*. The Old Testament prophecies are understood, as they are in the book of Daniel (9,2,22 f.; cf. 2,19,24), to be a 'mystery' *(raz)* in need of interpretation *(pesher)*, an interpretation that only the *maśkīlīm* can give[50].

(e) From midrash to *testimonia:* 'Words lifted from their scriptural context can never be a testimonium to the Jewish mind. The word becomes a testimonium for something or other after one has brought out its meaning with the aid of other parts of Scripture.'[51] With this perceptive observation J. W. Doeve goes beyond the thesis of C. H. Dodd, mentioned above (151), to contend that

---

[50] Cf. 1QpHab 7,1—8; 1QH 12,11 ff.; R. N. Longenecker, *Biblical Exegesis in the Apostolic Period*, Grand Rapids 1974, 41—45; F. F. Bruce in *Neotestamentica et Semitica*, ed. E. E. Ellis and M. Wilcox, Edinburgh 1969, 225 ff.; O. Michel, *Paulus und seine Bibel*, Darmstadt ²1972, 215 ff.; H. C. Kee, 'The Function of . . . Quotations . . . in Mark 11—16', in E. E. Ellis and E Grässer (ed.), *Jesus und Paulus*, Göttingen 1975, 179—82. See above, 57 ff.

[51] Doeve, *Hermeneutics*, 116.

12*

'testimony' citations in the New Testament are derived from midrashim, i. e. expositions of those particular Old Testament passages.

In support of Doeve are several examples of a 'Christian' interpretation of a text that is established in an exposition and presupposed elsewhere in a 'testimony' citation of the same text[52]. (1) The exposition in Acts 2,17—35 and that underlying Mk 13 (see above, 154) apply Ps 110,1 and Dan 7,13, respectively, to Jesus. This interpretation is presupposed in the use of the verses at Mk 14,62. (2) Hebr 2,6—9 establishes by midrashic procedures that Ps 8 is fulfilled in Jesus; in 1Cor 15,27 and Eph 1,20,22 this understanding of Ps 8 (and Ps 110) is presupposed. (3) Acts 13, 16—41 is probably a (reworked) midrash in which 2Sam 7,6—16 is shown to apply to Jesus[53]. This interpretation of 2Sam 7 is presupposed in the *testimonia* in Hebr 1,5 and 2Cor 6,18.

The midrashic expositions in these examples are not, of course, the immediate antecedents of the cited *testimonia* texts. But they represent the kind of matrix from which the 'testimony' usage appears to be derived. They show, furthermore, that the prophets and teachers in the early church were not content merely to cite proof texts but were concerned to establish by exegetical procedures the Christian understanding of the Old Testament.

We may proceed one step further. Rabbinic parables often are found in midrashim as commentary on the Old Testament texts. Christ's parables also occur within an exegetical context, e. g. in Mt 21,33–44 and Lk 10,25–37 (see 157 ff.); and elsewhere, when they appear independently or in thematic clusters, they sometimes allude to Old Testament passages[54]. Probably such independent and clustered parables originated within an expository context from which they were later detached. If so, their present context represents a stage in the formation of the Gospel traditions secondary to their use within an explicit commentary format.

---

[52] See chapters twelve and fifteen below, 192—197, 213—218 (cf. 1Cor 1,31 with 2Cor 10,17); Michel, *Paulus*, 213. Somewhat different perhaps is Hab 2,4; it appears with Gen 15,6 = Rom 4,3 as the initial text of a midrash, Rom 1,17–4,25, and is apparently interpreted in terms of the exposition of the same text in Gal 3,6–29.

[53] See note 35.

[54] E. g. Mk 4,1—22 (on Jer 4,3); Lk 15,3—6 (on Ez 34,11).

II. *The Presuppositions of New Testament Interpretation*

1. *General*

To many Christian readers, to say nothing of Jewish readers, the New Testament's interpretation of the Old appears to be exceedingly arbitrary. For example, Hos 11,1 ('Out of Egypt I called my son') refers to Israel's experience of the Exodus; how can Mt 2,15 apply it to Jesus' sojourn in Egypt? In Ps 8,4 ff. the 'son of man' *(ben-'adam)* given 'glory' and 'dominion' alludes to Adam or to Israel's king[55]; how can Hebr 2,8 f. and 1 Cor 15,27 apply the text to Jesus? If Gen 15,6 and 2Sam 7 are predictions of Israel's future, how can New Testament writers refer them to Jesus and to his followers, who include Gentiles as well as Jews?

As has been shown above, the method used to justify such Christian interpretations of the Old Testament represents a serious and consistent effort to expound the texts. The method itself, of course, may be criticized. But then, our modern historical-critical method also is deficient: although it can show certain interpretations to be wrong, it can achieve an agreed interpretation for virtually no biblical passage. 'Method' is inherently a limited instrumentality and, indeed, a secondary stage in the art of interpretation. More basic are the perspective and presuppositions with which the interpreter approaches the text.

The perspective from which the New Testament writers interpret the Old is sometimes stated explicitly, sometimes it can be inferred from their usage. It is derived in part from contemporary Jewish views and in part from the teaching of Jesus and the experience of the reality of his resurrection. Apart from its christological focus, it appears to be governed primarily by four factors: a particular understanding of history, of man, of Israel and of Scripture.

2. *Salvation as History*

Jesus and his disciples conceive of history within the framework of two ages, this age and the age to come[56]. This perspective ap-

---

[55] Cf. F. Delitzsch, *The Psalms*, Grand Rapids 1949 (1871), 154–157; (re the king) A. Bentzen, *Fortolkning ... Salmer*, Copenhagen 1939, cited in H. Ringgren, *The Faith of the Psalmists*, Philadelphia 1963, 98.

[56] E. g. Mt 12,32; Mk 10,30; Lk 20,34 f.

pears to have its background in the Old Testament prophets, who prophesied of 'the last *('aḥariṯ)* days' and 'the day of the Lord' as the time of an ultimate redemption of God's people and the destruction of their enemies[57]. It becomes more specific in the apocalyptic writers, who underscored the cosmic dimension and (often) the imminence of the redemption and, with the doctrine of two ages, the radical difference between the present time and the time to come. This point of view is clearly present in the message of the Baptist that 'the kingdom of God is at hand' and that the one coming after him, Jesus, would accomplish the final judgment and redemption of the nation (Mt 3,2,10 ff.).

The *two-fold* consummation of judgment and deliverance that characterized the teaching of apocalyptic Judaism becomes, in the teaching of Jesus and his disciples, a *two-stage* consummation. As 'deliverance' the kingdom of God that Judaism expected at the end of the age is regarded as already present in the person and work of Jesus[58]. As 'judgment' (and final deliverance) the kingdom awaits the second, glorious appearing of Messiah[59]. This perspective may be contrasted with that of Platonism and of apocalyptic Judaism as follows:

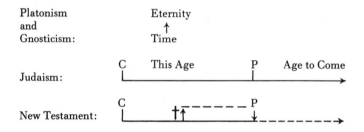

Platonic and later Gnostic thought anticipate a redemption from matter, an escape from time and history at death. The Jewish hope includes a redemption of matter within time: The present

---

[57] Num 24,14; Is 2,2; Dan 10,14; Hos 3,5; Am 5,18 ff.; Mi 4,1; Zc 14; cf. Hg 2,9; G. Kittel and G. von Rad, *TDNT* 2 (1964/1935), 697, 944 f.; U. Luz, *Das Geschichtsverständnis des Paulus*, München 1968, 53 ff.

[58] Cf. Lk 7,19–22; 11,20–22,31 par.; Rom 14,17; Gal 1,4; Col 1,13; O. Cullmann, *Christ and Time*, London 1952, 81–93; *Salvation in History*, London 1967, 193–209; Luz, *Paulus*, 5.

[59] Cf. Lk 11,2; 21,27; 22,16,28 ff.; Mt 25,31.

age, from creation (C) to the coming of Messiah (P), is to be succeeded by a future age of peace and righteousness under the reign
of God. The New Testament's modification of Jewish apocalyptic
rests upon the perception that in the mission, death and resurrection of Jesus the Messiah the age to come, the kingdom of God,
had become present in hidden form in the midst of the present evil
age, although its public manifestation awaits the parousia (P) of
Jesus. Thus, for Jesus 'the kingdom of God does not culminate a
meaningless history, but a planned divine process.'[60] Equally, for
the New Testament writers faith in Jesus means faith in the story
of Jesus, the story of God's redemptive activity in the history of
Israel that finds its high-point and fulfilment in Jesus.

For this reason the mission and meaning of Jesus can be expressed in the New Testament in terms of a *salvation history* 'con-
sisting of a sequence of events especially chosen by God, taking
place within an historical framework.'[61] Although the concept
οἰκονομία as used in Eph 1,10 represents this idea, that is, a divinely ordered plan, the term 'salvation history' does not itself
occur in the New Testament. The concept is most evident in the
way in which the New Testament relates current and future events
to events, persons and institutions in the Old Testament. That relationship is usually set forth as a typological correspondence.

3. Typology

(a) Typological interpretation expresses most clearly 'the basic
attitude of primitive Christianity toward the Old Testament.'[62] It
is not so much a system of interpretation as, in the phrase of Dr.
Goppelt, a 'spiritual perspective'[63] from which the early Chris-

---

[60] Cullmann, *Salvation*, 233, 236.

[61] *Ibid.*, 25. Cf. F. F. Bruce, 'Salvation History in the New Testament,' *Man
and his Salvation*, ed. E. J. Sharpe, Manchester 1973, 75–90; W. G. Kümmel,
Promise and Fulfilment, London 1957, 148: ... 'the New Testament message
itself is abrogated if a timeless message concerning the present as a time of
decision or concerning the spiritual nearness of God replaces the preaching of
the eschatological future and the determination of the present by the future.
For this would result in a complete degeneration of Jesus' message that man
... is placed in a definite situation in the *history* of salvation advancing toward
the end, and the figure and activity of Jesus would lose their fundamental
character as the *historical* activity of [God] ...'

[62] W. G. Kümmel, 'Schriftauslegung,' *RGG*[3] V, 1519.

[63] 'Pneumatische Betrachtungsweise.' L. Goppelt, *Typos: Die typologische*

tian community viewed itself. As a hermeneutical method it must be distinguished from τύπος ('model,' 'pattern') as it is widely used in the Greek world[64].

Only occasionally using the term τύπος typological interpretation appears, broadly speaking, as *covenant typology* and as *creation typology*. The latter may be observed in Rom 5, where Christ is compared and contrasted with Adam, 'a type (τύπος) of the one who was to come' (5,14). The former appears in 1Cor 10 where the Exodus events are said to be 'types for us', to have happened 'by way of example' (τυπικῶς) and to have been written down 'for our admonition upon whom the end of the ages has come' (10,6,11). Covenant typology accords with the Jewish conviction that all of God's redemptive acts followed the pattern of the Exodus[65]; it is, then, an appropriate way for Jesus and his community to explain the decisive messianic redemption. More generally, covenant typology approaches the whole of Old Testament as prophecy. Not only persons and events but also its institutions were 'a shadow of the good things to come.'[66]

(b) New Testament typology is thoroughly christological in its focus. Jesus is the 'prophet like Moses' (Acts 3,22 f.) who in his passion brings the old covenant to its proper goal and end (Rom 10,4; Hebr 10,9 f.) and establishes a new covenant (Lk 22,20,29). As the messianic 'son of David,' i. e. 'son of God,' he is the recipient of the promises, titles and ascriptions given to the Davidic kings[67].

Deutung des Alten Testaments im Neuen, Darmstadt 1969 (1939), 183, 243 f. An English translation is forthcoming from Eerdmans Publishing Co., Grand Rapids, Mich. USA.   [64] Cf. Luz, *Paulus*, 53.

[65] D. Daube, *The Exodus Pattern in the Bible*, London 1963; G. von Rad, *Old Testament Theology*, 2 vols., London 1960, 1965, II, 272.

[66] Hebr 5,1—10; 9,9; 10,1; Col 2,17; cf. Mt 7,11; Joh 3,14 f.; 6,32; Hebr 8,5 (cf. 9,24; Acts 7,44), reflecting Ex 25,40, reverses the usual typological imagery and identifies τύπος with the heavenly model for which the Old Testament institutions were 'anti-types.' Like John (6,31—39; 14,1—3) and unlike Philo, Hebrews incorporates the vertical typology into the horizontal, two-age schema by identifying the 'heavenly' with the age to come, that is, with the ascended and *coming* Jesus. Cf. Hebr 9,24—28; 10,37; L. Goppelt, *TDNT* 8 (1972), 258; Rev 21,2; Gal 4,25 f.: 'present Jerusalem ... Jerusalem above.' See also C. T. Fritsch, 'TO ANTITYΠON', *Studia Biblica [for] T. C. Vriezen*, ed. W. C. van Unnik, Wageningen 1966, 100—110.

[67] 2Sam 7,12 ff.; Ps 2; 16; 110; Am 9,11 f.; cf. Joh 7,42; Acts 3,25—36; 13, 33 ff.; 15,16 ff.; 1Cor 15,25; Hebr 1,5; E. Lohse, *TDNT* 8 (1972), 482—487. Re Moses cf. J. Jeremias, *TDNT* 4 (1967/1942), 856—873. Re Son of God cf. M. Hengel, *The Son of God*, London 1976, 42—5.

Because the new covenant consummated by Jesus' death is the occasion of the new creation initiated by his resurrection, covenant typology may be combined with creation typology: As the 'eschatological Adam' and the 'Son of man,' i. e. 'son of Adam,'[68] Jesus stands at the head of a new order of creation that may be compared and contrasted with the present one. This combination in Paul and Hebrews finds its immediate background in the resurrection of Jesus[69]. But it is already implicit in Jesus' own teaching, e. g. his temple saying, his promise to the robber and his teaching on divorce[70]. It is probably implicit also in his self-designation as the Son of man (Mk 14,62), a designation that is derived from Ps 8,4 and Dan 7,13 f., 27. The Son of man in Ps 8 refers not only to Israel's (messianic-ideal) king but also to Adam[71]; likewise the Son of man in Dan 7 is related not only to national restoration but also to a new creation[72]. In apocalyptic Judaism also Israel was associated with Adam and the new covenant with a renewed creation[73]. Jesus and his followers shared these convictions and explained them in terms of the mission and person of Jesus.

(c) The Old Testament type not only corresponds to the new-age reality but also stands in antithesis to it. Like Adam Jesus is the representative headman of the race; but unlike Adam, who brought death, Jesus brings forgiveness and life[74]. Jesus is 'the prophet like Moses' but, unlike Moses' ministry of condemnation, that of Jesus gives righteousness[75]. Similarly, the law 'is holy, just and good' and its commandments are to be 'fulfilled' by the believer[76]; yet as a demand upon man it can only condemn him[77].

---

[68] Ps 8,4, *ben-adam;* 1Cor 15,27,45; Eph 1,21 f.; Hebr 2,5–10; cf. Lk 3,38; Acts 7,44,48.   [69] Cf. also 1Petr 3,21 f.; Rev 2,7,26 f.

[70] Mk 14,58 (ἀχειϱοποιητός); Lk 23,42 f. ('kingdom,' 'Paradise'); Mt 19,4–9; cf. Lk 16,16–18.

[71] See note 55. Cf. W. Wifall, 'Gen 3,15 . . .', *CBQ* 36 (1974), 365: The Yahwist has presented Israel's prehistory within a 'Davidic' or 'messianic' framework.

[72] Dan 7,14 ('dominion,' 'glory'); cf. M. Hooker, *The Son of Man in Mark,* London 1967, 17 ff., 24–30, 71.

[73] Dan 7,13 f.,27; TestLevi 18; 2 Baruch 72–74; 1QS 4,22 f.; CD 3,13–20; 4, 20; 1QH 6,7 f.,15 f.; 17,12–15; IQ 34; cf. Is 43; 65,22.

[74] 1Cor 15,22; Rom 5,12,15.   [75] Acts 3,25; 13,39; 15,10; 2Cor 3,6–9.

[76] Gal 5,14; Rom 7,12; 13,8: 'Love' (Lev 19,18) is not a substitute for the commandments (Ex 20) but a means and guide by which they are interpreted and fulfilled. Cf. Hebr 10,1.

[77] 2Cor 3,6; cf. Gal 3,10–13. The failure to distinguish, among other things,

One may speak, then, of 'synthetic' and of 'antithetic' typology to distinguish the way in which a type, to one degree or another, either corresponds to or differs from the reality of the new age[78].

(d) Since the history of salvation is also the history of destruction[79], it includes a *judgment typology*. The flood and Sodom, and perhaps the A. D. 70 destruction of Jerusalem, become types of God's eschatological judgment[80]; the faithless Israelite a type of the faithless Christian[81]; the enemies of Israel a type of the (Jewish) enemies of the Church[82] and, perhaps, a type of Antichrist[83].

(e) In a brilliant and highly significant contribution to New Testament hermeneutics Leonard Goppelt has set forth the definitive marks of typological interpretation[84]. (1) Unlike allegory, ty-

---

between the law as an expression of God's righteousness, which it ever continues to be, and the (works of) law as a means of man's salvation, which it is not and never was, leads G. Klein (*Rekonstruktion und Interpretation*, München 1969, 210 = *Evangelische Theologie* 24 [1964], 155) to the totally misguided conclusion that for Paul Moses, the giver of the law, is 'the functionary of anti-godly powers ... [and] the historical realm based on him is not merely profaned but flatly demonized.' Cf. C. E. B. Cranfield, 'St. Paul and the Law', *SJT* 17 (1964), 43—68; 'Notes on Rom 9,30—33', in E. E. Ellis and E. Grässer (ed.), *Jesus und Paulus*, Göttingen 1975, 35—43.

[78] Luz, *Paulus*, 59 f. E. g. Abraham represents synthetic typology (i. e. his faith) but not antithetic (i. e. his circumcision, Gal 3). Moses and the Exodus can represent both (Hebr 11,28 f.; 1Cor 10,1—4,6—10; 2Cor 3,9); so can Jerusalem (Gal 4,25 f.; Rev 11,8; 21,2). The old covenant, i. e. the law, more often represents antithetic typology.

[79] Cullmann, *Salvation*, 123; cf. 127—135.

[80] Lk 17,26—30; 2Petr 2,6; Jude 7 (δεῖγμα); Mt 24,3.

[81] 1Cor 10,6—11; Hebr 4,5,11.

[82] Rev 11,8; 17,5; cf. Rom 2,24; Gal 4,29.   [83] 2Thess 2,3 f.; Rev 13,1—10.

[84] Goppelt, *Typos*. Cf. Cullmann, *Salvation*, 127—135; J. C. K. von Hofmann, *Interpreting the Bible*, Minneapolis 1972 (1880). Alternative approaches have been advocated by R. E. Brown (*The Sensus Plenior of Sacred Scripture*, Baltimore 1955), by the existentialist theologians (e. g. M. Rese, *Alttestamentliche Motive in der Christologie des Lukas*, Gütersloh 1969, 209; A. Suhl, *Die Funktion der alttestamentlichen Zitate ... im Markusevangelium*, Gütersloh 1965, 162—186) and by A. T. Hanson (*Jesus Christ in the Old Testament*, London 1965, 6 f., 172—178), who believes that 'the real presence of the pre-existent Jesus' best explains, for the most part, this area of New Testament exegesis. Cf. also his *Studies in Paul's Technique and Theology*, London 1974, 149 to 158. Whether *sensus plenior* is only a kind of allegorical interpretation, as J. L. McKenzie thinks (*JBL* 77, 1958, 202 f.), will depend upon the criteria used; cf. R. E. Brown, *CBQ* 25 (1963), 274 ff. Hanson's view does not pose an absolute alternative to typological interpretation, as he admits (177); it also does not appear to do justice to certain aspects of the two-age, apocalyptic frame-

pological exegesis regards the words of Scripture not as metaphors hiding a deeper meaning (ὑπόνοια) but as the record of historical events out of whose literal sense the meaning of the text arises (18 f., 243 ff.). (2) Unlike the 'history of religions' exegesis, it seeks the meaning of current, New Testament situations from a particular history, the salvation-history of Israel. From past Old Testament events it interprets the meaning of the present time of salvation and, in turn, it sees in present events a typological prophecy of the future consummation (235—248). (3) Like rabbinic midrash, typological exegesis interprets the text in terms of contemporary situations, but it does so with historical distinctions that are lacking in rabbinic interpretation (31—34). (4) It identifies a typology in terms of two basic characteristics, historical correspondence and escalation, in which the divinely ordered prefigurement finds a complement in the subsequent and greater event (244).

In a masterly essay[85] Rudolf Bultmann rejected Goppelt's conclusion that salvation history was constitutive for typological exegesis and sought to show that the origin of typology lay rather in a cyclical-repetitive view of history (cf. Barnabas 6,13). Although Judaism had combined the two perspectives, the New Testament, e. g. in its Adam/Christ typology, represents a purely cyclical pattern, parallels between the primal time and the end time.

However, Professor Bultmann (369 f.), in interpreting the New Testament hermeneutical usage within the context of the traditional Greek conception[86], does not appear to recognize that the recapitulation element in New Testament typology is never mere repetition but is always combined with a change of key in which some aspects of the type are not carried over and some are intensified. Exegetically Goppelt made the better case and established an important framework for understanding how the New Testament uses the Old.

---

work of New Testament thought. The setting of existential decision in opposition to salvation history *(Suhl)* is, in my judgement, a false dichotomy. See below, 171 f.

[85] R. Bultmann, 'Ursprung und Sinn der Typologie als hermeneutische Methode,' (*TLZ* 75 (1950), cols. 205—212 = *Exegetica*, Tübingen 1967, 369—380.

[86] See note 64.

4. Other Presuppositions

(a) In agreement with the Old Testament conception, the New Testament views *man as both individual and corporate existence.* It presents the corporate dimension, the aspect most difficult for modern Western man to appreciate, primarily in terms of Jesus and his church[87]. For the New Testament faith in Jesus involves an incorporation into him[88]: It is to eat his flesh (Joh 6,35,54), to be his body (1Cor 12,27), to be baptized into him (Rom 6,3), or into his name (1Cor 1,13; Acts 8,16), to be identified with him (Acts 9,4 f.), to exist in the corporate Christ (2Cor 5,17) who is the 'tent' (Hebr 9,11) or 'house' (2Cor 5,1) in the heavens, God's eschatological temple.

Corporate existence can also be expressed as baptism 'into Moses' (1Cor 10,2), existence 'in Abraham' (Hebr 7,9 f.) or 'in Adam' (1Cor 15,22) and, at its most elementary level, the unity of man and wife as 'one flesh' (Mt 19,5; Eph 5,29 ff.). It is not merely a metaphor, as we are tempted to interpret it, but an ontological statement about who and what man is. The realism of this conception is well expressed by the term 'corporate personality.'[89]

The corporate extension of the person of the leader to include individuals who belong to him illumines the use of a number of Old Testament passages. It explains how the promise given to Solomon

---

[87] Mk 14,22 ff.; Col 1,24; J. A. T. Robinson, *The Body*, London 1952; R. P. Shedd, *Man in Community*, London 1958; Ellis, *Paul's Use*, 88—98, 126—135; B. Gärtner, *The Temple and the Community in Qumran and in the New Testament*, Cambridge 1965, 138—142.

[88] Even the phrase 'in faith' appears to denote at times a sphere of existence, i. e. 'in Christ.' Cf. Acts 14,22; 16,5; 1Cor 16,13; 2Cor 13,5; Col 1,23; 2,7; 1Tim 1,2; 2,15; Jas 2,5; 1Petr 5,9. On baptism, however, cf. L. Hartman, 'Baptism "into the name of Jesus"', *Studia Theologica* 28 (1974), 24—28, 35 f.

[89] H. W. Robinson, *Corporate Personality in Ancient Israel*, Philadelphia 1964 (1935); cf. *Deuteronomy and Joshua* (The Century Bible), Edinburgh 1907, 266. Cf. J. Pedersen, *Israel*, London 1959 (1926), I—II, 263—269, 474 to 479; III—IV, 76—86; A. R. Johnson, *The One and the Many in the Israelite Conception of God*, Cardiff 1961, 1—13. J. W. Rogerson (*JTS* 21, 1970, 1—16) suspects that Robinson's concept may have been derived from a current theory about primitive man's thought. The theory may have stimulated Robinson's work, just as current psychological theory may have stimulated a recognition of the psychosomatic unity of man in Scripture. But it is hardly responsible for the exegetical conclusion that has been established with considerable probability by Robinson, Pedersen, Johnson and others. To set that aside one needs a more persuasive explanation of the texts, a task that Rogerson does not attempt.

(2Sam 7,12—16) can be regarded as fulfilled not only in the Messiah (Hebr 1,5) but also in his followers (2Cor 6,18) and, similarly, how the eschatological temple can be identified both wtith the individual (Mk 14,58; Joh 2,19 ff.) and corporate (1Cor 3,16; 1Petr 2,5) Christ. It very probably underlies the conviction of the early Christians that those who belong to Christ, Israel's messianic king, constitute *the true Israel*[90]. Consequently, it explains the Christian application to unbelieving Jews of Scriptures originally directed to Gentiles[91] and, on the other hand, the application to the church of Scriptures originally directed to the Jewish nation[92].

Corporate personality also offers a rationale whereby individual, existential decision (Mk 1,17; 2Cor 6,2) may be understood within the framework of a salvation history of the nation or the race. These two perspectives are considered by some scholars to be in tension[93] or to be mutually exclusive[94]. However, in the words of Oscar Cullmann[95], the 'now of decision' in the New Testament is not in conflict with the salvation-historical attitude but subordinate to it: 'Paul's faith in salvation history creates at every moment the existential decision.' For it is precisely within the context of the community that the individual's decision is made: Universal history and individual history cannot be isolated from one another[96].

The history of salvation often appears in the New Testament as the history of individuals — Adam, Abraham, Moses, David, Jesus; yet they are individuals who also have a corporate dimension embracing the nation or the race. The decision to which the New Testament calls men relates to them. It is never a decision between

---

[90] Cf. Ellis, *Paul's Use*, 136—139; Lk 19,9; Acts 3,22 f.; 15,14 ff.; Rom 9,6; Gal 6,16; Phil 3,3; Hebr 4,9; Rev 2,14. Otherwise: J. Jervell, *Luke and the People of God*, Minneapolis 1972, 41—69; P. Richardson, *Israel in the Apostolic Church*, Cambridge 1969.

[91] E. g. Acts 4,25 ff.; Rom 8,36; 11,9—10; cf. M.Simon, *Verus Israel*, Paris 1964, 104—24; W. Gutbrot, *TDNT* 3 (1965/1938), 384—388; H. Strathmann, *TDNT* 4 (1967/1942), 50—57.

[92] E. g. 2Cor 6,16 ff.; Hebr 8,8—12; 1Petr 2,9 f. The Qumran sect views itself similarly. In IQM 1,2 the Jewish 'offenders' are included among the pagan enemies. Cf. 1QpHab 2,1—4; 4Qtest 22,29 f.

[93] E. Dinkler, 'Earliest Christianity,' *The Idea of History in the Ancient Near East*, ed. R. C. Denton, New Haven 1955, 190.

[94] Klein, *Rekonstruktion*, 180—204.

[95] Cullmann, *Salvation*, 248.   [96] Luz, *Paulus*, 156.

the isolated individual and God but is, rather, a decision to 'put off the old man' and to 'put on the new man,' to be delivered from the corporeity 'in Moses' and 'in Adam' and to be 'immersed in' and to 'put on' Christ, i. e. to be incorporated into the 'prophet like Moses' and the eschatological Adam of the new creation in whom the history of salvation is to be consummated[97].

(b) The early Christian prophets and teachers explain the Old Testament by what may be called *charismatic exegesis* or, in the words of L. Cerfaux[98], 'spiritual interpretation.' Like the teachers of Qumran, they proceed from the conviction that the meaning of the Old Testament is a 'mystery' whose 'interpretation' can be given not by human reason but only by the Holy Spirit[99]. On the basis of revelation from the Spirit they are confident of their ability to rightly interpret the Scriptures[100]. Equally, they conclude that those who are not gifted cannot 'know' the true meaning of the word of God[101].

This view of their task does not preclude the New Testament writers from using logic or hermeneutical rules and methods. However, it does disclose where the ultimate appeal and authority of their interpretation lie. Correspondingly, an acceptance of their interpretation of Scripture in preference to some other, ancient or modern, also will rest ultimately not on the proved superiority of their logical procedure or exegetical method but rather on the conviction of their prophetic character and role.

---

[97] Eph 4,22 ff.; 1Cor 10,2; 15,22,45; Gal 3,27; Acts 3,22 ff.

[98] P. Auvray *et al.*, *L'Ancient Testament et les chrétiens*, Paris 1951, 132 to 148.

[99] 1Cor 2,6—16. See notes 15, 50.

[100] Cf. Mt 16,17; Mk 4,11; Rom 11,25 f.; 12,6 f.; 16,25 f.; 1Cor 2,12 f.; Eph 3, 3—6; 2Petr 3,15 f.

[101] Mt 22,29; 2Cor 3,14 ff.

10. MIDRASH PESHER IN PAULINE HERMENEUTICS

The priority of the LXX in Pauline quotations has long been recognized; slightly over half are in absolute or virtual agreement, often at variance with the Hebrew. However, more striking is the fact that thirty-eight of the apostle's citations vary both from the LXX and the M. T. The problem of divergent N. T. quotations has engaged the minds of many scholars from the Reformation to the present time, and attempts at solution have not been lacking. Some 250 years ago, in an argument strangely resembling some twentieth-century discussions, Whiston and Carpzov sought to resolve the issue[1]. Whiston argued that the N. T. was exact with first-century Greek and Hebrew texts but that the latter were corrupted. Having 'shrewdly suspected some pernicious practices of the Jews in this case', especially with regard to the Hebrew Bible, Whiston sought to correct the present O. T. text with the Samaritan Pentateuch, the N. T., Philo, Josephus, and other sources. Carpzov, in reply, defended the accuracy of the Hebrew text and attributed N. T. variations to hermeneutical purposes and literary convenience. In more recent times these two lines of thought have continued to play an important role in the study of N. T. quotations and are implicit in more comprehensive problems such as the origin of the LXX and the 'testimony hypothesis'.

Of the considerable number of Pauline quotations which vary from the LXX and/or the M. T., some may be explained on the basis of a variant textual source. However, agreements with the Targum, Peshitta, and various Greek texts are sporadic; and in some of these texts, at least, a Christian influence is probable. In any case it is very doubtful that all of the apostle's textual aberrations can be accounted for in this manner. Several variant read-

---

[1] W. Whiston, *An Essay toward Restoring the True Text of the Old Testament*, London 1722, 283; J. G. Carpzov, *A Defense of the Hebrew Bible*, London 1729, 104—83.

ings which have a direct bearing on the N. T. application suggest either an *ad hoc* rendering or an interpretive selection from various known texts. For example, the addition of πᾶς in Rom 10,11 (Rom 9,33 omits it) contributes directly to the argument; and there is little doubt that Paul is here inserting his own 'commentary' into the body of the text. In Rom 12,19 the variation apparently follows the rendering of the Targum; making this selection, Paul (or an earlier Christian exegete) secures the desired interpretation:

N. T.: Vengeance is mine, I will repay.
M. T.: To me belongs vengeance and retribution.
Targ.: Vengeance is before me and I will repay.

Also, לֹנֶצַח in Is 25,8, which Paul (1Cor 15,54) — against the LXX and Targum (לְעָלְמִין) — renders εἰς νῖκος, usually is translated 'forever' or 'utterly'[2]. The Aramaic נצח can mean 'excel' or 'overcome', and this connotation is probably not entirely absent from the Hebrew. The point of interest, however, is that Paul uses a selective interpretation; and this interpretation is essential for the application of the passage in 1Corinthians 15.

The same motive apparently is present in Rom 11,26 f. Where the M. T. reads 'to those who turn from transgression in Jacob', Romans (with the LXX) has 'and shall turn away ungodliness from Jacob'. The LXX itself is here an interpretive rendering of the Hebrew, an interpretation which accords with the argument in Romans. Possibly Paul merely follows the text which lay before him, but more likely he retains the LXX reading because it gives the sense which he himself finds in the passage. There are a number of indications favouring this supposition. In the same verse Paul departs from the LXX in the phrase ἐκ Σιών, evidently with a hermeneutical purpose in view. Furthermore, where the LXX text is followed elsewhere a distinctive interpretation of the Hebrew is sometimes involved; and upon this interpretation Paul's argument is built. For example, in Rom 1,17 πίστις stresses a particular aspect of אמונה ; in Gal 3,8 the N. T. and LXX 'be blessed' would, on the basis of statistical probability, better represent the Hebrew if it were reflexive rather than passive. These variations should not be viewed as capricious, or arbitrary, or merely inci-

---

[2] E. g. 2Sam 2,26; Job 36,7; Amos 1,11.

dental. Similar features found in other writings of the N. T. and of the Qumran sect indicate that this procedure has a more significant purpose: Paul utilizes *ad hoc* renderings and the deliberate selection and rejection of known readings to draw out and express the true meaning of the O. T. passage as he understands it.

In his dissertation, Dean K. Stendahl compared the texts of Matthew's 'formula' quotations with the M. T., LXX, Targum, and other Greek and Syriac versions[3]. He found that, in contrast to other O. T. citations in the Gospels, the 'formula' quotations peculiar to Matthew follow no one textual tradition but represent a selective targumizing procedure in which the interpretation is woven into the text itself. The rendering is not the result of a free paraphrase or looseness but arises out of a scholarly, detailed study and interpretation of the texts themselves[4]. Furthermore, the Matthaean type of midrashic interpretation closely approaches the *midrash pesher* of the Qumran sect[5]. To prove this contention Stendahl engages in a detailed examination of some of the exegetical procedures employed in the Habakkuk scroll (1QpHab).

In *pesher* quotation or midrash the interpretation or exposition is incorporated into the body of the text itself, thereby determining its textual form. Also, the method, as found in 1QpHab and in the N. T., has an apocalyptic feature in which the prophetic passage is viewed as 'fulfilled' in the present time and is applied to contemporary events[6]. As the Habakkuk 'Commentary' applies Habakkuk 1—2 to the Teacher of Righteousness and the events surrounding him, similarly Matthew's formula quotations view the O. T. as fulfilled in Christ. Stendahl, however, is concerned chiefly with the way in which *pesher* interpretation affects the text-form (as contrasted with the exposition proper) of 1QpHab. He finds more than fifty variants from the M. T., most of which form 'such an intimate and organic part of the exposition of the

---

[3] K. Stendahl, *The School of St Matthew*, Uppsala 1954, [2]1969. Cf. *NTS* I (1954—55), 155 ff. [4] *Ibid.* 195, 200 f.

[5] *Ibid.* 35. Pesher (פשר) occurs as a technical term in 1QpHab. Whether it should be rendered 'commentary', 'interpretation', or 'midrash' is uncertain; Stendahl classifies it as a midrash parallel to halacha and haggada. Cf. the discussion in B. J. Roberts, 'Some Observations on the Damascus Documents and the Dead Sea Scrolls', *BJRL* 34 (1951—2), 367 ff.; below, 189 f., 196 n.

[6] Roberts *(ibid.)* regards this factor as the chief link between the Dead Sea Scrolls and the N. T.

text that they cannot possibly be dismissed as [scribal errors]'[7]. Even though many of these readings appear to be created *ad hoc*, they nevertheless frequently coincide with one or more of the known versions; 'such coincidences occur where adaption to the dogma and situation of the sect could sufficiently explain the text of [1QpHab].'[8]

Stendahl classifies 1QpHab variants as to (1) alterations of number and suffix, and (2) more substantial changes[9]. Among the former, in Hab 1,13 M. T. has the singular (הביט), 1QpHab the plural (הביטו); in Hab 2,1 M. T. has מצור, 1QpHab מצורי; in Hab 1,10 M. T. has a feminine, 1QpHab a masculine; M. T. a second person suffix, 1QpHab a third person (Hab 2,15); M. T. a suffix where 1QpHab has none (Hab 2,18). Other variations are of greater weight: M. T. in Hab 1,9 has a locative *heh* with the idea 'eastward' or 'forward' (קדימה), 1QpHab takes the word as a noun (קדים); in Hab 2,5 M. T. has היין ('wine'), 1QpHab הון ('riches'); in Hab 2,6 M. T. has מליצה ('taunt'), 1QpHab מליצי ('interpreters'). In several places a reading or interpretation is omitted from the 1QpHab text only to be taken up in the exposition, e. g. 'they shall come' in Hab 1,8; this indicates the exegete's acquaintance with other readings or possible interpretations. After comparing the divergent readings with later O. T. texts and versions, which in many cases are in accord with 1QpHab, Stendahl evaluates the data as follows:

> The peculiar way in which [1QpHab] coincides both with those readings differing from the M. T. and with the M. T.'s own makes it inadequate to say that [1QpHab]'s Hebrew text was the one which is supported by the said versions. We must rather presume that [1QpHab] was conscious of various possibilities, tried them out and allowed them to enrich its interpretation of the prophet's message, which in all its forms was fulfilled in and through the Teacher of Righteousness[10].

Stendahl finds similar phenomena — variations in person and number, structural changes, and evident knowledge of divergent readings — in Matthew's quotations and regards this as arising from a scholarly interpretation of the texts by an early Christian 'school' of exegetes: they selected from various textual traditions,

---

[7] Stendahl, 185.   [8] *Ibid.* 189.
[9] *Ibid.*, 185—90.   [10] *Ibid.* 190.

and at times created *ad hoc,* readings which best expressed the meaning of the text as they understood it.

There are a number of Pauline quotations which indicate that the *pesher* method was employed not only by the apostle but in the pre-Pauline period of the Church as well[11]. The apocalyptic outlook, in its messianic expression, is implicit in the whole Pauline hermeneutic and is particularly obvious in 2Cor 6,2:

> For he saith, I have heard thee in a time accepted and in the day of salvation have I succoured thee: behold now is the accepted time, behold now is the day of salvation[12].

The interpreted or *pesher* text-form is also present in Paul's quotations. The apostle follows the LXX where it diverges from the M. T. in a number of places. Some of these probably have an exegetical purpose in view (e. g. πίστις in Rom 1,17; οἷς in Rom 15, 21)[13]; but since the LXX is his usual *vade mecum,* it is difficult to show 'a selective rendering of a chosen text' in most of the citations.

In some twenty quotations in which the LXX and M. T. agree and Paul's text varies, the evidence of *pesher* technique is more certain. In almost all of these the variation seems to be a deliberate adaption to the N. T. context; in some cases the alteration has a definite bearing on the interpretation of the passage. Changes in person and number are especially prevalent[14]. The deviations in the *catena* in 2Cor 6,16 ff. are evidently designed for a messianic-age interpretation of the prophecies. God's command to Israel regarding Babylon (αὐτῆς) is now applied to the relation of Christions with unbelievers (αὐτῶν); the promise given to Israel 'person-

---

[11] Stendahl recognizes that this type of interpretation is present in apocalyptic writings and occasionally in the rabbis (*ibid.* 195), and that it is found in other N. T. writings, especially the Fourth Gospel. But he concludes that there were fewer intentional changes based on the Hebrew, and 'thus the elaborate stage of the *pesher* found in Matthew scarcely existed' (*ibid.* 202).

[12] The manner in which this citation is parenthetically inserted suggests that the whole verse — the O. T. text plus the interpretation — was taken as a quotation by Paul. Cf. 1Cor 15,45; 1Tim 5,18; 2Tim 2,19.

[13] On Rom 1,17, cf. C. F. Burney, *The Gospel in the Old Testament,* Edinburgh 1921, 129 f.; the LXX 'to whom' in Rom 15,21 accords much more explicitly with Paul's application than the indefinite אשר of the M. T.

[14] E. g. Rom 3,18 (αὐτοῦ to αὐτῶν); 10,19 (αὐτούς to ὑμᾶς); 1Cor 15,27 (ὑπέταξας to ὑπέταξεν). See below, 191 n.

ified' in Solomon (αὐτῷ . . . αὐτός) is fulfilled in the true Israel, the members of Christ's body (ὑμῖν . . . ὑμεῖς). Similarly, σοφῶν in 1Cor 3,20 and ὁ πρῶτος ἄνθρωπος 'Αδάμ in 1Cor 15,45 show an elaboration or interpretation of the O. T. text to fit it to the N. T. context.

In a few instances the variations point to a selection from among several known readings. The present state of the whole textual problem cautions against any dogmatizing in this regard[15], and there appears to be no instance of a rejected reading being alluded to in the apostle's exposition. Nevertheless, the choice of a particular text for interpretive reasons appears probable in several Pauline quotations. Rom 12,19 modifies the Hebrew with the Targum; the Targum also may be the source of the rendering, 'confess', which is important for the sense of the citation in Rom 14,11[16]. Eph 4,8 substitutes the third person for the second and rejects the M. T. and LXX rendering 'take' or 'receive' in favour of the translation 'give' found in the Targum and Peshitta. Whether this represents an interpretation of לקח ('take', 'fetch'), or a variant Hebrew textual tradition (e. g. חלק, 'apportion', 'distribute') is uncertain, but the former is more probable.

1Cor 15,54 f. (Is 25,8; Hos 13,14) is perhaps the most notable instance of *pesher* quotation in the Pauline literature:

Death is swallowed up in victory.
Where, O Death, is your victory?
Where, O Death, is your sting?

The interrogative of the LXX is followed (the M. T. אהי is uncertain), and for the M. T. לנצח ('forever') εἰς νῖκος ('in victory') is substituted. The rendering εἰς νῖκος, which is found in other Greek texts[17], may originate in the Hebrew (or Aramaic) root itself (נצח, leader, success). The Peshitta conflation, 'to victory forever', witnesses to two known versions of the passage[18]; but whether the Peshitta, Theodotion, and like readings reflect a textual tra-

---

[15] E. g. Paul's citations from Job (Rom 11,35; 1Cor 3,19) may follow the Hebrew simply because it is the most familiar text.
[16] So C. H. Toy, *Quotations in the New Testament*, New York 1884, *in loc.* The *pael* תקים, used in the Targum, may have the meaning 'vouch' or 'confirm'.
[17] *Viz.* Theodotion and Aquila. The Targum has 'forever' (לעלמין).
[18] Cf. Toy, 180.

dition known to and used by Paul, or whether they represent a textual tradition derived from the Pauline usage, is a moot point. The variant εἰς νῖκος is interwoven into Paul's exposition and indicates that the merged quotation was probably known to him in this form. But the idea of death being 'swallowed up in victory' is so intimately connected with the 'victory' of Christ's resurrection that, if a conjecture must be made, the probability is that this interpretation of the Hebrew is one created (or recovered) in the early Church. As Manson has well remarked, the doctrinal and liturgical traditions of the first century were very influential in shaping the textual traditions themselves[19].

Taken as a whole, the Pauline citations reflect in substantial measure a *pesher*-type moulding of the text which in some cases is determinative for the N. T. application of the passage. While this at times involves a choosing and rejecting between texts and/or targums known to the apostle, more often the interpretive paraphrase appears to be created *ad hoc* by Paul or by the early Church before him. This type of *pesher* arises from the N. T.'s attitude toward and understanding of the concept of 'quotation' itself as Manson has noted:

> We are long accustomed to distinguish carefully between the text which — in more senses than one — is sacred, and the commentary upon it and exposition of it. We tend to think of the text as objective fact and interpretation as subjective opinion. It may be doubted whether the early Jewish and Christian translators and expositors of Scripture made any such sharp distinction. For them the meaning of the text was of primary importance; and they seem to have had greater confidence than we moderns in their ability to find it. Once found it became a clear duty to express it; and accurate reproduction of the traditional wording of the Divine oracles took second place to publication of what was held to be their essential meaning and immediate application. Odd as it may seem to us, the freedom with which they handled the Biblical text is a direct result of the supreme importance which they attached to it[20].

In selecting a particular version or in creating an *ad hoc* rendering Paul views his citation as thereby more accurately expressing the true meaning of the Scripture. For Paul, as for the rabbis, the 'letter' was sacred; but unlike some rabbis, Paul valued the 'letter'

---

[19] T. W. Manson, 'The Cairo Geniza: A Review', *Dominican Studies*, II (1949), 184. Other quotations such as 1Cor 2,9; 14,21; 15,45 also appear to involve interpretations which have a distinctively Christian origin.

[20] T. W. Manson, 'The Argument from Prophecy', *JTS* 46 (1945), 135.

not for itself alone but for the meaning which it conveyed. His idea of a quotation was not a worshipping of the letter or 'parroting' of the text; neither was it an eisegesis which arbitrarily imposed a foreign meaning upon the text. It was rather, in his eyes, a quotation-exposition, a *midrash pesher*, which drew from the text the meaning originally implanted there by the Holy Spirit and expressed that meaning in the most appropriate words and phrases known to him.

The *pesher* method is not used extensively in Paul's quotations; but where is does occur, it often appears to go behind the Greek to reflect an interpretation of the Hebrew Ur-text. Further, some of the most significant instances appear to point back to a pre-Pauline usage in the early Church. The presence of the method in λέγει κύριος quotations (e. g. Rom 12,19; 1Cor 14,21), the temple typology *catena* (cf. 2Cor 6,16 ff.), and such citations as 1Cor 15, 45 are cases in point[21]. Stendahl's valuable dissertation, by its comparison of *pesher* quotation in Matthew and 1QpHab, presents a strong argument that N.T. writers and the Christian exegetes behind them, in their use of this method, are not indulging in a novelty. Converted priests and rabbis, especially those formerly adhering to apocalyptic parties or sects, might be expected to be well acquainted with it. Having now the light of the gospel and the gifts of the Spirit, it is no surprise that they apply a *midrash pesher* method to the O. T. with conviction, confidence, and thoroughness. Stendahl envisions this exposition in its N. T. form as the product of early Christian 'schools of the prophets'. He suggests that the development may form 'an unbroken line from the School of Jesus via "the teaching of the apostles", the "ways" of Paul, the basic teaching of Mark and other ὑπηρέται τοῦ λόγου, and the more mature School of John to the rather elaborate School of Matthew with its ingenious interpretation of the O. T. as the crown of its scholarship'[22]. While the predilections of different

---

[21] The significance of the λέγει κύριος quotations are discussed below; there are some grounds for referring these texts to pre-Pauline *testimonia*. 1Cor 15, 45, as 2Cor 6,2, appears to have been already in 'quotation' form when Paul used it; cf. M. Black, 'The Pauline Doctrine of the Second Adam', *SJT* 7 (1954), 170 ff. On temple typology *testimonia*, cf. C. H. Dodd, *According to the Scriptures*, London 1952; A. Cole, *The New Temple*, London 1950; C. F. D. Moule, 'Sanctuary and Sacrifice in the Church of the New Testament, *JTS* 2nd ser. 1 (1950), 29—41.   [22] Stendahl, 34.

writers for particular introductory formulas, subject-matter, and text-forms do indicate different 'schools' of exegesis in the early Church; nevertheless, the developmental progression posited by Stendahl for the use of *midrash pesher* by the early Christians is open to some question. Since the method is not of Christian coinage, there is no reason why it could not have been employed even by individual exegetes (e. g. converted rabbis) from the earliest time. If *midrash pesher* is understood as an interpretive moulding of the text within an apocalyptic framework, *ad hoc* or with reference to appropriate textual or targumic traditions, then there is some evidence for its use on a rather advanced scale even in the pre-Pauline strata of the N. T.

11. ΛΕΓΕΙ ΚΥΡΙΟΣ QUOTATIONS IN THE NEW TESTAMENT

There are nine N. T. quotations — four of them in Pauline letters — within which the phrase, 'saith the Lord' (λέγει κύριος) occurs[1]; the equivalent phrase, λέγει ὁ θεός, occurs once[2]. Rom 12, 19 is a typical example:

For it is written: Vengeance is mine,
I will repay, saith the Lord.

The phenomenon ordinarily would be only of passing interest since any number of O. T. texts include this seal of authority. However, two facts are present which warrant a second look: (1) All of the citations vary, to one extent or another, both from the LXX and from the M.T. Furthermore, the variations are not only in the addition or omission of words but in the rendering of the text as well. (2) On at least six occasions the phrase, λέγει κύριος (as well as λέγει ὁ θεός in Acts 2,17), is a N. T. addition to the text[3]; the other five occurrences — all non-Pauline — have the phrase or its equivalent in the O. T. passage[4].

In the question of subject matter there is some affinity with earliest Church *testimonia*[5] although only one λέγει κύριος passage is used more than once (Rom 12,19; Hebr 10,30). The greater portion of the citations is related to the 'temple typology' in which the Christian community is viewed as God's new temple. This is

---

[1] Acts 7,49; 15,16 f.; Rom 12,19; 14,11; 1Cor 14,21; 2Cor 6,16 ff.; Hebr. 8, 8—12; 10,16 f.; 10,30. The phrase occurs twice in 2Cor 6,16 ff. and three times in Hebr 8,8—12. Its presence in Hebr 10,30 (= Rom 12,19) is textually uncertain; Codex A and the Antiochian texts have it, B and C omit it.

[2] Acts 2,17.

[3] If Hebr 10,30 be admitted, the total is seven. In Acts 7,49 the phrase may have been borrowed from the opening clause of the LXX or M.T.

[4] Acts 15,16 f.; Hebr 8,8,9,10; 10,16 f. The passages quoted in Hebrews all have φησὶ κύριος in the LXX.

[5] Cf. C. H. Dodd, *According to the Scriptures*, London 1952.

the probable import of Stephen's words (Acts 7,49), and it is the explicit purpose for the quotation of the catena in 2Cor 6,16 ff. Amos 9,11 f. (Acts 15,16 f.) is cited by James to show that the purpose of God includes the Gentiles; the introductory portion of the quotation concerns rebuilding 'the tabernacle of David'. As several writers have shown[6], these themes are a part of a pattern current in the earliest period, and their presence here suggests, at least, that this context of Scripture was understood as a part of the 'new temple' *testimonia*.

The New Covenant prophecy (Jer 31,31 ff.) cited in Hebrews (8,8—12; 10,16) also has more than a surface connection with the other λέγει κύριος quotations. The author of Hebrews sums up his argument by noting that Christ is the minister 'of the true tabernacle (τῆς σκηνῆς τῆς ἀληθινῆς), which the Lord pitched, not man'[7], and the mediator of a better covenant; then follows Jeremiah's prophecy concerning the New Covenant. It may be going too far to see in 'the house of Israel' (i. e. the Christian 'remnant') an allusion to the 'true tabernacle'[8] or to make a contrast between the law in the heart and the tablets (or scrolls) of the law in the temple. But the words, 'I shall be to them a God and they shall be to me a people', are a distinct echo of a verse in a Pauline 'new temple' quotation (2Cor 6,16 ff.); and the reference to the old covenant 'ready to vanish away' is probably an allusion to the old temple services[9] (Hebr 8, 10, 13).

The other λέγει κύριος quotations concern (1) the principle of vengeance or judgment as the prerogative of God alone (Rom 12, 19; 14,11; Hebr 10,30) and (2) the judicial significance of 'tongues' (1Cor 14,21). The latter may be considered within the framework of the anti-Jewish polemic to which Rendel Harris assigned the 'Testimony Book'[10]. The citation (Acts 2,17 ff.), λέγει ὁ θεός,

---

[6] See especially C. K. Barrett, 'Paul and the "Pillar" Apostles', *Studia Paulina*, Festschrift for J. de Zwaan, Haarlem 1953, 1—19; A. Cole, *The New Temple*, London 1950; C. F. D. Moule, 'Sanctuary and Sacrifice in the Church of the New Testament', *JTS* 1 (1950), 29—41.

[7] Hebr 8,2. It is an interpretive paraphrase of Num 24,6 (LXX).

[8] Taken in terms of the Jewish concept of solidarity, there is a closer relation than is apparent at first. Cf. Eph 2,19 ff.; *TDNT* 5 (1967), 126 f.

[9] Cf. B. F. Westcott, *The Epistle to the Hebrews*, London 1920, 226; Rev. 21,3.

[10] The passage is difficult. Robertson and Plummer, *First Corinthians*, Edinburgh 1911, 316 f., give perhaps the best explanation: As the Jews who scorned

is from a section of the O. T. listed by Dr. Dodd as a primary testimony source, and from which Paul also draws a quotation (Rom 10,13).

Taken as a whole, the λέγει κύριος quotations represent only a fraction of N. T. citations, and some of these merely repeat the phrase from the O. T. text; furthermore, most of the passages inserting the phrase *ad hoc* are Pauline. Yet the usage appears to be more than an idiosyncracy of any individual N. T. writer. The 'testimony' pattern into which most of the passages fall, the ever-present textual variations, and the significance of the phrase in the O. T. suggest that λέγει κύριος may have been characteristic in the proclamation of elements of the *kerygma*. Even if Hebr 10,30 be excepted, the words of Stephen and the essentially identical λέγει ὁ θεός of Peter remain independent witnesses to the practice. Its employment in Paul is too sporadic to construe the verses in Acts as a Lukan interpolation of Pauline phraseology. Nor is the explanation satisfying that the N. T. writers are merely stressing the fact that God is speaking. The introductory formula performs this function; and the λέγει κύριος is always an integral part of the citation, apparently already present in the text when it is introduced by the writer.

Λέγει κύριος is the badge of prophetic pronouncement in the O. T. Its presence in the N. T. probably has an equivalent significance and may give a clue for understanding the role which the N. T. exegete — or better, the N. T. prophet — considered himself to fill. The gift of prophecy was highly regarded in the apostolic age[11]; it was a specific gift or appointment of the Holy Spirit[12]; and it was not conferred upon all[13]. Early Christians without

---

Isaiah's clear and simple message were judged in God's speaking to them by means of a foreign-tongued Assyrian horde, so now those rejecting the simple message of the Gospel are, in effect, judged by the incomprehensible words of the Holy Spirit. On Harris's hypothesis cf. J. R. Harris, *Testimonies*, two volumes, Cambridge 1916 and 1920.

[11] Cf. Acts 2,17 ff.; 1Cor 14,1—5. Stress on the prophetic aspect is seen in the added phrase, καὶ προφητεύσουσιν in Acts 2,18.

[12] Cf. 1Cor 12,4,10,28.

[13] Cf. 1Cor 12,28. According to Swete 'only a relatively small number of believers were "established to be prophets", forming a charismatic order to which a recognized position was given in the Church. Such persons were said ἔχειν προφητείαν (1Cor 13,2) and known as οἱ προφῆται (Eph 2,20; 3,5; Rev 18,20; 22,6), being thus distinguished from those who occasionally "proph-

doubt used the word in full light of its O. T. significance, and, indeed, some of the functions most peculiar to O. T. prophets, such as predictive utterance, appear in their N. T. counterpart[14].

It is not unreasonable to expect that the N. T. 'prophet' would, at times, employ the prophetic epigraph, 'thus saith the Lord'. The equivalent phrase, 'thus saith the Holy Spirit' (τάδε λέγει τὸ πνεῦμα τὸ ἅγιον) introduces the prophecy of Agabus in Acts 21,11[15]. The occurrences in the Apocalypse are even more noteworthy. In Rev 14,13 the phrase, 'saith the Spirit', appears in much the same fashion as λέγει κύριος in the passages mentioned above:

And I heard a voice from heaven saying, Write: Blessed are the dead who die in the Lord henceforth. Yea, saith the Spirit, that they may rest from their labours; for their deeds follow them.

In the beginning of John's prophecy[16] the Lord Christ is quoted as follows:

I am the Alpha and the Omega, saith the Lord God (λέγει κύριος ὁ θεός), the One who is, and was, and is to come, the Almighty (ὁ παντοκράτωρ)[17].

This citation has no introductory formula and λέγει κύριος may only be the writer's way of introduction. If so, it evidences a type of introductory formula of which there are very few in the N. T.; even the other λέγει κύριος quotations have a formula of the ordinary type.

At first blush one is inclined to dismiss the whole matter as the idiom of the N. T. writers as they quoted, and it may well be that some instances are only the writer's formula of quotation. Such a case could be made, for example, of the two citations in the Apocalypse. This, however, does not explain why the pattern is not found more often; it certainly does not explain why Paul, whose introductory formulas are so consistently different, should have λέγει κύριος embedded in a few of his quotations which already contained an ordinary formula of introduction, and that he should

---

esied" (Acts 19,6; 1Cor 11,4 f.; 14,31).' H. B. Swete, *The Holy Spirit in the New Testament*, London 1909, 377. See above, 24—30.

[14] E. g., Acts 21,11.   [15] Cf. Hebr 3,7.   [16] Cf. Rev 1,3.

[17] Rev 1,8. The phraseology differs from the more usual introductory formula, e. g., 'these things saith he that . . .' Cf. Rev. 2,1; 3,1. It is perhaps worth noting that ὁ παντοκράτωρ occurs only once in the N. T. outside Revelation; it is in the λέγει κύριος citation in 2Cor 6,16 ff.

do this without any warrant from the O. T. text. It is more probable that this form of the quotation was most familiar to him. He may, certainly, have originated the particular text-form himself; but it is extremely unlikely that he did so as he wrote his epistle. That he introduced a double formula of introduction into his quotations sporadically and apparently without any reason is one of the least likely explanations of the matter.

The foregoing argument may be summed up as follows:

1. Λέγει κύριος is a characteristic phrase of prophetic pronouncement in the O. T.

2. The early Christian community also includes those with the office or appointment of 'prophet', and these 'prophets' sometimes use the same phrase, or its equivalent, in citing their own revelation.

3. The phrase also is inserted within some quotations in the N. T. in such a manner as to preclude its being considered an introductory formula or a part of the cited O. T. text.

4. These λέγει κύριος quotations are consistently divergent from extant O. T. texts and their O. T. source is often within a 'testimony' pattern evident elsewhere.

It is not an unreasonable conclusion that at least some of the Pauline λέγει κύριος texts were quoted by the apostle in a form already known and used in the early Church. The most natural origination for such paraphrases of the O. T. would be early Christian prophets — including not only leaders such as Paul but also minor figures.

The use of testimonies may be partly ascribed, as Dodd suggests, to the exposition of whole sections of the O. T. and their oral application to the facts of the Gospel. But this does not mean that no written and specific 'proof texts' were in use in the precanonical testimony tradition[18]. That there were 'schools of prophets' has been established above (3—62,115). How do they relate to the fact that many O. T. quotations in the N. T. evidence a careful working out of interpretive principles, and an incorporation of these principles into the text of the quotations themselves[19]?

---

[18] Dodd (126) argues against the hypothesis of a pre-canonical 'Testimony Book,' but he recognizes the possibility of occasional testimonies in written form. The presence of O. T. *florilegia* among the Qumran scrolls now demonstrates the first-century use of written testimonies.

[19] Cf. K. Stendahl, *The School of St. Matthew*, Lund 1969, 1954. Stendahl's conclusions are concerned mainly with Matthew, but he finds similar evidence in the Fourth Gospel: 'Thus the Johannine method is not what is usually meant

There is an activity of the Holy Spirit in the early Church which may well explain the source of some of these interpretations. It is the exercise of prophecy, and it occurs both in ecstatic utterance (cf. 1Cor 12—14) and the disclosure of the import of revelations from the Holy Spirit (e. g., Acts 21,11). There is now ample evidence that it also included the elaboration, interpretation, and application of O. T. Scriptures[20]. The fact that the prophetic λέγει κύριος was already present in some O. T. texts being used as *testimonia* may well have facilitated an *ad hoc* employment elsewhere. This extension appears at least in some degree to be related to *testimonia* of the same order or perhaps arising from the same group or 'school'[21]. There would be no hesitation in using these O. T. paraphrases — or any other matter spoken 'in the Spirit'; for they, as much as the O. T. itself, were the Words of God. This hypothesis is not without its problems, but it does seem satisfactorily to explain some of the phenomena found in N. T. quotation and to shed further light on the genesis and development of O. T. exegesis in the early Church.

---

by loose citations, or those more or less freely quoted from memory. It is rather the opposite since the form of John's quotations is certainly the fruit of scholarly treatment of written O. T. texts' (163). See above, 180 f.

[20] There is something similar to this in the reflection of O. T. prophets upon earlier Scriptures; cf. Ps 2; 105; Isa 48,21. The origin of some early Christian hymns — a few of which are incorporated into the N. T. cf. E. G. Selwyn, *The First Epistle of Peter*, London 1952, 267 — may also have been included within the exercise of the prophetic gift. Cf. 1Cor 14,15. See above, 135—140.

[21] E. g., the presence of λέγει κύριος (φησὶ κύριος) in Amos 9,11 f. (Acts 15,16 f.) and Jer 31,31 ff. (Hebr 8,8 ff.) may have occasioned the *ad hoc* usage in other 'new temple' *testimonia* such as the *catena* in 2Cor 6,16 ff.

12. MIDRASH, TARGUM AND NEW TESTAMENT QUOTATIONS

The two preceding chapters treated specific New Testament examples of what we shall now call implicit midrash, i. e. interpretive renderings of the Old Testament text. The present topic raises two broader questions. (1) How does this New Testament usage fit into a definition and classification of midrash generally? (2) Is there a discernable process of development in the New Testament from the use of an Old Testament passage in a midrash to its use as an independent quotation?

I.

Since mid-century increased attention has been given to the investigation and classification of midrash[1]. In part this has been stimulated by the interest in biblical literary genres and in biblical hermeneutics generally, in part by the manuscript discoveries at Qumran. More importantly, it has been marked by a shift away from the rabbinical Midrashim as the standard by which the genre is to be defined or measured. A. Robert (cf. *DBS* 5, 1957, 411—21) had noted in the Old Testament a 'procédé anthologique' in which Old Testament writers contemporized or reapplied to the present situation the phraseology and/or ideas of prior Scriptures[2]. Building upon these observations Miss R. Bloch[3] identified such contemporization (and reference to Scripture) as the essence of the mid-

---

[1] Cf. especially J. W. Doeve, *Jewish Hermeneutics in the Synoptic Gospels and Acts*, Assen 1954; R. Bloch, 'Midrash', *DBS* 5 (1957), 1263—81; G. Vermes, *Scripture and Tradition in Judaism*, Leiden 1961; A. G. Wright, *The Literary Genre Midrash*, New York 1967 = *CBQ* 28 (1966), 105—38, 417—57.

[2] Cf. Jer 32,18 with Ex 20,5 f.; Dan 11,30 with Num 24,24; Jer 7,21 f. with Am 5,25 f.; Jer 48,45 with Num 21,28; 24,17. See above, 133.

[3] Bloch, *op. cit.*, 1266; cf. Vermes, *op. cit.*, 7 f.; Doeve, *op. cit.*, 116.

rashic procedure. She saw it not only in the use of prior Scriptures by the Old Testament (and later) writers but also in the interpretive glossing in the LXX, the Targums, and the successive redactions of the Hebrew text[4]. Her broad definition of midrash has not found complete acceptance[5], but it does accord with the use of the term in intertestamental Judaism as an activity of biblical interpretation[6]. It may be helpful, however, to distinguish such implicit midrash[7], i. e., interpretive paraphrase of the Old Testament text, from explicit midrash, i. e., the lemma (a cited Old Testament text) plus its commentary. Both forms appear at Qumran.

In the Qumran literature the explanation of an Old Testament text often is preceded by the phrase, 'the interpretation *(pēšer = pesher)*', or 'its interpretation concerns'. The literary structure of the *pesher* texts has formal parallels with some rabbinic midrash[8], and the *pesher* is identified as midrash at 4Qflor 1,14,19. It appears in anthology (4Qflor), in consecutively interpreted Old Testament texts (e. g., 1QpHab), and in single Old Testament quotations (CD 4,14). Customarily used in connection with haggadic, i. e., non-legal midrash, Qumran *pesher* is distinctive not in its structure nor in its specific subject matter[9] but in its tech-

---

[4] So, also, Vermes, *op. cit.*, 176. Thus in Is 9,11(12) 'Aramaeans and Philistines' become in the LXX the contemporary 'Syrians and Greeks'; in Ex 4, 24 ff. 'Lord' becomes in the LXX and *Targum Onkelos* 'angel of the Lord', and 'the blood' is given explicit sacrificial merit. Vermes, *op. cit.*, 178—92, in agreement with Bloch, characterises the LXX and Targums as a 're-writing of the Bible' in which contemporary interpretations are woven into the text (179).

[5] A. G. Wright *(op. cit.)* apparently prefers to use the term of a literary genre in which the primary intention is to illumine a prior biblical text.

[6] It designates both an activity and a genre, a way of expounding Scripture and the resultant exposition. Cf. Sir 51,23; CD 20,6 (= 9,33 CAP); 4Qflor 1,14; W. Bacher, *Die exegetische Terminologie der jüdischen Traditionsliteratur,* Darmstadt 1965 (1899), I, 103; Doeve, *op. cit.*, 55.

[7] I am dependent here on M. Gertner *(JSS* 7, 1963, 268) who uses in a similar way the terms, covert and overt midrash.

[8] E. g., EcclR 12,1; cf. L. H. Silberman, *RQ* 3 (1961—62), 328. It also has affinities with the gnostic *Pistis Sophia,* e. g., 120a; cf. J. Carmignac, *RQ* 4 (1963 to 64), 497—522.

[9] I. e., the interpretation of Scripture. Cf. O. Betz, *Offenbarung und Schriftforschung,* Tübingen, 1960, 40—54, 80 ff. Silberman *(op. cit.),* following K. Elliger *(Studien zum Habakkukkommentar zum Toten Meer,* Tübingen 1953, 157), identifies *pesher,* in accordance with the use of term in Daniel, with the explanation of dreams and visions. But see 1Q22Moses 1,3 f.; Num 12,6 ff.; below, 201 f.

nique and, specifically, its eschatological perspective. In these passages the Old Testament text-form undergoes interpretive alterations[10], in order to fit it to a present-time eschatological fulfilment[11]. Strictly speaking, the cited Old Testament text is followed by exposition in which words from the text are repeated[12] and its 'mystery' therewith 'interpreted'. Qumran *pesher* reflects an eschatological perspective similar to the New Testament and unlike that in rabbinic midrash, and it combines characteristics of the implicit and explicit midrash mentioned above.

The so-called *Genesis Apocryphon* or *Genesis midrash* and *The Book of Jubilees* (1Q 17,18; 2Q 19,20; 4Q) offer examples at Qumran of a kind of implicit midrash. The former, in particular, illustrates the difficulty of specialists in this area in finding a satisfactory definition of targum and midrash in their relationship to one another. It was identified by some initially as a targum and then as a midrash[13]. The latter classification seems to be followed by most writers on the subject[14]. However, M. R. Lehmann (*RQ* 1, 1958—59, 249—63) suggests that it represents 'the oldest prototype of both', and J. A. Fitzmyer, apparently following the rabbinic models of Targum and Midrash, declines to classify it as either[15].

The problem is not new: on the similar *Book of Jubilees* (London, 1902, 13) R. H. Charles commented that as the 'most advanced pre-Christian representative of the midrashic tendency, which has already been at work in the Old Testament Chronicles, ... [it] constitutes an enlarged Targum ... in which difficulties

---

[10] Cf. W. H. Brownlee, *The Meaning of the Qumran Scrolls for the Bible*, New York 1964, 64; K. Stendahl, *The School of St. Matthew*, Lund 1969 (1954), 183—202. The changes most often are word-play alterations of letters. Cf. B. Gärtner, *ST* 8 (1954), 1—15; F. F. Bruce, *Biblical Exegesis in the Qumran Scrolls*, Grand Rapids, 1959, 32 f.

[11] I. e., to the 'last generation'. CD 1,12; 1QpHab 2,7; 7,2; Mk 13,30; cf. Mt 4,14—17; Lk 16,16; Acts 2,17; 3,24; 1Cor 10,11; 1Joh 2,18.

[12] B. Gärtner, *ST* 8 (1954), 13 f.

[13] Cf. M. Black, *The Scrolls and Christian Origins*, London, 1961, 192—98 with *An Aramaic Approach to the Gospels and Acts*, Oxford, ³1967, 40; cf. Brownlee, *op. cit.*, 81n: except for the use of the first person, 'the *Genesis Apocryphon* might be described as a sort of Targum'.

[14] See the annotated bibliography in J. A. Fitzmyer, *The Genesis Apocryphon of Qumran Cave 1*, Rome, 1966, 8 f.

[15] *Ibid.* On the problem cf. R. LeDeaut, *BTB* 3 (1973), 18—22.

... are solved ... and the spirit of later Judaism infused ...'[16] This does not appear far removed from Miss Bloch's (*DBS* 5, 1271, 1278 f.) conclusions about Chronicles, Jubilees, and the Palestinian Targum. The last is 'nearer midrash than version' (1279), and each in its own way is representative of the midrashic development of older Scriptures. Following Miss Bloch's broad definition of midrash, there are at Qumran at least three kinds, the *pesher*, the highly elaborated paraphrase of the *Genesis midrash* and *Jubilees*, and the (unpublished) more literal targums of Job and (fragments of) Leviticus[17]. According to P. Kahle, followed by others, the elaborated paraphrase of the Palestinian Targum represents an earlier stage of development than the more literal official rabbinic Targum Onkelos[18]. The presence of both literary forms at Qumran cautions against positing this (or its opposite) as a general law of development[19]. Nevertheless, it may represent one way in which the midrashic practice proceeded. Further, Kahle (*Geniza*[2], 202) contends that the so-called Fragment Targum largely represents midrashic commentary culled from the older Palestinian Targum[20]; *Targum Pseudo-Jonathan* apparently reflects a similar process, Scripture + commentary → detached commentary, after which the older midrash or commentary is grafted into a later biblical paraphrase (? Onkelos).

---

[16] Similarly, M. R. James (*The Biblical Antiquities of Philo*, London 1917, 33) viewed Chronicles as the 'chief model' of the *Biblical Antiquities*.

[17] Cf. Brownlee, *op. cit.*, 64 f., 81. He believes that the interpretations of 1QpHab are influenced by the Targum to the Prophets and that the *pesher* form, text + commentary, derives from the synagogue practice of Scripture reading + targum. G. Vermes (*RHPR* 35, 1955, 99—103) also found affinities between the Qumran *pesher* and the Targum.

[18] P. Kahle, *The Cairo Geniza*, London [1]1947, 125 f.; Oxford [2]1959, 200 ff.; cf. A. Wikgren, *JR* 24 (1944), 91 f.; contrast Fitzmyer, *op. cit.*, 32—35. Kahle is apparently supported by Neofiti I, a recently discovered Palestinian Targum to the Pentateuch. Cf. Black, *Approach*[3], 42; Vermes, *Scripture*, 6; R. Bloch (*DBS* 5, 1279) suggested that originally the Palestinian Targum was 'une sorte de midrash homilétique, ou simplement le canevas d'une suite d'homélies sur l'Ecriture, faites à la synagogue après la lecture publique de la Torah'. Cf. M. McNamara, *The New Testament and the Palestinian Targum to the Pentateuch*, Rome 1966, 31 f., 64; A. Diez-Macho in *Melanges E. Tisserant*, Città del Vaticano 1964, I, 184 f.

[19] Cf. McNamara, *op. cit.*, 25n.

[20] Cf. J. Z. Lauterbach, 'Midrash and Mishnah', *JQR* 5 (1914—15), 504—13. He sees a development in halachic literature from wholly midrash (Scripture + commentary) to the Mishnah form (independent halacha).

To one who is dependent on the specialists the above developments raise a number of questions. What are the guidelines to distinguish midrash as a literary genre and midrash as an activity?
Or is this distinction a later refinement that has no place in pre-
Christian or pre-rabbinic usage[21]? How much and what kind of
paraphrastic elaboration is required before a 'targum' becomes a
'midrash' (or 'midrash-targum')? As yet there seem to be no clear
answers to these questions of definition and classification. In spite
of this the New Testament student can only be grateful for the
progress achieved and seek to apply it judiciously to problems
within his own discipline.

The inquiry below addresses an issue raised by the presence of
midrashic techniques in certain New Testament quotations. Specifically, is there discernable a development or transition from an
earlier midrash form? What do the techniques signify for the use
of the Old Testament in the primitive Christian community?

II.

A number of Old Testament texts appear in the New Testament
both in an explicit midrash and as an independent citation. Among
them are Hab 2,3—4; Ps 8,6; 110,1; 118,22 f.; 2Sam 7,12—14. J. W.
Doeve has contended that words lifted from their Scriptural context
can never be a *testimonium* to the Jewish mind. What was required was a midrash, an exposition of that text in the context of other Scriptures. The *testimonia*, then, were a secondary phenomenon
for non-Jewish Christians growing out of, and extracted from
Christian midrash[22]. The presence of *testimonia* at Qumran shows
that such collections were used previously in Judaism. But it still
may be correct that their value depended upon a preceding
midrash.

A New Testament example that could illustrate this kind of devel-

---

[21] W. Bacher (*op. cit.*, 103 ff.) notes the difference in rabbinic (tannaitic)
usage. A. G. Wright's *(op. cit.)* restricted definition of the genre seems to reflect more a practical than an historical distinction.

[22] Doeve, *op. cit.* 116. B. Lindars in his closely argued *New Testament Apologetic*, London 1961, 186, 251–59, sought to trace the development topically,
e. g., in the consecutive application of the Old Testament to the resurrection,
the passion, and the birth of Jesus.

opment is Paul's use of Hab 2,4 in Gal 3,11 and, later, in Rom 1,17. Gal 3 includes the citation in a midrash on Gen 15,6, whose literary form is found also in the Rabbis and Philo[23]. Hab 2,4 appears in Rom 1,17 as a lead-line citation. The foundation of Paul's teaching of 'righteousness through faith' is the story of Abraham; Hab 2,4 is only an apposite expression of it[24]. Therefore, Rom 1,17 may assume the midrash of Gal 3 or something like it. But Paul does not presuppose that his readers knew this since in Rom 4 he presents a virtually identical midrash on Gen 15,6, but without the citation from Hab 2,4[25]. Therefore, unless Rom 1,17 (καθὼς γέγραπται) opens an exposition or is not intended for Jewish Christians, it would show that the force of a citation did not depend upon its previous establishment in the context of midrash[26]. Nevertheless, it may still be correct that the early Christian use of Scripture did in fact develop from midrash to *testimonia* in many instances and that the *apologetic* effectiveness of the latter depended in some measure upon a midrashic undergirding.

Hab 2,3 f. is cited again, independently of Paul[27], in Hebr 10, 37 ff. There, also, it appears to be the concluding text of an extensive midrash (? Hebr 10,5—38)[28]. In view of its affinities with 1 Qp-Hab, Hebr 10,37 ff. could equally well illustrate a Christian *pesher*-type midrash[29].

The use of Ps 8,6(7) and Ps 110,1 presents similar phenomena. With midrashic techniques Hebr 2,6—9 establishes (for the believer in Jesus' resurrection) that Ps 8 finds its fulfilment not in 'man in

---

[23] This has been shown in the recent investigation of P. Borgen, *Bread from Heaven*, Leiden 1965, 51 f.

[24] Cf. E. E. Ellis, *Paul's Use of the Old Testament*, Edinburgh 1957, 120.

[25] Cf. Borgen, *op. cit.*, 47—52; J. W. Bowker, *NTS* 14 (1967—68), 110.

[26] This may be the case also in 4Qtest; however, one of its citations (Jos 6,26) is midrashically elaborated. But on Rom 1,17 see below, 217 f.

[27] Cf. C. H. Dodd, *According to the Scriptures*, London 1953, 49 ff.

[28] A number of catchwords join Hebr 10,5 ff. (= Ps 40,7—9) to the subsequent citations and exposition: θυσίαν (8,26), προσφοράν (8,10,14,18), περὶ ἁμαρτίας (8,18,26), ἥκω (9,37). Note also the (? created) variants εὐδόκησας (6), necessary for a verbal tally with Hab 2,4(38), and ὁ ἐρχόμενος (37), important for an explicit connection with Dtn 32,35; Ps 135,14(30). There is a shift in theme, however, and commentators usually make a major division at Hebr 10,18.

[29] Note the tendentious alterations of the Old Testament text and the repetition of the text in the exposition (39), fitting it to a present-time eschatological fulfilment (ἡμεῖς). See above, 155.

general' (8) but in Jesus (9). In 1Cor 15,27 this understanding of Ps 8 (and Ps 110) is assumed, and the exposition is restricted to the meaning of the 'all things' that are subjected to Jesus. The allusions to Ps 8 and Ps 110 in Eph 1,20,22 apply the texts to Jesus as though the interpretation were self-evident.

Acts 2,16–36, perhaps in the form of a synagogue midrash and certainly using midrashic methods[30], includes a citation of Ps 110, 1 in which a traditional interpretation is disallowed and an application to Jesus is established. Thereby the pregnant question posed earlier by Jesus (Lk 20,42 ff.) finds its exegetical answer. This answer is presupposed in the frequent use of the verse elsewhere, including a catena of *testimonia* in Hebr 1, the exposition in Hebr 10, and the allusion to this text at the trial of Jesus[31].

In Mt 21,33–44 and parallels an allegory built on Is 5,1 ff. is applied to Jesus and concluded with a citation from Ps 118,22 f. and an allusion to Dan 2,34 f.,44 f. Although the matter is disputed, it appears probable that the allegory originated in the pre-resurrection mission[32]. The introductory formula ἀνέγνωτε (42) suggests that the Psalm citation also goes back to Jesus[33]. The coupling catchwords, οἰκοδομέω (33,42) and λίθος (42,44) favour the supposition of an originally unified midrash of some kind[34]. Dif-

---

[30] Doeve, *op. cit.*, 171 f.; Bowker, *op. cit.*, 105 ff. See below, 199–205.

[31] Mk 14,62. N. Perrin (*NTS* 12, 1965–66, 150–55) argues that the verse represents the 'historicizing' of Christian *pesher* traditions on Ps 110 and other Old Testament texts. For a similar approach to Mt 4,1–11 cf. B. Gerhardsson, *The Testing of God's Son*, Lund 1966. If the texts were culled from some form of Christian midrash, they may still only summarize (and thus not 'historicize' in the radical sense) Jesus' actual trial response, in biblical words whose exegesis was understood in the Christian community. But the opposite is equally possible: Jesus' application to himself, then and earlier, of such passages pointed his disciples to them. On this reading their altered, i. e., contemporized, post-resurrection interpretation was only an extension of Jesus' usage. Cf. Doeve, *op. cit.*, 153 f.

[32] Cf. E. E. Ellis, *The Gospel of Luke*, London ²1974, 232; see below, 206.

[33] It is found in the New Testament only on the lips of Jesus, usually in midrashic exposition (cf. Doeve, *op. cit.* 105 f., 163 ff. on Mt 12,3,5; 22,29,31). It may reflect a well-known rabbinic distinction between reading and knowing Scripture. Cf. D. Daube, *The New Testament and Rabbinic Judaism*, London 1956, 422–36; Ac 8,30; 13,27; 2Cor 3,14 f. See above, 149.

[34] In Hebrew/Aramaic there may have been a word-play on 'to stone' (35) and 'to clear stones' (*sql;* Is 5,2; cf. 62,10) and, with a change of synonym, an additional word tally with Ps 118 and Dan 2 (*'bn*). Cf. Is 62,10 Targum. Cf. also B. Gerhardsson, *NTS* 14 (1967–68), 165–93, on Mk 4,1–20. See below, 251 f.

ferently understood, Ps 118,22 is introduced as a testimony in Acts 4,11, much in the manner of the ἵνα πληρωθῇ quotations in Matthew[35]. There the application to Jesus is not so much explained as it is asserted. The same is true in 1Petr 2,7, where the text appears in a mosaic of *testimonia* with their *pesher*-type elaboration. The allusion to Ps 118 in Eph 2,10 ff. simply takes the Christian reference for granted.

2Sam 7,6—16 offers a clearer example. Acts 13,16—41 alludes to it (22 f.), probably as the haphtarah text of a synagogue homily[36]. Its application to Jesus is confirmed by other Scriptures and by the events of Jesus' Davidic descent and his resurrection. The messianic use of 2Sam 7 is pre-Christian[37]; what is interesting is that the early Church was not content simply to appropriate it but established its interpretation by means of midrash. Such exegesis may undergird the *testimonia* use of 2Sam 7 in 2Cor 6,18 and Hebr 1,5, where the Christian reference of the text is assumed.

III.

In these and similar contexts, some closer in structure to synagogue midrash and some closer to the Qumran *pesher*, the text of the Old Testament citation is sometimes shaped to fit the contigu-

---

[35] I. e., the tendentious rendering (ὑμῶν), the present-time eschatological application (οὗτός ἐστιν), and the sequence, Current Event→Scripture (cf. Mt 3,3; 11,10; Ac 2,16; 1QpHab 3,2; 4QpIs^b 2,7). The sequence is opposite to that of the New Testament midrash considered thus far, i. e., Scripture→Current Event. (I am indebted to Professor R. N. Longenecker for calling this distinction to my attention.) Cf. Joh 6,31,50; Rom 9,7 f.; 10,6,8; Hebr 13,15; 1QpHab 12,3 ff.,7—9; 4QpIs^b 2,6 f.,10; 4QpNah 1,11; 4Qpatr 2; 4Qflor 1,2 f.; CD 6,4,7. As the references indicate, the latter sequence is more frequent in the Qumran *pesher*. The formula, 'this is', or its equivalent is found in the Old Testament, Qumran, and the rabbinical writings. Cf. Is 9,14 f.; Ez 5,5; Dan 4,24(21); 5,25. In Dan and the DSS it is used in conjunction with or as an equivalent of *pesher*. Cf. McNamara, *op. cit.*, 72.

[36] The midrash form of the passage has been demonstrated, to a fair degree of probability, by J. W. Bowker (*NTS* 14, 1967—68, 101—4) and J. W. Doeve (*op. cit.*, cf. 172—76). They take 2Sam 7 to be the underlying haphtarah text. Regarding the allusion to 2Sam 7 cf. Egypt (17), judges (20), Saul (21), David (22), raise up (22), my son (33). The verbal tallies between texts and exposition also reflect a midrashic procedure: Δαυίδ (22,34 ff.), ἐγείρω (22,23D,30,37) and perhaps ὑψόω (17) = ἀνίστημι (33 f.) in an underlying Semitic text-form.

[37] Cf. 4Qflor 1,7—11; 4Q 243 Son of God 2,1. Cf. *NTS* 20 (1974), 393.

ous exposition[38]. *Testimonia* in the New Testament also are characteristically tendentious in their text-form, but they often lack any accompanying exposition or elaboration[39]. In the light of the above discussion such independent citations may represent lemma texts that have been excerpted from midrash. Some quotations that combine texts from the Law and the Prophets (and the Writings)[40] or that merge an Old Testament text with a snippet of another[41] may have a similar background. However, the Targums and, as W. H. Brownlee has pointed out, the Isaiah text at Qumran (1QIsᵃ) also have assimilated related Old Testament passages. Whether behind a merged citation in the New Testament lies such a targumizing implicit midrash, an explicit midrash, an *ad hoc* assimilation by the New Testament writer, or some other explanation is not easy to determine. For example, behind Rom 9,33; 10, 11; 1Petr 2,6 ff. (Is 28,16; 8,14) there may have been a *testimonium*[42] or, on the other hand, an earlier midrash similarly re-employed in Romans and 1 Peter.

If some New Testament quotations represent the lemma texts of an explicit midrash, it is equally possible that the midrashic commentary, with or without its Old Testament allusions, also was detached and used. Taking this approach, M. Gertner (*JSS* 7, 1962, 267—92) and others identified as midrashic commentary a number of New Testament passages, including parables of and stories

---

[38] Cf. σημεῖα, Acts 2,19,22; καθίζω, Acts 2,30, cf. 34; δίδωμι, Acts 13,34,35 (cf. Bowker, *op. cit.*, 104; Dtn 4,38); προσκυνεῖν, βαβυλῶνος, Acts 7,43; ἐλευθέρας, Gal 4,30 f.,22 f.; σοφῶν, 1Cor 3,20,19; παιδεύει, Hebr 12,6,7—10. Further, see my article, 'Quotations', *International Standard Bible Encyclopedia*, Revised ed., ed. G. W. Bromiley, Grand Rapids, forthcoming. The New Testament appears to be more radically creative in reshaping the text than is the Qumran midrash. Interpretive variants in 1QpHab depend largely on wordplay; but cf. 4Qtest 22,29 f. which makes a significant omission of Jericho.

[39] E. g., some of the ἵνα πληρωθῇ citations in Mt. The lack of elaboration occasioned B. Gärtner's (*ST* 8, 1954, 12 f.) criticism of the identification of them as *pesher* midrash *contra* K. Stendahl (*op. cit.*, 194—202).

[40] Cf. Ellis, *Testament*, 49 f., 186; Stendahl, *op. cit.*, 216.

[41] Cf. Rom 11,26 f. (Is 59,20 f.; 27,9); Hebr 10,37 ff. (Is 26,20; Hab 2,3 f.); Mt 2,6 (Mi 5,2(1); 2Sam 5,2); Lk 19,38a (Ps 118,26; ? Zec 9,9) with Jn 12,13,15; Mt 21,5 (Zec 9,9; Is 62,11) with Joh 12,15 (Zec 9,9; ? Zeph 3,14,16). Mt 21,13 (Is 56, 7; Jer 7,11) and Mt 21,42 ff. (Ps 118,22 f.; Dan 2,34 f.,44 f.) are somewhat different.

[42] Dodd, *op. cit.*, 43; Ellis, *Testament*, 89; B. Lindars, *ExpT* 75 (1963—1964), 173.

about Jesus[43]. It is true that in some Gospel narratives there is a tendency for Old Testament allusions to fade in transmission[44]. But in the absence of a clear allusion or an explicit quotation it is, in the nature of the case, difficult to establish a midrashic background for a New Testament passage.

In conclusion, the presence of different types of midrash — targum, *pesher*, synagogue homily – is most likely reflected in the use of the Old Testament in the New. Also, some New Testament writers used midrash to establish a Christian interpretation of Old Testament texts, an interpretation that is assumed in the *testimonia* use of the same texts. The results of the above study are not as conclusive as one might wish. But they do underscore the plausibility if not the probability that some independent New Testament quotations have been extracted from an earlier context of Christian midrash.

---

[43] Mk 4,1—22 (on Jer 4,3); 7,31—37 (on Is 35,5); Joh 10 (on Ez 34),15 (on Ez 19,10—14); 2Cor 3 (on Ex 34); Jas (on Ps 12).

[44] Cf. Lk 20,9; 21,20; (12,53) with the Markan parallels. See below, 206.

13. MIDRASHIC FEATURES IN THE SPEECHES OF ACTS

Since mid-century research in the use of the Old Testament in the New has concentrated on three issues, the relation of quotations to midrash, the use of *testimonia* and the nature of New Testament typology. The comments below address the first two, elaborating observations made in the last chapter, with special reference to quotations in Acts 2;4 and 13. In the nature of the case the textual problem is deeply involved in the issues of midrash and *testimonia*. Some thirty years ago Lucien Cerfaux[1] investigated the problem and concluded that the eleven single citations in Acts generally follow the Septuagint and seven combined citations tend to vary from it. The variations in the latter probably are to be traced to the use of *testimonia* collections. The variations in single citations, e. g., Acts 2,17—21 (Joel 3,1—5) and 7,42 f. (Amos 5, 25–27), reflect a concern to emphasize in the text-form the application of the quotations to present circumstances. Cerfaux thus qualified the older judgment of H. B. Swete who, while noting the variants, derived the quotations in Acts 'from the Septuagint exclusively'[2]. Recently M. Wilcox also has suggested a *testimonium* in Acts 13,22. More generally, however, he concludes that in the speeches of Acts 1—15 a number of the variants in Old Testament quotations and allusions may be traceable to the original

---

[1] L. Cerfaux, *Citations scripturaires et tradition textuelle dans le livre des Actes*, in *Tradition Chrétienne* (Mélanges M. Goguel), Paris 1950, 41—51. F. F. Bruce, *The Speeches in the Acts of the Apostles*, London 1943, 20, also referred to *testimonia* as an explanation of some textual variations in Acts 15, 16—18.

[2] H. B. Swete, *An Introduction to the Old Testament in Greek*, Cambridge 1914, 398. He counts 23 citations in Acts, L. Venard 24 and Turpie 28. Cf. D. M. Turpie, *The Old Testament in the New*, London 1868, 276 f.; L. Venard, in *DBS* II (1934) 24—28. W. K. L. Clarke, in *Beginnings of Christianity* (ed. F. J. F. Jackson and K. Lake) II, London 1922, 95, 97 f., who lists the texts in parallel columns, agrees with Swete with the possible exception of Acts 2,24,30; 4,11.

speaker. That is, the speaker's idiom, which incorporated Semitic textual traditions known to have been current, remained as 'unrevised elements' in the Greek traditions preserved by Luke[3].

This leads to the observation that virtually all of the Old Testament quotations in Acts are in the speeches, and almost all are in Acts 1—15[4]. Recent developments in the origins of Jewish midrash and in the relation of midrash to New Testament quotations, particularly to *testimonia,* justify another look at the speeches of Acts from this perspective[5].

In catchword connections and in the literary form of Acts 2 and 13, J. W. Bowker and J. W. Doeve saw features of midrashic exegesis[6]. In Acts 2 the Pentecost event (14 f.) is explained by Joel 3,1—5 which then is *peshered* to apply to Jesus (22) and to Pentecost (33). The speech is interspersed with citations from Ps 16, 8—11 (25 ff.) and Ps 132,11(30), allusions from Ps 116,3(24) and Ps 68,19 (33: cf. Eph 4,8), and is concluded with a citation from Ps 110,1. Similarly in Acts 13 a summary of Israel's history, alluding to Dtn 4,37 f.(17) and Jer 30,9(22), is climaxed by a citation of 1Sam 13,14(16—22). Its application to the mission and resurrection of Jesus (23—31) is supported by an allusion to 2Sam 7,6—16(22 f.) and by subsequent citations of Ps 2,7(33), Is 55,3 (34) and Ps 16,10(35). After further commentary the whole is climaxed with a citation of Hab 1,5(41).

Bowker compares the form of these passages with that of the 'proem' and *yelammedenu-rabbenu* ('let our rabbi teach us') midrashim, the two major types of homilies in the rabbinic literature, which survive chiefly in the Tanḥuma and the Pesiqtas. In the proem homily a freely chosen opening ('proem') text was followed by an exposition often beginning with the words, 'its interpretation *(pesher)* is'. It included a string of texts *(haruzim)* in which the day's lectionary text from the Prophets (the *Haftarah*) was cited or alluded to. The homily concluded with the day's

---

[3] M. Wilcox, *Semitisms in Acts,* Oxford 1965, 23,54 f.; contra: J. A. Emerton, in *JSS* 13 (1968) 282—297.

[4] Cf. Acts 23,5; 28,26 f. Acts 8,32 f. (= Is 53,7 f.) is within Luke's narrative.

[5] See above, 161 f., 192—195.

[6] J. W. Doeve, *Jewish Hermeneutics in the Synoptic Gospels and Acts,* Assen 1954, 168—76; J. W. Bowker, in *NTS* 14 (1967—68), 96—111; cf. E. Lövestam, *Son and Saviour . . . (Acts 13,32—37),* Lund 1961, 7.

reading from the Law (the *Seder*) or another text pointing to it.
The proem served as a bridge text illustrating the connection between the *Seder* and *Haftarah* texts and contained a verbal tally
with the *Haftarah* text. The similar *yelammedenu-rabbenu* homily
began with an enquiry which was answered by a string of texts
concluding with a reference to the *Seder* for the day.

In Acts 13, according to Bowker, 1Sam 13,14(22) is the Proem;
the allusions to Dtn 4,37 f.(17) and 2Sam 7,6–16[7] reflect the *Seder*
and *Haftarah* readings respectively. While it does not fully accord
with the rabbinic models, Acts 13 shows clear traces of the 'proem'
type homily. With certain reservations Bowker reaches similar conclusions with regard to Acts 2, Acts 7 and Acts 15,14—21[8].
In spite of several problems[9] his general interpretation has a considerable degree of probability.

If the midrashic form of these speeches is established, the research will have moved a long step towards the solution of some
problems of the Old Testament quotations in Acts, e. g., the nature
and cause of certain textual alterations and combinations. Such a
conclusion also will have a bearing on the estimate placed upon
the speeches as a whole. Specifically, it will serve to define more
precisely their role in what P. Schubert has called 'Luke's theology based on the "proof from prophecy" '[10]. And it will call for
renewed consideration of the pre-Lukan background of the speeches, in form as well as content.

---

[7] So also regarding 2Sam 7, Doeve, *op. cit.*, 172, who believes that it forms
the background for the argument of the first part of the sermon.

[8] Acts 15 represents a *yelammedenu* response, and possibly a fragment of
a longer homily of that type, to the halachic question, 'Is it necessary for proselytes to be circumcised and to keep the Law of Moses'?

[9] For example, Dr. Bowker builds partly upon the theory of J. Mann that
the *yelammedenu* homilies were derived exclusively from the *haftarah* readings
and not from the *sedarim*. This was found to be true in only a portion of the
collected homilies, and the problem is further complicated by the fact that the
selected *sedarim* (and therefore the *haftaroth*) seem to have varied from place
to place. However, the fact remains that the pattern is present and offers considerable support for a midrashic interpretation of the speeches of Acts in
which a similar pattern appears. Cf. J. Mann, *The Bible as Read and Preached
in the Old Synagoge*, I, Cincinatti 1940; II, New York 1966; cf. the review of
volume 2 by N. M. Sarna, in *JBL* 87 (1968) 100—105. U. Wilckens, *Die Mis-
sionsreden der Apostelgeschichte*, Neukirchen 1961, does not give a great deal
of attention to the role of the quotations in these speeches.

[10] P. Schubert, *The Final Cycle of Speeches in the Book of Acts*, in *JBL* 87
(1968) 1—16 (1).

In the present chapter I wish simply to call attention to two other midrashic features in the use of the Old Testament in Acts. The first serves to strengthen the hypothesis advanced by Doeve and Bowker. The second argues that even *testimonia* texts in the speeches may be drawn from earlier midrashic traditions. Both features support the traditional character of the material in Acts and raise considerable doubt about any evaluation of the speeches that does not take full account of these phenomena.

I.

There are in Acts a number of affinities with the *pesher* technique, which is usually defined in terms of its use in certain Qumran writings. There the explanation of an Old Testament text is prefaced by the phrase, 'its interpretation' or 'the interpretation *(pesher)* concerns'. The phrase is used of Moses' interpretation of the Law[11], and in the commentary on consecutive Old Testament texts[12], *florilegia*, and individual quotations[13]. It appears at Qumran in conjunction with the term midrash[14], and the literary structure has formal parallels with some rabbinic midrash[15] and, more loosely, with certain expositions of Scripture in the New Testament[16]. In the Qumran *pesher* the Old Testament text-form often undergoes an interpretive alteration — usually based on wordplay — in order to apply it to a present-time eschatological fulfilment. In making the application the commentary repeats the words of the (altered) text. The eschatological perspective distinguishes the *pesher* from the simple contemporization[17] of the text that is common to all midrash, and it constitutes an important similarity between the *pesher* and certain New Testament quota-

---

[11] 1Q22Moses 1,3 f.   [12] E. g., 1QpHab; 4QpNah; 4QpPs 37.
[13] 4Qflor; CD 4,14.   [14] 4Qflor 1,14,19.
[15] Cf. L. H. Silbermann, in *RQ* 3 (1961–62) 328. Parallels also with the Gnostic *Pistis Sophia* were noted by J. Carmignac, in *RQ* 4 (1963–64) 497–522.
[16] For example, the lemma + commentary pattern in Joh 6,31–48; Hebr 2, 5–10; 10,5–10. Cf. P. Borgen, *Bread from Heaven*, Leiden 1965, 41; B. Gärtner in *ST* 8 (1954) 13 f.
[17] An interesting example of this in Acts is the change of 'Damascus' to 'Babylon' at Acts 7,43 (= Amos 5,27). Cf. R. Bloch, 'Midrash', *DBS*, V (1955), 1266, 1280. Contrast the *pesher* technique in Acts 4,25 ff. in which Jesus is set forth as the eschatological fulfilment of Ps 2.

tions[18]. Indeed, if *pesher* is understood in terms not of literary structure but of technique and eschatological perspective, it may be recognized in various forms of midrash.

We may observe the *pesher* pattern in a number of Old Testament quotations in Acts 2 and Acts 13, all of which are eschatologically applied to the present. Acts 2,17—21, citing Joel 3,1—5, contains a number of interpretive variations from the Septuagint and the Masoretic Text including a built-in introductory formula, 'says God', and a specific reference to 'the last days' (17). Ἐκχέω (17) and the added word σημεῖα (19) are repeated in the following exposition (33,22). In Acts 2,25—28 (Ps 16,8—11) the words δεξιός (25,33 f.), ᾅδης (27,31), σάρξ (26,31), ἰδεῖν διαφθοράν (27,31) are similarly repeated in the exposition. For the most part these applications do not require any interpretive alteration of the Old Testament text-form. For example, at Acts 2,27 the Septuagint reading διαφθοράν ('corruption'), rendering the Hebrew שחת, well serves Luke's or his source's exegetical purpose. But at Acts 2,30 (Ps 132,11) instead of the Septuagint reading 'place' (τίθημι; MT: שית) there occurs the word καθίζω, perhaps shaping the text to the adjoining quotation of Ps 110,1 (κάθημαι; MT: ישב, 34) or reflecting such a change in an underlying Hebrew or Aramaic text-form[19]. Some of these alterations, and others elsewhere, leave the impression that early Christian writers were more radically creative in reshaping the biblical text than those at Qumran, who show greater dependence on word-play[20].

Paul's speech in Antioch-Pisidia provides further examples. In the textually-altered citation at Acts 13,22, probably from 1Sam

---

[18] Both the Qumran sect and the primitive Church regard themselves as the elect company out of which God's final redemptive and judging action is now proceeding. For both the end-time is impending. Cf. 1QpHab 7,1—13; Lk 16, 16; Mt 4,14—17. Their time is the 'last generation' to which the Old Testament prophecies referred. Cf. CD 1,12; 1QpHab 2,7; 7,2; Mk 13,30; Acts 2,17; 3,24; 1Cor 10,11; 1Joh 2,18.

[19] The Hebrew שית is never in the Septuagint rendered by καθίζω which is, however, a most frequent translation of ישב, the word used in Ps 110,1.

[20] Cf. J. G. Harris, *The Qumran Commentary on Habakkuk*, London 1966, 28—35. Word-play is not, of course, absent from New Testament quotations and allusions. In Acts compare ἀνείλατε/ἀνέστησεν (2,23 f.) and ἀνεῖλαν/ἤγειρεν (10,39 f.). M. Black, in *BJRL* 45 (1963) 315 ff., believes that they may reflect an allusion to an Aramaic text of Is 52,13 using זקף, which carries both meanings, exalt and hang. Cf. Acts 13,28,30 (ἀναιρέω/ἐγείρω). A similar double entendre may be present at Acts 3,22,26 ('raise up').

13,14, the words εὗρον (22,28) and Δαυίδ (22,34 ff.) are repeated in the subsequent citation and commentary, where the text is applied to Jesus[21]. Significant also is the repetition of ἐγείρω (23D, 30,37) which, however, initially appears in verse 22 not in quotation but only as an Old Testament allusion (2Sam 7,12: קום, ἀνίστημι). Both ἐγείρω and the interpretive ὑψόω (17, cf. Dtn 4,34,37) may represent the same word in an underlying Semitic text-form, a word repeated, perhaps, at verse 33 (ἀναστήσας).

One further affinity with the *pesher* technique may be noted. Acts 2,16 introduces the quotation from Joel with the words τοῦτό ἐστιν, '*This is* that which was spoken'[22]. Equivalent terms, הוא, זו, זאת ('that', 'this' = οὗτος LXX), are used in the Old Testament, especially in the later strata. They appear in explanations of divine revelation given through prophetic oracle (Is 9,14 f.), parable (Ez 5,5), vision (Zech 1,10,19; 5,3,6), dream (Dan 4,21(24)) and strange writing (Dan 5,25 f.). In Daniel and the Dead Sea Scrolls the expression is used in conjunction with and/or as an equivalent of *pesher*.

And this is (זו) the writing that was written
'Mene, Mene, Tekel, Upharsin'
This is (זו) the interpretation (פשר) . . .

Dan 5,25 f.

. . . (2Sam 7,10 f.). This is (הואה) the House . . . as it is written . . ., 'In the House that your hands have established . . .' (Ex 15,17).
. . . (2Sam 7,14). This is (הואה) the Shoot of David . . . as it is written, . . . (Amos 9,11).
. . . (Ps 1,1). The interpretation (פשר) is . . .

4 Qflor 1,2 f.,11 f.,14

It will be observed that in Acts 2,16 the movement is from Current Event to Scripture, whereas usually in the Qumran *pesher*

---

[21] If the quotation merges 1Sam 13,14 with words from Ps 89,21 and Is 44, 28, 1Sam 13,14 is still the basic text. M. Wilcox, *op. cit.*, 22 ff., suggests that it has been conflated by a targumic tradition. The Targum has similarly 'a man doing His will' (גבר עביד רעותיה). The repetition of εὑρίσκω at Acts 13,22,28 may be coincidental; but note the similar estimates, 'according to my heart' (22) and 'no cause of death' (28), coupled to opposite actions, 'raised up' (23D) and 'hanged' (28).

[22] Elsewhere, compare the formula quotations, Mt 3,3; 11,10. In the rabbinical writings compare the references in J. Bonsirven, *Exégèse rabbinique et exégèse paulinienne*, Paris 1939, 42–46. Cf. Mt 13,19 f.,22 f.

texts, Scripture is the starting point[23]. Indeed the order, Scripture → Current Event, is characteristic of explicit midrash. Perhaps one should not make too much of it since both sequences are present in the Qumran midrash:

They shall march..., smiting and plundering...
For this is (הוא) that which was spoken,
'to take possession of dwellings which are not their own'
(Hab 1,7). Its interpretation (פשרו) is the Kittim...

1QpHab 3,1 ff.

... (Is 5,11—15). These are (אלה הם) the men of
scoffing in Jerusalem, Those are (הם) they who
'have rejected...' (Is 5,24 f.).

4QpIs[b] 2,6 f.[24]

However, most *testimonia* in the New Testament follow the sequence, Current Event → Scripture:

This took place to fulfill what the Lord had spoken by the prophet.

Mt 1,22

They said... 'let us... cast lots for it'... This was to fulfill the scripture.

Joh 19,24

... by the name of Jesus Christ of Nazareth whom you crucified... this man is standing before you well.
This is (οὗτός ἐστιν)...

Acts 4,10 f.

Then follow the Old Testament citations. Acts 2,16—36 represents a mixed pattern. The quotation from Joel is introduced like a testimony text but then, like midrash, the quotation itself becomes the starting point for a wider exposition[25].

The Christian interpretation of certain Old Testament quotations is established exegetically in the New Testament by midrashic exposition; in the *testimonia* citations of the same texts it is simply asserted and applied to the appropriate current event[26]. I

---

[23] The order, Scripture → Current Event, also is present in the New Testament. Cf. Joh 6,31,50; Rom 9,7 f.; 10,6,8; Hebr 13,15 with 1QHab 12,3 ff.,7—9; 4QpIs[b] 2,6 f.,10; 4Qflor 1,2 f.; CD 6,4,7.

[24] This text is taken from the report of J. M. Allegro, in *JBL* 77 (1958) 217. Note the similarity in form between 1QpHab 3,1 ff. and Acts 2,15 ff.,22.

[25] A mixed pattern appears also in 4Qtest where several *testimonia* texts are followed by a *pesher* on the final text. See above, 150 f., 159—162.

[26] E. g., Hab 2,4 in Gal 3,11 and ?Rom 1,17; Ps 8,5—7 in Hebr 2,6 f. and 1Cor 15,27, Eph 1,22; Ps 110,1 in Acts 2,34 f. and 1Cor 15,25, Eph 1,20.

have argued earlier[27] that some *testimonia* texts may be derived from the biblical texts of Christian midrash. This hypothesis would account for the change in sequence discussed above; at the second stage, i. e., Current Event → Scripture, priority is given to the current event to which the Scripture, rightly interpreted, bears witness. If this is so, Acts 2 may represent not only a mixed pattern but a transitional pattern in the early Christian use of Scripture.

II.

This hypothesis, suggested earlier by J. W. Doeve (*op. cit.*, 116), is difficult to establish beyond a plausibility or, in a few instances, a certain probability. However, it may be strengthened if a *testimonia* text in Acts can be shown to have been extracted from an earlier midrash[28]. Peter's speech in Acts 4,11 applies Ps 118,22 to Jesus without further elaboration or exegetical justification. 1Petr 2,7 similarly gives a Christian interpretation of the verse in a catena of *testimonia*. However, the episode in Mt 21,33—44, which is found in Q[29] and Mark, ties Ps 118 to Dan 2,34 f., 44 f. and Is 5,2 via midrashic techniques. The context is the 'parable of the wicked tenants' which, apparently, was an application of the Isaiah text to the treatment given Jesus[30].

In the nature of the case the parable does not speak of the vin-

---

[27] See above, 161 f., 192 ff.

[28] Three other texts that may reflect this kind of development may be mentioned. In the midrashic setting of Acts 2,14—36 the traditional interpretation of Ps 110,1 is disallowed and a Christian interpretation is exegetically established; this interpretation, although not necessarily the tradition of Acts 2, is presupposed in the *testimonia* use of Ps 110,1 in Hebr 1,5; 10,12 f.; Mk 14,62. To establish the Christian meaning of 2Sam 7,6—16 is probably one goal of the midrash in Acts 13 (see above, 199); this kind of exegesis may lie behind the *testimonia* use of 2Sam 7 in 2Cor 6,18 and Hebr 1,5. With lesser certainty the testimony text in Acts 28,26 f. may be traceable to a midrash by Jesus using Is 6,9; the possibly midrashic character of Mk 4, in which the quotation occurs, is argued by M. Gertner, in *JSS* 7 (1962) 267—292. Cf. B. Gerhardsson, in *NTS* 14 (1967—68) 179.

[29] Besides the citation of Dan 2 note the non-Markan parallels in Matthew and Luke at Lk 20,10 (οἱ γεωργοί), 14 (ἰδόντες δέ), 15 (sequence: 'cast out ... killed'). The presence of a Q tradition, in turn, supports as the original reading the allusion to Dan 2 in Mt 21,44. See below, 251 f.

[30] Cf. the catchwords (and cognates) λίθος in Is 5,2 (סקל); Mt 21,35,42,44; and οἰκοδομέω in Mt 21,33,42. Cf. 4QpIs[b].

dication of the owner's murdered son. If the 'stone' citations from
Ps 118 and Dan 2 are understood of the son's vindication — and
this is quite common[31] — it is probable that those citations were
appended later (in Q) by Christian tradition-bearers. However,
that interpretation is not supported in the context[32], and it probably has been read in from the 'stone' *testimonia* elsewhere, e. g.,
in Acts 4,11. In the Gospels the point of the citation is not the
identity of the 'stone' nor the fact of its exaltation. It is rather
that 'the King and Ruler' (Ps 118,22 Targum), whom the leaders
of Israel reject, displaces them and becomes the keystone in God's
new Temple; in the Gospels Ps 118,22 is an 'eschatologisches Drohwort'[33]. J. Jeremias recognizes, rightly in my judgment, that the
original form of the parable goes back to Jesus, a form in which
the messianic significance of the 'son' is veiled. He supposes, however, that the Old Testament citations and the allegorical features
are secondary[34]. It is more likely, all things considered, that an
allegorical meaning was present in the parable from the beginning
even though it has been expanded by the traditioners[35]. Also,
while it is not impossible that the citations (which are present in
both Mark and Q) were added later to the parable to create a
commentary framework, this procedure is without parallel in the
Synoptic tradition. Such an explanation probably reads the historical development backwards. The allusion to Is 5 has virtually
disappeared in Luke, and in the apocryphal Gospel of Thomas
(65—66) both the messianic and the Old Testament references
have been lost. That the Gospel of Thomas represents an earlier
stage of the tradition is scarcely to be accepted, especially since
it shows a clear dependence on the Lukan text-form: the absence
of an allusion to Is 5, the singular καρπός, the sending of individual servants, the word 'perhaps' (Lk 20,13, ἴσως = *meshak*)
and the abbreviated form of Ps 118,22[36].

---

[31] So recently, C. K. Barrett, *Jesus and the Gospel Tradition*, London 1967,
27; B. Lindars, *New Testament Apologetic*, London 1961, 174.

[32] The reading 'marvellous' (Mk 12,11; Mt 21,42 AV; RSV) is somewhat
misleading; the translation 'shocking', 'astonishing', is preferable.

[33] J. Jeremias, in *TWNT* 4 (1942), 279.

[34] J. Jeremias, *The Parables of Jesus*, London ⁶1963, 70—77.

[35] E. E. Ellis, *The Gospel of Luke*, London ²1974, 232; K. Snodgrass in *NTS*
21 (1974—75), 142—144.

[36] See below, 251 n. Cf. Snodgrass (note 35).

It is the judgment theme that ties Ps 118 to the Daniel citation and to the parable, and this is the explicit reason given in the Synoptic Gospels for introducing the citation. The stone in Daniel that judges the nations is identified with the rejected stone for whom God judges Israel and gives its heritage to another 'nation'. This is the astonishing and, to the churchmen, the infuriating element in Jesus' application[37].

The Gospel tradition probably had an abbreviated midrash using Ps 118,22. This raises the possibility that the textually interpretive *testimonium* from the same verse in Acts 4,11 also had its origin in a Christian midrash. But, if so, it was not the midrash reflected in Mt 21 where Ps 118 is interpreted quite differently[38]: the shift is not only from a judgment word to a word of exaltation; there is also a change of reference from the destruction of Israel's leaders to the passion/resurrection of Jesus. The text-form also is altered:

This is (οὗτός ἐστιν) the stone set at nought (ἐξουθενηθείς) by you (ὑφ' ὑμῶν) the builders, which has become the head of the corner.

Both οὗτός ἐστιν and ὑφ' ὑμῶν are midrashic features. Also: Ἐξουθενέω and the Septuagint reading ἀποδοκιμάζω (Ps 117 (118) 22 LXX) are synonyms; and both are used elsewhere in the Septuagint to translate the Hebrew word מאס. Behind 4,11 W. K. L. Clarke (*op. cit.*, 97) suggested an independent Greek translation that used ἐξουθενέω. However, the introductory formula (οὗτός ἐστιν) and other alterations point to a more complex background. Father Barnabas Lindars calls attention to the fact that ἐξουθενέω is employed with reference to the sufferings of Jesus in Mk 9,12 and Lk 23,11, the former text perhaps an allusion to Is 53,3 (נבזה; ἐξουθενώμενος, Aq. Sym. Theod.). He attributes the variant in Acts 4,11, therefore, to the use of the verse in 'the Passion apolo-

---

[37] God's judgment upon the nation is deeply imbedded in the Gospels' presentation of the pre-resurrection mission. Favouring this setting is the different interpretation of the Psalm elsewhere in the New Testament, i. e., of the exaltation of Jesus. Also it is perhaps significant that the judging 'stone' is not (explicitly) identified with the murdered 'son'. This calls to mind the ambiguity preserved between the Son of Man and Jesus in Lk 12,8 and Mk 8,38.

[38] The Gospel tradition may have a closer relation to the *testimonia* in 1Petr 2,7—10 where the judging 'stone' is joined with the conception of a new nation or people of God that receives Israel's heritage. Cf. also Eph 2,19 ff.

getic'[39]. More specifically, ἐξουθενέω may represent a selected or *ad hoc* variant in a Christian (Greek) midrash or, if one may venture further, a common translation of בזה (Is 53,3) and מאס (Ps 118,22), creating a verbal tally in a (Greek) midrash using those texts[40].

The use of Ps 118,22 of Jesus' exaltation probably originated in the post-resurrection mission and is secondary to its interpretation as an eschatological judgment on Israel. But this fact itself suggests that Luke did not make the secondary application *ad hoc* but rather made use of a standing exegetical tradition. He may have inserted Acts 4,11 from such a tradition in the process of summarizing (or composing) the speech. However, the midrashic features of Acts 2 and 13 favor a further conjecture: that the citation in Acts 4 also is drawn from a midrash of similar traditional material.

---

[39] Lindars, *op. cit.*, 81 f., 170 f. Cf. Lk 23,11; Wilcox, *op. cit.*, 173.

[40] Both words are translated by ἐξουθενέω elsewhere in the Septuagint. The catchword ὅσιος (Acts 13,34 f.), on the other hand, has its rationale in an 'inference from Hebrew roots', i. e., חסד (Doeve, *op. cit.*, 173—76; Lövestam, *op. cit.*, 53—71). A combined use of Is 53,3 f. and Ps 118,22 may be reflected in the words πολλὰ παθεῖν and ἀποδοκιμάζω in Mk 8,31; Lk 17,25. Cf. W. Michaelis, in *TDNT* 5 (1967), 913 ff.

14. A NOTE ON 1COR 10,4

The following exegetical exercise probes the possible historical background of an unusual bit of Pauline exegesis. As has been observed above (156 n., 161), 1Cor 10,1—13 is a midrash on certain Exodus events that Paul applies typologically to the church. One verse, 1Cor 10,4, speaks of a 'spiritual' rock which followed (πνευματικῆς ἀκολουθούσης πέτρας) the Israelites in the wilderness and identifies this rock with Christ. There is a cumulative legend in rabbinic literature to which the Pauline phrase has been related in one degree or another[1]. Thackeray, who is certain that Paul has this legend in mind, traces the source of the tradition to a targumic interpretation of Num 21,17[2]. It does appear that, throughout, the rabbinic references to the story have to do almost exclusively with this text[3].

In full flower the legend went somewhat as follows[4]: A movable well, rock-shaped and resembling a sieve, was given to the Israelites in the desert. As to origin, it was one of the ten things created on the evening of the Sixth Day. About the size of an oven or beehive, it rolled along after the wanderers through hills and valleys and, when, they camped, settled at the tent of meeting. When the princes called, 'Rise up, O well' (Num 21,17), water flowed from its many openings as from a flask[5]. The well performed many services: Occasionally it gave everyone a drink at

---

[1] Envelopment in the cloud (1Cor 10,1 f.) is also mentioned in Jewish sources; however, Paul's reference probably stems directly from an interpretation of Exod 40,34,38, or Ps 105,39. Cf. Wisdom 10,17; Josephus, *Antiquities* 3,79; Ta'an. 9a. See below, 226 n.

[2] H. St. John Thackeray, *The Relation of St. Paul to Contemporary Jewish Thought*, London 1900, 205 ff.; cf. Targum of Onkelos on Num 21.

[3] LevRab 10,9 on Num 20,10 most probably does not refer to the well.

[4] This synthetic reconstruction naturally has no facsimile in the rabbinic material.

[5] Tosefta Sukka 3,11 ff.; NumRab 1,2; Shab 35a; NumRab 19,26; Aboth 5,6; Pes 54a.

the door of his tent[6]. Sending forth a river of water to the sea, it brought back all the delights of the world[7]. The fertile ground along the banks of the stream grew grass which served as an effective deodorant[8]; fruits, vegetables, and trees which produced a perfume for the women also grew along its course[9]. The water, too, had healing properties for all who used it[10]. Though no larger a beehive, this devoted servant of Israel once swelled up and filled a whole valley; thus it killed and collected the bones of Israel's enemies in a victory not equaled since the Red Sea swallowed Pharaoh[11]. At the death of Miriam the well dried up and disappeared; for it was given for her merit[12]. But for the sake of the Patriarchs it was restored, and continued with the Israelites until they reached the Sea of Tiberias; there it found its final resting place. And if one has clear eyes, he can stand on a summit and see its reflection in the depths to this day[13].

Such is the story of the 'well.' There seem to be two distinct strands of tradition — the following beehive or rock and the following stream; the latter is probably the earlier of them. The Targum of Onkelos is not clear in this regard[14]; Midrash Sifre (*ca.* 125 A.D.?) on Num 11,21 is certainly in the 'stream' tradition: 'Did not a brook follow them in the wilderness and provide them with fat fish more than they needed?'[15] Pseudo-Philo (*ca.* 100 A.D.?) strikes a similar note[16]. It is quite difficult to determine the precise character of the fable in the first century; apart from the sources mentioned above there is little evidence[17]. Certainly

---

[6] Targum of Jerusalem on Num 21.   [7] Tosefta Sukka 3,11 ff.
[8] DeutRab 6,11.   [9] SS Rab 12,3; 14,1.
[10] NumRab 18,22; EcclesRab 5,8,5.   [11] NumRab 19,25.
[12] Ta'an 9a; LevRab 27,6; NumRab 1,2; SSRab 5,2; 12,3; cf. Num 20,1 f.: 'And Miriam died ... and there was no water.'
[13] Shab 35a; LevRab 22,4; NumRab 18,22; 19,26.
[14] J. W. Etheridge, *The Targums of Onkelos and Jonathan*, London 1865, 300: '... and from [the time] that it was given to them it descended with them to the rivers, and from the rivers it went up with them to the height' (Num 21).
[15] P. P. Levertoff, *Midrash Sifre on Numbers*, London 1926, 77. On its ancient origin see VIII f.
[16] M. R. James, *The Biblical Antiquities of Philo*, London 1917, 7, 105 ff.: '... well of water following them, brought He forth for them' (10,7); '... The water of Marah was made sweet and followed them in the desert 40 years, and went up into the hills and came down into the plains...' (11,15 on Exod 15,23).
[17] The supposed connection of the Targum on Is 16,1 with the legend is

the rabbinical references are not lacking, and their abundance points to the early existence of the legend in some form. The story grew erratically with each writer so as to preclude any definite classification at a given date; but it is not improbable that the first century version spoke only of a following stream of water. While the well is spoken of in two later accounts[18] as being in the shape of a rock or crag (סלע), it is nowhere called a rock; also, 'it is to be noticed that the legend is based entirely upon the well of Num 21,17 f. and is unrelated either with the rock (צור) of Ex 17,5 f. or with the crag (סלע) of Num 20,7—11 (though it is brought into connection with the latter by some later writers, e. g., Rashi).'[19]

Between 1Cor 10,1 ff. and the Well Legend there are one or two points of comparison. Both refer to water from which Israel drank, Paul from one passage (Ex 17,6; cf. Num 20,7 ff.) and the legend from another (Num 21,16 ff.; cf. Ex 15,23 ff.). Paul speaks of a 'spiritual following rock' in the wilderness; the legend concerns a following stream or, later, a rock-shaped well. The correspondence is not especially close, but the phraseology, 'spiritual following rock,' is peculiar enough to be suggestive. When the story of a following stream exists in a closely parallel context, some relationship appears probable. As Driver has rightly noted, the adoption of such a puerile fable would be 'totally out of harmony' with the character of Paul's mind[20]; but his suggestion of a merely verbal relationship is a possible explanation:

St. Paul views the water which the Israelites drank in the wilderness as provided for them by Christ in his pre-existent Divine nature, who attended and watched over his people, whom he represents under the figure of a rock, accompanying them through their journeyings. The particular expression chosen by the apostle may have been *suggested* to him by his acquaintance with the legend current among the Jews; but it is evident that he gives it an entirely different application, and that he uses it not in a literal sense, but figuratively[21].

---

quite improbable: 'They shall bring tribute to the annointed one of Israel, who has prevailed over him who was as a wilderness...' J. F. Stenning, *The Targum of Isaiah*, Oxford 1949, 52.

[18] NumRab 1,2; Tosefta Sukka 3,11 f. The Numbers Rabbah is very late, probably 12th century (H. Freedman, ed., *Midrash Rabbah*, 10 vols., London 1951, V, VII).

[19] S. R. Driver, 'Notes on Three Passages in St. Paul's Epistles,' *The Expositor*, 3rd Series, 9 (1889), 17.

[20] *Ibid.*, 18. See above, 168 n. (A. T. Hanson).

[21] *Ibid.* Cf. Deut 32,4,10 ff.,15,18,30 ff.

However, the relationship may not be so direct as Driver supposed. The word-play of the Targum of Onkelos on Num 21,16 ff. accounts for a part of the legend's inception, but it is not the ultimate or most important factor in the origin of the 'following stream' tradition[22]. In Isaiah and the Psalms there are several references to the water from the rock:

...the waters gushed out (ἐρρύησαν), and the streams overflowed (κατεκλύσθησαν). — Ps 77,20; cf. vs. 16.

... the waters gushed out and ran (ἐπορεύθησαν) in the dry places like a river. — Ps 104,41; cf. Ps 113,8.

...and if they thirst, through (διὰ) the desert he will bring (ἐξάξει) water to them... and the waters will gush out. — Isa 48,21. [MT has the perfect tense.]

'Following rock' and 'following stream from the rock' are admittedly a loose equation, but by no means an impossible one; and taking into account the priority of the 'stream' tradition in rabbinic material, it is a likely key to the apostle's thought. Such an interpretation could also have provided the inspiration for the Targum's word-play on another passage; if so, Paul and the Targum are related more directly to a particular interpretation of the passages of the prophets than to each other. The Targum, applying it to Num 21,16 ff., either sets the legend in motion or applies an inchoate form of it to this particular passage. Paul takes a similar exegesis of the prophetic writings and employs it for his own typological purpose[23].

---

[22] *Contra* Thackeray, *op. cit.*, 206 ff.

[23] Beside Philo's equation of the rock with the wisdom or word of God (Philo, *Leg. alleg.* 2,86; *Quod deter.* 115 ff.), a further parallel with 1Cor 10,4 has been observed in the figure of Metatron. The following presence of Metatron is compared to Paul's following presence of Christ; cf. Sanh 38b (on Exod 33,15). A. Murtonen ('The Figure of Metatron,' *VT* 3 [1953], 409—11) concludes that the Talmudic Metatron in origin and evolution is a sort of Jewish counterpart to Jesus.

15. EXEGETICAL PATTERNS IN 1 CORINTHIANS AND ROMANS

Within 1Cor 1,18–3,20 two passages, 1,18–31 and 2,6–16, display similar exegetical patterns. The first opens with a citation (19 f.) of Is 29,14, supplemented by Is 19,11 f., and is followed by a christological exposition making use of two concepts in the opening texts, σοφία/μωρία (μωραίνειν). This leads to a final quotation (31) of Jer 9,22, whose motif-word, καυχᾶσθαι, also has been caught up in the exposition (29). Similarly, 1Cor 2,6–16 gives a composite and highly interpreted citation (9, ?10a) followed by an eschatological exposition containing a repetition of words from the cited text (εἶδεν, 9, cf. 12), including at least one word that has been interpolated, *pesher*-like, into the citation (ἄνθρωπος, 9, cf. 11; ? πνεῦμα, 10a, cf. 10b–14. This leads to a final quotation (16), Is 40,13, whose term γινώσκειν also has been caught up in the exposition (14).

There are some grounds for supposing that 1Cor 1,18–31 and 1Cor 2,6–16 are independent expositions, i. e., midrashim in their origin. That is, Paul is probably not himself creating the two pieces in the process of writing the letter but is adapting to his own purposes a midrash (or midrashim) already in hand. The several non-Pauline expressions in each passage[1] as well as an examination of the larger context support this conclusion.

1Cor 1,18–3,20 consists of five sections: 1,18–31; 2,1–5; 2, 6–16; 3,1–17; and 3,18–20. The first and third, i. e., the mid-

---

[1] E. g., in 1Cor 2,6–16: 'rulers of this age' (6), 'before the ages' (7), 'the spirit of the cosmos' (12), 'the spirit that is from God' (12); there is one Pauline hapax διδακτός. 1Cor 1,18–31 is somewhat more Pauline in word and idiom and is, perhaps, more likely to have been created by the Apostle; Pauline hapaxes are συζητητής (20), ευγενής (26), ἀγενής (28); in the quotation: συνετός, γραμματεύς (19 f.). Expressions occurring only in the pericope, 1 Cor 1,18 to 3,20, are μωρία (18,21 ff.); 'wisdom of the cosmos' (20, cf. 3,19), 'wisdom from God' (30).

rashic sections, appear to be used as foundation 'texts', which are then applied to the Corinthian situation in the second and fourth sections. The 'application' sections are distinguished by a shift to the past tense and to the first person singular, by personal and Corinthian allusions, by an absence of Old Testament references, and by similar introductory phraseology:

κἀγὼ ἐλθὼν πρὸς ὑμᾶς, ἀδελφοί, . . . (2,1)
κἀγώ, ἀδελφοί, οὐκ ἠδυνήθην λαλῆσαι ὑμῖν . . . (3,1)

At the same time they are verbally tied to the expository or midrashic sections. The fifth section concludes the piece with a final quotation-commentary (3,18—20) and application (3,21—4,21) into which are incorporated the words and motifs of the earlier midrash: σοφία, μωρία, καυχᾶσθαι, ἄνθρωπος. The passage thus discloses the following form:

1,18—31	Midrash
2,1—5	Application
2,6—16	Midrash
3,1—17	Application
3,18—20	Concluding Texts

The midrashic sections appear to form authoritative foundation 'texts' from which the application to the Corinthian situation proceeds. As such, key-words of the first 'text' (1,18—31), e. g., σοφία/μωρία, ἄνθρωπος, are repeated not only in the second 'text' (2,6 f., 9,11,13 f.) and the concluding text (3,19,20), but also in the application sections (2,1,4 f.; 3,3 f., cf. 10). 1Cor 3,21—4,21 appears to continue (the application of) the midrash beyond the concluding text. Thus, the Apostle's dismissal of the Corinthians' judging (4,3) of his work is related to his earlier exclusion of them from the pneumatics, whose role is to judge all things (2,13,15; cf. 3,1)[2]. And his warning not to go beyond what is written (4,6) likewise refers to the texts that he has just expounded to them. From these observations one may conclude that the first division of 1

---

[2] Later (1Cor 9,3; cf. 14,37) it is on the basis of apostolic privilege that Paul dismisses their judging him. In 1Cor 14,24,29 judging is similarly used of the prophets' role in discerning (24, ἀνακρίνειν) a person's true state before God or discerning (29, διακρίνειν) the measure of divine truth in another prophet's message (cf. Rom 12,6). The Corinthian pneumatics apparently wish to test Paul's word and work in this way.

Corinthians not only contains midrashim but also reflects in its own literary formation a midrashic pattern.

Professor Wuellner has shown[3] that the pattern in 1Cor 1,18 to 3,20 is not unlike that found in some rabbinic discourses on Scripture. The literary form of the two pericopes, 1Cor 1,18—31 and 1Cor 2,6—16, also is similar to a rabbinic pattern in which the appointed text of Scripture is supplemented by a second text and followed by commentary (repeating certain words in the texts) and by a concluding citation, usually but not always a repetition of the initial text. An example may be drawn from Pesikta Rabbati 17,1[4]:

> 'And it came to pass at *midnight,* that the Lord smote all the first-born in the land of Egypt' (Exod 12,29). R. Tanhum of Jaffa, in the name of R. Mana of Caesarea, began his discourse by citing the verse, 'When I pondered how I might *apprehend* this, it proved too *difficult* for me' (Ps 73,16). By these words David meant that no creature could be so knowing as to *apprehend* the instant of midnight — only the Holy One, blessed be He, could. For the likes of me, said David, it is too *difficult*. And so because no creature can be so knowing as to apprehend the instant of *midnight* — only the Holy One, blessed be He, can — therefore Scripture says, "And it came to pass at *midnight,* that the Lord smote.'

Often, of course, the piskas are more elaborate, containing additional supporting texts, parables, and longer commentary. But the above example is sufficient to show the basic pattern of a considerable number of these expositions. S. Maybaum[5] found a pat-

---

[3] W. Wuellner ('Haggadic Homily Genre in 1 Corinthians 1—3,' *JBL* 89 [1970], 199—204) limits the midrash to 1Cor 1,19—3,20. He regards this traditional theme, divine sovereignty and God's judgment on all wisdom, to have its *Sitz im Leben* in school or synagogue 'discussion with disciples' (202 f.; cf. Pirke Aboth 6,6; D. Daube, *The New Testament and Rabbinic Judaism,* London, 1956, 158—169). Midrashic procedures appear elsewhere in Corinthians, e. g., 1Cor 10; 15; 2Cor 3; 6,14—7,1. In some instances they may reflect Paul's use of a pre-existing piece of exposition; in some they may provide the literary frame for the Apostle's argument. But, if so, the pattern is neither as clear nor as comprehensive as that which one observes in 1Cor 1—4. On 1Cor 2,1—5 as exposition cf. L. Hartman in *SEA* 39 (1974), 111 ff., 118 ff.

[4] Cf. W. G. Braude, *Pesikta Rabbati,* 2 vols., New Haven 1968, I, 361, cf. 300 f. Piskas 15—18,32 represent 'fairly unified expositions of single themes' (4). Braude regards the *Pesikta* as a seventh-century compilation of the teachings of third- and fourth-century Palestinian Amoraim (26). For a midrash whose concluding text is not a repetition of the initial text cf. I, 363—365 (Piska 17,3); II, 591—597.

[5] S. Maybaum, *Die ältesten Phasen in der Entwicklung der jüdischen Predigt,* Berlin 1901, 15 ff.

tern like this to be typical in Palestinian midrashim, i. e., an initial (Pentateuchal) text plus a second (proemial) text from the Prophets or Writings, followed by exposition, and concluded by a further reference to the initial text.

A commentary-pattern in Philo, which Professor Borgen[6] has shown to be comparable to that in Rom 4,1—22 and Gal 3,6—29, also is somewhat similar to the pattern in 1Cor 1,18—31 and 2,6 to 16. An example is provided by *leg. alleg.* III, 169—173, in which an initial citation (Ex 16,13—15) is followed by commentary utilizing words from the text, supplemented by a subordinate text (Ex 15,8), and concluded by an allusion back to the initial text.

The rabbinic and Pauline exegetical patterns are too similar to be independent developments, and yet they scarcely show a direct dependence. Therefore, even though the rabbinic pattern is extant only in (later compilations of) third or fourth-century homilies, it may be presumed to reflect a type of exegesis used in first-century Judaism. The similar literary form in Philo confirms this.

As might be expected, the Pauline pattern in 1Cor 1,18—31; 2, 6—16 varies somewhat from both Philo and the rabbinic midrash. Like some rabbinical patterns, but unlike Philo, it uses a second opening text (1,20) and concludes with a citation different from the initial text[7]. Also unlike Philo, it lacks subordinate texts and moves from the initial text(s) and commentary directly to a concluding text. Unlike the rabbis, the 'second text' is little more than an allusion at 1,20 and only part of a composite citation at 2,9. However, these variations cannot conceal the basic affinity of these literary forms. 1Cor 1,18—31; 2,6—16 are midrashim, i. e., pieces of exposition with characteristics similar to the commentary-patterns used elsewhere in first-century Judaism. Furthermore, they appear to constitute the 'texts' on which the larger midrash, 1Cor 1,18—3,20, is constructed. This observation is im-

---

[6] P. Borgen, *Bread from Heaven*, Leiden 1965, 47—50, cf. 51 to 58.

[7] W. Bacher, *Die Proömien der alten jüdischen Homilie*, Farnborough (Eng.) 1970, 1913, 19, believes that the second opening text, the proem, developed from the earlier practice of supplementing an initial text with subordinate, non-Pentateuchal quotations. However, 1Cor 1,19,20 (cf. Gal 3,6,8) suggests that a second opening text may have been an acceptable pattern from a very early time, even if it did not have the formal character of a rabbinic proem.

portant for the analysis of the commentary-pattern in Romans 1—4.

In Romans, two sections, which on other grounds have been recognized to be distinctive literary units[8], also display a midrashic structure. The first, Rom 1,17—4,25, is like 1 Corinthians 1—4 in its commentary pattern and in employing a (?pre-formed)[9] expository piece as the concluding 'text' of the midrash (4,1—25). Furthermore, it uses as a supporting text (3,10—18) a combination of Old Testament passages or, if Professor Otto Michel is right[10], a Christian hymn or a part of a hymn created out of such passages. In either case, this thematic and interpretive summary of Old Testament verses, essentially an implicit midrash that interpolates the key-word *dikaios* into the summary, is used as an authoritative 'text' for the larger exposition. The concluding 'text' (4,1—25) is an explicit, proem-like midrash that, as Professor Peder Borgen has shown[11], is in some ways more similar to Philo's exegetical practice. The section as a whole, and the verbal connectives among the various elements, reveals the following sequence:

Proem text[12]:	1,17 (Hab 2,4, δίκαιος, πίστις)
Exposition:	1,18—2,5 (2,1, 3, κρίνειν)
?Supporting text:	2,6 (Prov 24,12, ἔργον)
Exposition:	2,7—23 (7, ἔργον; 13, δίκαιος, δικαιοῦν; 12, 16, κρίνειν)
?Supporting text:	2,24 (Is 52,5, βλασφημεῖν)
Exposition:	2,25—3,3 (2,26, cf. δικαίωμα, λογίζεσθαι; 3,3, πίστις)
Supporting text:	3,4 (Ps 51,6, δικαιοῦν, κρίνειν)
Exposition:	3,5—9 (5 ff., δικαιοσύνη, κρίνειν; ?8, βλασφημεῖν)

---

[8] P. Minear (*The Obedience of Faith*, London 1971, 46—56) sees a close connection between Rom 1,18—4,25 and 14,1—15,13, a section that also exhibits some characteristics of a commentary-pattern.

[9] This would account for the awkward transition at Rom 4,1.

[10] O. Michel, *Der Brief an die Römer*, Göttingen 1955, 85.

[11] Borgen, *op. cit.*, 29—33, 48n. Like Paul (e. g., Rom 4,23—25; 1Cor 3,21 to 4,21; 10,8—13; Gal 4,31—5,1), Philo (e. g., *leg. alleg.* III, 162—168: *de mut.* 253—263) adds to the concluding text of the exposition a further comment or application. It should be observed that, unlike the midrash on Gen 15,6 in Galatians (3,6—?29, cf. 11), Romans 4 contains no explicit reference to Hab 2,4, the text that opened the exposition (Rom 1,17), although the catch-words provide an allusion to it. See above, 157 n.

[12] Rom 1,17 not only concludes the preceding section but also serves as an 'opening' for the following one. This is evident from the literary connection with 1,18 and from the verbal tallies with 1,18—4,25.

Supporting text: 3,10—18 (10, δίχαιος)
Exposition: 3,19—31 (20, 27, ἔργον, διχαιοῦν; 21 f., 25 f., διχαιοσύνη; 22,
                   πιστεύειν; 22, 25 f., 27 f., 30 f., πίστις; 28, 30, διχαιοῦν;
                   26, δίχαιος)
Concluding 'text': 4,1—25 (2, διχαιοῦν; 3, πιστεύειν; 3, 8 f., λογίζεσθαι, διχαιο-
                   σύνη; 9, πίστις; χτλ)

In sum, the first part of Romans, like that of 1 Corinthians, is
a commentary, a teaching piece built upon an elaborate midrashic
pattern. It is true that the linguistic tallies in the exposition are
not so specifically related to the elucidation of the cited texts as
they are in the more compact forms of midrashim. But the commentary-pattern and the general exegetical intention are unmistakable.

The second section, Romans 9—11, has affinities with the *yelammedenu*-type discourse in which a question or problem is posed
and then answered by a biblical exposition. The basic questions in
Romans 9—11 are not difficult to identify:

9,6—29:   Do all those from Israel belong to Israel?
9,30—10,21:   Why have the Gentiles achieved righteousness and the Jews
              stumbled?
11,1—36:   Has God abandoned his people?

However, unlike the rabbinic homilies, the questions proceed more
from a current event — Israel's rejection of the Messiah — than
from a problem in the biblical text[13]. They also lack the stylized
form of the rabbinical pattern and are more interwoven, the second question arising out of the answer to the first, the third out
of the second. Also, they are supplemented by subordinate questions (e. g., 9,14; 10,18 f.) that add to the complexity of the whole
passage. In spite of the differences the pattern and techniques in
Romans 9—11 reflect sufficient similarities with the rabbinic discourses to suggest that they arose in a common milieu. In the following excerpts the procedures in Rom 9,13,14—23 may be compared with those in Pesikta Rabbati 50,1[14]:

...(Hos 14,2). This verse is to be   As it is written, 'Jacob have I loved...'
considered in the light of what Isaiah   (Mal 1,2 f.).

---

[13] But the sequence, current event → scripture, is occasionally present in
Qumran midrash. See above, 203 ff.
[14] Braude, *op. cit.*, II, 770, 843.

was inspired by the Holy Spirit to say, 'For Sheol cannot praise thee...' (Is 38,18). Can this verse in Isaiah really mean what it seems to be asserting of the Holy One, blessed be he, ... that a man who has merit... will go down into Sheol? Of course, this is not what the verse means. ... As it is said, 'Everyone that calls... upon my glory, [for this] I created him...' (Is 43,7), any man who calls upon my name... will be safe from the punishment of Sheol. Isaiah asked further..., Is it not thy delight to forgive so that the man lives... [for] as David said, 'The dead praise not the Lord' (Ps 115,17)? The Holy One ... replied to Isaiah, 'My son, what David said applies to the wicked....'

What shall we say then? Is there unrighteousness with God?

God forbid. For he says to Moses, 'I will have mercy....' So it is not of him who wills... but of God who shows mercy. For the Scripture says to Pharaoh, 'Even for this purpose. ...' Then you will say to me, 'Why does he still find fault? For who can resist his will?'

But who are you, a man, to answer back...? Will the pot say... (Is 29, 16; 45,9)?

A further comparison may be drawn between the pattern in Piska 44,1 and that in Rom 9,29,30–33:

'Return, O Israel...' (Hos 14,2). Let our master teach us. If one who keeps committing sin keeps saying that through repentance he will be forgiven, what answer shall be made to him? Our masters taught thus, 'He who keeps saying, 'I will sin and then repent...', will never have strength enough to repent' (Yoma 8,8).

Why not? Because if a man repents and then goes back to his transgressions his repentance was not true repentance ... [parable]. Scripture says, 'Let the wicked forsake his way...' (Is 55,7).

'Except the Lord Sabaoth had left us a seed...' (Is 1,9).

What shall we say then? That the Gentiles who followed not after righteousness, attained... righteousness that is from faith. But Israel who followed after the law of righteousness did not attain to the law of righteousness. Why? Because they sought it not from faith but as though it were from works. They stumbled over the stumbling stone. As it is written, 'Behold, I lay in Zion...' (Is 28,16).

The pattern in the larger pericope, Rom 9,6–29, also is somewhat similar to that found in the rabbis. The opening text, Gen 21,12, is supplemented by Gen 18,10. The key-words, καλεῖν, σπέρμα, and υἱός are repeated in the exposition (8,12,24) or in the supporting quotations (25–27). The word σπέρμα (29) in the concluding citation (Is 1,9, LXX) refers back to the opening text[15].

---

[15] A number of commentators mark Rom 9,29 as the conclusion of a section, e. g., Michel, *op. cit.*, 205 f.

In conclusion, the exegetical patterns in 1 Corinthians and Romans are suggestive both for the formation of the Pauline letter and for the structure and interpretation of a number of individual passages. They probably point not only to the creative mind of the Apostle but also to that of some of his co-workers, the circle of prophets and teachers whose exegetical labors Paul participated in and used.

16. PROPHECY AND HERMENEUTIC IN JUDE

I.

Both the literary form and the historical setting of the letter of Jude offer unusual insights into the theology and praxis of the early Christian mission. The literary form can be perceived best in the light of the analysis of 1Cor 1—4 and Rom 1—4,9—11 in the preceding chapter[1]. In those passages two remarkable phenomena in earlier Christian literature manifest themselves. (1) Expositions of Scripture, using 'commentary', i. e. 'midrash' patterns common to first century Judaism, not only are present in the early Christian letter but also determine in certain instances its literary form. (2) Moreover, the expositions employ not only quotations but also explicit and implicit midrashim on the Old Testament as their authoritative texts[2]. Both phenomena, which can be clearly observed in the commentary-format below, appear in thorough-going fashion in the letter[3] of Jude:

ΙΟΥΔΑ

1 Ἰούδας Ἰησοῦ Χριστοῦ δοῦλος, ἀδελφὸς δὲ Ἰακώβου, τοῖς ἐν θεῷ πατρὶ ἠγαπημένοις καὶ Ἰησοῦ
2 Χριστῷ τετηρημένοις κλητοῖς. ἔλεος ὑμῖν καὶ
εἰρήνη καὶ ἀγάπη πληθυνθείη.

3 Ἀγαπητοί, πᾶσαν σπουδὴν ποιούμενος γράφειν
ὑμῖν περὶ τῆς κοινῆς ἡμῶν σωτηρίας, ἀνάγκην
ἔσχον γράψαι ὑμῖν παρακαλῶν ἐπαγωνίζεσθαι τῇ

---

[1] See above, 213—220.

[2] For examples and the definition of implicit midrash see above, 151—154, 189.

[3] Like a number of New Testament writings Jude may be classified as a 'letter' only in a very general sense. It is described as a 'circular' by several writers. Cf. F. Spitta, *Der zweite Brief des Petrus und der Brief des Judas*, Halle 1885, 484n; A. Loisy, *The Origins of the New Testament*, London 1950, 279 ff.: Jude is 'a fragment of a diatribe (3—23) set in the frame (1—2,24 f.) of an epistle' (279).

4 ἅπαξ παραδοθείσῃ τοῖς ἁγίοις πίστει. παρεισεδύησαν γάρ τινες ἄνθρωποι, οἱ πάλαι προγεγραμμένοι εἰς τοῦτο τὸ κρίμα, ἀσεβεῖς, τὴν τοῦ θεοῦ ἡμῶν χάριτα μετατιθέντες εἰς ἀσέλγειαν καὶ τὸν μόνον δεσπότην καὶ κύριον ἡμῶν Ἰησοῦν Χριστὸν ἀρνούμενοι.

5 Ὑπομνῆσαι δὲ ὑμᾶς βούλομαι, εἰδότας ἅπαξ πάντα,

Num 14,35   ὅτι κύριος λαὸν ἐκ γῆς Αἰγύπτου σώσας τὸ δεύτερον τοὺς μὴ πιστεύσαντας ἀπώλεσεν,

Gen 6,1—4   6   ἀγγέλους τε τοὺς μὴ τηρήσαντας τὴν ἑαυ
1En 10,4—6   τῶν ἀρχὴν ἀλλὰ ἀπολιπόντας τὸ ἴδιον οἰκητήριον εἰς κρίσιν μεγάλης ἡμέρας δεσμοῖς ἀϊδίοις ὑπὸ ζόφον τετήρηκεν.

7   ὡς Σόδομα καὶ Γόμορρα καὶ αἱ περὶ αὐτὰς
Gen 19,4—25   πόλεις, τὸν ὅμοιον τρόπον τούτοις ἐκπορνεύσα
2Pet 2,6,10   σαι καὶ ἀπελθοῦσαι ὀπίσω σαρκὸς ἑτέρας, πρόκεινται δεῖγμα πυρὸς αἰωνίου δίκην ὑπέχουσαι.

8 Ὁμοίως μέντοι καὶ οὗτοι· ἐνυπνιαζόμενοι, σάρκα μὲν μιαίνουσιν, κυριότητα δὲ ἀθετοῦσιν, δόξας δὲ βλασφημοῦσιν.

9   Ὁ δὲ Μιχαὴλ ὁ ἀρχάγγελος, ὅτε τῷ διαβόλῳ
?AssmMos   διακρινόμενος διελέγετο περὶ τοῦ Μωϋσέως
Zech 3,2   σώματος, οὐκ ἐτόλμησεν κρίσιν ἐπενεγκεῖν βλασφημίας ἀλλὰ εἶπεν, ἐπιτιμήσαι σοι κύριος.

10 οὗτοι δέ· ὅσα μὲν οὐκ οἴδασιν βλασφημοῦσιν, ὅσα δὲ φυσικῶς ὡς τὰ ἄλογα ζῷα ἐπίστανται, ἐν τούτοις φθείρονται.

11 οὐαὶ αὐτοῖς,

jTgGen 4,8   ὅτι τῇ ὁδῷ τοῦ Κάϊν ἐπορεύθησαν, καὶ τῇ
Dt 23,4   πλάνῃ τοῦ Βαλαὰμ μισθοῦ ἐξεχύθησαν, καὶ
Num 16   τῇ ἀντιλογίᾳ τοῦ Κόρε ἀπώλοντο.

12 Οὗτοί εἰσιν οἱ ἐν ταῖς ἀγάπαις ὑμῶν σπιλάδες συνευωχούμενοι ἀφόβως, ἑαυτοὺς ποιμαίνοντες, νεφέλαι ἄνυδροι ὑπὸ ἀνέμων παραφερόμεναι, δένδρα

φθινοπωρινὰ ἄκαρπα δὶς ἀποθανόντα ἐκριζωθέντα,
13 κύματα ἄγρια θαλάσσης ἐπαφρίζοντα τὰς ἑαυτῶν
αἰσχύνας, ἀστέρες πλανῆται, οἷς ὁ ζόφος τοῦ
14 σκότους εἰς αἰῶνα τετήρηται. Ἐπροφήτευσεν
δὲ καὶ τούτοις ἕβδομος ἀπὸ Ἀδὰμ Ἑνὼχ λέγων,

ἰδοὺ ἦλθεν κύριος ἐν ἁγίαις μυριάσιν αὐτοῦ,
15 ποιῆσαι κρίσιν κατὰ πάντων καὶ ἐλέγξαι
πάντας τοὺς ἀσεβεῖς περὶ πάντων τῶν ἔργων
ἀσεβείας αὐτῶν ὧν ἠσέβησαν καὶ περὶ
πάντων τῶν σκληρῶν ὧν ἐλάλησαν κατ᾽
αὐτοῦ ἁμαρτωλοὶ ἀσεβεῖς.

1En 1,9
GenAp 2,20—22

16 Οὗτοί εἰσιν γογγυσταὶ μεμψίμοιροι, κατὰ τὰς
ἐπιθυμίας αὐτῶν πορευόμενοι, καὶ τὸ στόμα
αὐτῶν λαλεῖ ὑπέρογκα, θαυμάζοντες πρόσωπα
ὠφελείας χάριν.

17 Ὑμεῖς δέ, ἀγαπητοί, μνήσθητε τῶν ῥημάτων τῶν
προειρημένων ὑπὸ τῶν ἀποστόλων τοῦ κυρίου
18 ἡμῶν Ἰησοῦ Χριστοῦ, ὅτι ἔλεγον ὑμῖν

2Pet 3,3
2Tim 3; 4,3
Acts 20,29 f.

ἐπ᾽ ἐσχάτου τοῦ χρόνου ἔσονται ἐμπαῖκται
κατὰ τὰς ἑαυτῶν ἐπιθυμίας πορευόμενοι τῶν ἀσεβειῶν.

19 Οὗτοί εἰσιν οἱ ἀποδιορίζοντες, ψυχικοί, πνεῦμα μὴ
ἔχοντες.

20 Ὑμεῖς δὲ, ἀγαπητοί, ἐποικοδομοῦντες ἑαυτοὺς τῇ
ἁγιωτάτῃ ὑμῶν πίστει, ἐν πνεύματι ἁγίῳ προσευ-
21 χόμενοι, ἑαυτοὺς ἐν ἀγάπῃ θεοῦ τηρήσατε,
προσδεχόμενοι τὸ ἔλεος τοῦ κυρίου ἡμῶν Ἰησοῦ
22 Χριστοῦ εἰς ζωὴν αἰώνιον. καὶ οὓς μὲν ἐλεᾶτε
23 διακρινομένους, σώζετε ἐκ πυρὸς ἁρπάζον-
τες, οὓς δὲ ἐλεᾶτε ἐν φόβῳ, μισοῦντες καὶ τὸν ἀπὸ
τῆς σαρκὸς ἐσπιλωμένον χιτῶνα.

24 Τῷ δὲ δυναμένῳ φυλάξαι ὑμᾶς ἀπταίστους καὶ
στῆσαι κατενώπιον τῆς δόξης αὐτοῦ ἀμώμους ἐν
25 ἀγαλλιάσει, μόνῳ θεῷ σωτῆρι ἡμῶν διὰ Ἰησοῦ
Χριστοῦ τοῦ κυρίου ἡμῶν δόξα μεγαλωσύνη κράτος
καὶ ἐξουσία πρὸ παντὸς τοῦ αἰῶνος καὶ νῦν καὶ εἰς
πάντας τοὺς αἰῶνας· ἀμήν.

In addition to the observations made earlier on expository forms in 1 Corinthians and Romans four further considerations support in more detail the above format for the letter of Jude. (1) The suggested citations, i. e. the indented verses, are introduced by the formulas δέ (9), ὅτι (5,11) and λέγειν (14,17), formulas that are used elsewhere in the New Testament to introduce quotations, e. g. 2Cor 10,17; Gal 3,11; Mk 12,26. (2) The suggested citations are also similar in form and content to recognized quotations elsewhere. The first (5—7) represents express, thematic summaries of Old Testament passages, i. e. implicit midrashim, that are similar to the merged quotation-interpretations in Rom 3,10—18; 2Cor 6,16 ff. and to specified texts within the commentary-forms in 1Cor 2,9; Gal 4,22; 2Petr 3,5, cf. 8 (λανθάνειν τοῦτο ὅτι). The third citation in Jude 11 is less clear and may be the author's own continuing invective against the false teachers. But the shift in tense and the generalized wording suggest rather an application by Jude of an earlier (prophet's) condemnation of disobedient persons.

The second, fourth and fifth citations (9,14 f.,18) are apocryphal elaborations of the Old Testament and an apostolic prophecy, each of which is regarded as inspired in its own right and/or as a faithful interpretation of inspired teachings. The summary of the apostolic teaching (18) is no different from the quotation of Christian prophetic writings and/or oracles on the same subject in Acts 20,29 f.; 1Tim 4,1; 2Tim 3,1; 2Petr 3,3; cf. 2Thess 2,3—5[4] and on other subjects in Lk 11,49—51; Eph 5,14; ?Jas 4,5. The express citation of the non-canonical book of 1 Enoch in Jude 14 f. is more far-reaching and is unique in the New Testament. But it is essentially only an extended application of the principle found elsewhere that faithful interpretations of (canonical) Scripture are equivalent to Scripture[5]. That is, like Scripture the interpretations mediate God's teaching although, unlike Scripture, they do not in

---

[4] 1Tim 4,1 and 2Tim 3,1; 2Petr 3,3 appear to be citations of (traditioned) prophetic sayings or oracles. The formula, τὸ πενῦμα λέγει (1Tim 4,1), elsewhere introduces prophetic oracles (e. g. Acts 13,2; 21,11; Rev 2,7; cf. 14,13) and writings (Acts 28,25; Hebr 3,7; 10,15). The formula, (τοῦτο) γινώσκειν ὅτι, occasionally introduces revelatory words (Lk 10,11; Acts 2,36) or maxims (Jas 1,3; 5,20), some of which appear to have been traditioned teaching-pieces (cf. Eph 5,5 with 1Cor 6,9). On the similar phrase, 'let this be known,' see Acts 2,14; 4,8 ff.; 13,38; 28,28.

[5] See above, 156 n.

themselves have canonical status[6]. The principle is present in the New Testament wherever targumic and perhaps apocryphal (? 1Cor 2,9) interpretations and expansions of the Old Testament are cited like canonical writings[7].

(3) The distinctive form of the commentary following each of the proposed citations also argues for the midrashic character of Jude. Each commentary-section is marked by a shift in tense[8] and is introduced by the repeated and quasi-formulaic employment of οὗτος (8,10) and οὗτός ἐστιν (12,16,19). These terms or their equivalents are used in the Old Testament, New Testament and other contemporary Jewish literature to introduce *inter alia* commentary on sacred writings[9]. Similarly in Jude, they signal the application of the preceding citation to the current eschatological situation.

(4) The commentary-pattern is confirmed, finally, by the extraordinarily abundant catchword connections[10]. Such verbal links are the hall-mark of the midrashic procedure and, in the textform of Jude produced above, they are indicated by the s p a c e d words (including cognate forms). The catchwords join quotation to quotation (e. g. κρίσις, 6,9,15), quotation to commentary (e. g. λαλεῖν, 15,16), quotation to Jude's introduction (e. g. κύριος, 4,15), quotation to Jude's final application (e. g. σῴζω, 5,23), or they may join all four elements (τηρεῖν, 1,6,13,21; κύριος, 4,5,14,17,21). They include not only individual words but also clauses, i. e. in verses 6 and 13,16 and 18. They reinforce the impression that the whole piece (5—19) is a carefully worked-out commentary that Jude has then introduced (1—4) and supplied with a concluding exhortation (20—23).

---

[6] On the broader implications of this matter cf. E. E. Ellis, 'The Conception of the Old Testament in Early Christianity,' *Compendia: Rerum Judaicarum ad Novum Testamentum*, ed. M. de Jonge et al., Kampen 1974—, II, i, forthcoming.

[7] E. g. Mt 2,23; Joh 7,38; Rom 12,19; Eph 4,8; cf. E. E. Ellis, *Paul's Use of the Old Testament*, Edinburgh 1957, 34—37. An apocryphal writing is cited in 1Cor 2,9 according to Origen (*Comm.* on Mt 27,9); in Eph 5,14 according to Jerome (*ad Eph*, in loc.). In a change of mind I now think that Jas 4,5 probably cites a Christian prophetic writing.

[8] I. e. past (5—7a) to present (8) to past (9) to present (10) to past (11) to present (12); past (15) to present (16); future (18) to present (19).

[9] E. g. Dan 5,26; Rom 9,8; 1Cor 10,6; Gal 4,24; Eph 5,32. See above, 189 f., 203.

[10] See above, 155, 156 n.

Jude's writing, then, is a midrash on the theme of judgment for which the letter-form provides a convenient dress. In structure and theme it is very much like 1Cor 10,1–13[11]. Since it employs rather general examples (5–7,11)[12] and is introduced as a reminder of things that his readers already know (5), it may be a reworking of an existing, more general exposition on the outcome of disobedience[13]. As it stands, the midrash is similar not only to other New Testament commentary on Scripture but also to biblical exposition at Qumran. Like the Qumran texts, it (1) is oriented to a present-time eschatological fulfilment, (2) joins an alternating sequence of quotation and commentary with the *pesher* formula, 'this is[14],' (3) occasionally alters a citation to accomodate it to the desired interpretation (χύριος, 15; ἀσεβείας, 18)[15] and (4) cites non-canonical traditions alongside biblical texts[16].

It has been established above that the kind of exposition that appears in the letter of Jude occurs elsewhere in the New Testament as the activity of pneumatics or prophets[17]. Whether the exposition here falls into this category will require a closer look at the place of the letter within the early Christian mission, including the identity of the author and of the false teachers that he combats.

II.

Commentators have usually identified the author of the letter of Jude with the brother of Jesus[18] or with a pseudepigrapher writing under his name[19]. They base this conclusion on the phrase

---

[11] Note especially the (non-canonical?) allusion to the following rock and the concluding exhortation in 1Cor 10,1–13: introduction (1), opening text = Christianized summary of Old Testament (and non-canonical?) passages (2–5), commentary (6–7a), supporting text (7b), concluding exhortation (8–13). There is a similar conclusion in Gal 4,31–5,1; see above, 156.

[12] Cain, Balaam and Sodom are widely used paradigms for the outcome of ungodliness.

[13] The implications of this view of the matter for the broader question of the relationship of Jude to 2 Peter cannot be explored here.

[14] E. g. 4Qflor. See above, 159 ff.   [15] See above, 173–181.

[16] 4Qtest 22 f.   [17] See above, 26 f., 130–138.

[18] This Judas is mentioned by name in Mk 6,3 = Mt 13,55 and in Hegesippus (Eus *HE* 3,19). He is first identified with the author of the letter by Clement of Alexandria (fragment, *Adum. in ep. Judae*, beginning).

[19] For the references cf. W. G. Kümmel, *Introduction to the New Testa-*

ἀδελφὸς Ἰακώβου in Jude 1, taking the first word to mean 'blood brother' and the second to refer to the leader of the Jerusalem church and brother of Jesus. On the latter identification they cannot be faulted since, among other reasons, James of Jerusalem seems to be the only prominent person of that name long active in the early Christian mission[20]. The meaning of ἀδελφός is another matter.

Against the traditional interpretation of ἀδελφός here as physical brother are two important considerations. First, 'the brothers of the Lord' were active in the mission of the church and were known by that name[21] or as 'the brothers of Jesus.'[22] If Jude were such, why does he not so identify himself? The answer of Clement of Alexandria[23], that Jude was too modest to do so, involves an unlikely affectation since Jude (on this reading) identifies himself in any case as the brother of the brother of Jesus. More improbably, this explanation reads back a later reverence for the relatives of Jesus that is quite absent from the attitudes of the first-century church.

Second, the term ἀδελφός is often used in the New Testament to mean not 'relative' but 'co-worker.' This connotation, which has been demonstrated in an earlier chapter[24], is particularly applicable to Jude 1 since it is the usual meaning of the word in opening (and closing) greetings of a letter and since it applies to 'the brothers' associated with James in Acts.

In this regard the book of Acts gives significant pointers to author of the letter of Jude[25]. (1) A number of passages in Acts use the term 'the brothers'(οἱ ἀδελφοί) for workers in or from the

---

ment, Nashville 1975, 428. Fatal to the pseudepigraphal hypothesis is the name itself, as Zahn has rightly observed: Who could induce anyone to defend the Christian faith in the name of Jude? The phrase, 'Jude the brother of James,' is so obscure and so vaguely identified that it could never have served a pseudepigrapher's purposes. Cf. T. Zahn, *Introduction to the New Testament*, 3 vols., Edinburgh ³1909, II, 268—270.

[20] Gal 1,19; 2,12; 1Cor 15,7; Acts 12,17; 15,13; 21,18; cf. Jas 1,1. Cf. the discussion of J. N. D. Kelly, *The Epistles of Peter and of Jude*, London 1969, 231—234.

[21] 1Cor 9,5; cf. Gal 1,19.   [22] Acts 1,14; cf. Mk 3,31 f.; Joh 2,12; 7,3 ff.

[23] See note 18.   [24] See above, 13—17.

[25] On the historical reliability of Luke's depiction of the council in Acts 15 cf. F. F. Bruce, *The Book of Acts*, London 1954, 298—302; C. W. Emmet, *BC* II, 271—286.

Jerusalem church. Although some of them have been considered earlier[26], several require a closer examination. Acts 11 is introduced by the phrase 'the apostles and the brothers who were throughout (κατά) Judaea' (11,1). These persons or a part of them designated 'those of the circumcision' (11,2) sharply criticize Peter, when he comes to Jerusalem, for eating with Gentiles in Caesarea. That is, the apostles *and the brothers*, including Peter, appear to be workers in the Christian mission based on the church in Jerusalem but laboring throughout the region (9,31 f.). This meaning is supported by the reference to 'these six brothers' (11,12) from Joppa, who accompanied Peter to Caesarea and then to Jerusalem. It also accords with the theological critique and response of Peter, which Luke would less likely ascribe to the church or to the believers generally. Of course, the brothers are 'believers' (10, 45; cf. 15,5) or 'disciples' (cf. 21,16), but in Acts 11 they appear to be a special group of believers gifted and set apart for ministry.

(2) Acts 12,17 agrees with this usage and explicitly associates the brothers of the Jerusalem church with James. It quotes Peter, after his escape from prison and before his departure elsewhere, as instructing certain disciples to report these things 'to James and to the brothers.' Like 'the apostles and the brothers' in Acts 11,1, 'James and the brothers' is best understood of a select group within the Jerusalem church. The technical connotation of 'the brothers' corresponds with its use elsewhere. Also, if the idiom were intended to refer to believers generally, one would expect a phrase like James and 'the church' (12,5; cf. 14,27; 15,4) or 'the disciples' (6,2) or, at least, 'the other brothers.' Furthermore, the instruction is given (and is underscored by Luke) not to inform the church of answered prayer, which under the circumstances would be quite pointless, but to inform the Christian workers threatened by the official reaction to the escape and (in Luke's plan) to signal a change in the leadership of the mission. That is, after the death of James the brother of John (12,1) and the departure of Peter, the mission of the Jerusalem church will no longer be conducted by 'the apostles and the brothers' but by 'James and the brothers'.

(3) Acts 15, which depicts the council of Jerusalem, identifies one of these brothers of James with a prophet named Jude. He is

---

[26] On Acts 9,30; 21,17 see above, 15 f.

appointed, together with others, to draft[27], distribute and interpret a circular letter giving the decision of the council to the Gentile 'brothers' in Antioch, Syria and Cilicia (15,22 f.).

In Acts 15, then, there is a Jude who is a brother, i. e. a coworker of James and, thus, an active minister and indeed a prophet of the ritually-strict Hebrews, the dominant party of the Jerusalem congregation. Yet, to fulfill his commission, he clearly must
be bilingual with a special fluency in Greek. If he has participated
in drafting the decree, he also has ability in writing Greek. After
his present mission he will have a personal acquaintance with Paul
and his theology. He will also have a personal relationship with
many Jewish and mixed Jewish-Gentile churches of the Hellenist
mission, particularly those Pauline or Pauline-influenced churches
in Syria and in a part of Asia Minor that have been disturbed by
(gnosticizing) Judaizers coming from the Hebraist mission of the
Jerusalem church (ἐξ ἡμῶν, 15,24)[28]. He will be known, furthermore, as a representative of that mission or, in a word, as 'the
brother of James.'

In a number of ways the personal attributes and the historical
situation of the Jude in Acts 15 fit the author of the letter of
Jude. (1) The author is known as the brother of James. (2) He invites the supposition that he is a prophet by the form of his exposition, by the 'prophetic' description of his opponents (see below) and by identifying himself as 'a slave' (δοῦλος, 1), a term
that in Judaism and in the early church was associated with prophets[29]. (3) By his use of the Old Testament and Jewish apocrypha
the author reveals that he is a Jew steeped in his ancestral traditions. (4) Yet he writes competent Greek[30] and, although the re-

---

[27] Acts 15,23: γραψάντες διὰ χειρὸς αὐτῶν. The meaning of the clause is not
clear. But T. Zahn (*Die Apostelgeschichte*, Leipzig 1927, 534 f.) is probably
right to interpret it of the writing (cf. 1Petr 5,12) and not merely of the delivery of the decision: 'The council gave Judas and Silas the task of bringing
the decision of the assembly into a finished form' (535). It is not improbable
that the same Silas = Silvanus is 'the faithful brother' who is the amanuensis in
writing 1 Peter. J. B. Lightfoot (*The Apostolic Fathers*, 3 vols. in 5, London
1885, II, ii, 1, 281 on Ignatius, *ad Philad* 11,2) takes a similar idiom to refer to the
amanuensis. On the role of Jude also see above, 132, 137.
[28] See above, 107—112.
[29] See note 17; see above, 11 n., 17 n. If the opponents were pneumatics, Jude
must have had similar endowments to be an effective spokesman against them.
[30] For examples of good Greek idiom and of Semitisms cf. J. Chaine, *Les*

cipients most likely include Jewish Christians, he does not address them as though they come from a strictly Jewish background[31]. (5) Including no personal greetings or messages, he gives the impression that he is writing a circular letter to a considerable number of communities, nevertheless to specific communities that are facing a common problem from the same dangerous persons. (6) He directs his letter against false teachers who, as we hope to show below, display unmistakable affinities with the false teachers (and their diaspora adherents) opposed in the Jerusalem decree.

The last point must now be examined in detail. The affinities between the false teachers in Jude and the Judaizers opposed at the Jerusalem council (A. D. 50) depend upon the relationship of the latter to the opponents in the Pauline letters. The Judaizers in Acts 15 (1,23 f.) have come, without authorization, from the Hebraist mission of the Jerusalem church and are active teachers not only in Antioch but also in Asia Minor, i. e. Cilicia. They have the same traits and are undoubtedly the same group that in Galatians are designated 'those of the circumcision' (2,12), i. e. a part of the Hebraist mission, who have 'slipped in' (παρεισῆλθον, 2,4) and, already before the Jerusalem council, have promoted a judaizing praxis in Jerusalem, Antioch and Asia Minor, i. e. Galatia[32]. However, as has been shown earlier[33], the opponents in Galatia are a part of a broad front of opposition, a counter-mission that is active or potentially active in various churches from Galatia to Rome. Before the decision of the Jerusalem council, i. e. in Galatians (c. A. D. 49), they stressed judaizing demands. After that decision and in the variegated atmosphere of the diaspora they altered certain of their emphases. But in the other Pauline letters, no less than in Galatians, they are the same group that was censured in Acts 15.

Épitres Catholiques, Paris 1939, 274—278. The Greek of the introduction (1—4) and the concluding exhortation and doxology (20—25) is sufficient to show Jude's facility whether the midrash proper (5—19) has been created or only re-worked by him.

[31] The force of the examples from the Old Testament and the Jewish apocrypha would be well perceived not only by Jewish believers but also by instructed Gentiles, especially mission workers if such are the primary addressees.

[32] Gal 3,1 f.; 5,10; 6,12 f. In Gal 2 Paul relates the problem in Antioch precisely because it is analogous to the problem in Galatia. One may assume, then, that the same type of false teacher, if not the same persons, are active in both places. See above, 110 n.   [33] See above, 101—115.

The counter-mission in the Pauline letters reveals a number of features that are remarkably similar to the false teachers in Jude, features that are sometimes depicted in almost the same idiom:

Jude: They 'abandoned themselves to Balaam's error for the sake of reward' (11), 'flattering people to gain advantage' (16).

Paul: We are not, like them, 'peddlers of the word of God' (2Cor 2,17). 'They serve their own belly and deceive by fair and flattering words' (Rom 16,18), 'teaching for shameful gain' (Tit 1,11).

Jude: They have 'slipped in' (4) and 'set up divisions' (19) contrary to 'the doctrine (ἡ πίστις) once for all delivered to the saints' (3).

Paul: They 'came in stealthily' (Gal 2,4) and 'cause divisions... contrary to the doctrine (ἡ διδαχή) that you learned' (Rom 16,17).

Jude: They 'carouse at your love-feasts without fear, shepherding themselves' (12), and 'their mouth speaks boastfully' (ὑπέρογκα, 16).

Paul: They are 'insubordinate men, empty talkers' (Tit 1,10), who 'boast in appearance' and 'according to the flesh' (2Cor 5, 12; 11,18; cf. Phil 3,3).

Jude: 'On the basis of their visions (ἐνυπνιαζόμενοι) they defile the flesh' (8).

Paul: They take their stand 'on visions, vainly puffed up by their fleshly mind' (Col 2,18). Since they boast of visions, I am forced also to boast of mine (cf. 2Cor 12,1,11).

Jude: 'They are worldly (ψυχικοί) and do not have the (holy) Spirit' (19).

Paul: They impart 'a different spirit' (2Cor 11,4). Unlike true pneumatics, 'the worldly person (ψυχικὸς ἄνθρωπος) does not receive the things of the Spirit of God' (1Cor 2,14).

In addition the false teachers in Jude, like those in Paul's letters, interpret immoral conduct as a manifestation of Christian freedom (4)[34] and, as pneumatics, appeal to their 'dreamings' or vi-

---

[34] This is also the case with certain Corinthians (1Cor 5–6), who later support Paul's opponents (2Cor 12,11,21), and it is probably to be inferred of the opponents themselves. Gal 5,13,20 is a less certain parallel. See above, 104, 112 n.

sions to justify it (8)[35]. Like certain Corinthian pneumatics and the false teachers who are active in Corinth[36], they focus on and misuse the angelic powers, who are apparently present in their visions (8). In this way and in their immoral conduct they 'displace' Christ's lordship (8) and deny him (4)[37]. Other Pauline parallels are present[38], but the above examples are sufficient to establish the close relationship if not the identity of the false teaching in Jude with that opposed in the Pauline letters and, thus, in Acts 15. They are reinforced by the similar response of both writers to the error: strong invective against the false teachers[39] and a deliberate stress on the centrality of the lordship of Jesus Christ[40].

The letter of Jude differs considerably from many Pauline theological emphases and in some measure from Paul's description of his opponents. In some respects it has closer affinities with other Christian literature, e. g. 2 Peter. But these facts, which cannot be investigated here, are not at variance with the very substantial resemblances between Jude and Paul. Nevertheless, the close historical proximity of the two writers has been denied on other grounds.

Two principal objections to identifying the author of the letter of Jude with the prophet in Acts 15 (or with the brother of Jesus

---

[35] So, Kelly (note 20), 261 f.; H. Windisch–H. Preisker, *Die katholischen Briefe*, Tübingen 1951, 41. The term 'dreamings' is used in the Septuagint of prophetic visions in Joel 2,28 (= Acts 2,17) and, of false prophets, in Dtn 13, 2–5; Jer 23,25–32; 34,7 = 27,9. For a similar attitude among Paul's opponents cf. 2Cor 12,1,11; Col 2,18. See above, 105, 110, 113.

[36] Cf. 1Cor 3,10 f.; 12,3; 2Cor 11,4,13 ff.; Gal 1,8; Col 2,3,18 f.; Tit 1,16. See above, 102–114; J. A. T. Robinson, *Redating the New Testament*, London 1976, 171.

[37] The denial also may have wider, christological implications.

[38] E. g. their misuse of the Lord's supper (12; cf. 1Cor 11,20 f.) and προ-γράφεσθαι (4; Rom 15,4), used of Old Testament Scripture as it typologically refers to present eschatological events (5–7,8). Also, Jude 11 may possibly reflect a denial by the false teachers of the parousia and future judgment (cf. 1Cor 15,12; 2Thess 2,2; 2Tim 2,17 f.).

[39] E. g. Jude 9–12; 2Cor 11,13–15.

[40] See note 36. The strong christological emphasis of Jude, which has often been overlooked or denied, becomes clear in the commentary-format above in which the role of the κύριος = Jesus is repeatedly underscored. Jesus was the Lord who redeemed Israel from Egypt (5), and he will be the final redeemer (21). It is he who judged Israel in the wilderness (5), who presently keeps the rebellious angels in chains (6; cf. Col 2,15; 1Cor 15,24 ff.; Eph 1,22; 4,8; Hebr 2,14; 2Petr 2,4; Rev 20,1 f.), and who alone rightly exercises judgment in that realm (9). He is the Lord who will come in his glorious parousia to execute judgment on all the ungodly (15).

for that matter) are the author's competence in Greek and the use of Greek writings (1 Enoch), and the indications in the letter of a post-A. D. 70 date. The first objection assumes that in first-century Palestine a ritually-strict Jew would not be fluent in Greek, much less use Greek translations of Jewish writings. This assumption is not only undemonstrated but, as has been argued elsewhere in this volume, historically improbable[41].

Indications of a later date are thought to be present in the use of ἡ πίστις (3,20) as a formally transmitted (παραδίδοσθαι) deposit of teaching, in the reference to the condemnation of the false teachers being 'prescribed long ago' (πάλαι προγεγραμμένοι, 4), and in the citation of an apostolic prophecy (17 f.). The first two matters can, in fact, be understood better as further affinities with Pauline thought. For Paul also spoke of the Christian teaching as a known content of tradition transmitted (παραδίδοσθαι) to his readers and he underscored the importance of their adherence to it, especially in the face of erroneous teachings[42]. On occasion he used the term ἡ πίστις for the content of Christian teaching, i. e. *fides quae creditur*[43]. If this usage of πίστις was more common in the later patristic church, it should not for that reason be assigned a later *origin* than the meaning 'trust' that is more common in Pauline and Reformation usage. As for the second matter, it becomes clear from the commentary format of Jude that the condemnation of the false teachers 'prescribed long ago' reflects a typological understanding of the Old Testament (5—7), precisely in accord with Paul's theology and with his use of the same verb, and therefore does not indicate a later date for the letter[44].

That the citation of an apostolic prophecy (17 f.) points to a post-apostolic date for Jude is a tradition going back to Luther[45]. But on several grounds the tradition must be regarded as mistaken. First, already in A. D. 50 an apostolic tract, which had the character of a prophetic word (Acts 15,28), was issued against a judaizing aberration among certain Hebraist apostles and mission

---

[41] See above, 106 n., 116; below 245 ff.

[42] 2Thess 2,15; 3,6; 1Cor 15,3; Rom 16,17; cf. Rom 6,17; 1Cor 11,2.

[43] E. g. Gal 1,23.

[44] See note 38; see above, 96, 166.

[45] M. Luther, 'Vorrede auf... Judas,' *Die Deutsche Bibel*, 12 vols., Weimar 1931, VII, 387. Luther also thought that, though the letter speaks of Christ, it teaches us nothing about him (385). But see note 40.

workers. In the face of the persistence of this teaching, compounded in many areas by libertine attitudes and practices, prophetic oracles or sayings that warned of such errors[46] would, on this pattern, very likely have been circulated during the following decade (A. D. 50—60)[47] by faithful apostles[48]. Second, the formal introduction, 'the apostles of our Lord Jesus Christ,' found only here in the New Testament and not at all in the apostolic Fathers, does not itself suggest the perspective of a post-apostolic writer unless one reads later patristic connotations into the phrase[49]. Formal literary expression was not unknown to the primitive church (cf. 2Cor 1,3), and appeal to apostolic authority was already common in the fifties or earlier (e. g. 1Cor 9,1; 2Cor 11,13; Acts 15; cf. Gal 2,2).

Third, the words 'remember' and 'they said to you' (17) must be read in the light of the earlier, similar expressions: 'remember' and 'you were informed of all these things' (5)[50]. Thus read, they show that Jude's recipients are the same persons who had been instructed by apostles not only about the fate of disobedient persons (5—15) but also about the coming of the scoffers (18). Jude's readers, then, are the contemporaries of the apostles and they differ, e. g. from the Galatians only in that they are addressed by someone other than the apostles who introduced them to the Christian faith. With these considerations in mind, the above objections

---

[46] Such prophecies, one of which (2Petr 3,3) is remarkably similar to Jude 18, are cited in several New Testament books. Cf. Mk 13,19—22; Acts 20,29 f.; see note 4. The relationship between 2Petr 3,3 and Jude 18 affects the date of Jude suggested here only if Jude is here directly dependent on 2 Peter and the latter is given a post-apostolic date.

[47] I. e. the period in which Paul is first embattled by such errors. According to Rom 3,8 (c. A. D. 56) Paul's doctrine of salvation by grace was then possibly being utilized by false teachers to sanction libertine practices. Similarly, before the Jerusalem council some teaching or act of his, perhaps something like the circumcision of Timothy (Acts 16,3), was used to claim him as a Judaizer (Gal 5,11). Cf. C. D. Osburn, *NTS* 23 (1976—77), 339 ff.

[48] C. Bigg *(St Peter and St Jude,* Edinburgh 1910, 316) envisions a more formal manifesto similar to that of Acts 15. Jude 17 lends some support to this, but the citation itself is styled more like a prophetic saying.

[49] E. g. 'the apostles' identified with 'the Twelve' and conceived of as a kind of apostolic college. For the first-century church the Twelve were a select group within a much larger body of apostles of Christ, i. e. missionaries commissioned by the (risen) Lord. See above, 12 f., 16 n., 143 n.

[50] Cf. Kelly (note 20), 254.

to dating the letter of Jude during the pre-A. D. 70 Christian mission can be seen to be without merit.

III.

A proper historical method requires that, before a writing is judged to be pseudonymous, it should be examined within the context from which it professes to originate. The above investigation has endeavored so to understand the writing called Jude. If it has succeeded, this writing is the exposition of a Hebraist prophet, a mission worker from the Jerusalem church and a sometime companion of Paul[51]. Addressed to communities in Asia Minor and perhaps Syria[52], it is directed especially to the 'brothers' of these communities who have benefited from the author's ministry[53] and whose congregations have now been infiltrated by the same deviant Hebraists who have disturbed Paul's churches.

These Hebraists apparently have reversed certain teachings of the Hellenists. The latter, while holding firmly to the ethical teaching of the Old Testament, believe that with the coming of the messianic age its ritual laws are no longer binding. With a perverse twist the deviant Hebraists, while holding to the traditional rituals, are teaching that with the liberating presence of the messianic age the ethical and particularly sexual codes of the Old Testament are no longer binding.

The letter of Jude attacks the false teachers vehemently. Considering its affinities with the Pauline controversies, it is most

---

[51] So, E. C. Selwyn, *The Christian Prophets*, London 1900, 148, who thought that Jude was also the blood brother of James. See above, 137 f.

[52] Asia Minor seems to have been the focal point of the controversy. M. Schneckenburger (*Beiträge zur Einleitung ins Neue Testament*, Stuttgart 1832, 225) took the destination to be Colossae. However, his perception of two opposing groups of false teachers, and probably the special connection with Colossae, were mistaken. A Syrian destination, although appropriate to the known missionary labors of Jude, is rendered less probable by the fact that the Syrian church, which was based on Antioch, was very slow in accepting the prophetic, i. e. canonical status of Jude's letter.

[53] The rather complex literary form, the blunt and rather strong language, the apparent distinction of the recipients from the 'saints', i. e. the believers (3), and the exhortations to the recipients to exercise their ministry (20,22 f.) favor a leadership group as the primary addressees. In Acts 15, also, Jude's ministry was primarily directed to 'the brothers' although the congregations were not excluded (Acts 15,23,32 f.,30 f.).

likely to be dated within the decade A. D. 55—65. Favoring a relatively early date within this period are the author's recent appre-
hension of the situation (3 f.) and his reference to James († 62) as
though he is still the active leader of the Hebraist mission (1). The
urgency of the matter may explain why Jude did not return to
Jerusalem and pen a weighter introduction like 'James ... and
Jude the brother' (cf. 1Cor 1,1). On the other hand, it may be
that James has already been martyred and that the false teaching
in these particular communities, or Jude's knowledge of it, has
been slow in coming. One can only say that the letter, as it has
been interpreted above, is unlikely to have been written after the
late sixties since with the Christians' flight from Jerusalem (c. A.
D. 65) the Hebraist mission of the Jerusalem church, as it was
constituted under James, came to its end.

In an earlier chapter it has been suggested that the letter to the
Hebrews (3,1; 6,10; 13,22) is a prophetic 'word of exhortation'
(παράκλησις) from a Hellenist to certain Hebraist 'brothers' who,
out of loyalty to their traditions, are in danger of falling away
from Christ[54]. It is suggested here that the letter of Jude also is a
prophetic word of exhortation (παρακαλεῖν, 3), but here a word
from a Hebraist to certain Hellenist 'brothers' who are in danger
of seeing their congregations subverted and destroyed. Both letters
reveal something of the praxis of the early Christian mission and
the relationship of its two major components. While the Hebraist
and Hellenist missionaries followed different life-styles and in
some measure pursued their tasks separately, they also co-operated
with one another and continued to manifest a mutual Christian
love and concern. The letter of Jude gives an eloquent witness to
this ecumenical brotherhood. When the churches of Asia Minor no
longer have Paul or Peter among them and when, perhaps, the
voice of James has been silenced by death, the endangered believers have still a champion, a prophet who has worked among them
some time before and who again speaks to them the Word of God
with passion and in power.

---

[54] See above, 127 f.

17. NEW DIRECTIONS IN FORM CRITICISM

It is now almost sixty years since German scholars introduced form criticism to the study of the Synoptic Gospels. They drew upon similar studies in Old Testament criticism[1] and, in the Gospels, were preceded by the suggestive comments of a number of scholars[2]. Nevertheless, they first applied form criticism, as a discipline, deliberately and systematically to the Gospels. Most influential among them were Martin Dibelius of Heidelberg and Rudolf Bultmann of Marburg[3]. Standing at the beginnings of the inquiry they exercised a decisive influence in determining the principles that would govern it for the next generation. Also, by the comprehensive scope of their contributions they, more than others,

---

[1] H. Gunkel, *Genesis*, Göttingen 1917.

[2] J. G. Herder, *Vom Erlöser der Menschen*, Riga 1796, 149–233; J. Wellhausen, *Einleitung in die drei ersten Evangelien*, Berlin 1905, [2]1911. Cf. also K. L. Schmidt, *Der Rahmen der Geschichte Jesu*, Darmstadt 1964 (1919), which may perhaps be best regarded as a prolegomenon rather than as a part of the discipline. Cf. W. G. Kümmel, *The New Testament: ...Investigation of its Problems*, London 1973, 330. Of the English writers cf. B. F. Westcott, *An Introduction to the Study of the Gospels*, London [7]1888 (1851): 'The oral Gospel ... centred in the crowning facts of the Passion and the Resurrection, while the earlier ministry of the Lord was regarded chiefly in relation to its final issue. [The] last stage of Christ's work would be conspicuous for detail and fulness, and ... its earlier course would be combined together without special reference to date or even to sequence. Viewed in the light of its end the whole period ... would be marked not so much by divisions of time as by groups of events' (208). '[The Gospels] seem to have been shaped by the pressure of recurring needs and not by the deliberate forethought of their authors. In their common features they seem to be ... the summary of the Apostolic preaching ...' (209). '[The argument that oral] tradition is the parent of fable ... disregards ... the traditional education of the age [in oral learning], and arbitrarily extends the period during which the [oral] tradition was paramount' (211).

[3] R. Bultmann, *Die Geschichte der synoptischen Tradition*, Göttingen [5]1961, [1]1921 (ET: [3]1963); M. Dibelius, *Die Formgeschichte des Evangeliums*, Tübingen [2]1933, [1]1919 (ET: [2]1935).

excited the imagination of the scholarly world and became the touchstones from which its work proceeded.

In this frame of reference form criticism was both a success and a failure. As a method for the analysis of the literary units of the Gospels it was well received by most scholars throughout the world[4]. However, as a critique of the historical value of the Gospels it was identified with a particular 'school' and was, as Professor Conzelmann has rightly noted, widely unacceptable to non-German scholarship. Even among German scholars, where the form critical approach became a dominant point of view, it soon experienced a 'gewisse Stagnation[5].'

A number of studies in the present generation have sought to renew and redirect the discipline along more fruitful lines. Some have proceeded from the general framework of the early form criticism[6] but others, especially among Scandinavian and Anglo-American writers, represent a more radical break or a quite different departure. The present chapter is written within the latter context although not without criticism of it and, it is hoped, with full recognition of the achievement and abiding contribution of the pioneers of form criticism. In criticizing the classical formulation of the discipline the essay intends (1) to review the issues causing many scholars to follow new directions and (2) to offer, within the context of several recent studies, a sociological context, i. e. a *Sitz im Leben*, in which certain Gospel traditions were formed and developed. It concludes (3) with an examination of two exegetical 'forms' that appear to have originated within the pre-resurrection mission of Jesus and his disciples.

---

[4] E. g. B. S. Easton, *The Gospel before the Gospels*, New York 1928; V. Taylor, *The Formation of the Gospel Tradition*, London 1933, 9—21; F. V. Filson, *Origins of the Gospels*, New York 1938, 85—114; L. de Grandmaison, *Jesus Christ*, 3 vols., New York 1937, I, 39—56; L. J. McGinley, *Form Criticism of the Synoptic Healing Narratives*, Woodstock (Md.) 1944; P. Benoit, *Jesus and the Gospel I*, New York 1973, 11—45 (= *RB*, 1946, 481—512); M. D. Hooker, 'Christology and Methodology,' *NTS* 17 (1970—71), 485; G. B. Caird, 'Form Criticism,' *ExpT* 87 (1975—76), 137—141.

[5] H. Conzelmann, *VF* 7 (1956—57), 151 f.; cf. *ZTK* 54 (1957), 279 f.; *Jesus*, Philadelphia 1973, 9 (= *RGG³* III, 621).

[6] H. W. Kuhn, *Ältere Sammlungen im Markusevangelium*, Göttingen 1971, 11—14.

I.

Among the assumptions with which the form criticism of the Gospels began were (1) views widely received in New Testament scholarship, (2) views *in statu nascendi* among German scholars of the early twentieth century, (3) philosophical tendencies and commitments traditional within an influential segment of (mainly) German scholarship. Each set of assumptions, questioned by some from the outset, has been increasingly eroded by subsequent research and critiques. The first includes *inter alia* the two document hypothesis and the conviction that a considerable 'oral period' preceded the writing of any Gospel material.

While the two document hypothesis has been rejected outright by some scholars[7], it probably remains the starting point for the majority. However, even by its adherents it has been modified by the recognition of other sources besides Mark and 'Q.' Such sources include collections behind Mark[8], written Matthean and Lukan traditions[9], and 'Q' viewed as several tracts[10] or a stratum of tradition[11] rather than as one document. The demonstration that 'Q,' i. e. non-Markan parallels in Matthew and Luke, considerably overlaps Mark in both narrative and sayings material[12] shows that the extent of the Q material is greater and its literary character more complex than was earlier supposed. It thus effectively undermines the two document hypothesis as it was originated, appar-

---

[7] E. g. A. M. Farrer, 'On Dispensing with Q,' *Studies in the Gospels*, ed. D. E. Nineham, Oxford 1955, 55—86; W. R. Farmer, *The Synoptic Problem*, New York 1964. They correctly pointed out certain tenuous elements in the two document hypothesis, however one may judge their own alternative reconstructions. Cf. B. Orchard, *Matthew, Luke and Mark*, Manchester 1976, 3—36.

[8] Kuhn, *Sammlungen*; E. B. Redlich, *Form Criticism*, London 1939, 37—50; R. H. Lightfoot, *History and Interpretation in the Gospels*, London 1935, 110; Easton, *Gospel*, 71 f.

[9] B. H. Streeter, *The Four Gospels*, Oxford 1924, 227—270.

[10] W. L. Knox, *Sources of the Synoptic Gospels*, 2 vols., Cambridge 1953, 1957, II, 3—6.

[11] G. Bornkamm, *RGG³*, II, 756; cf. Dibelius, *Formgeschichte*, 235 f. (ET: 234 f.).

[12] T. Schramm, *Der Markus-Stoff bei Lukas*, Cambridge 1971; cf. E. E. Ellis, 'The Composition of Luke 9 and the Sources of its Christology,' *Current Issues in Biblical and Patristic Interpretation*, ed. G. F. Hawthorne, Grand Rapids 1975, 121—127 (FT in *Jésus aux origines de la christologie*, ed. J. Dupont, Gembloux 1975, 193—200).

ently by Herbert Marsh of Cambridge[13], and traditionally developed.

The demise or radical modification of the two document hypothesis throws into question the form critical 'laws of development' since they were constructed on the assumption that the Matthean and Lukan variations from Mark were 'developments' that provided (written) illustrations of such laws. More importantly, it throws into question the entire theory of an 'oral period,' a fundamental postulate of the early form criticism: since an extensive complex of written Gospel material must be assumed for the pre-Markan period, i. e. pre-65, it is more difficult to suppose that none of it extended back into the ministry of Jesus.

II.

The sharp discontinuity that some early form criticism postulated between Jesus and the earliest post-resurrection church has been widely and rightly regarded as resting more on theological than on historical considerations[14]. Rejecting this assumption, several recent investigators have located the beginnings of the Gospel tradition in the oral teachings of Jesus to his disciples. Professor Riesenfeld[15] and Gerhardsson have underscored the fact that Jesus is represented in all strata of the tradition as a rabbi, a teacher, and

---

[13] H. Marsh, 'Origin and Composition of our Three First Canonical Gospels' (Cambridge 1801), appended to volume V of J. D. Michaelis, *Introduction to the New Testament*, 5 vols., Cambridge 1793–1801: 'In addition to the document א which contained a series of *facts* another document [ב] was drawn up containing a collection of *precepts, parables,* and *discourses* which ... was used only by St. Matthew and St. Luke ... [in] different copies ...' (202, cf. 194–211). The Hebrew document א was used in different forms by the three Evangelists and was best reproduced by Mark; ב, the non-Markan parallels in Matthew and Luke, was also recognized by Eichhorn (1804) to be one document and was later assigned the symbol Q.

[14] For Bultmann the discontinuity is a theological postulate: cf. E. Heitsch, *ZTK* 53 (1956), 196. For the confessional, i. e. philosophical considerations involved cf. also Conzelmann, *Jesus*, 90–96; Benoit, *Jesus*, 38 ff. Within this context there is justification for Benoit's (28–38), Albright's and Hengel's complaint about the 'anti-historical' attitude of the early form criticism. Cf. W. F. Albright and C. S. Mann, *Matthew*, Garden City (N. Y.) 1971, v–vi; M. Hengel, *ZTK* 72 (1975), 204.

[15] H. Riesenfeld, 'The Gospel Tradition and its Beginnings,' *The Gospel Tradition*, Philadelphia 1970, 1–29 (= *TU* 73, 1959, 43–65).

that 'all historical probability favors the conclusion that Jesus' disciples would have valued his words at least as highly as the pupils of the famous rabbis valued theirs'[16]. Professor H. Schürmann[17] sought a sociological setting for the earliest transmission of Jesus' teachings: (1) The disciple-circle constituted a sociological and confessional continuity between the pre-resurrection and post-resurrection community (46—50). (2) The confessional continuity, in the value placed on Jesus' word, implies a continuity of tradition: the disciples would have kept and protected, shared and transmitted that which they regarded as a final 'word of revelation' of a God-sent prophet or of the Messiah (51—53). (3) Jesus gave both individual sayings and blocks of teaching in easily remembered poetic form[18]. Since form criticism has shown that the 'form' had a sociological function, we may presume that Jesus taught thus not only for the disciples' retention but also for their transmission of his teaching not only after his death — for them an artificial setting lacking existential, contemporary meaning — but also during his present mission (56 f.)[19]. (4) The transmission had its sociological 'setting' in the sending out (and co-working) of disciples, a tradition attested in all strata of the Gospel material[20]. It was 'official' and consciously nurtured, not folkloric[21]; it was the work of the *shaliah*, i. e. the 'apostle' who de-

---

[16] B. Gerhardsson, *Memory and Manuscript*, Uppsala 1961, 258; cf. his response to criticisms in *Tradition and Transmission*, Lund 1964. Whether the analogy offered by Gerhardsson, i. e. the 'oral Torah' in (Pharisaic) rabbinic tradition, is fully adequate to explain the transmission of the Gospel tradition is another question. For criticisms cf. W. G. Kümmel, *Jesu Antwort an Johannes den Täufer*, Wiesbaden 1974, 18 f.; E. Güttgemanns, *Offene Fragen zur Formgeschichte des Evangeliums*, München 1971, 151; W. D. Davies, *The Setting of the Sermon on the Mount*, Cambridge 1964, 464—480; M. Smith, *JBL* 82 (1963), 149—176; J. A. Fitzmyer, *TS* 23 (1962), 442—457; see below, 243 f.
[17] H. Schürmann, 'Die vorösterlichen Anfänge der Logientradition,' *Traditionsgeschichtliche Untersuchungen*, Düsseldorf 1968, 39—65.
[18] C. F. Burney, *The Poetry of our Lord*, Oxford 1925.
[19] B. S. Easton, *JBL* 50 (1931), 149.
[20] I. e. not only in (later formed) Gospel narrative but also in individual sayings (Mk 1,17; 3,14 f.; Lk 5,10), blocks of teaching (Mt 10,5—23; Lk 10,1 to 20; cf. 12,22—31) and parables (Mt 24,45—51; cf. 13,24—30; Lk 11,5—8; 19, 12—27). More significant are multiple attestation in the oldest sources, i. e. overlapping Markan and Q material (e. g. Lk 9,1—6), and the association of 'sending' with the twelve, whose existence in the pre-resurrection mission is virtually certain (cf. E. E. Ellis, *The Gospel of Luke*, London ²1974, 136 f.).
[21] The incorrectness of using folk tradition as an analogy to explain the

livered not his own message but that of the sender. It must have
included teachings elaborating the 'kingdom of God' proclamation
since the proclamation alone would be meaningless, and it probably included some narrative about Jesus since the sender's message would inevitably raise questions about the sender (57—60).

Schürmann has shown, convincingly in my judgment, that the
historical circumstances of Jesus' mission presuppose for certain
of his teachings a *Sitz im Leben Jesu*, i. e. a sociological locus in
which the teachings were given typical transmission-forms. The
present essay builds upon the observations of Schürmann and offers two theses to modify and extend them. (1) Some Gospel traditions were transmitted not only in oral but also probably in
written form during the earthly ministry of Jesus. (2) Some exegetical patterns in the Gospels are among the earliest transmitted
'forms' of Jesus' teachings.

III.

The postulate of an 'oral period,' i. e. antecedent to any written
accounts of Jesus' words and works, became increasingly accepted
during the nineteenth century[22]. In the early form criticism it was
attached to an apocalyptic interpretation of Jesus and of the early
church. This interpretation, which supposed that writing would

---

transmission of Gospel traditions has now been made clearer by Güttgemanns
(*Offene Fragen*, 119—150). Cf. also McGinley, *Form-Criticism*, 4—10; Benoit,
Jesus, 34—38; W. Manson, *Jesus the Messiah*, London 1943, 27—29.

[22] It apparently arose from the tradition (Papias, in Eus. *HE* 3, 39, 15), from
the influence of J. G. Herder's conception of the Gospel tradition as 'oral
saga' and from the complexity and inadequacy of solutions to the Synoptic
problem via written sources. Cf. Kümmel, *Problems*, 80—83; Westcott, *Gospels*,
165—194, 207—212: The Apostles 'seem to have placed little value upon a
written witness... [for] the outward fashion of the world... was passing
away' (166); 'the whole influence of Palestinian [rabbinic] habits was most
adverse to [a written Gospel]' (167); 'the faithful zeal of the Galileans may be
rightly connected with their intellectual simplicity.' And 'the art of writing itself was necessarily rare among the peasantry... while they were oral teachers
by inclination and habit' (168); '... the characteristic work of the Apostles was
preaching and not writing' (183). However, there was not a consensus: cf. W.
M. F. Petrie, *The Growth of the Gospels*, New York 1910, 4—8 (sketchily); W.
M. Ramsay, 'The Oldest Written Gospel,' *The Expositor: Seventh Series* 3
(1907), 410—432, 424; 'The lost common Source of Luke and Matthew... was
written while Christ was still living.'

begin only when the expectation of an imminent end of the age subsided[23], foundered with the discovery of the Dead Sea Scrolls: the Qumran sect viewed itself to be in the 'last generation' (1Qp-Hab 2,7; 7,2), expected an imminent end but, nevertheless, produced a large body of literature. Other traditional grounds for the postulate also are open to some doubt[24].

A number of considerations favor the supposition that some written formulations of Jesus' teachings were being transmitted among his followers already during his earthly ministry.

1. Teaching Jewish children to read and write was regarded in the first century as essential and, according to Josephus, was commanded by the Law[25]. The synagogue, where such training was given, was present in every Palestinian village and assures us that literacy was widespread. The picture of Jesus' followers as simple, illiterate peasants is a romantic notion without historical basis. Unless it can be shown otherwise, it must be assumed that some of the disciples and/or their converts were capable of composing written traditions.

2. Jesus and his community had more in common with a prophetic (Schürmann) than with a rabbinic (Gerhardsson) attitude to-

---

[23] Dibelius, *Formgeschichte*, 9 (ET: 9): 'Eine Gemeinde unliterarischer Menschen, die heute oder morgen das Weltende erwartet, hat zur Produktion von Büchern weder Fähigkeit noch Neigung...' This apocalyptic viewpoint was not able to sustain itself in the subsequent discussion. Cf. W. G. Kümmel, *Promise and Fulfilment*, London 1957; A. L. Moore, *The Parousia in the New Testament*, Leiden 1966, and the literature cited; E. Linnemann, *Parables of Jesus*, London 1966, 132–136.

[24] (1) Doubts about the learning (γράμμα, Joh 7,15; Acts 4,13) of Jesus and his disciples do not refer to their literacy, a meaningless observation in the contexts, or to their biblical knowledge but to their 'unprofessional' status and the lack of sophistication associated with it (cf. R. J. Knowling, *Acts: Expositor's Greek Testament*, 5 vols., ed. W. R. Nicoll, London 1901, II, 128; F. J. F. Jackson and K. Lake, *Beginnings of Christianity*, 5 vols., London 1920–1932, IV, 44. (2) Papias' (Eus. *HE* 3, 39, 4) preference for the 'living and surviving voice' was not a preference for oral tradition but for firsthand testimony. The comments that Mark wrote down the teachings (διδασκαλίας, Eus. *HE* 3, 39, 15) of Peter and that the barbarians received the gospel without written documents (Iren. *a. Haer.* 3, 4, 2) are irrelevant to the question of the prior existence and origin of written Gospel traditions. (3) Creative variations in the traditions and sources of the synoptic Gospels are as explicable in written as they are in oral form if the traditioners (or the Evangelists) handled 'holy word' Jesus-traditions in as creative a fashion as they did 'holy word' Old Testament traditions.

[25] Jos. *c. Apion.* 2, 204; *Ant.* 4, 211; Test. Levi 13,2; Philo, *ad Gaium* 115, 210. On early written rabbinic traditions cf. J. Neusner, *JSJ* 4 (1973), 56–65.

ward the biblical tradition. The former attitude, observable in first century Judaism in the apocalyptic Qumran community[26], lacked the inhibitions[27] about written, midrashic alterations of and commentary on sacred texts, inhibitions that apparently characterized the early (Pharisaic) rabbinic transmission.

3. Oral folk traditions, on which the early form criticism drew its analogies, were inappropriate to understand either the nature or the transmission of the Gospel traditions. (a) The transmission of folk traditions over one or more centuries is *ipso facto* a very different thing from the transmission of 'holy word' traditions over three decades within a closely knit religious movement originating in a nation with rather firm conceptions and exalted attitudes about such traditions[28]. (b) Recent studies of the technique and transmission of oral folk traditions, especially of the problems inherent in a shift from their oral to written transmission[29], make clear that this kind of analogy is of little value for understanding the development of the Gospel traditions[30].

4. The circumstance that gave rise to written teachings in early Christianity was not chronological distance but geographical distance, not the death of the eyewitnesses but the absence of the teaching leadership. This is evident in the case of Paul's letters and of the Jerusalem Decree (Acts 15), but a similar situation on a smaller scale was also present in the mission of Jesus. Mark cannot be used as a yardstick for the length of that mission, and one must probably reckon with a period of several years[31]. According to

---

[26] See above, 45—62.

[27] As Gerhardsson (*Memory*, 31) recognizes.

[28] At this point Gerhardsson's (*Memory*, 14, 56—70) critique of the early form criticism is quite correct and his further observations instructive, however one may wish to modify his own reconstruction.

[29] A. B. Lord, *The Singer of Tales*, Cambridge (Mass.) 1964 (1960), 123, 124 to 138: 'the two techniques [of oral and written style] are ... contradictory and mutually exclusive' (128 f.). In the change from oral to literary transmission the stimulus is usually a foreign literary tradition (133). The written tradition 'supplanted [the] native oral traditions; it did not develop out of them' (138).

[30] Güttgemanns, *Fragen*, 104 f., 140—150: Either the Gospel-form is genuine, i. e. a mature written-form from an individual conscious of the results, in which case the evidence for a collective oral-form disappears; or the written-form, and with it the literary individuality, is lightly dismissed in order to maintain a continuity of tradition from 'forms' to Gospel (104).

[31] C. A. D. 28/29—33. Cf. H. E. W. Turner in *History and Chronology*

the traditions in the Gospels and Acts Jesus taught and presumably gained followers in both Galilee and Judea[32]. The twelve are appointed to be 'with him' (Mk 3,14) and the replacement for Judas must also be one who accompanied him (Acts 1,21 f.). But that role was a distinction. Many followers who 'listened to his teaching' (Lk 10,39) remained in their villages and towns. They were in no less need of continued teaching, especially in the face of the rising tide of opposition to Jesus and to his eschatological and ethical message. As has been observed above, certain disciples were trained and sent out by Jesus to transmit his teachings orally. But did they, in the brief mission tour, so train their hearers? It is more plausible to suppose that at least some written paradigms of the Lord's pronouncements would be left with those who received his message of the kingdom. There existed in any case a *Sitz im Leben* for such literary forms.

5. The use of Greek in Palestinian Judaism[33] and, probably, among Jesus' pre-resurrection followers favors the formulation of written traditions about Jesus from the earliest period.

a) A Jerusalem synagogue inscription[34] and numerous ossuary and other funerary inscriptions throughout Jewish Palestine attest to the widespread use of Greek in the first century[35]. The syna-

---

in the New Testament, ed. D. E. Nineham, London 1965, 59—74; B. Reicke, *The New Testament Era*, Philadelphia 1968, 183 f.

[32] Mt 21,23; 26,6 f.; Mk 6,6; 12,35; Lk 4,15; 13,10,22,26; 19,8 ff.,37,39; Joh 4,1; 7,3; 19,38 f.; Acts 1,14D; 10,39; 18,24 f.; 19,1 ff. Some such notices are editorial; but one must not, in dialectic fashion, suppose that 'editorial' and 'traditional' are mutually exclusive categories. For example the journey structure in Lk 9—19 is 'editorial;' however, it is not editorial *de novo* but a Lukan formulation of a journey tradition that he knows from Mk 10. The same is true of some other geographical notices in the Gospel narrative. Cf. Lk 19,11 with Mt 25,14—30.

[33] On the broader influence of Hellenism in Jewish Palestine cf. I. H. Marshall, 'Palestinian and Hellenistic Christianity,' *NTS* 19 (1972—73), 271—287; M. Hengel, *Judaism and Hellenism*, 2 vols., Philadelphia 1974, especially I, 58 to 106.

[34] E. L. Sukenik, *Ancient Synagogues in Palestine and Greece*, London 1934, 69 f.

[35] For a good summary and evaluation of the evidence cf. J. N. Sevenster, *Do You Know Greek?*, Leiden 1968, 23—38 (New Testament), 96—175, esp. 131—134, 143—149, 152 ff., 171—175 (Jewish Palestine). He rightly observes that Luke regards it noteworthy, not that Paul spoke Greek in Jerusalem, but that he spoke 'in the Hebrew language' (Acts 22,2). One may add that Philo (*Vita Mos.* II, 31) accepts without question that the Jerusalem high priest should

gogue, where apparently 'the reading of the Law' and 'the teaching of the commandments' (lines 4,5 in the inscription) were done in Greek, 'may well have been one of the synagogues of the "Hellenists" mentioned and even listed in Acts 6,1–9[36].' 'Hellenists' probably refers to Jews who lived like Greeks, with special reference to their rather loose attitudes toward the Jewish cultus, ritual and customs[37]; but the Greek language would clearly be a component of such a life-style. Such persons appear without explanation in Acts 6 as a significant minority within the earliest Jerusalem church, and in all likelihood they were among Jesus' followers during his earthly ministry.

b) According to the Evangelists Jesus had hearers, and presumably converts, from the thoroughly hellenized Decapolis, Transjordan, and Gadarene districts. He centered a part of his ministry on Galilee where, in the judgment of G. Dalman, a knowledge of Greek was common and therefore to be expected of Jesus also. In any case, he included among the twelve several — e. g. Philip, Andrew, Simon — whose hellenized names and home town (Bethsaida-Julias) 'beweisen ihre Beziehung zum griechischen Kulturkreise[38].' Furthermore, his (eschatological) detachment from Jewish rituals doubtless had special appeal for Hellenists with their (cultural) detachment from the same laws. If he attracted such followers, he must have been concerned to mediate his teachings — and they to have them — in their own language[39].

c) When they were sent out, some of the disciples or their bilingual converts would have used Greek in transmitting the proclamation of Jesus to interested Greek-speaking Hellenists. On the

---

send *Hebraioi* 'educated in Greek' to Alexandria to translate the Old Testament into Greek. Cf. Joh 20,16.

[36] E. R. Goodenough, *Jewish Symbols*, 12 vols., New York 1953–65, 12 (1965), 41.

[37] See above, 118–121; Sevenster, *Greek*, 28 f. But see M. Hengel (note 14), 161 to 172.

[38] G. Dalman, *Jesus-Jeschua*, Leipzig 1922, 5 Cf. Mt 4,25; Mk 3,8; 5,1; 7,31; Joh 1,44; R. Gundry, *The Use of the Old Testament in St. Matthew's Gospel*, Leiden 1967, 174–178; J. A. Fitzmyer in *CBQ* 32 (1970), 507–518; A. W. Argyle in *NTS* 20 (1973–74), 87 ff.; P. E. Hughes, 'The Languages Spoken by Jesus,' *New Dimensions in New Testament Study*, ed. R. N. Longenecker, Grand Rapids 1974, 141 ff.; Hengel (note 33), I, 102.

[39] Whether Jesus taught in Greek is a moot question; it is probable at least that he used it occasionally in personal encounters. Cf. Mk 7,26 (the Syro-Phoenician Ἑλληνίς); 15,2 (Pilate).

assumption that Jesus usually taught orally in Aramaic (or Hebrew), they had a twofold task of translation and transmission. It is not impossible that they did this orally also, carrying over the key words, rhyme and other mnemonic devices that C. F. Burney has shown to be characteristic of some of Jesus' teaching[40]. But oral translation *for purposes of wider transmission* would be cumbersome and difficult at best. On balance it is likely that the apostles (and/or their converts) used the translation of Jesus' teachings as an occasion for the writing of at least some of them. Where they translated sayings or biblical expositions relating Jesus' message to the Old Testament promises, they could have employed the Septuagint which, from the Qumran library, is known to have been used in pre-destruction Palestine. Since both the reduction to writing and written transmission could have occurred simultaneously in different circles, written no less than oral transmission would account for the variants that one observes in parallel Gospel pericopes.

In conclusion, it is a mistake in method, as Schürmann has shown[41], to restrict form criticism *a priori* to a post-resurrection setting. This applies equally to the *written* transmission of Gospel traditions. The above arguments have sought to establish a plausible pre-resurrection *Sitz im Leben* for such writing within the circle of Jesus' followers. They also show the difficulties in the traditional postulate that a sudden shift to written forms occurred after an extended 'oral period.' The arguments vary in weight but, cumulatively, they raise a considerable degree of probability for some written transmission of Gospel traditions from the time of Jesus' earthly ministry.

IV.

As a number of writers have noted[42], certain literary forms in the Gospels are similar to those found in rabbinic and apocalyptic (Qumran) literature. Among them, exegetical patterns and techni-

---

[40] See note 18.

[41] Schürmann, *Untersuchungen*, 40—46.

[42] E. g. J. W. Doeve, *Jewish Hermeneutics in the Synoptic Gospels and Acts*, Assen 1954; D. Daube, *The New Testament and Rabbinic Judaism*, London 1954, 55—201.

ques have received particular attention[43]. Two patterns, the proem and the *yelammedenu* midrash, which also appear in Acts[44] and in the Pauline literature[45], occur in several Synoptic passages. As used in the synagogue, the proem midrash ordinarily had the following form:

The (Pentateuchal) text for the day.

A second text, the proem or 'opening' for the discourse.

Exposition containing additional Old Testament citations, parables or other commentary that are linked to the initial texts by catchwords.

A final text, usually repeating or alluding to the text for the day.

The *yelammedenu rabbenu* ('let our master teach us') midrash poses a question or problem that is then answered by the exposition. Apart from the interrogative opening it follows in general the pattern of the proem midrash[46].

The dialogue on the greatest commandment (Mk 12,28—31 parr) and the parable of the wicked tenants (Mk 12,1—12 parr) present, in underlying and probably more primitive Q material[47], a struc-

---

[43] E. g. K. Stendahl, *The School of St. Matthew*, Lund ²1969 (1954); P. Borgen, *Bread from Heaven*, Leiden 1965; 'Logos was the True Light,' *NovT* 14 (1972), 115—130; B. Gerhardsson, *The Testing of God's Son*, Lund 1966; L. Hartman, *Prophecy Interpreted*, Lund 1966; 'Scriptural Exegesis in . . . Matthew,' *L'évangile selon Matthieu*, ed. M. Didier, Gembloux 1972; B. Olsson, *Structure and Meaning in the Fourth Gospel*, Lund 1974, 282 f.; H. C. Kee, 'The Function of Scriptural Quotations and Allusions [in Mark],' *Jesus und Paulus. Festschrift W. G. Kümmel*, edd. E. Grässer et E. E. Ellis, Göttingen 1975, 165 ff. See note 64; cf. M. P. Miller, 'Targum, Midrash and the Use of the Old Testament in the New Testament,' *JSJ* 2 (1971), 29—82 and essays cited. J. A. Sanders, 'Luke 4,' *Christianity, Judaism . . . Studies for M. Smith*, 4 vols., ed. J. Neusner, Leiden 1975, I, 75—106.

[44] J. W. Bowker, 'Speeches in Acts,' *NTS* 14 (1967—68), 96—111; see above, 198—208.

[45] W. Wuellner, 'Haggadic Homily Genre in 1 Corinthians 1—3,' *JBL* 89 (1970), 199—204; see above, 213—220.

[46] Also the second, opening text is sometimes lacking. On the *yelammedenu* and four similar patterns cf. W. G. Braude, *Pesikta Rabbati*, 2 vols., New Haven 1968, I, 3—6; on the proem midrash cf. Bowker, 'Speeches,' 97—101; W. Bacher, *Die Proömien der alten jüdischen Homilie*, Farnborough 1970 (Leipzig 1913).

[47] As Dr. T. Schramm (*Markus-Stoff*, 47 ff., 160 ff., 166 f.) has noted, both passages in the Lukan parallel use a non-Markan source. In all probability the source is Q. This assumes the priority of Mark and the mutual independence of Matthew and Luke. It is not certain that Lk 10,25—29 is parallel to Mark: (1) Discussion of 'the greatest commandment' was widespread in later Judaism,

ture similar, respectively, to the *yelammedenu* and proem patterns. The passage on the greatest commandment reveals a Q source in the non-Markan verbal agreements in Matthew and Luke[48], even though in Matthew Q has been assimilated to the context and largely to the content of Mark. In the Lukan parallel the passage includes the parable of the Good Samaritan (Lk 10,29—37) which many suppose[49] to have been attached to the dialogue (Lk 10,25 to 28) by the Evangelist. This supposition is highly unlikely since (1) the dialogue on the commandment continues in the parable section (29 f.,36 f.), (2) Lk 10,29 does not appear to be a Lukan editorial coupling[50], (3) catchword connections show that the dialogue and parable were worked out as a set piece of exposition and (4) the Evangelist does not customarily re-work Jesus' parables into an intricate midrashic pattern.

Lk 10,25—37, then, comes to the Evangelist as a single piece as Gerhardsson, on other grounds, has suggested[51]. Since both the dialogue and the parable are probably sayings of the earthly Jesus[52], the whole piece is composed of very old material. Possibly

---

and it very likely occurred more than once both in Jesus' ministry and in the circles traditioning his teaching. Cf. (H. L. Strack and) P. Billerbeck, *Kommentar zum Neuen Testament*, München 1920—28, I, 901—908; Daube, *Judaism*, 247; J. Jeremias, *The Parables of Jesus*, London ⁶1963, 202. (2) Since Luke is very careful to keep to the Markan sequence for Markan material and since he does not do so here, we must conclude that 'Luke did not take the pericope from Mark' (B. Gerhardsson, *The Good Samaritan*, Lund 1958, 8). (3) Luke's omission of the dialogue in the section corresponding to Mk 12,28—31 may be to avoid repetition of a similar episode. However, Lk 10 reveals unmistakable affinities with Matthew's version (see note 48) which is clearly paralleled to Mark. Probably Luke is using a Q source in which the dialogue and parable formed one piece. Whether Q here represents a parallel to Mark is doubtful.

[48] Cf. Mt 22,35 ff. with Lk 10,25 (νομικός, [εκ]πειράζων, διδάσκαλος), 26a (with slight variation in tense and case), 26b (ἐν τῷ νόμῳ), 27 (ἐν + dative). Against Mk 12,29 Matthew and Luke omit the credo.

[49] Apparently following A. Jülicher, *Die Gleichnisreden Jesu*, 2 Bde., Freiburg 1888, 1889, II, 596.

[50] Of four other occurrences of δικαιοῦν in Luke one (7,35) or probably two (7,29) are from Q material and two are from special Lukan traditions (16,15; 18,14). In Acts (13,39 f.) the term appears only in Paul's sermon, i. e. a (pre-Lukan) proem midrash. Cf. Bowker, 'Speeches,' 101—104; see above, 200. The term and/or motif is clearly not a Lukan editorial interest and, in Lk 10,29, is received from the tradition.

[51] Gerhardsson, *Samaritan*, 28.

[52] Note (1) the Jewish context of the question (e. g. Shab. 31a; see note 47) and of the parable, (2) the commendation of the νομικός (10,28), (3) the unlike-

it was formed into a midrash out of separate sayings, but since parables were commonly used in the exposition of Scripture, the midrash form is more likely to be original. It may have been formulated and transmitted within the pre-resurrection circle of disciples as a teaching piece contrasting Jesus' ethic to that of other Jewish groups in terms of his radically new interpretation of Scripture: 'you have heard it said ... but I say.' As such, it presents a dialogue (25—29)[53] that employs Dtn 6,5; Lev 19,18; 18,5 and culminates by posing a problem — in the *yelammedenu* fashion — about the text of Lev 19, a problem that Jesus proceeds to answer by means of the parable (30—35)[54]. The section concludes (36 f.) with a return to the dialogue and with verbal allusions to the earlier texts, Lev 19,18; 18,5. The similarity to the pattern of the rabbinic commentary is clear:

25–28	– Dialogue including a question and initial texts: Dtn 6:5; Lev 19:18.
29	– A second text: Lev 18:5.
30–36	– Exposition by means of a parable, linked to the initial texts by the catchwords πλησίον (27, 29, 36) and ποιεῖν (28, cf. 37a, 37b).
37b	– Concluding allusion to the second text (ποιεῖν)[55].

Precise agreement with the *yelammedenu* form is, of course, not to be expected. But the correspondence is remarkable enough and suggests that the two forms have a common root. In the words of

---

lihood that this kind of material would be part of the risen Lord's teaching through a Christian prophet, and (4) the misconception in the earlier view of an uncontrolled, folkloric development of Jesus-traditions (see notes 28, 29, 30).

[53] The form in Lk 10,25—29 is what Daube (*Judaism*, 151—157) terms 'socratic interrogation': hostile question (25), counter question (26), reply (27) and rejoinder (28). In all probability it was taken over by the rabbis from hellenistic rhetoric before the first century.

[54] The parable itself is sometimes taken to allude to Scripture: Ez 34 (roeh, shepherd becomes via word play → rēeh, neighbor: Gerhardsson, *Samaritan*, 20) or Hos 6,6—9 (חסד, mercy = אהבה, love: J. D. M. Derrett, *Law in the New Testament*, London 1970, 210, 223, 227 = NTS 11 (1964—65), 23 f., 32 f., 36 f.). Cf. 2Chr 28,15; C. H. Cave, 'The Parables and the Scriptures,' NTS 11 (1964 to 65), 379: in rabbinic parables the substance of the parable is derived from Scripture rather than from the contemporary scene.

[55] Derrett, *Law*, 222 n. The midrash in Gal 3,6—29 similarly concludes with a mere allusion to the opening text, 'Abraham's seed' (29).

Professor Derrett, Lk 10,25—37 is 'a highly scientific piece of in-struction clothed in a deceptively popular style[56].'

The pericope containing the parable of the wicked tenants also reflects an exegetical pattern in both its Markan and Q[57] forms. It best corresponds to what Billerbeck has called the oldest type of synagogue address: the speaker reproduces a part of the Scripture lesson for the day, illumines it with a parable, and underscores his words with a further biblical passage[58]. More loosely, it corre-sponds to the pattern of the proem midrash. The proem or 'open-ing' text of Is 5,1 f. (or an allusion to it) is illumined by a parable, and the exposition is underscored by concluding texts from Ps 118, 22[59] and Dan 2,34 f.,44 f. All elements are joined by catchwords. In Mt 21,33—44, which appears to have best preserved the text of Q, the midrash has the following form:

33   – Initial text: Is 5,1 f.
34–41   – Exposition by means of a parable, linked to the initial text by the catchwords ἀμπελών (39, 40, 41), λιθοβολεῖν (35, cf. Is 5,2, סקל).
42–44   – Concluding texts (Ps 118,22; Dan 2,34 f., 44 f.), linked to the initial text by the catchwords οἰκοδομεῖν (42, cf. Dan 2,44, קים) and λίθος (42, 44, cf. 35).

---

[56] Derrett, *Law*, 227.

[57] Note the non-Markan parallels in Matthew and Luke: Lk 20,10c (γεωρ-γοί), 14 (ἰδόντες δὲ αὐτόν), 15 (sequence: cast out → kill), 16 (dialogue), 17 (cf. αὐτοῖς εἶπεν), 18 (verse). Schramm(*Markus-Stoff*, 165 ff.) rightly recog-nizes that Luke uses a non-Markan *Vorlage*. But he is apparently unaware of the midrashic pattern, overlooks the significance of the Q parallels, mistakenly dismisses Mt 21,44 as a gloss (150 n.), and conjectures that it is the Gospel of Thomas that represents 'ein vorsynoptisches Stadium, aus dem die synoptischen Fassungen leicht entstanden sein können...' (165). However, the Matthean parallels in Luke themselves make that conjecture doubtful since they reveal a pre-Synoptic midrashic pattern. The Thomas logion is in all probability depend-ent on Luke (cf. H. Schürmann, *BZ* 7 (1963), 236—260; see above 206; other-wise: Jeremias, *Parables*, 70—77, 74 n.). Cf. M. Hengel, *ZNTW* 59 (1968), 6. Also, it is a questionable procedure to take second or third century Gnostic material, containing clear allusions to New Testament literature, and read it back (via a conjectural *Vorlage*) behind first century, i. e. New Testament texts.

[58] Billerbeck (*Kommentar*, IV, 173) considers this form to have been current in the first century.

[59] The concluding citation of Ps 118 could allude to a seder reading, i. e. the Pentateuchal text for the day, including Ex 17,4,6 in which the rejected Moses is threatened with stoning. If so, the passage would conform even more closely

The pericope appears to have had a 'commentary' form from the beginning. The alternative is the improbable supposition that the parable, attached later to the quotations, has been carefully reworked even to incorporate words from Is 5 that are lacking in the Synoptic reference to that passage[60]. Furthermore, although the pericope may have been altered in transmission, it was probably first formed during the pre-resurrection mission: (1) Ps 118 is used here as a judgment, an *'eschatologisches Drohwort;'* in the post-resurrection community it is used with reference to Christ's exaltation[61]. (2) A messianic allegory is inherent in the parable, yet no allegory formed after the resurrection would have stopped short at the murder of the 'son[62],' nor would it have placed the murder *in* the vineyard. (3) The introductory formula ἀνέγνωτε (42) is found in the New Testament only on the lips of Jesus.

The exegetical patterns in Lk 10,25—37 and Mt 21,33—46 were widespread in Judaism and are found elsewhere in the Gospels[63]. The former reflects the form (and substance) of Jesus' exegetical discussion with the theologians; the latter is representative of a pattern of address that Jesus very likely used in his synagogue ministry, the context in which he probably gave many of his parables[64]. Apparently, the tendency of the Gospel tradition often was to separate the parable from its exegetical framework. In the parable of the wicked tenants this tendency, *pace* Professor Jeremias, finds its end product in the Gospel of Thomas (65,66) in which the allusions to Is 5 have disappeared and the quotation of Ps 118 has become simply a saying of Jesus. Correspondingly, some Old Testament quotations originally employed within a

---

to the usual pattern of the proem midrash. Ps 118,22 does indeed offer a remarkable pointer to the Israelites' rejection of and (implied) threat to stone (סקל) Moses, and it is not difficult to visualize a Christian or dominical midrash on Ex 17,4 (סקל)י, 6 (צור) utilizing Is. 5 (סקל), Ps. 118 (אבן), and Dan 2 (אבן).

[60] I. e. λιθοβολεῖν/סקל, τί ποιήσει (Mt 21,35,40; Is 5,2,5).

[61] J. Jeremias, *TDNT* 4 (1967/1942), 275; see above, 206.

[62] On the pre-Christian messianic use of 'son' cf. 4Qflor 1,11; 4Q243Son of God 2,1. On allegory in Jesus' parables cf. R. E. Brown, *NovT* 5 (1962), 36—45; I. H. Marshall, *Eschatology and the Parables*, London 1963, 10—13.

[63] E. g. Mt 15,1—9; 19,3—8; 22,23—33; cf. 11,4—11; 19,16—26; see above, 154—159. For the pattern in Philo and the rabbis cf. Borgen, *Bread*, 28—58.

[64] So, Cave, 'Parables,' 374—387. He is too restrictive, however, in regarding the original context as 'always a sermon' or necessarily 'centered upon the Synagogue' (376). Cf. Bowker, 'Speeches,' 97 f.

midrashic framework may have become, in the Gospels, independent *testimonia*[65].

'Jesus lived in the Old Testament[66].' And nothing is more certain than that our Lord was a teacher, a rabbi who taught in the synagogues and disputed with the establishment-theologians. In such situations he undoubtedly taught in an exegetical context[67]. Furthermore, in his ethic and in his conception of the kingdom of God he posed a challenge to the Jewish theologians and churchmen precisely at the exegetical level, a challenge to their interpretation of the Old Testament. One must suppose, therefore, that in the face of the theological opposition he instructed his followers in his new understanding of Scripture. If so, biblical exposition like that in Lk 10,25—37 and Mt 21,33—46 must be reckoned as one classification or 'form' in which his teaching was transmitted from the beginning. The present chapter has taken up only two, rather obvious, examples. Future studies will need to give further attention to the role of biblical exposition in the origin and history of the Gospel tradition.

---

[65] Cf. Mk 14,62 with Mk 12,35—37 (Ps 110,1); 13,6—28,26 (Dan 7,13). Cf. Acts 2,34 f.; Hebr 10,12. Rabbinic commentary may have a similar history: see above, 191.

[66] J. Jeremias, *New Testament Theology I*, London 1971, 205.

[67] See above, 133—137. On the identification of διδάσκαλος and ῥαββί in first century Palestine cf. H. Shanks, *JQR* 53 (1963), 343 f.

INDEX OF AUTHORS

INDEX OF PASSAGES

I. Old Testament

II. New Testament

III. *Apocrypha and Pseudepigrapha*

IV. Dead Sea Scrolls

V. Ancient Christian Writings

IX. Other Jewish Writings